Enterprise Security® with EJB™ and CORBA™

Bret Hartman
Donald Flinn
Konstantin Beznosov

Wiley Computer Publishing

John Wiley & Sons, Inc.

NEW YORK • CHICHESTER • WEINHEIM • BRISBANE • SINGAPORE • TORONTO

Publisher: Robert Ipsen
Editor: Robert M. Elliott
Assistant Editor: Emilie Herman
Managing Editor: John Atkins
Associate New Media Editor: Brian Snapp
Text Design & Composition: Publishers' Design and Production Services, Inc.

This book is printed on acid-free paper. ♾

Published by John Wiley & Sons, Inc.

Published simultaneously in Canada.

Library of Congress Cataloging-in-Publication Data

Hartman, Bret.
Enterprise security with EJB and CORBA / Bret Hartman, Donald Flinn, Konstantin Beznosov.
p. cm.
Includes bibliographical references and index.
ISBN 0-471-40131-5 (pbk. : alk. paper)
1. Electronic commerce—Security measures. 2. Business enterprises—Computer networks—Security measures. 3. Java (Computer program language) 4. JavaBeans. 5. CORBA (Computer architecture) I. Flinn, Donald, 1935- II. Beznosov, Konstantin. III. Title.

HF5548.32.H372 2001 2001017818

Printed in the United States of America.

10 9 8 7 6 5 4 3 2 1

Advance Praise for *Enterprise Security with EJB and CORBA*

"In today's new Web world, a typical server system consists of a Web application server full of things like Java applets, JSPs, CORBA objects, EJB containers full of Enterprise JavaBeans, and other strange artifacts we never imagined a couple of years ago. Some of them migrate from the server to its clients, others work while they sit in the server, and others hand work off to older servers further inside the enterprise. Putting applications together in this environment is fairly complicated. It would be nice if once you figured out how to build your application, security would "just work." But the current environment is not nice. Until this book came along, you needed to read many different documents—and figure some stuff out for yourself—to learn how to make your security services work together.

Bret Hartman, Don Flinn, and Konstantin Beznosov are uniquely qualified to explain how security works in today's complex environment. They are insiders who have been involved in the development of many of the security standards and technologies you'll need to use to integrate security across a modern Web-enabled enterprise. Together they have decades of security experience.

This is the first book I know of that talks about how to make Java security, EJB security, and CORBA security all work together in the same server. It's the first book I know of that covers the important new OMG RAD technology. And it's the first book I know of that explains the specifics of how to implement Role-Based Access Control in a CORBA or EJB business environment. *Enterprise Security with EJB and CORBA* gives specific advice about where to use specific features and how to use them.

I hope you enjoy the book and find it useful. I did."

Bob Blakley
Chief Scientist, Enterprise Solutions Unit, Tivoli Systems, Inc. (an IBM Company)

"The authors have made a significant contribution to the continuing discussion on establishing, securing, and integrating distributed components at the enterprise level. This is not an abstract, theoretical treatise, but an immensely practical guide, packed with concrete working examples and written in a crisp, accessible style. This is an important and stimulating piece of work."

Ted Gerbracht
Chief Information Security Officer, Credit Suisse First Boston

"Leveraging their strong implementation and standards committee experience, the authors have delivered the definitive guide to enterprise distributed object security. This book is a comprehensive guide for architects and developers who need to plan, implement, and sustain a flexible application security architecture that enables secure, rapid solutions delivery in the highly complex world of distributed components. Their excellent exploration of distributed object security makes this an essential companion for practitioners faced with the challenge of implementing security architecture in a multi-tier, components-based environment."

Wing K. Lee
Technical Specialist, Sprint

"While Java and EJB are rapidly becoming the component development platform of choice, CORBA has become firmly established as the only multi-language, multi-platform solution for distributed systems. Together these specifications provide just the right mix of portability and interoperability. A significant number of the thousands of deployed CORBA and EJB systems, however, are discovering the real need for security in those systems. For the first time, Enterprise Security with EJB and CORBA brings together those two worlds to review the security solutions provided by each, comparing and contrasting and exploring how to provide secure application and content delivery in the CORBA/EJB world. This book is indispensable for distributed application developers with security and protection requirements and belongs on the bookshelf of every distributed systems engineer."

Richard Mark Soley, Ph.D.
Chairman and Chief Executive Officer, Object Management Group, Inc.

To Dana, Sarah, and Will.

Bret

To Jane.

Don

To Alla, Vladimir, Valerij, Olga, and Alissa.

Konstantin

OMG Press Advisory Board

OMG Press Books in Print

(For complete information about current and upcoming titles, go to www.wiley.com/compbooks/omg/)

- ***Building Business Objects*** by Peter Eeles and Oliver Sims, ISBN: 0471-191760.
- ***Business Component Factory: A Comprehensive Overview of Component-Based Development for the Enterprise*** by Peter Herzum and Oliver Sims, ISBN: 0471-327603.
- ***Business Modeling with UML: Business Patterns at Work*** by Hans-Erik Eriksson and Magnus Penker, ISBN: 0471-295515.
- ***CORBA 3 Fundamentals and Programming, 2nd Edition*** by Jon Siegel, ISBN: 0471-295183.
- ***CORBA Design Patterns*** by Thomas J. Mowbray and Raphael C. Malveau, ISBN: 0471-158828.
- ***Enterprise Application Integration with CORBA: Component and Web-Based Solutions*** by Ron Zahavi, ISBN: 0471-32704.
- ***Enterprise Java with UML*** by CT Arrington, ISBN: 0471-386804
- ***The Essential CORBA: Systems Integration Using Distributed Objects*** by Thomas J. Mowbray and Ron Zahavi, ISBN: 0471-106119.

- ***Instant CORBA*** by Robert Orfali, Dan Harkey, and Jeri Edwards, ISBN: 0471-183334.
- ***Integrating CORBA and COM Applications*** by Michael Rosen and David Curtis, ISBN: 0471-198277.
- ***Java Programming with CORBA, Third Edition*** by Gerald Brose, Andreas Vogel, and Keith Duddy, ISBN: 0471-247650.
- ***The Object Technology Casebook: Lessons from Award-Winning Business Applications*** by Paul Harmon and William Morrisey, ISBN: 0471-147176.
- ***The Object Technology Revolution*** by Michael Guttman and Jason Matthews, ISBN: 0471-606790.
- ***Programming with Enterprise JavaBeans, JTS and OTS: Building Distributed Transactions with Java and C++*** by Andreas Vogel and Madhavan Rangarao, ISBN: 0471-319724.
- ***Programming with Java IDL*** by Geoffrey Lewis, Steven Barber, and Ellen Siegel, ISBN: 0471-247979.
- ***UML Toolkit*** by Hans-Erik Eriksson and Magnus Penker, ISBN: 0471-191612.

About the OMG

The Object Management Group (OMG) was chartered to create and foster a component-based software marketplace through the standardization and promotion of object-oriented software. To achieve this goal, the OMG specifies open standards for every aspect of distributed object computing from analysis and design, through infrastructure, to application objects and components.

The well-established CORBA (Common Object Request Broker Architecture) standardizes a platform- and programming-language-independent distributed object computing environment. It is based on OMG/ISO Interface Definition Language (OMG IDL) and the Internet Inter-ORB Protocol (IIOP). Now recognized as a mature technology, CORBA is represented on the marketplace by well over 70 ORBs (Object Request Brokers) plus hundreds of other products. Although most of these ORBs are tuned for general use, others are specialized for real-time or embedded applications, or built into transaction processing systems where they provide scalability, high throughput and reliability. Of the thousands of live, mission-critical CORBA applications in use today around the world, over 300 are documented on the OMG's success-story web pages at http://www.corba.org.

CORBA 3, the OMG's latest release, adds a Component Model, quality-of-service control, a messaging invocation model, and tightened integration with the Internet, Enterprise JavaBeans and the Java programming language. Widely anticipated by the industry, CORBA 3 keeps this established architecture in the forefront of distributed computing, as will a new OMG specification integrating

CORBA with XML. Well-known for its ability to integrate legacy systems into your network, along with the wide variety of heterogeneous hardware and software on the market today, CORBA enters the new millennium prepared to integrate the technologies on the horizon.

Augmenting this core infrastructure are the CORBAservices, which standardize naming and directory services, event handling, transaction processing, security, and other functions. Building on this firm foundation, OMG Domain Facilities standardize common objects throughout the supply and service chains in industries such as Telecommunications, Healthcare, Manufacturing, Transportation, Finance/Insurance, Electronic Commerce, Life Science, and Utilities.

The OMG standards extend beyond programming. OMG Specifications for analysis and design include the Unified Modeling Language (UML), the repository standard Meta-Object Facility (MOF), and XML-based Metadata Interchange (XMI). The UML is a result of fusing the concepts of the world's most prominent methodologists. Adopted as an OMG specification in 1997, it represents a collection of best engineering practices that have proven successful in the modeling of large and complex systems and is a well-defined, widely-accepted response to these business needs. The MOF is OMG's standard for metamodeling and metadata repositories. Fully integrated with UML, it uses the UML notation to describe repository metamodels. Extending this work, the XMI standard enables the exchange of objects defined using UML and the MOF. XMI can generate XML Data Type Definitions for any service specification that includes a normative, MOF-based metamodel.

In summary, the OMG provides the computing industry with an open, vendor-neutral, proven process for establishing and promoting standards. OMG makes all of its specifications available without charge from its website, http://www.omg.org. With over a decade of standard-making and consensus-building experience, OMG now counts about 800 companies as members. Delegates from these companies convene at week-long meetings held five times each year at varying sites around the world, to advance OMG technologies. The OMG welcomes guests to their meetings; for an invitation, send your email request to info@omg.org.

Membership in the OMG is open to end users, government organizations, academia, and technology vendors. For more information on the OMG, contact OMG headquarters by phone at +1-508-820 4300, by fax at +1-508-820 4303, by email at info@omg.org, or on the web at www.omg.org.

Contents

Foreword xix

Introduction xxiii

Acknowledgments xxxi

Chapter 1 An Overview of Enterprise Security Integration 1

Components and Security 1
Security as an Enabler for E-Business Applications 3
E-Business Applications Increase Risks 4
Information Security Goals: Enable Use, Bar Intrusion 4
E-Business Solutions Create New Security Responsibilities 5
Risk Management Holds Key 6
Information Security: A Proven Concern 7
Distributed Systems Require Distributed Security 8
Security Challenges in Distributed Component Environments 9
End-to-End ESI 12
ESI Requirements 13
ESI Solutions 14
ESI Framework 15
Applications 15
APIs 17
Core Security Services 17
Framework Security Facilities 18
Security Products 19
ESI Benefits 19
Principles of ESI 20

Example of a Secure Component Architecture 22
Business Scenario 22
eBusiness.com Object Model 22
eBusiness.com Security Requirements 24
Summary 26

Chapter 2 Securing EJB Components 27
An Overview of EJB Security 28
Players and Their Duties in the EJB Lifecycle 30
Roles 32
The Bean Provider 34
Application Assembler 39
Defining Roles 41
Assigning Method Access 42
Assigning Roles to Role References 44
Security Identity 45
Deployer 47
Principal Delegation 50
EJB Container Provider 51
Deployment Tools 51
Security Domains 51
Principal Naming 52
ejbContext 52
Auditing 54
Using the Deployment Descriptor 54
Recommended Permissions 57
The Beans Themselves 57
Authentication 58
Authorization 59
Transport 59
Security with Container-to-Container Interoperability 60
Association Options 62
Who's Running the Show? 64
Summary 66

Chapter 3 Securing CORBA Components 69
Benefits of CORBA Security 72
A Brief Review of CORBA 76
Declarative Part 76
Runtime Part 78
Wire Protocol 81
Object Reference 83
Runtime CORBA Security 84
Identification and Authentication 84
Policy Enforcement 86
Wire Protocol 89
Functionality Levels 91
Level 1: Security-Unaware Applications 92
Level 2: Security-Aware Applications 92
Declarative CORBA Security 93
Why You Need Rights, Domains, and Attributes 93

The Role of Rights 95
The Role of Domains 101
The Role of Privilege Attributes 102
Setting Audit Policies 104
Using Programmatic Security 106
Summary 108

Chapter 4 Enterprise Security Technologies 109
Perimeter Security Technologies 112
Firewalls/VPNs 112
Authentication 113
Authorization 113
Accountability 114
Security Administration 114
Cryptographic Protocols 114
Authentication 115
Web-Based Security Servers 116
Authentication 116
Authorization 117
Accountability 118
Security Administration 118
Intrusion Detection 118
Mid-Tier Security Technologies 119
Component-Based Security Servers 119
Cryptographic Protocols 120
Authentication 120
Authorization 121
Cryptography 121
Delegation 121
Accountability 121
Security Administration 121
Entitlements Servers 122
Authentication 122
Authorization 122
Legacy Security Technologies 123
Mainframe Security 123
Authentication 123
Authorization 124
Cryptography 124
Accountability 124
Security Administration 124
Database Security 124
Summary 124

Chapter 5 Interoperability of Cross-Domain Components 127
What Is Interoperability of EJB and CORBA? 128
Intracompany and Intercompany Security 131
Security Technology Domains Relative to Security Tiers 133
Security Domains in the Perimeter Tier 138
Security Domains in the Mid-Tier 139
EJB and CORBA in the Mid-Tier 139

Security Domains in the Legacy Tier 140
Rationale for Mixed Security Technology Domains 140
Mixed Domains in the Perimeter 141
Mixed Domains in the Mid-Tier 141
Mixed Domains in the Legacy Tier 143
Auditing 143
Security Administration 143
Bridging the Security Tiers 143
Perimeter to Mid-Tier Interoperability 145
Browser to Web Server Interaction 146
Passing Data from the Browser 148
An Example of Perimeter to Mid-Tier Interoperability 148
The Critical Web Server 151
Mid-Tier to Legacy Interoperability 152
Security Policy Domains 157
Modifying Architectures for Security 161
Summary 164

Chapter 6 Interoperability of EJB and CORBA Components 167
Making EJB and CORBA Work Together Securely 168
Advantages of Combined Technologies 170
Packaging Security for the Component Developer 171
JNDI Security 172
Container Security 173
Security between Containers 174
EJB and CORBA Transport Protocols 174
RMI 176
IIOP 178
RMI over IIOP 181
Common Secure Interoperability Version 2 182
CSIv2 Attribute Layer 185
The Authorization Token 185
The Identity Token 189
CSIv2 Authentication Layer 190
CSIv2 Transport Layer 191
Credentials and Privilege Delegation in CSIv2 192
CSIv2 Association Options in the IOR 196
Conformance to CSIv2 197
Interoperable Security Layers 198
Authentication 198
Extending EJB to CORBA Authentication 199
Authorization 201
How Rich Does It Need to Be? 203
Extending EJB to CORBA Authorization 204
Summary 206

Chapter 7 Protecting Application Resources 209
Beyond Middleware Access Control 209
Refining Access Control in the Example 210
Authorization Server 212
Resource Access Decision Facility 214

Pros and Cons of Using RAD 215
Middleware or RAD Authorization? 217
RAD Standard 217
RAD Interfaces and Data 218
RAD Architecture 220
Access Decision Object 220
Policy Evaluator 224
Decision Combinator 225
Policy Evaluator Locator (PEL) 227
Dynamic Attribute Service 230
Putting It All Together 233
What Belongs to RAD and What Does Not 236
Runtime Model 236
Administrative Model 236
Summary 240

Chapter 8 Scaleable Security Policies 243
Using Rights Wisely 244
Using Attributes Wisely 246
An Argument for Roles 247
Overview of RBAC 248
$RBAC_0$: Just Roles 250
$RBAC_0$ Using CORBA 252
$RBAC_0$ Using EJB 255
$RBAC_1$: Role Hierarchies 260
$RBAC_1$ in CORBA 261
$RBAC_1$ in EJB 263
$RBAC_2$: Constraints 266
$RBAC_3$: $RBAC_1$ + $RBAC_2$ 267
Concluding Remarks on RBAC 268
Using Domains Wisely 268
Using Domain Structures for Composing Security Policies 272
Assigning Object Instances to Policy Domains 274
Delegation 276
Motivations for Using Delegation 277
Levels of Delegation 278
Product Support for Delegation 279
Delegation in EJB 281
When and How to Use Delegation 281
General Recommendations 281
Risks of Delegation 282
Summary 283

Chapter 9 Planning a Secure Component System 285
Making the Jump from Application to System 286
Interaction of Applications 286
What Is Security? 286
Security Evolution—Losing Control 288
Dealing with the "ilities" 289
eBusiness.com's Approach 290
Determining Requirements 291

Functional Requirements 291
Security Requirements 291
Limit Visitor Access 292
Eliminate Administration of New Customers 292
Grant Members More Access 293
Protect the Accounts of Each Individual 293
Administrator Control of Critical Functions 294
Restrict Administrators Abilities 294
Nonfunctional Requirements 295
Manageability 295
Extensibility 295
Reliability 296
Availability 296
Scalability 297
Applying the Framework 297
Application Components 299
Security APIs 299
Core Security Services 299
Framework Security Facilities 300
Summary 300

Chapter 10 Building an Integrated Security System 303
Security Architecture 305
Deploying the Example 308
The Underlying Protection Layer 309
Perimeter Security 310
Using Component Security with Firewalls 312
Using Component Security with Web Servers 313
A Caution Against Proprietary Solutions 315
Mid-Tier Security 315
Legacy Security 320
Advantages of Using a Security Server 321
Administration 322
Multiple Security Servers 324
Authentication 325
Securing the Infrastructure 325
Naming 326
Persistence of Security Data 327
LDAP 328
Relational or Object Databases 330
File Systems 331
Security Gotchas at the System Level 331
Scaling 331
Performance 332
Summary 334

Glossary 337

References 351

Index 353

Foreword

When I visit customers interested in purchasing my company's CORBA and EJB middleware products, the conversation invariably turns to security. More often than not, the conversation follows the same pattern. First, the customer asks for a description of our security products. After hearing it, the customer then declares that those products will never fulfill his needs unless they fully support everything specified for Level 2 of the CORBA Security Specification. When he says everything, he means everything: he wants to build and deploy security-aware applications that make heavy use of delegation, authorization, authentication, encryption—the whole nine yards, and with all the possible buzzwords. When I proceed to inquire as to why his applications require such thorough security support, the customer tends to mumble a few words and quickly change the subject. Later, after the customer has purchased the software and built and deployed his applications, it almost always turns out that he chose not to use any middleware security whatsoever. "Of course, that's only for the first version," is the customer's typical excuse. "I'll secure the application later, once I prove that it works properly." As we all know, "later" almost never arrives in these cases.

Building and deploying secure applications is probably the least understood area of the whole middleware industry. Like the customer described above, nobody wants to show his ignorance when it comes to computer security. We all want to say, "Of course my applications are secure! Naturally, I designed security into them from the start." We all know why the small padlock icon pops up in our browser when we place an online order with a secure Web site. Many of us have a basic understanding of authorization, encryption, and authentication. Unfortunately, it's not enough. What little most of us know about middleware security is inadequate for creating secure middleware applications in the real world.

Years ago, you could get away with not building security into your middleware applications. This was because such applications tended to live on the wrong side of the tracks, often near some smoke-belching mainframes. Nobody except the hard-core system developers and administrators would even go near them. You could simply use a single system account as the identity for all the applications, and as long as they stayed up and running, the users in your company didn't care.

The rapid growth of the Web changed all that, and you can no longer ignore security in this manner. Those same back-end middleware applications (or more likely, their descendants) are now powering your e-business Web site. Between the Web server and your back-end legacy applications, you've got EJB applications and CORBA applications that are tying together diverse systems in a continually expanding heterogeneous environment. You've got the new Java code talking to the tried-and-true C++ code talking to the aging but solid COBOL, and it all works, and you wish you could just stop there. But you can't. You also need to make sure that your customers can register on your Web site, log in, and supply sensitive data such as credit card numbers without fear of being taken for a ride by the teenage hacker down the street.

One way to break the cycle of middleware security ignorance is for us to educate ourselves. Unfortunately, books on security tend to fall into one of two categories: they are either so high-level that they are practically useless, or so low-level that they are impossible for mere mortals to understand. The high-level books inform us of what we don't know, but don't teach us anything practical about it. As for the low-level books, well, let's be honest—we never finish reading them because they're too thick and boring.

This book is different. Not surprisingly, the authors of this book have achieved a fine balance between theory and practice. Bret, Don, and Konstantin have been among the few participating on both sides: they have not only contributed heavily to defining the specifications for CORBA and J2EE security, they have actually designed and built real-world, practical, and working secure middleware systems based on those specifications. Because this is a book written by developers for developers, it's full of practical and up-to-date information about EJB and CORBA security, and how to actually apply it in your own applications. They describe the contents of the relevant specifications, and then they show you some code to help put it all in perspective. They even include advice on scalability and performance as it relates to security, which is rare. Personally, I have always tried to cater to developers in my own writings about CORBA and distributed object systems, and I am thrilled that Bret, Don, and Konstantin have chosen this approach as well.

As the Web continues to evolve, it will outgrow its current (and relatively simple) two-tier architecture based on browsers and servers, and become a multi-tier system based around Web services. A Web service, similar to a CORBA or EJB application, is invokable by remote programmatic clients who wish to make requests. For example, an automated business client application might notice that inventory is running low on a certain part and contact the supplier's Web services to order more. In this context, end-to-end security is an absolute must, from the client application, across the Internet, through the Web service, and into the supplier's back-end legacy systems. This is an example of secure business-to-business integration, and it won't be long before it's common on the Internet. However, unless you learn and master this book's lessons and advice regarding practical middleware security, you needn't worry about Web services. Like your competitors, they will have passed you by.

Steve Vinoski
Chief Architect and Vice President Platform Technologies
IONA Technologies
February 2001

Introduction

E-business—which uses Internet technology to help businesses streamline processes, improve productivity, and increase efficiencies—is emerging as a vibrant force in the world's commerce. A necessary prerequisite to a successful implementation of an e-business site—whether it is a business-to-business or consumer-to-business site—is that the transactions to, from, and within the site be executed securely. It is not sufficient to regard e-business security as stopping at the perimeter firewall of your company. In today's e-business environments, customers, suppliers, remote employees, and at times even competitors are all invited into the inner sanctum of your enterprise computing system. Consequently, e-business security is an end-to-end requirement—from the browser through the perimeter firewall, into your application servers and applications in the heart of your enterprise system to the persistent store of your sensitive data in legacy systems.

This book shows you how to apply enterprise security integration (ESI) to secure your enterprise from end-to-end, using theory, examples, and practical advice.

Underlying e-business is the broader technology of distributed computing and the various distributed security technologies. Everybody in the computing field and many ordinary computer users have heard of HTML and SSL but few have heard of Enterprise JavaBeans (EJB) and even fewer have heard of the Common Object Request Broker Architecture (CORBA). But these two technologies are at the heart of modern distributed computing systems that support application servers running behind the perimeter firewall. This area, which we call the mid-tier, is the most complex and most neglected area of end-to-end enterprise security. Several surveys have shown the mid-tier to be highly vulnerable to break-ins resulting in significant financial loss. With the increasing e-business movement towards letting outsiders into the mid-tier, the mid-tier is becoming even more sensitive to break-ins, with the potential of greater financial loss and privacy violations.

If you have any responsibility, direct or indirect, for any part of the security of your site you owe it to yourself to read and study this book. Distributed security is not an easy subject, and it follows that parts of this book are not easy; but the returns to yourself and your company are significant if you master this complex subject.

We present material on how to use the programming tools and models, and how to understand the specifications that are available to build a secure system. Since this technology is rapidly changing, we present the theory behind the models and explain the thinking behind many of the security specifications that are at the forefront of the technology today. The authors are well positioned to do this as we are members of many of the committees and organizations writing these specifications as well as doing hands-on work designing and building enterprise security products. We have also helped many large enterprise clients in banking, manufacturing, and telecommunications develop their ESI frameworks.

Our emphasis is in showing you how to build and understand the complexities of an end-to-end secure enterprise system. Consequently, we do not cover in-depth some of the more arcane aspects of security such as cryptography, Public Key Infrastructure (PKI), or how to build the security services themselves. We discuss these specialized security technologies in the context of their use in a distributed system so that you can judge how and where to use them.

This book gives you both a detailed technical understanding of the major components of an end-to-end enterprise security and a broad description of how to deploy and use these technologies to secure your corporation and its interaction with the outside world.

Overview of the Book and Technology

Enterprise security is an ongoing battle. On one side are those who want to break into your system, either for fun or for some advantage to themselves or their organization. On the other side are people like you who are putting up defenses to prevent break-ins to your system. This continuing battle results in continuing changes to security solutions. Another dimension is the evolving set of business security requirements, such as giving a new group of outsiders controlled access to your system for e-commerce purposes. For these reasons we have concentrated on explaining the underlying thinking behind today's enterprise security solutions so that you can judge the worth of new solutions as they come on the scene and judge when old solutions are no longer good enough.

We emphasize server-side technologies that are used to secure the middle tier, which is the most critical yet generally neglected area of distributed enterprise security. Unlike many other security books, we do not explain how to secure a user's desktop machine. Although desktop security is important, it is a relatively easy problem to solve compared to *enterprise* security, where the sensitive resources generally reside in mid-tier applications and legacy databases. Consequently, we have devoted a good portion of this book to securing EJB and CORBA, which are the most popular distributed technologies used by mid-tier servers.

Further, we believe that developers should *avoid* using security application programming interfaces (APIs) whenever possible. This is a rather unusual position compared to most other security books, which spend most of their time explaining how developers should use security APIs such as the `java.security` package, the Java Cryptography Extension (JCE), and the Java Authentication and Authorization Service (JAAS). We believe that application developers should generally not use custom solutions based on these APIs, and consequently we do not describe how to use them. Instead, we advocate *container-based* security, in which the EJB and CORBA security services enforce security for mid-tier applications, thus usually sparing the application developer from having to write any security code at all.

This fundamental shift away from writing custom security solutions to transparent mid-tier security makes life much easier for the application developer, but it can complicate security integration. Most large enterprises use several different middleware technologies, so an important task is to securely interoperate between mid-tier object models as well as to interoperate between the perimeter security and the mid-tier and between the mid-tier and legacy systems. To this end, we give significant detail describing the problems of secure interoperability and how you can overcome these problems. Both the Java and CORBA communities have offered the solutions to some of these problems in specifications that have been developed by their cooperative efforts. Other solutions have been worked on by organizations such as the Internet Engineering Task Force and the World Wide Web Consortium, to name a couple. We cover many of these solutions to bring to you all the pertinent distributed security work and thinking.

We look at solving the security problem from an end-to-end corporate viewpoint as well as from the major technical viewpoints of authentication, authorization, secure transport, and security auditing. By presenting enterprise security from these two viewpoints, we give you both a top-down and bottom-up approach to understanding the problems and the solutions.

In some cases there are no standard solutions. In these cases we bring you the latest thinking and guidance towards solutions. The best solution is one where there is an open standard, since in order to reach the status of a standard the solution will have gone through a rigorous examination and debate among the security experts. However, standardization is a slow process, and we all are under pressure to solve the problem now. In situations where there is not yet a consensus, we put forth solutions that we have implemented, and/or we describe the different possible solutions under debate in the distributed security community.

We also recognize that there are security solutions offered by other server-side middleware technologies, particularly Microsoft COM+ and message-based technologies (e.g., IBM MQSeries). We wish we could cover other mid-tier security solutions in this book, but we must limit our scope by necessity. COM+ provides a fully featured mid-tier security solution that is a viable alternative to EJB/CORBA. However, COM+ security exists in a separate universe from the open standards defined by EJB/CORBA security; interoperability between COM+ security and EJB/CORBA security requires difficult low-level integration techniques. That advanced topic deserves a separate book on its own, so we do not attempt to cover COM+ in this book. Message-based technologies tend to support basic product-specific and proprietary security mechanisms, so there is little general advice we can give on this topic. We do touch on the security of XML-based messaging, which shows great promise. However, as of this publication the standards for XML security in the mid-tier are at a formative stage and are too immature to discuss.

We have tried to balance the theory and understanding of e-business security to give you the ability to determine when you can use today's solutions or when you should reject an inadequate solution and find something better. There is a saying to the effect that it is better to teach someone how to farm than to just give him today's meal. This is the philosophy that we have tried to follow. We hope that the knowledge you get from this book will prepare you to build secure systems that are ready for the new solutions, requirements, and threats that will always be coming down the road.

How This Book Is Organized

This book starts out with an introduction to distributed security and then explains the security aspects of the two main component technologies in use in the security mid-tier today, EJB and CORBA. Next is a description of other security technologies in use in an end-to-end secure enterprise system. We then explain how to make these technologies interoperate to get the best capabilities of each. In the process, we dig into some of the most forward-thinking of today's security experts in distributed security as expressed in recent specifications and technical committees and consortia. We finish up with an explanation of how to plan a secure distributed system; and using our example company, eBusiness.com, we discuss how you would go about deploying a secure system.

Chapter 1 introduces the subject of distributed security and the new technologies that are used to solve the distributed security problem. We lay the groundwork for understanding how the subsequent chapters fit into the whole solution. We introduce the concept of risk management in balancing system performance and complexity on the one hand and the value of the resources on the other hand. We introduce the concept ESI and how it supports end-to-end enterprise security. We wrap up with a description of our fictional enterprise, eBusiness.com, which is used as a running example throughout the rest of the book.

Chapter 2 takes an in-depth look at Enterprise JavaBean security. The technological underpinnings are described using the EJB version 2.0 specification as the authoritative source for EJB security. We use example code to tie the theory to reality. We follow the long-standing EJB approach of using the major players—the bean provider, the application assembler, and the deployer—to describe EJB security. Along the way we give specific advice on what problems to look for when purchasing and using an EJB container and third-party EJB applications. We cover authentication, authorization, secure transport, and auditing as applied to EJB and explore some of the more difficult aspects of using EJB such as delegation.

Chapter 3 takes an in-depth look at CORBA security. Similar to the approach to EJB security, the technical underpinning of CORBA Security is described referencing the CORBA security specification, CORBASec, developed by security architects from academia and industry. We describe how CORBA security supports the basic distributed security principles of authentication, authorization and secure transport. We delve into security policy and how CORBA uses security policy to great advantage. We also describe the trio of rights, domains, and attributes that CORBA uses to produce its strong scaling capabilities.

Chapter 4 takes a step back and looks at the bigger picture of the many security technologies that are necessary to build a complete enterprise security system. We discuss these technologies in the context of the perimeter, the middle, and the legacy tiers and show how the sum of the parts fit together to give us end-to-end security. We discuss how firewalls, VPN, and Web Servers work to protect your enterprise at the perimeter boundary; how component-based security servers (discussed in Chapters 2 and 3) and entitlement servers support the mid-tier; and how mainframe and database security in the legacy tier are tied into the full end-to-end security model.

Chapter 5 discusses the difficult problem of interoperability between the different tiers in use in modern security deployments and the interoperability between the different technical domains in use today. We spend some time discussing why you would want to use different security techniques and technologies. After describing the wisdom and benefits and in some cases the necessity of using a heterogeneous mix of security technologies we describe the specifications and standard approaches of bridging the differences. We point out that specifications are somewhat weak in a number of the areas of secure interoperability. In these cases this chapter gives non-standard ways to bridge the security domains and tiers. We also enumerate and describe the work that is underway in these areas.

Chapter 6 covers the interoperability between EJB and CORBA. This is an area where the two communities have put a lot of effort into solving the interoperability problem. The result of this effort, the Common Secure Interoperability Version 2 (CSIv2) specification, is described. This description will help you understand some of the hard problems in distributed security and how they can be solved. Understanding these complex security problems and how the security experts solved them is a good way for you to acquire the knowledge to attack security problems yourself. We also give you practical examples for solving these problems. In keeping with our general approach we look at the EJB/CORBA secure interoperability problem from the top-down, tier interoperability, and the bottom-up security technology points of view.

Chapter 7 delves into a somewhat different security technology, the Resource Access Decision (RAD) specification. This is a CORBA specification, applicable to EJB as well, that applies to protecting resources when the solutions presented in the previous chapters are not sufficient. A case in point would be when dynamic attributes are necessary for an application access decision. In these cases RAD comes to the rescue. As we point out in this chapter, RAD is not a panacea, and because it moves some of the responsibility up into the application, it is not an optimal solution. However, there are some security requirements that cannot be solved by a pure middleware solution and require a RAD or RAD-like approach.

Chapter 8 provides guidance on a variety of security policy issues for dealing with large-scale applications. We describe the trio of mechanisms underlying CORBA security that produce its scaling capabilities and a lot of its power: access rights, security attributes, and security policy domains. We describe their advantages and how to use them. We also go into some of the theory behind these concepts. We then present several models for role-based access control (RBAC) that show how access rights and security attributes can be used to define hierarchical access using organizational roles. Finally, we discuss credential delegation that is commonly required for chains of invocations across many components. These mechanisms underlie much of the modern thinking in distributed security. Therefore, understanding these concepts is important to anticipating the future directions for distributed security.

Chapter 9 uses the ideas and concepts of the previous chapters to show you how to plan a secure system. We use the idea of an ESI framework, which was introduced in Chapter 1, to help you plan your enterprise security system. We also use our e-business example, eBusiness.com, to make the planning more concrete. We lay out the requirements that you should pay attention to so that you may assess how your system will interact with other systems.

Chapter 10 walks you through the actual deployment of the eBusiness.com application. This chapter brings together the theory and approaches from the previous chapters in a practical example of securely deploying a consumer to business enterprise to support today's new electronic business scenarios. We point out many of the pitfalls that could snare you in your deployment and describe how to avoid them. By following a realistic deployment scenario we describe how firewalls, Web servers, browsers, EJB containers, CORBA applications, the middleware infrastructure, and legacy systems all have to work together to ensure a secure system.

If you have trouble finding or remembering any of the multitudes of definitions and acronyms we use in this book, we also provide an extensive glossary. To help keep all these terms straight, we recommend that you keep the glossary as a handy reference while you read each of the chapters.

Who Should Read This Book

This book should be read by anyone who has a responsibility for the security of a distributed enterprise computing system. This includes managers, architects, programmers, and security administrators. We assume that you have some experience with distributed computing as applied to enterprise systems, but we do not expect you to have experience with security as applied to large distributed systems. In addition some experience with EJB and CORBA is helpful but not necessary.

Be forewarned that distributed security is not an easy subject, so don't expect to absorb some of the more technical chapters in a single reading. We also don't expect each category of our audience to read all of the parts of the book with equal intensity.

Managers should read Chapters 1, 4, 9, 10, and the introductions and summaries for the other chapters. For areas where a manager has a special responsibility or interest we invite them to delve into the pertinent chapters.

Architects should read all the chapters, while programmers might want to skim Chapters 1 and 4. Also those who are familiar with EJB security can skim Chapter 2 and those familiar with CORBA can skim Chapter 3 and Chapter 7. We recommend skimming these chapters even though you are familiar with the technology because some of the information is quite new and not readily available elsewhere.

Security administrators should pay particular attention to Chapters 9 and 10. They should also read Chapters 4, 5, 6, and 7 while reading at least the introduction and summary to the other chapters.

What's on the Web Site

Our Web site at www.wiley.com/compbooks/hartman contains the complete source code for securing the fictional corporation eBusiness.com that we used as an example throughout this book. The Web site also contains any errata and updates to this book.

Since distributed security is an active, growing technology we will from time to time keep you up to date on those security technologies that are expanding, those that are of less interest, and new technologies that come on the scene.

Summary

If you don't want your company to appear on the nightly news with the lead, "<Your company> has reported a break-in by hackers. The break-in resulted in large financial losses and disclosure of privacy information of thousands of their customers including stolen credit card numbers," you should learn how to protect your enterprise system. That is the purpose of this book, to teach you how to protect your enterprise. While we put emphasis on the two most popular distributed enterprise systems, EJB and CORBA, the technologies and concepts that we teach using these component models are applicable to the security of all distributed systems.

One weak link in the security of your enterprise can result in the failure of its security. Consequently, we describe the security of each part of your company from the customers, suppliers, and partners beyond your perimeter firewall to securing the heart of your corporate system. By using both theory and examples we teach you how to build a secure distributed system today and how to anticipate and be ready for the security systems of tomorrow.

We trust that you will be able to apply the theory, concepts, and approaches to distributed enterprise security that we have discussed as you deploy and upgrade the security of your company's enterprise system. As we move deeper into this new computing paradigm of cooperative computing you will need all the skills that you can muster to beat the bad guys. We hope our efforts in describing enterprise security will help you in this regard.

Acknowledgments

The concepts discussed in this book represent the work of many people. In particular, an enormous amount of credit goes to the architects and engineers at Concept Five Technologies, Inc., who were instrumental in producing new solutions for difficult enterprise security problems before many people realized that the field of Enterprise Security Integration even existed.

First, we would like to thank the Concept Five development team who created an ambitious full-featured implementation of the CORBA Security service called *C5Sec*: Julio Barros, Jeff Berger, Kevin Callan, Paul Campbell, Mark Cannava, Chris Chaney, Diane Coe, Mark Cornwell, Ani Dutta, Steve Evans, Joe Faber, Kevin Foley, Ian Foster, Glen Goodwin, Chuck Grayer, Tom Herron, Henry Hom, Jane Huan, Chris Irwin, Gerry Jones, Melony Katz, Lynette Khirallah, Jason Knapp, Vidya Laxman, Julie LeMoine, Catherine Li, Kent Lockhart, Steve Lowing, FengMin Lu, Richard Lu, John Marsh, Geri Micek, Liz Miller, Steve Popkes, Aarthi Prasad, Mindy Rudell, Dan Sharp, Ruth Sigel, David Solomon, Lisa Strader, Mark Taylor, Lynda Thimble, and Pratik Wadher.

Next, we thank the Concept Five consultants who have contributed toward creating the Enterprise Security Integration techniques that have solved problems for a lot of enterprise clients: Tom Amlicke, Larry Anderson, Jay Brennan, Henry Ching, Michael Etkind, Robert Frazier, Harriet Goldman, Lakshmi Hanspal, Matthew Hicks, John Horsfield, Ken Hudok, Celia Joseph, Shirley Kawamoto, Alexander Kotylev, John Laskar, David Miller, Rick Murphy, Cathy Petrozzino, Terry Reed, Brian Seborg, and Phillip Wherry.

We would also like to thank Concept Five management, who actively encouraged and supported the creation of a strong e-business security consulting practice: Kevin Dougherty, Rick Frier, Barry Horowitz, Helen Ojha, Tana Reagan, Bill Ruh, and Kim Warren.

Hitachi was Concept Five's development partner for the CORBA Security service. We appreciate the technical support from many Hitachi, Ltd., and Hitachi Computer Products (America), Inc., contributors including: Michinori Amemori, Fred Dushin, Robert Freund, Tadashi Kaji, Akira Kito, Kazuaki Masamoto, Makoto Oya, Narizumi Shindo, Takuma Sudo, Satoru Tezuka, Katsuyuki Umezawa, David Warren, and Hiroshi Yagi.

Next, we thank the Iona people for their long discussions on security implementation and architecture: Donal Arundel, Brendan Holmes, Stephen Keating, Neil Kenealy, Bob Kukura, Mat Mihic, and Steve Vinoski.

The Common Secure Interoperability Version 2 (CSIv2) and Security Domain Membership Management (SDMM) Services are two important Object Management Group (OMG) specifications that greatly influenced this book. Contributors to the development of these specifications include: Konstantin Beznosov (SDMM editor), Bob Blakley, Gordon L. Buhle, Ted Burghart, David Chang, Don Flinn, Bret Hartman, Rob High, Jr., Heather Hinton, Henry Hom, Polar Humenn, Gene Jarboe, Tadashi Kaji, Paul Kyzviat, Christopher Milsom, Jeff Mischkinsky, Ron Monzillo (CSIv2 editor), Jishnu Mukerji, Mindy Rudell, and Kent Salmond.

Thanks to Ron Monzillo and Jishnu Mukerji for reviewing various parts of this book and helping us keep at least most of our facts straight. Thanks also to the folks at Wiley who made this book possible: John Atkins, Bob Elliott, Emilie Herman, and Anne Marie Walker. We appreciate all of their support and feedback for these many months.

Professor Yi Deng was instrumental for Konstantin Beznosov's Ph.D. research on the engineering of access control for distributed enterprise applications, which, among other results, led to the better understanding of the Resource Access Decision service paradigm in the enterprise application security. Thanks go to the research group at the Center for Advanced Distributed Software Engineering (CADSE), directed at the time of the research by Dr. Deng of the Florida International University, for their contribution to research and development.

Finally, we especially want to thank our families: Dana, Sarah, and Will Hartman; Jane and Jason Flinn; and Olga and Alissa Kniazeva. We know this writing exercise hasn't been much fun for you, as you patiently put up with all of the late nights and lost weekends. We thank you for your understanding and support.

An Overview of Enterprise Security Integration

This chapter explores groundbreaking technology that supports rapid deployment of secure e-business applications. This technology, based on the integration of distributed component computing and information security, represents new power to mount secure, scalable e-business services. We begin by discussing the basic relationship between security and components. We then describe how security enables new e-business applications that were not previously feasible and how e-business solutions create new security responsibilities. Next, we describe the many challenges of enforcing security in component-based applications. Finally, we introduce *Enterprise Security Integration* (ESI), which we use to tie together many different security technologies, and as a result, provide the framework for building secure component architectures.

Components and Security

Application servers, which provide a convenient environment for building component-based distributed business applications, are now widely available. Most middleware vendors have application server products on the market today. Application servers provide environments for building and deploying components.

A *component* is the fundamental building block of distributed software applications. Each component has one or more interfaces that provide the points of entry for calling programs. An interface, which is defined in terms of operations (also called methods), encapsulates a component and ensures that a component is modular. That is, a developer may replace one implementation of a component for another, and as long as the new component preserves the interface and expected behavior of the old one, there will be no impact on programs that use the component. Figure 1.1 illustrates the component architecture.

Component architectures include a rich runtime environment called a *container*. Containers provide an array of application services that allow the application developer to concentrate on building the application rather than the supporting infrastructure.

In the Java world, the Enterprise JavaBeans (EJB) specification, which is part of the Java 2 Enterprise Edition (J2EE) from Sun Microsystems, has gained broad acceptance as the standard for Java server component architectures. Products based on the EJB specification have compelling advantages: They shield application developers from many of the low-level component service details (such as transactions and security), they enable enterprise Beans to be moved to another environment with minimal effort, and they are interoperable with other EJB products.

Beyond Java, the Object Management Group (OMG) has defined the Common Object Request Broker Architecture (CORBA) Component Model. The CORBA Component Model, which has been designed to be consistent with EJB, extends the notion of EJB to allow components to be built in other languages,

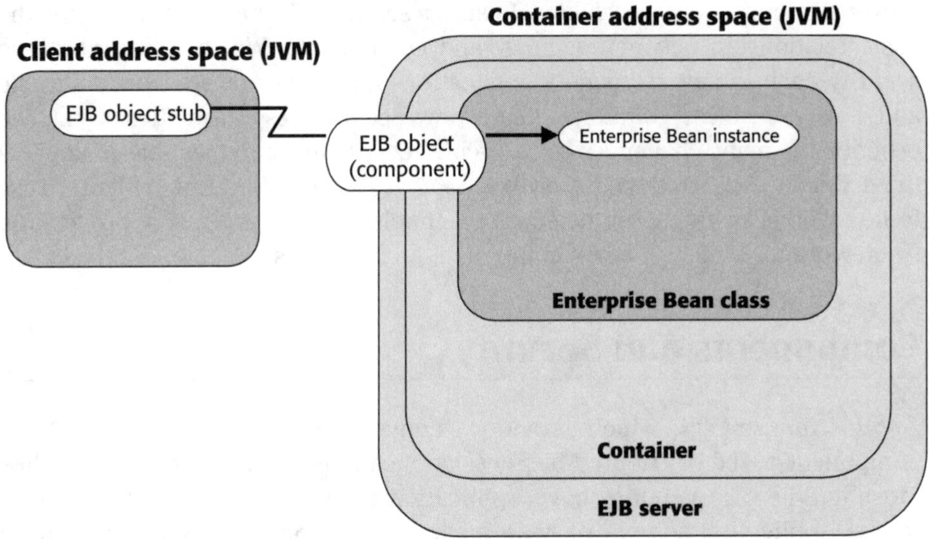

Figure 1.1 Component architecture.

such as C++. Fully compliant EJB products also support the OMG Internet Inter-ORB Protocol (IIOP), allowing EJB components and CORBA components to interoperate.

Because application servers are targeted at enterprise deployment, it's no surprise that security is generally addressed in these architectures. Without a good security solution protecting corporate data on an application server, most businesses would not be willing to make their data accessible to Internet Web clients.

Distributed component computing and information security are complex technologies that are naturally in conflict. A distributed environment makes data widely accessible and thus introduces potential security holes at multiple points in the enterprise. Security protection confines systems and reduces data accessibility. As a result, distributed systems require trade-offs between the degree of distributed computing and the degree of security.

Technologies are resolving the conflict between distributed computing and security, particularly in EJB and CORBA. This book explores how deploying security services in support of EJB and CORBA address security integration. This book addresses an audience of enterprise technical managers, software architects, security architects, software developers, and security administrators—particularly those now moving to distributed environments and those new to the issues of information security. We explore new ways of thinking about information security in distributed environments—focusing on how to develop practical, comprehensive approaches using new and existing technologies.

Security as an Enabler for E-Business Applications

Corporations are discovering the power of online services to increase customer loyalty, support sales efforts, and manage internal information. The common thread in these diverse efforts is the need to present end users with a unified view of information stored in multiple systems, particularly as organizations move from static Web sites to the transactional capabilities of electronic commerce. To satisfy this need, legacy systems are being integrated with powerful new e-business–based applications that provide broad connectivity across a multitude of back-end systems. These unified applications bring direct bottom-line benefits. For example:

- **On the Internet.** A bank cements relationships with commercial customers by offering increased efficiency with online currency trading. This service requires real-time updates and links to back-office transactional and profitability analysis systems.

- **On extranets.** A bank and an airline both increase their customer bases with a joint venture—a credit card that offers frequent flyer credits sponsored by the bank. This service requires joint data-sharing, such as purchase payment and charge-back information, as well as decision support applications to retrieve, manipulate, and store information across enterprise boundaries. Additionally, employees from both companies need to access information.
- **On an intranet.** A global manufacturer accelerates the organizational learning curve by creating a global knowledge sharing system for manufacturing research and development. Plant engineers on one continent can instantly share process breakthroughs with colleagues thousands of miles away.

E-Business Applications Increase Risks

These new e-business applications can have a dark side. They can open a direct pipeline to the enterprise's most valuable information assets, presenting a tempting target for fraud, malicious hackers, and industrial espionage.

Appropriate protections are a prerequisite for doing business both for an organization's credibility with its stakeholders and its financial viability. For example:

- The bank offering currency trading needs to protect the integrity of its core systems from unauthorized transfers or tampering.
- The bank and airline in a joint venture may compete in other areas or through other partnerships. A secure barrier, permitting authorized transactions only, must be erected between the two enterprise computing environments.
- The manufacturer posting proprietary discoveries needs to ensure that competitors or their contractors cannot tap into the system. Attacks from both the outside and inside must be blocked.

Information Security Goals: Enable Use, Bar Intrusion

Information security focuses on protecting valuable and sensitive enterprise data. To secure information assets, organizations must open availability to legitimate users while barring unauthorized access. In general, secure systems must provide the following protections:

- **Confidentiality.** Safeguard user privacy and prevent the theft of enterprise information both stored and in transit.

- **Integrity.** Ensure that electronic transactions and data resources are not tampered with at any point, either accidentally or maliciously.
- **Accountability.** Detect attacks in progress or trace any damage from successful attacks (security audit and intrusion detection). Prevent system users from later denying completed transactions (non-repudiation).
- **Availability.** Ensure uninterrupted service to authorized users. Service interruptions can either be accidental or maliciously caused by denial-of-service attacks.

To provide these four key protections, information security must be an integral part of system design and implementation.

E-Business Solutions Create New Security Responsibilities

The breadth of information security in e-business applications is broader than you might expect. Many system architects and developers are accustomed to thinking about security as a low-level topic, dealing only with networks, firewalls, operating systems, and cryptography. However, e-business is changing the risk levels associated with deploying software, and as a consequence, security is becoming an important design issue for any software component.

The scope of e-business security is so broad because these applications typically cut across lines of business. There are many examples of new business models that drive security needs:

- **E-Commerce Sites on the Internet.** Rely on credit card authorization services from an outside company. A federated relationship between an e-commerce company and a credit card service depends on trustworthy authenticated communication.
- **Cross-Selling and Customer Relationship Management.** Rely on customer information being shared across many lines of business within an enterprise. Cross-selling allows an enterprise to offer a customer new products or services based on existing sales. Customer relationship management allows the enterprise to provide consistent customer support across many different services. These e-business services are very valuable, but if they are not properly constrained by security policies, the services may violate a customer's desire for privacy.
- **Supply Chain Management.** Requires continuing communication among all of the suppliers in a manufacturing chain to ensure that the supply of various parts is adequate to meet demand. The transactions describing the supply chain that are exchanged among the enterprises

contain highly proprietary data that must be protected from outside snooping.

- **Bandwidth on Demand.** Allows customers to make dynamic requests for increases in the quality of a telecommunications service and get instant results. Bandwidth on demand is an example of *self-administration,* in which users handle many of their own administrative functions rather than relying on an administrator within the enterprise to do it for them. Self-administration provides better service for customers at a lower cost, but comes with significant security risks. Because corporate servers, which were previously only available to system administrators, are now accessible by end users, security mechanisms must be in place to ensure that sensitive administrative functions are off-limits.

In each of the preceding cases, one enterprise or line of business can expose another organization to increased security risk. For example, a partner can unintentionally expose your business to a security attack by providing its customers access to your business resources. As a result, security risk is no longer under the complete control of a single organization. Risks must be assessed and managed across a collection of organizations, which is a new and very challenging security responsibility.

Risk Management Holds Key

A large middle ground exists between the extremes of avoiding e-business applications altogether, fatalistically launching unprotected systems, or burdening every application with prohibitively costly and user-unfriendly security measures.

This middle ground is the area of risk management. The risk-management approach aims not to eliminate risk but to control it. Risk management is a rigorous balancing process of determining how much and what kind of security to incorporate in light of business needs and acceptable levels of risk. It unlocks the profit potential of expanded network connectivity by enabling legitimate use while blocking unauthorized access. The goal is to provide adequate protection to meet business needs without undue risk, making the right trade-offs between security and cost, performance and functionality.

Consider four different e-business users: an Internet Service Provider (ISP), a hospital administrator, a banker, and a military officer. Each has a different security concern.

- The ISP is primarily concerned about availability, that is, making services available to its customers.
- The hospital administrator wants to ensure data integrity, meaning that patient records are only updated by authorized staff.

- The banker is most concerned about accountability, meaning that the person who authorizes a financial transaction is identified and tracked.
- The military officer wants confidentiality, that is, keeping military secrets out of the hands of potential enemies.

The challenge is to implement security in a way that meets business needs cost-effectively in the short term and as enterprise needs expand. Meeting the challenge requires a collaborative effort between corporate strategists and information technology managers. Understanding the business drivers for information security helps clarify where to focus security measures. Understanding the underlying application architecture—how components work together—clarifies the most practical approach for building system security. Distributed applications in particular require new ways of thinking.

Industrial experience in managing e-business information security is generally low. Security technology is changing rapidly, and corporate management is not well equipped to cope with risk management changes caused by technology changes. New versions of interconnected e-business systems and software product versions continue to appear, and with each release, a whole new set of security vulnerabilities surface.

Managing security risk in distributed e-business applications is daunting, but following some basic rules for building security into component-based applications lays the groundwork for a solid risk management approach. Although this book does not provide detailed advice on security risk management, we do describe principles for building secure applications that are independent of any specific technology and will continue to be a guide for you as technologies evolve. Near the end of this chapter, we provide basic principles for ESI, which are security integration themes that we have seen addressed repeatedly by many enterprises. Other chapters in this book, particularly Chapter 9, "Planning a Secure Component System," and Chapter 10, "Building an Integrated System," supply many insights on ESI that will place your risk-management approach on a firm foundation.

Information Security: A Proven Concern

Information security is a serious concern for most businesses. Even though reporting of computer-based crime is sporadic because companies fear negative publicity and continued attacks, the trend is quite clear: Information security attacks continue to be a real threat to businesses. According to a recent Computer Security Institute Survey, 90 percent of interviewed businesses reported that they had detected computer security breaches in the last year. In addition, 74 percent of the businesses reported that the attacks caused financial losses, such as losses due to financial fraud or theft of valuable intellectual property.

The threats to businesses are from both internal and external attacks. In the same survey, 71 percent of businesses said that they detected insider attacks (by trusted corporate users). This last statistic is very important from the perspective of this book—to meet corporate needs, a complete end-to-end security solution *must* address insider attacks.

Most e-business solutions today blur the line between the inside world containing trusted users and the outside world containing potentially hostile attackers. As we've discussed, the primary purpose of multitier architectures is to open up the corporate network to the external world, thus allowing valuable corporate resources to be accessible to outsiders. Outsiders (such as business partners, suppliers, or remote employees) may have very similar data access rights to corporate information as many insiders. As a result, protection mechanisms must be in place not only at the external system boundaries, but also throughout the enterprise architecture.

According to a META Group survey, 70 percent of businesses view information security as critical to their corporate mission. Due to the continuing threat, many businesses are increasing their spending on security; large corporations are increasing their spending the most.

We're concerned about the way businesses spend their money on security. We've seen many of them address security using a fragmented, inefficient approach, in which various corporate divisions each build their own ad hoc security solutions. Piecemeal security solutions can be worse than no security at all because they can result in:

- Redundant spending across the organization
- Point solutions that don't scale or interoperate
- Increased maintenance, training, and administration cost

Applying security products without thinking about how they all fit together clearly does not work. We believe that businesses should build and leverage a common security infrastructure that is shared across the enterprise. An integrated approach to security is the only way to address complex multitier e-business applications, which we'll explain in the following sections.

Distributed Systems Require Distributed Security

Component technology, which closely groups data and the business logic that makes use of the data, is having a dramatic impact on the business computing landscape. Developments in the field of distributed component computing allow cooperating components to reside in different machines, networks, or even enterprises. These developments enable businesses to enhance and reuse installed applications rapidly and represent new power to tap the immense value of legacy resources. As a result, many organizations are migrating from traditional single layer client/server applications to multitiered application architectures.

Distributed component technology provides the foundation for next generation e-business applications because it offers so much versatility. Distributed components that encapsulate code and data can reside anywhere on the network. Client software only needs to know about the component's interface; how the component is implemented and where it is running is transparent to the invoking application. Transparency and reusability give distributed component computing environments great power, but they present new challenges for information security. These challenges require new ways of thinking and new tools.

Security Challenges in Distributed Component Environments

Traditionally, computer security has worked effectively in systems in which sensitive data can be isolated and protected in a central repository. Distributed components promote the opposite philosophy by making distributed data widely accessible across large networks. Simply put, the more accessible data is, the harder it is to protect. Ordinarily, it's a good idea to keep your crown jewels locked up in a vault. Distributed components encourage you to pass them around to all your friends for safekeeping.

The traditional notion of computer security is embodied in the concept of a *trusted computing base* (TCB). The TCB consists of the hardware and software mechanisms that are responsible for enforcing the security policy, which defines when a user may access a resource. The TCB must be:

- Tamper-proof
- Always invoked (nonbypassable)
- Small enough to be thoroughly analyzed

The TCB is usually implemented within an operating system that is under strict configuration control. This architecture permits very tight security because the TCB is the mediator through which all user accesses to resources must pass. Everything within the TCB is trusted to enforce the security policy; everything outside of the TCB is untrusted. Figure 1.2 illustrates a traditional TCB.

Distributed component systems, on the other hand, have a more complex security architecture as shown in Figure 1.3. Security functionality (the shaded areas of the diagram) in component systems is distributed throughout the architecture rather than residing in a central TCB. Because distributed

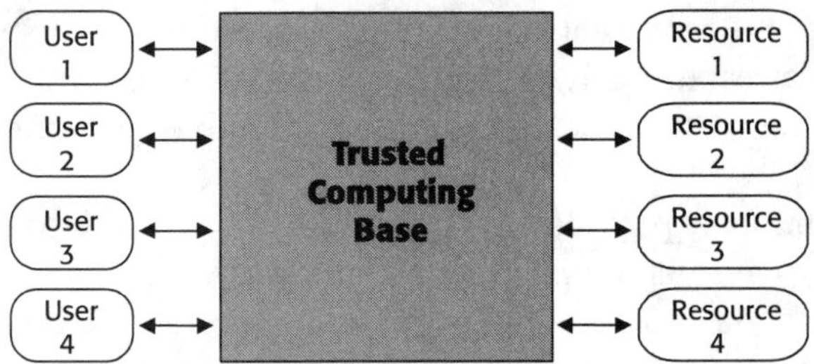

Figure 1.2 Traditional TCB.

component systems are frequently heterogeneous, security may be implemented differently on different platforms. Security might be enforced by the application components, middleware, operating system, hardware, or any combination thereof. Some platforms may contain a great deal of code that is trusted to enforce the security policy, whereas other platforms may have very little.

Distributing security in this manner means that a particular distributed application may be secure, but that fact is hard to confirm. In a distributed component system, the combination of all of this trusted code together theoretically embodies a *distributed TCB*. But is this really a distributed TCB? Probably not. It may be tamper-proof and always invoked, but it may not be small enough to be analyzed easily. That's a concern because if we can't analyze the system, we can't be certain that the valuable data is being protected.

Some security traditionalists believe that it is not possible to build highly secure distributed component systems. We disagree and question whether a TCB model is even appropriate for distributed component environments.

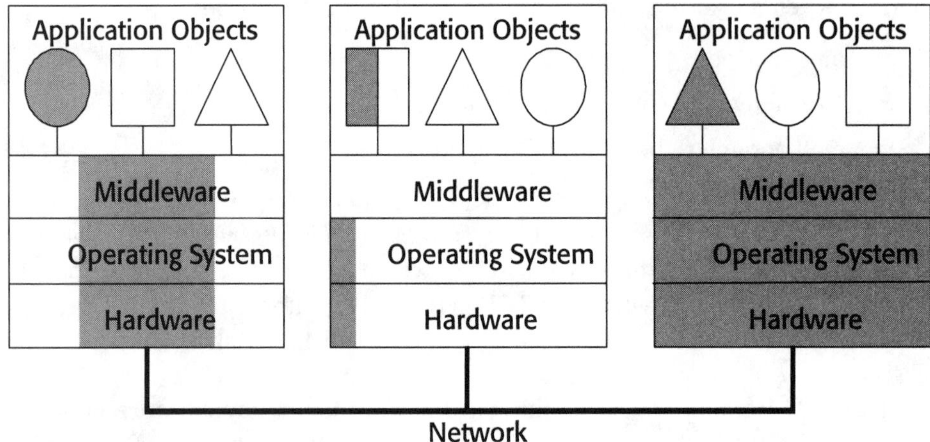

Figure 1.3 Distributed component security architecture.

Although we agree with the philosophy of TCBs, which is that TCBs are great for enforcing security, they aren't sufficiently flexible to support component-based systems. This book presents a number of techniques that integrate security into a distributed component environment. Although the end result of our approach does not resemble a traditional TCB model, we do recommend an integrated approach that is consistent with TCB principles and simplifies the analysis of distributed system security.

The flexibility and openness of distributed component systems make security administration a real challenge. Systems managers with experience administering security in Unix or Windows NT environments know how difficult it is to get it right. Many security attacks on these systems are not due to obscure security vulnerabilities but instead are due to inadvertent administrative errors or "leaving the barn door open."

Several other characteristics of distributed component systems also complicate security enforcement. These system characteristics include:

- **Layered.** Systems consist of many security layers (applications, middleware, operating system, hardware, and network) that must fit together.
- **Exposed.** Many distributed component systems are designed to work over the Internet or large intranets. Data going over networks is subject to packet-sniffing interception.
- **Dynamic.** Component systems are designed to be dynamic, allowing new application components to be created on the fly. Components can play both client and server roles and can interact in multiple and unpredictable ways. This means that security policies must also be dynamic, adding complexity.
- **Multi-enterprise.** Distributed component computing allows the sharing of information among enterprises. Enterprise security policies will be different (say, between a hospital and a bank), which means that data sharing requires translations between enterprise policies.

Configuring and administering security for distributed component systems is potentially far more complex than for a traditional system. Without special tools, security has to be administered manually for each layer independently, leaving room for mistakes and inconsistencies. For instance, an application may correctly confirm that a loan officer is authorized to access a record before allowing changes. However, if supporting operating system calls have not been set up with complementary file permissions, access protection is not complete.

The challenge is to create an environment in which the complexity is minimized, ensuring that security administration is enforced automatically and consistently.

End-to-End ESI

As e-business environments have evolved to distributed component models, security technologies have been trying to keep up. As you'll see throughout this book, we believe that most of the pieces of the security puzzle exist, but that it still takes considerable effort to put all these pieces together to build an integrated solution. Figure 1.4 provides an overview of the different security technologies that need to be integrated.

Twenty years ago life was reasonably simple for the security professional. Sensitive data resided on monolithic back-end data stores. There were only a few physical access paths to the data, which were protected by well-understood operating system access control mechanisms. Policies, procedures, and tools have been in place for many years to protect legacy data stores.

Several years ago, Web-based applications burst onto the scene. With the advent of e-commerce in this environment, secure access to Web servers was extremely important. Today, there are many mature perimeter security technologies, such as Secure Sockets Layer (SSL), firewalls, and Web authentication/authorization servers that enforce security between browser clients and corporate Web servers.

Huge numbers of companies are now building complex e-business logic into application servers in the mid-tier. As we've discussed, the business motivation

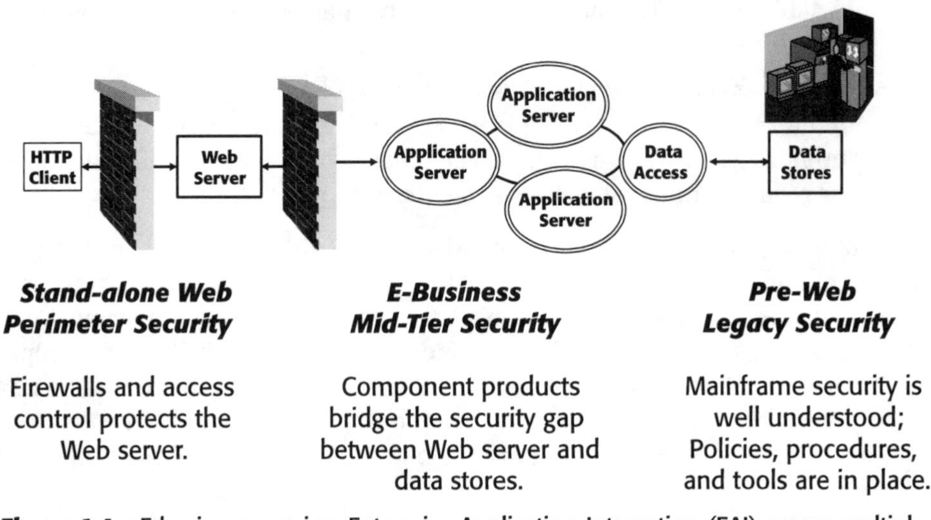
HTTP Client
Web Server
Application Server
Application Server
Application Server
Data Access
Data Stores
Stand-alone Web Perimeter Security
E-Business Mid-Tier Security
Pre-Web Legacy Security
Firewalls and access control protects the Web server.
Component products bridge the security gap between Web server and data stores.
Mainframe security is well understood; Policies, procedures, and tools are in place.

Figure 1.4 E-business requires Enterprise Application Integration (EAI) across multiple security technologies.

for this development is compelling: Mid-tier business logic allows accessibility to back-end legacy data in ways never imagined; the opportunities for increased interaction among all kinds of buyers and suppliers seem endless.

Security gets much more interesting when we introduce components in the middle tier. Although there are many mid-tier technologies that hook up Web servers to back-end legacy systems, the security of these approaches is often nonexistent. In fact, several recent publicized attacks have been caused by weaknesses in mid-tier security that have exposed sensitive back-end data (e.g., customer credit card numbers and purchase data) to the outside world. Companies are usually at a loss for solutions to middle tier security.

To solve the thorny issue of securely connecting Web servers to back-end data stores, we introduce the concept of end-to-end ESI. ESI is a special case of EAI (Ruh, Maginnis, Brown, 2000).

EAI is a technique for unifying many different applications by using a common middleware infrastructure. EAI provides an application "bus" that allows every application to communicate to others via a common generic interface. Without EAI, an application would need a separate interface for every other application, thus causing an explosion of pairwise "stovepipe" connections between applications. EAI allows application development to scale to a large number of interchangeable components.

We recognize that integration of end-to-end security requires EAI techniques. Many different security technologies are used in the perimeter, middle, and legacy tiers. Typically, these security technologies do not interoperate easily. As a result, we face exactly the same problem that application integrators face: A separate ad hoc interface to connect one security technology to another causes an explosion of pairwise stovepipe connections between security technologies.

ESI provides a common security framework to integrate many different security solutions. We use mid-tier component security, specifically EJB and CORBA security, to bridge the security gap between perimeter and legacy security. By using ESI, new security technologies in each tier may be added without affecting the business applications. We'll further explore the concept of ESI in the next few sections.

ESI Requirements

A key issue in enterprise security architectures is the ability to support end-to-end security across many application components. End-to-end security is the ability to ensure that data access is properly protected over the entire path of requests and replies as they travel through the system. The scope of end-to-end security begins with the person accessing a Web browser or other client program, continues through the business components of the middle tier, and ends at the data store on the back-end legacy system. The path of data may travel through both public and private networks with varying degrees of protection.

In the enterprise architecture, shown in Figure 1.4, a user accesses an application in the presentation layer (e.g., a Web browser client sends requests to a Web server), which communicates to mid-tier business components (e.g., application servers). Frequently, the client request is transmitted through a complex multitier chain of business components running on a variety of platforms. The request finally makes it to one or more back-end legacy systems, which accesses persistent data stores on behalf of the user, processes the request, and returns the appropriate results.

To provide end-to-end security, each link in the chain of requests and replies must be properly protected: from the initiating client, through mid-tier business components, to the legacy systems, and then back again to the client. There are three security tiers that comprise any end-to-end enterprise security solution:

- **Perimeter security technologies.** Used between the client and the Web server. Perimeter security enforces protection for customer, partner, and employee access to corporate resources. Perimeter security primarily protects against external attackers, such as hackers, that are outside of the organization.
- **Mid-tier security technologies.** Used between the mid-tier business components. Mid-tier security focuses primarily on protecting against insider attacks, but also provides another layer of protection against external attackers.
- **Legacy security technologies.** Address protection of databases and operating system specific back-end systems, such as mainframes, Unix, and Windows NT server platforms.

ESI Solutions

ESI solutions integrate security technologies across the perimeter, middle, and legacy security tiers. An ESI solution first and foremost consists of a security framework, which describes a collection of security service interfaces that may be implemented by an evolving set of security products. We'll spend most of this section describing our approach for defining an enterprise security framework. As you read the rest of this book, keep in mind that we use this security framework to integrate interfaces into all of the security technologies discussed.

In addition to the framework, an ESI solution also contains the software and hardware technologies for securing e-business components. Chapters 2, 3, 4, and 7 describe EJB, CORBA, and many other security technologies that may be used to secure components.

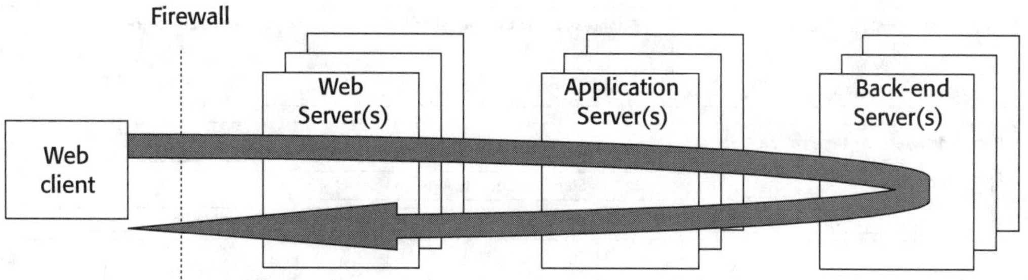

Figure 1.5 Key e-business challenge: end-to-end ESI.

Finally, an ESI solution contains integration techniques, such as bridges, wrappers, and interceptors, that developers can use to plug security technologies into a middleware environment. To hook together different security technologies, ESI must solve a key problem: defining a secure association between clients and targets that establishes a common security context. The security context consists of a user's privileges, which must be transferred across the system to a target application. A user's privileges, which form the basis for authorization decisions and audit events, must be protected as they are transmitted between perimeter, middle, and legacy tiers, as shown in Figure 1.5. Because each technology in these tiers represents and protects a user's privileges differently, integration of security context can be a rather difficult problem. Chapters 5, 6, and 10 describe some examples of commonly used integration techniques that address interoperability of security context.

ESI Framework

The ESI framework specifies the interactions among the security services and application components that use those security services. By using common interfaces, it's possible to add new security technology solutions without making big changes to the existing framework. In this way, the ESI framework supports "plug-ins" for new security technologies. Key aspects of the framework are shown in Figure 1.6.

Applications

The security framework provides enterprise security services for presentation components, business logic components, and legacy data stores. The framework supports security mechanisms that enforce security on behalf of *security-aware* and *security-unaware* applications.

- **Security-Aware Application.** An application that uses the security Application Programming Interfaces (APIs) to access and validate the

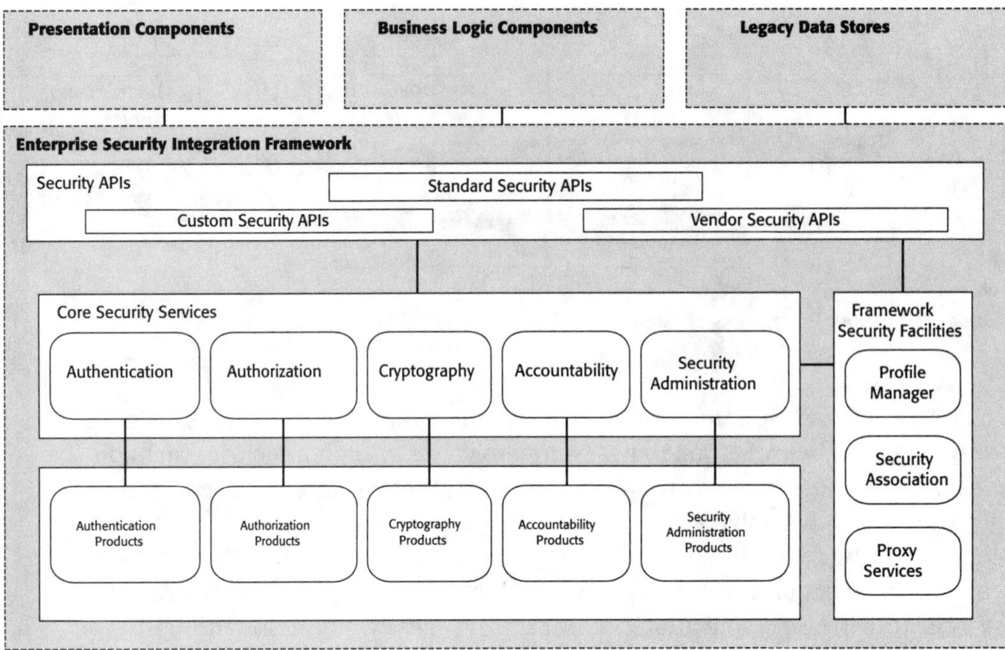

Figure 1.6 ESI framework.

security policies that apply to it. Security-aware applications may directly access security functions that enable the applications to perform additional security checks and fully exploit the capabilities of the security infrastructure.

- **Security-Unaware Application.** An application that does not explicitly call security services, but is still secured by the supporting environment (e.g., an EJB or CORBA Container). Security is typically enforced for security-unaware applications by using interceptors, which transparently call the underlying security APIs on behalf of the application. This approach reduces the burden on application developers to develop security modules within the application and lessens the chance of security flaws being introduced.

Other applications, called *security self-reliant applications*, do not use any of the security services provided by the framework. A security self-reliant application may not use the security services for two reasons: because it has no security relevant functionality and thus does not need to be secured or because it uses separate independent security functions that are not part of the defined ESI security framework.

APIs

The framework security APIs are called explicitly by security-aware applications and implicitly by security-unaware applications via interceptors. Security APIs provide interfaces for access to the framework security services. The framework supports standard, custom, and vendor security APIs.

- **Standard Security API.** We encourage support for APIs based on open standards or industry *de facto* standards. Examples of such standards are the EJB and CORBA security APIs described in this book in Chapters 2, 3, and 7. These standards should be used whenever possible because they are likely to provide the most stability and the most flexibility across many different vendors' products.
- **Custom Security API.** Custom APIs may be implemented when an enterprise's needs cannot be met by existing standard APIs. Custom APIs are required especially when an enterprise uses a security service that is tailored to its business, for example, a custom rule-based entitlements engine developed internally by an investment bank.
- **Vendor Security API.** As a last resort, vendor specific proprietary APIs may be used where open standards have not yet been defined. We recommend avoiding the use of proprietary security APIs in applications if at all possible. Proprietary APIs make it very difficult for the developer or administrator to switch security products. Although vendors may think this is a great idea, we believe that security technology is changing much too rapidly to be confined to any one product. As an alternative, we recommend wrapping a vendor's proprietary API with a standard or custom API.

Core Security Services

The next layer of the security framework provides core security services enabling end-to-end application security across multitier applications. Each of the security services defines a wrapper that sits between the security APIs and the security products. The security services wrappers serve to isolate applications from underlying security products. By creating a new wrapper, switching security products without affecting application code if the need arises is straightforward. The key security services are authentication, authorization, cryptography, accountability, and security administration.

- **Authentication.** Verifies that principals (human users, registered system entities, and components) are who they claim to be. The result of authentication is a set of *credentials*, which describes the attributes (e.g., identity, role, group, and clearance) that may be associated with the authenticated principal.

- **Authorization.** Grants permission for principals to access resources, providing the basis for access control. Data integrity and confidentiality access controls enforce restrictions of access to prevent unauthorized use. Data integrity controls ensure that only authorized principals may modify resources. Data confidentiality controls ensure that resource contents are disclosed only to authorized principals.
- **Cryptography.** Provides cryptographic algorithms and protocols for protecting data and messages from disclosure or modification. Encryption provides confidentiality by encoding data into an unintelligible form with a reversible algorithm, which allows the holder of the encryption key(s) to decode the encrypted data. Digital signature applies cryptography to ensure that data is authentic and has not been modified during storage or transmission.
- **Accountability.** Ensures that principals are accountable for their actions. *Security audit* provides a record of security relevant events and permits monitoring of a principal's actions in a system. *Nonrepudiation* provides irrefutable proof of data origin or receipt.
- **Security Administration.** Defines the security policy maintenance lifecycle embodied in user profiles, authentication, authorization, and accountability mechanisms as well as other data relevant to the security framework.

Framework Security Facilities

The framework provides general security facilities that support the core security services. The framework security facilities include the profile manager, security association, and proxy services.

- **Profile Manager.** Provides a general facility for persistent storage of user and application profile and security policy data that can be accessed by other framework services.
- **Security Association.** Handles the principal's security credentials and controls how they propagate. During a communication between any two client and target application components, the security association establishes the trust in each party's credentials and creates the security context that will be used when protecting requests and responses in transit between the client and the target. The security association controls the use of *delegation*, which allows an intermediate server to use the credentials of an initiating principal so that the server may act on behalf the ini-

tiating principal. (Delegation is discussed in considerably more detail in Chapters 6 and 8.)

- **Security Proxy Services.** Provides interoperability between different security technology domains by acting as a server in the client's technology domain and a client in the target's domain.

Security Products

Implementation of the framework generally requires several security technology products that collectively comprise the enterprise security services. Sample security products required include firewalls, Web authentication/authorization products, component authentication/authorization products, cryptographic products, and directory services. Several of these product categories are discussed in this book; we describe EJB and CORBA security in Chapters 2 and 3, and we survey other relevant security technologies in Chapter 4.

ESI Benefits

At this point, the benefits of using a framework to address enterprise security integration should be clear. Our approach focuses on standards, which are the best way to maintain application portability and interoperability in the long run. Products and technologies will come and go, but generally accepted security standards for fundamental security services will be much more stable. A standards-based set of security APIs allows you to evolve security products over time without needing to rewrite your applications. Designing your applications for evolving security products is important because we believe that your business requirements and new security technologies will continue to be a moving target. You might choose a great product that satisfies your needs for the present, but you'll probably want to change the product in the future, and most people don't want to be stuck with any one vendor's product for too long.

Having a security framework also means that you don't need to implement everything at once. The framework allows you to start small by selecting the security services you need and building more sophisticated security functionality when and if it's required. The framework provides you with a roadmap for your security architecture, helping to guide you on how to choose products and technologies that match your needs over time.

Finally, the framework puts the security focus where it should be—on building a common infrastructure that can be shared across the enterprise. Custom-built security that is hand coded within applications is expensive to implement and maintain and is likely to have more security vulnerabilities. A single security infrastructure with APIs that can be used by all of your applications avoids multiple, duplicate definitions of users, security attributes, and other policies. You can focus your limited time and money on building a few critical interoperable security technologies rather than coping with a mass of unrelated security products that will never work together.

Principles of ESI

We finish our discussion of ESI by giving you some basic principles to follow when integrating security into component-based e-business applications. We've learned these rules over the years as we applied ESI techniques to many large customers' problems in banking, telecommunications, and manufacturing. In the chapters that follow, we'll point out examples that illustrate these principles.

- **Authentication**
  - **Trust no one.** In distributed systems, authentication isn't just about people. A client request bounces through many applications in a multitier architecture, so there are many points of vulnerability. Each component that is a part of a request chain should be authenticated on its own. If not, an attacker may be able to insert a new component in this chain and cause serious damage. The more complex the application architecture, the more serious the threat.
  - **Balance cost against threat.** On the other hand, the best authentication isn't for everyone. The most secure authentication, such as public-key certificates on smart cards, is probably too expensive to deploy and manage for many applications. If authentication techniques are *too* strong, people may just give up and not use the system. It's better to have authentication that people will use rather than building a secure boat anchor. Single sign-on is an example of this principle; no one likes to login more than once.
- **Authorization**
  - **Application driven.** Authorization policies aren't really to protect URLs or files: They protect business data that resides in those files. A lot of time and money is wasted blindly setting up security products that do little to protect important application data. To secure a system, don't lose sight of the fact that the most important thing to understand is the purpose of the business application. Once you understand what the business application is for and what security failures you are worried about, you can *then* figure out the best way to protect the data.
  - **Push security down.** After you know what application data is really important to protect, look to enforce authorization at the lowest practical level in the architecture. The least desirable location is within the application, although some policies cannot be enforced anywhere else.

(Chapter 7 discusses this topic at length.) By pushing authorization down to the lower layers of the architecture, you're more likely to produce robust common security mechanisms that can be shared across many applications.

- **Accountability**
  - **Audit early, not often.** Auditing is expensive in distributed systems, so for performance reasons, it's better to do it as little as possible. Unlike authorization, it's preferable to push the source of an audit event to the *upper* layers of the architecture near the application. Low-level auditing (e.g., at the operating system level) is extremely difficult to analyze because it takes several low-level events to match to a single business transaction. Low-level auditing is fine for discovering an attack on your operating system, but correlating low-level audit data across multiple audit logs to detect an application attack can be close to impossible. As a result, the most effective auditing is done as soon as an application recognizes that a potentially dangerous event has occurred.
- **Security Administration**
  - **Collections for scale.** E-business applications are all about managing huge numbers: millions of users and resources; thousands of servers. The best way to deal with large numbers is to collect users and resources into groups and make those groups hierarchical. (We discuss this topic in Chapter 8.) By defining collections, administrators can set policies on lots of users and resources at the same time and delegate security responsibilities across many administrators. Note that collections do not just contain people; services and data also should be grouped to handle scale.
  - **Centralized management, distributed enforcement.** Administering distributed applications is difficult because components are widely scattered, and manually setting up policies for each component across a large network isn't practical. The easiest way to administer security is when the security policy is in one place. However, a centralized policy may not be very efficient to enforce if the security infrastructure must check a central policy every time a remote component executes. In addition, fully centralized management creates a single point of failure and an opportunity for denial of service attacks. The best approaches provide the best of both worlds by offering security administration that is logically centralized, but uses distribution techniques to get the policy out near the components where it's needed. Beware of synchronization issues: Many products use caching, which speeds up access, but could mean that policies are sometimes out-of-date.

- **Security Association**
  - **Think end-to-end, not point-to-point.** As we mentioned previously, e-business applications are implemented by chains of requests, which are much more complex than the client/server model. Transport security mechanisms, such as SSL or Internet Protocol Security (IPSEC), are inadequate in multitier environments because they cannot secure a chain of requests—they only secure two end-points. It's for this reason that these protocols don't deal with delegation, as we'll explain in later chapters. Protocols that are built upon transport security, such as Common Secure Interoperability v2 (CSIv2) (discussed in Chapter 6), are the best way to secure applications end-to-end.
  - **Design for failure.** A simplistic component model assumes that all applications trust each other to protect data. That may be okay for small systems, but it's a dangerous assumption when the applications are more distributed. If one component is compromised in this scenario, then the entire set of distributed components is vulnerable. A better approach is to view collections of components as mutually suspicious islands—if one collection of components is compromised, then others will still be safe.

Example of a Secure Component Architecture

Throughout this book, we use a simple e-commerce example to illustrate component security topics. In this section, we introduce the example and provide an overview of its business security requirements.

Business Scenario

Our application is a simple online storefront called *eBusiness.com*. The store sells its products to *customers* who can electronically place and settle orders for products through *customer accounts*. *Members* are a category of customers who get special treatment: Members have access to product deals that are not available to regular customers.

eBusiness.com Object Model

The eBusiness.com object model contains the interfaces and operations shown in the class diagram in Figure 1.7. We assume that the reader is generally familiar with the Unified Modeling Language (UML) notation for a class diagram. For simplicity, we have omitted the complete operation signatures that describe

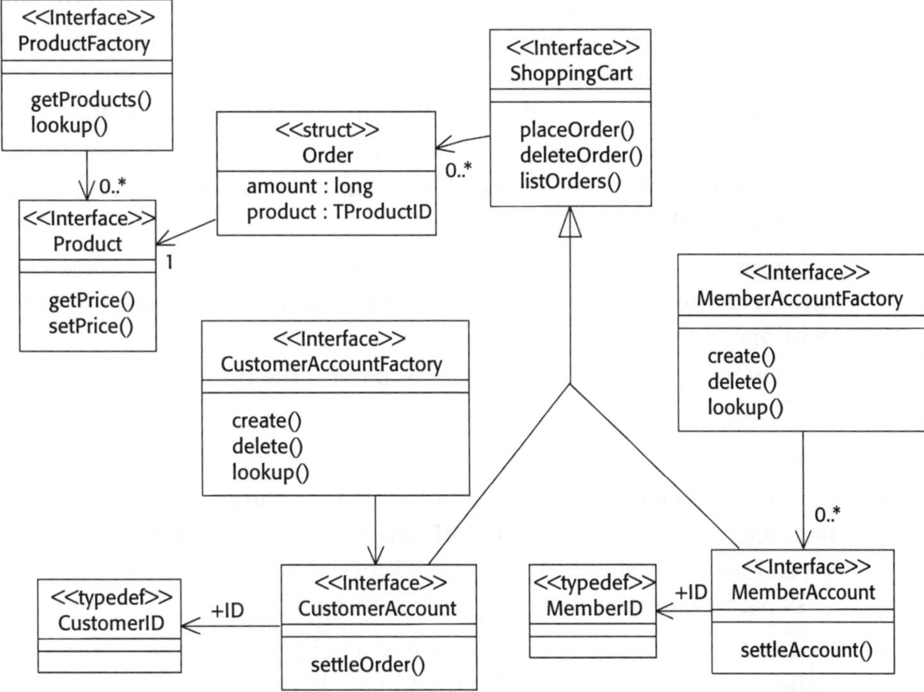

Figure 1.7 eBusiness.com: example of secure component object model.

arguments and return values because these have little relevance to the security policies that we will define.

- **ProductFactory** is the object factory that returns **Product** instances.
  - **getProducts** returns a list of **ProductIDs** that represents the inventory of products that eBusiness.com is selling. (To keep the example simple, we don't provide an interface to add new products to the list.)
  - **lookup** returns a **Product** instance based on a supplied **ProductID**.
- **Product** represents a product that eBusiness.com is selling.
  - **getPrice** returns the price of **Product**.
  - **setPrice** sets the price of **Product**.
- **ShoppingCart** represents a customer's list of product orders.
  - **placeOrder** puts an order into **ShoppingCart**.
  - **deleteOrder** deletes an order from **ShoppingCart**.
  - **listOrders** lists the orders in **ShoppingCart**.
- **Order** represents the data that describes a product order.
  - **amount** attribute describes the quantity of **Product** ordered.
  - **product** attribute is the **ProductID** of the ordered **Product**.

- **CustomerAccountFactory** is the object factory that returns **CustomerAccount** instances. This factory stores customer accounts so a customer may retrieve them for later use.
  - **create** makes a new **CustomerAccount** based on the **CustomerID**.
  - **delete** removes an existing **CustomerAccount**.
  - **lookup** retrieves an existing **CustomerAccount** based on the **CustomerID**.
- **CustomerAccount** represents the state of a customer's account. **CustomerAccount** inherits from **ShoppingCart** and adds the following operation.
  - **settleOrder** allows the customer to pay for the orders in the account with a credit card.
- **CustomerID** represents a unique identifier for a customer.
- **MemberAccountFactory** and **MemberID** have the same signatures and functionality as **CustomerAccountFactory** and **CustomerID**. The member versions of these interfaces make it easier for us to define different access permissions for members and customers.
- **MemberAccount** represents the state of a member's account. **MemberAccount** inherits from **ShoppingCart** and adds the following operation.
  - **settleAccount** allows the member to pay for the orders in the account with a credit card.

For this scenario, we assume that the preceding interfaces have been implemented on an application server as EJB or CORBA components. A typical interaction would go something like this: A customer first authenticates to the security service, and then gets a list of products and prices using the **ProductFactory** interface. The customer then places orders for products into his or her account using the **CustomerAccount** interface and sometime later settles the order with a credit card number.

eBusiness.com Security Requirements

The EJB and CORBA security policies that we define in later chapters are based on the business requirements for this eBusiness.com example. We describe the business requirements for each class of user in the next section.

ESI AUTHORIZATION PRINCIPLE: APPLICATION DRIVEN

We first ensure that we understand the purpose of the eBusiness.com application before we try to figure out how to secure it. Our definition of EJB and CORBA authorization policy is closely aligned with the following business requirements.

- **Visitors.** To entice new customers, eBusiness.com permits visitors who are unauthenticated users to browse the site. Visitors are permitted very limited access. Visitors may:
  - See the product list, but not their prices.
  - Self-register to become a customer. Visitors may create a **Customer-Account**, which turns the visitor into a **Customer**.
- **Customers.** Most users accessing eBusiness.com are customers who are permitted to order regular products. Customers may:
  - See the product list and prices for regular products, but not the prices for special products, which are only offered to members.
  - Place, delete, and settle (pay for) an order. A customer may not delete his or her **CustomerAccount**, however, and must ask someone on the eBusiness.com staff to perform this task. eBusiness.com wants to make it difficult for customers to remove their affiliation with the company.
- **Members.** If approved by eBusiness.com staff, some customers may become members. Members have a longstanding relationship with eBusiness.com and are offered price breaks on special products. Other than having access to special products and prices, members exhibit the same behavior as customers. Members may:
  - See the product list and prices for regular and special products.
  - Place, delete, and settle (pay for) an order. A member may not delete his or her **MemberAccount**, however, and must ask someone on the eBusiness.com staff to perform this task. eBusiness.com wants to make it difficult for members to remove their affiliation with the company.
- **Staff.** eBusiness.com company staff members are responsible for administering all aspects of the site. However, eBusiness.com is concerned about someone on the staff committing fraud by creating fictitious customers and using stolen credit card numbers to order merchandise. To prevent this exposure, people on the staff are not permitted to settle orders on behalf of customers or members. Staff may:
  - See the product list and prices for regular and special products and set product prices.
  - Assist a customer or member by placing, deleting, or listing orders on their behalf. Staff may not settle an order, however—customers and members must settle their own orders.
  - Administer customer and member accounts including creation, deletion, and lookup of the accounts.

Summary

In this chapter, we covered a large expanse of material to introduce you to the wide world of component-based enterprise security using EJB and CORBA. We started with a quick overview of components and security and described how components and security often have conflicting goals.

We then described how security is an enabler for many e-business applications: Without a good security solution in place, many new e-business opportunities would not be feasible. We also discussed the concept of risk management, which balances the level of security that is required in light of the business needs of cost, performance, and functionality. We showed that information security is a serious concern for many businesses both in terms of external and internal (insider) attacks.

Next, we described the many challenges of enforcing security in component-based applications. We defined the notion of a TCB and showed that the TCB concept is not a very good match for distributed component environments.

We introduced Enterprise Security Integration (ESI), which we used to tie together many different security technologies. We defined perimeter, middle, and legacy tiers of security and described how they all work together to provide end-to-end security. We defined an ESI solution in terms of a security framework, technologies, and integration techniques that hook those technologies together. Recall that the ESI framework consists of a number of layers including the applications, APIs, core security services, framework security services, and underlying security products. We also described a number of basic ESI principles that we will refer to in future chapters.

Finally, we introduced the eBusiness.com object model and security requirements. This example will be used as the basis of our security discussions in several of the later chapters.

In the rest of this book, we'll expand on many of the concepts that we've just introduced. Hopefully, this chapter has laid the groundwork for your basic understanding of the security issues in component-based systems.

In several of the chapters, you'll see code fragments that refer to security integration technology. Rather than focus on any specific set of products, this book addresses issues that are relevant to many different application servers and security products. At Concept Five, we have worked on both EJB and CORBA security solutions, so we explain what we have learned about integrating security into EJB and CORBA environments. Our work is based on security integration in many application server environments including Hitachi TPBroker, Iona Orbix, Inprise Visibroker, BEA WebLogic, and IBM WebSphere. We've integrated application servers with many different security products including Hitachi TPBroker Security, Netegrity SiteMinder, Entrust getAccess, and IBM/Tivoli PolicyDirector to name a few.

CHAPTER 2

Securing EJB Components

In the Java world, Enterprise JavaBeans (EJB) from Sun Microsystems appears to be gaining acceptance as the open standard for server component architectures. Products based on the EJB specification have compelling advantages: they shield application developers from many of the low-level object service details (such as transactions and security), they enable enterprise beans to be moved to another environment with minimal effort, and they are interoperable with other EJB products. Fully compliant EJB products support the Internet Inter-ORB Object Protocol (IIOP) protocol, allowing Common Object Request Broker Architecture (CORBA) clients to access enterprise bean objects.

The software system that supplies these services to the application developer is the application server. Application servers, which provide a convenient environment for building distributed business applications, are appearing everywhere. It seems that every middleware vendor has one under development, if not already on the market.

This chapter assumes that you have worked with EJB and have written programs for some application servers, but that you have not necessarily done anything with EJB security. We are going to take a thorough look at EJB security, concentrating on the security features in the EJB version 2.0 specification. We will look at both client and server security. Although EJB is for the most part a server-side protocol, an enterprise bean can act as a client and call upon other beans.

Version 1.0 of the EJB specification did not devote much space to security, whereas version 1.1 added a lot of the security infrastructure for EJB. When Sun Microsystems introduced version 2.0, it put a significant effort into the security component, especially in the area of interoperability between containers and between beans within a container. A container is the working component of an application server that interacts directly with EJB and supplies low-level support, such as transactions and security. As with the other parts of the EJB specification, writers divided the responsibility for security among the players that they defined for EJB: the bean provider, the application assembler, the deployer, and the container provider.

The EJB specification puts most of the responsibility for security on the server-side of a message exchange, that is, the container. The responsibilities of the EJB client and the system administrator are of less importance in EJB. This chapter follows the same approach.

Because EJB is a server-side protocol, we mostly discuss the server-side of an interaction. However, remember that security is an end-to-end problem and that all the pieces must work together. In the later chapters of this book, we will bring the other parts of the security picture into the discussion, but for now let's concentrate on the security aspects of EJB alone.

We also cover how security is handled when one container calls on another container, especially when containers are built by different providers.

In Chapter 1, we introduced the example of an e-business company called eBusiness.com, which we use throughout this book. In this chapter, we use this example to illustrate various aspects of EJB security to tie the description of specifications and protocols to concrete code.

An Overview of EJB Security

The basic security model for EJB, as depicted in Figure 2.1, is a simple and elegant access control policy. When the client program invokes a method on a target EJB object, the identity of the user (i.e., principal) associated with the calling client is transmitted to the EJB object's container, which is delivered as the major piece of an application server. The container checks to see whether the caller's identity is in the access control entry associated with the bean's method. If the caller's identity is in the access control entry, the container permits the invocation on the method.

The security mechanism used between the client and the EJB server determines how the user's identity is passed from the client to the server. For example, if Secure Sockets Layer (SSL) is used for client authentication, SSL passes the client's identity in the form of a public key certificate. Message confiden-

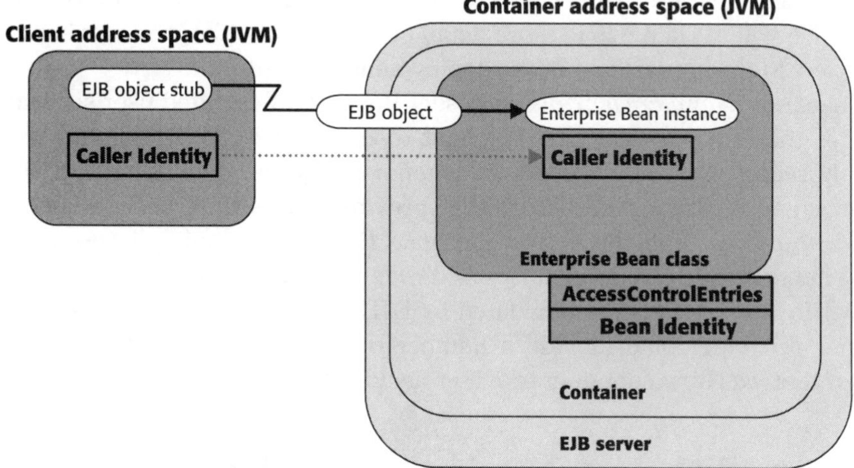

Figure 2.1 The EJB model.

tiality (encryption) and message integrity (digital signature) are not explicitly provided by the EJB security model and are assumed to be provided by the underlying security mechanism.

The container provides the caller's identity as part of the bean's context. If an enterprise bean instance needs to determine the caller identity (say, to perform additional checking), the bean can call *getCallerPrincipal* and *isCallerInRole* on the javax.ejb.EJBContext interface. Defining which callers are in which roles is not specified by the EJB security model and is left up to each implementation. EJB does specify that the container provider supply a tool that the deployer can use to map identities to roles, but it doesn't say how the result of the mapping is to be captured.

The enterprise bean provider sets up the security policy for the bean as part of the deployment descriptor in the EJB jar file. When the bean is deployed, container tools read and interpret the security policy in the deployment descriptor to enable the container to enforce the specified security policy for all bean instances. The container may allow the deployer and system administrator to modify the bean security policy so that it may be customized beyond what was originally set up by the bean provider. More and more container providers, for example, furnish an EJB deployment wizard, which includes the security policy setup for the deployment descriptor. The EJB deployment wizard may be used at a later time to modify the security policy.

Access control entries are an aspect of security policy defined in the bean's deployment descriptor. The deployment descriptor may include a *method permission* for each individual bean method. The descriptor may also include a method permission for the entire bean that applies to all methods. A method permission associates a bean's method with a list of logical privileges or roles.

The user identities are mapped to the roles that are allowed to invoke the method. We will explain this in more detail as we describe the jobs of the various *players* in the preparation of the deployment descriptor.

In a secure system, *credentials* represent the system certified user security attributes that are passed from the client to the server. Credentials are not explicitly represented in EJB, but are supported by the underlying security mechanism (e.g., SSL or Kerberos) that provides the secure authentication between the client and the server. Because EJB access policy is normally defined in terms of the user identity, the credentials usually contain only that identity. However, this is not mandated by EJB. In the credentials object, the container provider could include a number of attributes pulled from some source if that was how container provider decided to implement the container.

Players and Their Duties in the EJB Lifecycle

One of the goals of EJB security stated in the EJB specification (EJB V2.0) is "Lessen the burden of the application developer (i.e., the Bean Provider) for securing the application." We heartily agree with the principle espoused by EJB and also CORBA security that in a distributed environment, security should not be coded into each application, but instead should be handled beneath the application in the middleware layer. Security in a distributed system is difficult and—as much as possible—should be implemented by security experts. Because the security of an application depends on the activity of servers and clients that execute both before and after the application in question, it becomes extremely difficult for an application writer to get the security right. By enforcing security in the middleware layer, the application developer can focus on building his or her application.

You might be thinking, "No need to worry about security, on to my next task." Not so fast! Security is an end-to-end problem; the reason that you are reading this book is because you have a responsibility in one way or another for distributed applications that live in a large system. Consequently, you should have an understanding of the way security is implemented in EJB in order to determine whether it is sufficient for the applications you are building. You also need to understand how EJB security fits in with the rest of the software security. In today's corporations, there is a heterogeneous mix of software models and

ESI AUTHORIZATION PRINCIPLE: PUSH SECURITY DOWN

EJB pushes most security functionality down into the container, thus relieving the developer from the burden of writing security code.

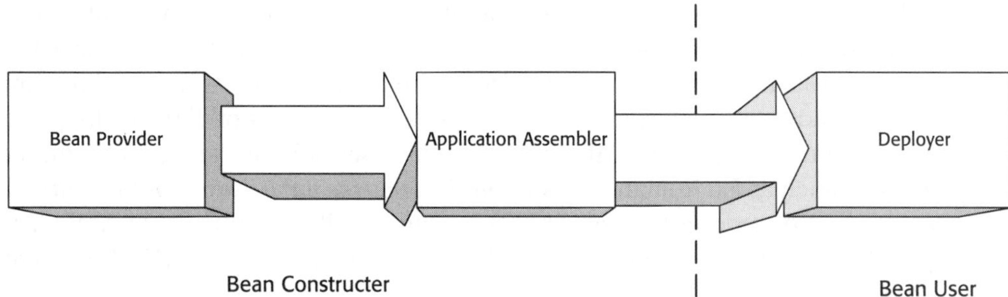

Figure 2.2 Players in the lifecycle of an EJB.

environments. A bad hand off from one part of the system to another can compromise the whole system. As you will see in this chapter, instructions must be given to the container security system. These instructions are put in the deployment descriptor, and you are responsible for some aspect of this work even if it's only in an advisory capacity.

One of the ideas behind EJB is that you can buy an EJB from a company that specializes in a particular business function, put that bean in your container, and it will run in harmony with your container. In order to do this smoothly, the duties of building and installing the bean are split between the people who know the different parts of the bean lifecycle. Figure 2.2 shows this hand off between the various players.

The *bean provider* builds the bean and should have a limited hand in the security of the bean. The *application assembler* combines beans into a larger application and is responsible for defining the security aspects of each bean, which means defining the secure interactions of the code. To do this, Assemblers need to understand the code. In a model in which the beans are purchased from one company and used by other companies, this means that the application assembler and the bean provider are from the company that builds and sells the bean. After all, as a user of beans, you want to buy a bean as a black box and just use it. There is still some work to be done to adjust the security of the bean to work with your particular environment. This work is done by the *deployer*, who works for the company that purchases the EJB.

As you know from your work with EJB, beans run in containers that are provided by EJB middleware server providers, or as the specification calls them, *container providers*. Containers provide the bulk of the infrastructure for EJB including such things as transport, transactions, and security. Most of the security coding that users of EJB Containers perform consists of adding sections to the deployment descriptor, which is used to transmit information about your specific site environment to the container. Additional information is added to the deployment descriptor as it moves from bean provider to application assembler to deployer.

Version 1.1 of the EJB specification changed the format of the deployment descriptor to an XML document. Previously, the deployment descriptor was a serialized Java object. You should already be familiar with XML-based deployment descriptors, as they are used extensively in all parts of EJB deployment. If you need an update on XML, there are a number of books and articles on the subject, such as Ed Roman's *Mastering Enterprise JavaBeans and the Java 2 Platform, Enterprise Edition* (1999) has an excellent summary of XML. The granddaddy of XML books is Goldfarb and Prescod, *The XML Handbook* (2000).

You should be able to follow the XML in our examples with a little background. XML is similar to HTML in that it has tags that identify the data. XML tags are user defined, whereas HTML has a fixed set of tags. The data is encompassed within a tag set as follows: <tag1> data </tag1>, where the <tag1> defines the beginning of tag1 and the </tag1> defines the end of tag1. Also, tags (called elements in XML) may be nested. We'll give you more help when we get to our first XML example.

Roles

One of the major security attributes that are used in EJB are roles. Roles are an important concept, especially in a large enterprise. They aid in reducing the amount of security data that must be managed and, in their guise of logical privileges, they are used by the container for access control. We will go into some detail to explain the concept and use of roles in this section.

Roles are used both to define collections of users and to enforce access control. The deployer assigns an individual to a role, and by that action the role becomes a privilege attribute of the individual that is the basis of access control. Let's look at an example to help explain this concept. The deployer at eBusiness.com could assign the customer Henry Mudd to the role member, to which he has assigned a number of other customers. This assignment of many principals to a role gives roles their scaling capabilities. The assignment itself gives Henry Mudd the privilege attribute of member, which can be used by Henry for accessing the special products offered by eBusiness.com.

The EJB specification leaves it up to the container provider to determine how the deployer assigns the roles and how these roles are used in the access

ESI SECURITY ADMINISTRATION PRINCIPLE: COLLECTIONS FOR SCALE

EJB roles simplify deployment descriptor access policies by enforcing security on collections of users.

decision. Therefore, be sure to understand how your container provider uses roles and how the provider performs access decision.

In addition to their use in scaling and access control, roles in EJB are used for portability of a bean from a producer company that creates and provides the bean to a number of companies to which the producer of the EJB sells that bean. The producer of the bean does not know the specifics of how a particular role will fit into the company purchasing the bean. Therefore, a role defined by the producer is a logical privilege that can be used by the different purchasers of the bean. The purchaser of the bean can then provide a meaningful assignment of individuals to the role created by the producer.

Another way of looking at a role is as a set of clients who can be treated the same with respect to security for the application under consideration. It should be noted that the relationship between the client and the role only takes place when the purchaser assigns individuals to a role. For example, the producer could define the abstract role "customer." The purchaser could then assign individuals to that role and then treat that set of individuals as represented by that role. A term that is closely associated with roles is *principal*. Security terminology uses principal to mean a person or computer process that makes a request on a distributed object.

Another important use of roles is that they can provide scaling capabilities to the authorization aspects of an EJB installation. In order to grant this permission to a principal, you have to tell the security service to whom you have granted the permission and to which resources, which are classes or methods.

Let's assume that our example, eBusiness.com, is a successful e-business with hundreds of thousands of customers. If our business had to list each customer as well as the resources they could access, then eBusiness.com would probably no longer be successful. On the other hand, if eBusiness.com studied its customer base and decided that it could group customers into two sets—ordinary customers and special customers, called members—then the hundreds of thousands of rules could be reduced to two for each resource. This is one of the reasons that roles were introduced in EJB. eBusiness.com could define two roles for each of the customer types—for example, with the role names of customers and members. Then, rather than individually naming each customer, eBusiness.com could just use these two roles.

There are a couple of caveats (aren't there always?). Each of the principals assigned to a role must have the same security privileges to access all the resources to which that role is granted rights. If there is any deviation of the rights needed between a given set of principals, then you'll need to create another role. A principal can be assigned to more than one role, so that isn't a problem. The problem arises if you define the role too narrowly. In the extreme case, you could have as many roles as principals, which brings you back to the original problem. Therefore, be sure to put a lot of thought into how you define your roles and try to look towards future uses of your system when defining the roles so you don't have to redefine them later.

A second problem is that although roles reduce the number of rules, they still have to be expressed for each resource. If you have a large number of resources, there may still be a maintenance problem. In Chapters 5 and 6 we discuss ways to reduce this problem by introducing interoperability with CORBA.

The Bean Provider

When it comes to security, the bean providers have the least to do among the cast of characters responsible for the EJB application. This is as it should be if EJB is to live up to its goal of relieving the bean providers from the responsibility of security. They don't get off scot-free, however.

Application assemblers and deployers define most EJB security policies in the deployment descriptor, which uses a declarative model. However, there are some security situations that can not be expressed in a declarative format, such as when using an access check that depends on a variable within the application. In these cases, security has to be written into the application code. Therefore, one of the bean provider's responsibilities is to write any needed dynamic security checks using the methods supplied for this purpose by EJB and declare all the security entities that are used in his or her code in the deployment descriptor.

It is not good security practice to write security into the application itself. Security is best handled in the middleware. This is because security is hard to get right and most application programmers are not security experts, so it is best to buy security middleware that has been written by security experts. A second reason for not putting security into the application is that security is an end-to-end proposition, and it depends on the beans that precede and follow the one a provider is writing. These beans may not even be written prior to when the provider is writing a particular bean, or conversely, the particular application writer may not have knowledge of the security needed or provided by the other beans.

We will use our example, which was introduced in Chapter 1, to construct a portion of the deployment descriptor that represents the bean provider's declaration of the security roles used in his code and describe the mechanics of a deployment descriptor. The first snippet of the deployment descriptor for our business looks at how the bean provider declares the administrator role to the security system.

As mentioned earlier, the producer of the bean does not know the specifics of how a particular role will fit into the purchasing companies. Therefore, a role defined by the producer has to be a logical role, so that it can be used by the different purchasers of the bean, and the purchasers can then provide a meaningful assignment of principals to the role. In addition, bean providers, when they do have to write the security code into the application, do not have to declare each individual, but instead can use roles for scaling purposes. Later in this section, we'll use the role "admin" for an administrator and show an example of how the bean provider would write application level security code to check the role of a caller.

Rather than giving rights to each administrator individually, you can give the necessary rights to the admin role, and then use the admin role when writing the security into the application. The bean providers define the roles that they have used in their application code by using the EJB defined security-role-ref element in the deployment descriptor. The providers can optionally supply a description of the roll name when declaring the security-role-ref. The important point is that the bean providers declare the dependencies on privileges that are embedded in the code in a way in which the container can answer questions that are asked by the application.

The deployment descriptor starts with the tag <enterprise-beans>, and then lists the tag <entity>. Note in the following code snippet that each element ends with an ending tag, such as </enterprise-beans> at the bottom of the example. Also, elements can be nested. The entity element is nested within the EJB element. Nested within the entity element is the ejb name followed by the ejb class, which is the full class name of the bean. Between the beginning and ending tag for <ejb-name> is string CustomerAccount. This is the value of the <ejb-name>. After the <ejb-class>, we reach the information that we are interested in declaring, the security-role-ref. Nested within the security-role-ref element is the role name "admin" as it is used in the code. The name used in the code is declared in the deployment descriptor via the security-role-ref, so that the assembler can link this name to the security role that will be used when the bean is assembled together with other beans.

There is also an optional description of the role. There are nuances and other constructs in XML so pick up and read one of the many XML books.

```
...
<enterprise-beans>
          ...
          <entity>
               <ejb-name>CustomerAccount</ejb-name>
               <ejb-class>com.account.CustomerAccountBean</ejb-class>
               ...
               <security-role-ref>
                    <description>
                         This role encompasses the administrators of
                         the on-line shopping company.
                    </description>
```

```
                    <role-name>admin</role-name>
                </security-role-ref>
                ...
            </entity>
            ...
</enterprise-beans>
...
```

Later you'll see how the assembler can add an additional tag in the security-role-ref to link the role declared by the bean provider to the one defined by the assembler. In this case, the assembler will link the security role reference "admin" to the security role "staff."

The reason that bean providers make the roles in the deployment descriptor visible is that they use these roles in their application code. Remember that writing security code in the application is discouraged unless the declarative methods for defining security in the deployment descriptor are not sufficient. For example, there might be a security check, which uses a conditional based on a parameter value of a method call. The check could be that if the value of the transaction, which is passed as a parameter, is greater that $5,000, then only users associated with the role of admin can approve that expense. There is no way to put this runtime information or the procedural statements in the deployment descriptor.

EJB supplies a few security programmatic interfaces that the bean provider can use. One of these is the security context. From this interface, the programmer can retrieve the principal or find out if the calling principal is in a particular role. The connection between the principals is made in the deployment descriptor code that the bean provider has written, as shown previously, and the eventual linking to the individual principals is done by the assembler and the deployer. The following calls can be used by the bean provider in the application code to check whether a principal is in a role.

```
public interface javax.ejb.EJBContext {
            ...
                //
                // The following two methods allow the EJB class
                // to access security information.
                //
            java.security.Principal getCallerPrincipal();
            boolean isCallerInRole(String roleName);
}
```

Note that version 1.1 of the EJB specification has deprecated the following two EJB 1.0 methods.

```
java.security.Identity getCallerIdentity();
boolean isCallerInRole(java.security.Identity role);
```

Specification writers use the word *deprecated* as a way of saying, "Don't use these methods any longer as they will disappear some time in the near future." Deprecated methods are usually held for one or two releases by the container providers, but this is not guaranteed. So be forewarned, don't use deprecated methods.

In order to make additional security checks beyond those specified in the deployment descriptor, the bean provider can use the method isCallerInRole, passing it a role name. isCallerInRole returns true if a particular principal, which may have been passed into an EJB from another EJB, was assigned a particular role by the assembler and the deployer.

The container security service checks whether the principal is in the named role and returns the appropriate boolean. If the principal is not in the specified role, the bean provider can throw an exception. The following code snippet shows how this can be done.

```
public class CustomerAccountBean implements SessionBean {
            EJBContext ejbContext;

            public void deleteOrder(int amt) {
                 // The deployment descriptor will ensure that only
                 // customers or admin are permitted to delete orders.
                 // However, this code makes an additional restriction:
                 // orders greater than $5000 may only be deleted by
                 // admin, not customers.
                 if (amt > 5000) &&
                      !ejbContext.isCallerInRole("admin")){
                           throw new SecurityException(...);
                 }
                 ...
            }
            ...
}
```

The programmer can also get the principal's name:

- Use getCallerPrincipal, which returns a java.security.Principal interface that represents the current principal
- Get the principal's name from the java.security.Principal by calling the getName method

The following code snippet shows how these calls may be used. In this snippet, an instance of a principal whose primary key is the same as the caller's identity is returned.

```
public class CustomerAccountBean implements SessionBean {
     EJBContext ejbContext;
     public void settleOrder(...) {
```

```
            ...
            // Obtain the default initial JNDI context.
            Context initCtx = new InitialContext();
            // Look up the home interface of the CustomerRecord
            // enterprise bean in the environment.
            Object result = initCtx.lookup(
                 "java:comp/env/ejb/CustomerRecord");
            // Convert the result to the proper type.
            CustomerRecordHome customerRecordHome =
                 (CustomerRecordHome)
                 javax.rmi.PortableRemoteObject.narrow(
                 result,CustomerRecordHome.class);
            // obtain the caller principal.
            callerPrincipal = ejbContext.getCallerPrincipal();
            // obtain the caller principal's name.
            callerKey = callerPrincipal.getName();
            // use callerKey as primary key to CustomerRecord finder
            CustomerRecord myCustomerRecord =
                 customerRecordHome.findByPrimaryKey(callerKey);
            // update the account
            myCustomerRecord.settleOrder(...);
            ...
      }
      ...
}
```

Much of the code snippet should be familiar to you from your nonsecurity EJB work. The new items show how we get the principal's name.

In the example, we first get the initial Java Naming and Directory Interface (JNDI) context from the container. Using this context, we look up and narrow to the customer record's home interface.

The next two steps are new concepts. We get the principal object that was passed into the server from the caller. From the principal object, we get the principal's name.

We designate the principal's name, callerKey, because the user's name is the primary key by which the container finds the record of the user. This is done in the next step, where we use findByPrimaryKey, passing it the principal's name. Having the record, we can now settle the order for this customer.

There is another complication that we will cover in more detail later. If desired, the deployer can change the principal who is used for an outgoing call from the bean. This is done using the *runAs* clause in the deployment descriptor. The runAs identity is called the *invocation identity.* Note that the runAs declaration only changes the principal for outgoing calls; within the calling bean, the value of getCallerPrincipal remains unchanged. If needed, the assembler can provide guidance to the deployer on how to set runAs.

As we mentioned earlier and will mention again—avoid putting security into the application itself. Even this simple example exposes some problems. For example, suppose we wanted to increase the value to $7,000 in the preceding code? In that case, the bean code would have to be modified. If you purchased this bean from a bean provider, you would be out of luck because you don't have the source code. If you built the bean yourself, it means a maintenance problem every time you want to change the value.

Even worse, a malicious programmer could code an added conditional that permitted another role, known only to that programmer, to buy something you didn't want. This may not seem that bad at first because you can just reject the order. But suppose this was done for thousands of orders. It could be disastrous for our online business. Of course, that is what code reviews are for. Be sure to look for security holes or backdoors when you carry out your code reviews. On the other hand, if you purchase the bean, you don't have access to the source code, so you should test the purchased code looking for security abnormalities.

In order to use this clandestine role, the assembler and probably the deployer would have to be in on the deception. This is another reason for separating roles in sensitive situations.

The best course is to build your own EJBs or purchase ones that avoid application level security.

Application Assembler

The application assembler and the bean provider are usually responsible for packaging a combination of a number of beans to solve a business problem, which their company then sells to other companies. For example, the package the assembler constructs may be an accounts receivable .jar file that is comprised of dozens of beans built by the bean provider(s) from the same company as the assembler. The assembler usually supplies the security aspects of the package as well as other parts of the package, but is not required to. The deployer is ultimately responsible for the security aspects of an EJB application.

One of the assembler's security tasks is to provide sufficient information to the deployer so that the deployer can secure the EJB. The information supplied by the assembler is intended to make the job of the deployer easier. One of the major security attributes that are used are roles. When we discuss the deployer's duties, you'll see that they are not obliged to use only the roles defined by the assembler. The deployer may also add new roles or change the definition of a role. The changing of a definition of a role by a deployer is not advised because the assembler is the person who knows, or should know, the intricacies and intent of the code, whereas the deployer may be in a company that has simply purchased the EJB.

The application assembler might define the role "customers." Consequently, when the assembler wants to assign access rights for a bean or a method, he can assign them to the customer role rather than to each individual in that role. The assignment of roles makes the application assembler's job easier as well as reduces the maintenance task.

The assembler can split the task into two efforts, which can be maintained separately:

- Define roles that can be used by the deployer
- Allow roles access to a bean or a method in a bean

We have covered the first task. For the second task, once the assembler has assigned the logical roles, his next security task is to define permissions to access a particular method for each role. The specification calls these method permissions. Note that permissions are not necessarily organized by role. They can be defined either per role or per method group because both roles or methods can be held constant while the other is varied. In this way, EJB can support either a permissions or a capabilities model.

A method permission can be set on both the enterprise beans' home and remote interfaces. Therefore, the assembler can control who can create or destroy a bean as well as who can access the bean or its methods.

There is an important distinction to be made in what the assembler creates with respect to roles and what the deployer defines with respect to roles. The assembler may have no knowledge of the environment in which a bean is to be deployed. For example, the bean or set of beans may be sold to a number of different companies. On the other hand, the deployer who works for the company purchasing the bean may not know what the relationship between a particular role and method should be because he does not have the source code. Therefore, the assembler creates what the specification calls a logical role, and the deployer assigns principals to the logical role.

The following example might help to clarify this difference. An assembler of an EJB product creates a role "customer" and a role "member" and gives the customer role permission to the placeOrder method for a regular product, whereas the member is given permission to the placeOrder method for a special product. The assembler has no idea what defines a member nor what differentiates the products that they can order. However, in eBusiness.com, the company that buys the EJB product, the criteria for recognizing members in the online store and the identification of special products is well understood as part of its business. So the eBusiness.com deployer sets the principals Mary, Joe, and Harry to the role member, and sets the book *Enterprise Security* to a special product. This topic is further described in the "Deployer" section later in this chapter.

The assembler uses the deployment descriptor to provide a consistent view of the application by describing roles and using them in method permissions to logically define who should be able to do what. The following section gives an example of a deployment descriptor that would be created by an assembler.

Defining Roles

The following fragment of a deployment descriptor depicts the security portion of a deployment descriptor that would be created for our eBusiness.com company. The assembler writes the portion of the deployment descriptor in this section. It starts with the tag <assembly-descriptor>, and then defines a security role <security-role>. Each element ends with an ending tag as described in our previous example, and the elements are nested. For instance, there are a four security roles nested in the <assembly-descriptor> element, and a description and a role name are nested in each <security-role>. The description element is optional. Also, note that the names of the tags, such as <assembly-descriptor>, have been defined by the specification and should be used as specified.

```
...
<assembly-descriptor>
     <security-role>
          <description>
               This role includes the members of the on-line
               business who are allowed to access the
               special products application. Only users
               who have the role member can access the special
               products.
          </description>
          <role-name>member</role-name>
     </security-role>

     <security-role>
          <description>
               This role includes the customers of the on-line
               business. This role is only allowed to
               access the regular products.
          </description>
          <role-name>customer</role-name>
     </security-role>
     <security-role>
          <description>
               This role should be assigned to the personnel
               of the on-line store who are authorized
               to perform administrative functions.
          </description>
          <role-name>staff</role-name>
     </security-role>
          ...
</assembly-descriptor>
```

This portion of the deployment descriptor defines the security roles member, customer, and staff. It also provides a description of each of these roles. It is important that the assembler provide a clear description of each of the roles as this is the way the assembler communicates the use of the roles in the code to the deployer.

Assigning Method Access

The assembler portion of the deployment descriptor defined three roles: a customer role, a member role, and a staff role. Now, we will define the methods that each of these roles are permitted to access by constructing another part of the deployment descriptor. In this portion of the deployment descriptor, the logical role that was previously defined is assigned the methods that it is permitted to access. The specification refers to this association as a (Role,Method) or R,M pair. A role may be defined in more than one R,M pair.

Just to complicate things a little further, the specification defines three legal styles for declaring methods in these R,M pairs. Examples of each of these styles follows.

The first style of declaring methods is used to refer to the whole bean, that is, to all the remote and the home interface methods of the named bean. We use the tag <method>, and then explicitly nest the name of the bean using the tag <ejb-name>. Notice that the method name uses the meta character * as the name. In regular expressions, * means 0 or more occurrences. However, the specification interprets it to mean all the methods in this bean.

STYLE 1

```
<method>
<ejb-name>EJBNAME</ejb-name>
<method-name>*</method-name>
</method>
```

In the second style, a specific method name of the remote and home interface of a specified enterprise bean is used. If you have multiple overloaded methods with the same name, the method name used refers to all of the overloaded methods. This means that you cannot put different access permissions on different overloaded methods using this style. You can use Style 3 for those situations.

STYLE 2

```
<method>
<ejb-name>EJBNAME</ejb-name>
<method-name>METHOD</method-name>
</method>
```

Style 3 is an extension of Style 2, which allows you to refer to different methods in the overloaded case. This is done by nesting the parameters within the <method-name> tag.

STYLE 3

```
<method>
<ejb-name>EJBNAME</ejb-name>
<method-name>METHOD</method-name>
<method-params>
<method-param>PARAMETER_1</method-param>
...
<method-param>PARAMETER_N</method-param>
</method-params>
</method>
```

There is also an optional `<method-intf>` element that can be used to differentiate methods with the same name and signature that are defined in both the remote and home interfaces.

Now that we have shown how to code the methods in a deployment descriptor, we will show how to define permissions for these methods. (The specifications prior to version 1.1 used access control lists, which effectively only supported Style 2.) As usual, we start with a tag that defines what we are going to do. In this case, the tag is <method-permission>, which is the name the specification gives to the process of associating the permission for a role to access a given method. The first tag that is nested within a <method-permission> is a <role-name>, in this case, customer.

Following the <role-name> are the methods that a customer can access. In this example, we use Style 1. Using this style, the customer can access all the methods in the bean named CustomerAccount because the method name is defined by an "*".

```
...
<method-permission>
     <role-name>customer</role-name>
     <method>
          <ejb-name>CustomerAccount</ejb-name>
          <method-name>*</method-name>
     </method>
</method-permission>
```

Under the next <method-permission>, we give staff of the online business permission to access three of the methods in the CustomerAccount bean: listOrder, deleteOrder, and placeOrder. We will not permit staff to settle orders on behalf of customers, however, to avoid possible fraudulent purchases initiated by untrustworthy staff members. (This business requirement was discussed in Chapter 1.)

```
<method-permission>
     <role-name>staff</role-name>
     <method>
```

```
        <ejb-name>CustomerAccount</ejb-name>
        <method-name>listOrder</method-name>
    </method>

    <method>
        <ejb-name>CustomerAccount</ejb-name>
        <method-name>deleteOrder</method-name>
    </method>

    <method>
        <ejb-name>CustomerAccount</ejb-name>
        <method-name>placeOrder</method-name>
    </method>
</method-permission>
```

Up to this point, we have defined roles and have given permission to the customer role to access all the methods on one bean, CustomerAccount. And we have given permission for the role, staff, to access specific methods on the CustomerAccount bean.

It is important to note that we have only given permission to the logical roles. We have not yet concretely assigned principals to these roles. We also have not yet linked these roles to those declared by the bean provider. This last statement might seem a bit obtuse, but remember that the assembler may need to use beans that have been implemented by different bean providers, and each of those beans may use different naming conventions for the roles. You'll see how this is done in the next section.

Assigning Roles to Role References

There is another concept related to security roles, namely, security role references. Recall that in the discussion of the bean provider's security duties, they declare security role references, which are called security-role-ref in the specification. The assembler links the security-role-ref declared by the bean provider to a role defined by the assembler. The role link essentially provides an alias to the role name that was used in bean code. This approach allows the assembler to handle role naming differences among beans and define role names that are more appropriate to the package of beans that is supplied to the deployer.

This task is pretty simple. The assembler finds the security-role-ref defined in the deployment descriptor by the bean provider and adds a tag <role-link> and a name to the role-link. The assembler must assign a role-link to all the security-role-ref s declared by the bean provider, even if the role-link name is the same as the role ref name declared by the bean provider. The assembler may only link to a role that the assembler defined as a role in the deployment descriptor.

In our previous examples, the assembler defined a role of `staff`, while the bean provider used the role `admin` in his code. The following deployment descriptor example shows how to link the security role reference named `admin` to the security role named `staff`. The tag <role-link> is used for this purpose. If you compare the deployment descriptor below with the one shown previously that was declared by the bean provider, you will see that the assembler has added description text in addition to the <role-link> definition for staff. As a result of adding this role link, the container will automatically map the role reference of admin that is used in the bean to the role name of staff without requiring code changes in the bean.

```
...
<enterprise-beans>
     ...
     <entity>
          <ejb-name>CustomerAccount</ejb-name>
          <ejb-class>com.account.CustomerAccountBean</ejb-class>
          ...
          <security-role-ref>
               <description>
                    This role encompasses the administrators of
                    the on-line shopping company.
                    The role reference has been linked to the
                    staff role.
               </description>
                    <role-name>admin</role-name>
                    <role-link>staff</role-link>
          </security-role-ref>
               ...
     </entity>
          ...
</enterprise-beans>
     ...
```

Security Identity

EJB supports a form of delegation called *impersonation*. Delegation is the property of assigning some or all of your rights to another entity such as a bean in an application. For example, you might give someone else the right to impersonate or act as you. In *unconstrained delegation* this means that the bean would be able to deposit money to your bank account, which is a positive outcome from your point of view. But the bean would also be able to withdraw money from your account, which is not exactly what you intended. The <security-identity> tag in the deployment descriptor is used to set the identity that is used by a bean in outgoing calls to another bean or another container. In our example, if a normal customer was set to run as a member, then that customer could purchase products from the special list of products. This would discourage people from paying an additional fee to become members of our online store, hurt the store's reputation, and eventually its business.

ESI AUTHENTICATION PRINCIPLE: TRUST NO ONE

EJB's use of security identity allows the assembler and deployer to control how user credentials are propagated from bean to bean. If delegation is used by setting use-caller-identity, the principal of the calling bean may be passed along an entire call-chain of beans, allowing each bean to impersonate the original principal. As beans pass the calling principal's identity down the chain, each bean trusts the other and assumes that no malicious bean abuses that trust by substituting some other principal. A benefit of impersonation is that each bean makes authorization checks based on the original principal. A risk of delegation is that one of those beans may abuse its privilege and access a resource on behalf on the original principal that wasn't intended. Currently the EJB specification does not require each bean in the chain to individually authenticate, which would minimize the risk of impersonation by constraining delegation. Future versions of the EJB specification are likely to address this topic.

Setting the security identity is not quite that open in EJB. Constructs in the deployment descriptor determine what type of delegation is used and where it is used. The deployment descriptor is scoped or limited to the .jar file, so that any delegation is allowed only for beans within the .jar file. Furthermore, delegation can be scoped to the bean. However, there is still the possibility of abuse when delegation is permitted. The bean in question might be a bank account bean, which has both deposit and withdrawal methods. The assembler must be careful when permitting delegation in such a bean.

The security identity constructs in EJB establish the way a principal security identity is passed by a calling bean, and is described by means of the deployment descriptor. As with the other definitions put into the deployment descriptor by the assembler, the role defined by the security identity is a logical one that is made concrete by the deployer by assigning principals to the role. The ultimate responsibility for delegation does not lie with the assembler but with the deployer. However, the assembler brings about the possibility of delegation.

The assembler has one other task related to delegation. He decides whether the principal or some other role should be used to make outgoing calls. The identity defined by the assembler is used to determine authorization for the method on the called upon bean. That is, when the security identity is set by the assembler, that identity is used to make a call on the next component in the call chain. Therefore, the security identity does not affect the authorization in the component in which the assembler defined the new identity, but does affect the authorization in the target component.

There are two XML elements that can be used in defining which principal is used for authorization, use-caller-identity and runAs-specified-identity. When use-caller-identity is specified, the principal in the calling bean is passed to the target bean. That is, use-caller-identity specifies that the form of delegation known as impersonation should be used. When runAs-specified-identity is used, the principal that is passed to the target bean is defined by the assembler using the specified element.

The following example illustrates the use of a runAs-specified-identity in the deployment descriptor. When a principal makes a call on the CustomerAccount bean, the role staff will be used rather than the original principal for any outgoing calls from this bean.

```
...
<enterprise-beans>
    ...
    <session>
        <ejb-name>CustomerAccount</ejb-name>
        ...
        <security-identity>
            <runAs-specified-identity>
                <role-name>staff</role-name>
            </runAs-specified-identity>
        </security-identity>
        ...
    </session>
    ...
</enterprise-beans>
...
```

In the preceding deployment descriptor snippet, the assembler specifies the role name that is to be used as the principal for accessing other beans called by the CustomerAccount bean. To be more specific, this tells the deployer that principals that have the role staff may be used in place of the true caller to the next component. The deployer must follow these instructions.

Deployer

Deployers are members of an organization that are going to use a particular EJB. The EJB product may have been purchased from some other company, which is a supplier of the EJB application. Deployers, not the producers of the EJBs, know how the EJB product will be used in their company's specific environment and how the product will meet the security requirements of their company.

The deployer's responsibility is the point in the security of an EJB application "where the buck stops." Although the bean provider may perform some application level security and the assembler makes security information such as logical roles available, the deployer must ensure that the application is secure by assigning the right principals to the logical roles. If the other two members of the process do not define an element that is necessary for the security of the EJB application, then it is the responsibility of the deployer to supply the missing ingredient. For example, if there is a certain role for which access rights must be defined to protect a resource, and that role has not been defined, then the deployer must define that role. This might be difficult or impossible if the bean provider and the assembler have not done a thorough job, and the deployer is in a different company than the provider and assembler. When you purchase an EJB product, make sure that the company from which you are buying the beans has a reputation for conscientious work. However, don't take them on faith, test the products that you purchase.

From a security point of view, the deployer has the following responsibilities:

- Assign principals or groups of principals to the roles defined by the application assembler
- Define roles that have not been defined by the application assembler and assign principals or groups of principals to those roles
- Assign principals to the runAs identity
- Determine principal mapping for resource management and inter-enterprise beans

The deployer may ignore some or all of the logical security roles defined by the application assembler. If principals are not assigned to a logical role, that logical role is ignored in the security of the application. Ignoring a logical role should not be done lightly as the manufacturers of the EJB product most likely had a reason for defining the roles as they did.

You, as the deployer, should not be left to guess the intent of some unknown assembler. The container manufacturer should supply a good set of tools that you can use to deploy the application successfully. The tools should let you read the rules that the assembler created to direct how the roles, in this case, should be used. Remember that you, the deployer, are responsible for the security of the purchased application once you have deployed it. This means that you should make sure that the application server you are using supplies a comprehensive and easy to use tool set for reading the rules of the assembler.

In addition, you must ensure that the EJB application has defined the security rules and that the tools your application server supplies can read them. Not everybody follows specifications as closely as they should, and sometimes specifications are too vague and leave some leeway as to the implementations, which can lead to incompatibilities. Consequently, those in your company that are responsible for purchasing the application server should be aware of these potential problems and perform due diligence when purchasing the application server as well as the EJB applications to be used by the application server. The specification leaves the format and the means of storing the deployment descriptor up to the container manufacturer, so the EJB application provider must test new EJB applications against the container to ensure compatibility. Ask bean providers whether they have tested their product against the container that you are using. If everybody faithfully follows the specification, there should be no problem.

Once deployers define any needed roles, they must associate principals or groups of principals with each of the roles. The specification leaves this up to the container provider. This is another area where you must read the documentation of the container provider, in this case, to determine how to assign principals or groups of principals to the logical roles defined by the assembler.

The specification states that the scope of principal assignment to roles is the .jar file. Usually a .jar file contains a single application. In these cases, name clashes between applications are prevented by the scoping rule of .jar files. This means that you can assign the same name to a different role or assign a different set of principals to the same role in different applications. It is up to the container provider to determine how to enforce this separation.

The deployer can use this scoping capability to solve a potential problem. Let's say that in eBusiness.com, members are defined differently in the Toy department than they are in the Hardware department. Won't this cause a problem? No, the specification writers cover this situation with the scoping rules of EJB. The practical result means that the role member in the Toy department will be distinct from the role member in the Hardware department, as long as the EJB application for the two departments are in different .jar files. Keeping this straight is the job of the deployer, who knows the customer prerogatives in the two departments in eBusiness.com.

There are two ambiguities in the EJB specification. The specification talks about the responsibility of the deployer to "assign the security domain and principal realm to an enterprise bean application," but does not define either of these terms, probably assuming that the terms are self-evident. They are not. You will see a number of definitions of security domains later in this book. The specification explicitly does not define the scope of a security domain by using following words: "The EJB specification does not define the scope of the security domain. For example, the scope may be defined by the boundaries of the application, EJB server, operating system, network, or enterprise." The specification writers did at least limit it to the planet earth.

Where the specification uses the term "realm," it usually means technology domain, and where it uses the term security domain, it usually means policy domain. We'll talk more about these terms in Chapter 5.

Realms are specified as principal realms and probably refer to the Kerberos definition of a principal realm, which is a Distributed Computing Environment (DCE) cell. The specification leaves the interpretation up to the container providers, and as expected, the container providers will formulate their own interpretations. As a result, you will have to read your container providers' documentation closely to understand how they interpret domains and realms and how they want you to use them. For example, BEA's WebLogic has a construct called a security realm in its container, which contains the security code for authorization and supports insertion of a third-party security model.

The specification should tighten its definition of security domains and realms to support interoperability between containers from different vendors. Without an independent definition of domains and realms, different vendors will inevitably define and use containers differently, which can lead to confusion when the different vendors products are used together.

Principal Delegation

We discussed delegation in the "Application Assembler" section and pointed out its potentially complex nature. In this section, we cover the subject of delegation in more detail.

There are two choices in deciding which principal is used when one component calls another: It is either the principal associated with the calling component (i.e., delegation) or another principal that was specified by the assembler. The delegation specification is quite emphatic in declaring that the deployer must follow the instructions of the assembler. The rationale is that the assembler not the deployer knows the details of the code, and this is especially true in the area of delegation.

Recalling the specific example that was used in the "Application Assembler" section, the assembler declared that the CustomerAccount bean would act as the staff principal. The staff role was set by using the runAs-specified-identity element in the deployment descriptor and by explicitly declaring the role using the role-name element. Be sure you examine the deployment descriptor to identify the places where a runAs-specified-identity has been declared by the assembler. You, the deployer, must define roles for any runAs-specified-identity clauses without role names, and assign principals to all roles. Check the container provider's tools to see if they search the deployment descriptor for any unsatisfied runAs-specified-identity clauses. Because the container providers are responsible for the means of assigning principals, they should supply a tool that identifies an unsatisfied condition in this important area.

Not only is the deployer responsible for setting the principal for calls from one bean to another in the same container, but he is also responsible for assigning principals in calls between containers where the runAs-specified-identity element is declared in a bean that is receiving a call from another container. The requirement for following the assembler's instructions for calls from one container to another is mandatory in this case.

EJB Container Provider

As far as EJB is concerned, the container is one of the most important items in an application server. The container handles all the low-level, specialist tasks, such as security, transactions, and inter-process communication. Having all of these messy tasks taken care of allows application programmers to concentrate on writing the business logic that their corporation hired them for. It also relieves the corporation of the necessity of hiring experts in each of these areas.

In the following sections, we discuss the security aspects that are handled by the containers. The intent is to describe the functionality that containers should supply and how the developer interacts with a container, not describe how container providers should build containers. We explain the process that the container goes through, so that you can make intelligent decisions in purchasing the container that is best for your needs and in coding your interaction with that container. The EJB specification does not tell the container provider how to implement, manage, or administer the container, but it does specify the intent of what is expected of the container. You will have to judge which capabilities of a container are important to you and judge the container against your requirements.

Deployment Tools

A container is responsible for supplying a set of tools that makes deployment of an EJB product easy. The quality of the deployment tools is important in making the jobs of the bean provider, the assembler, and the deployer easier. These tools are most important to the deployer. Keep in mind that the deployer may not have any knowledge of the code as it may be a purchased product, so he needs a good set of tools to guide him through the deployment process.

The deployment tools take the information from the deployment descriptor, which was supplied by the bean provider and the assembler, and present it to the deployer. The ease and clarity of this presentation determines whether the deployer's job is easy or very difficult.

A good set of tools should guide you through the process of deploying an EJB application, catch errors in the deployment process, report on these errors clearly, and guide you in correcting deployment errors. Therefore, it is important that those responsible for purchasing an application server for use in your company assess the quality of the deployment tools.

Security Domains

As mentioned earlier, the EJB specification does not define a security domain except to imply that it is a means of scoping. The specification leaves the implementation, management, and administration of security domains up to the container provider. The specification does say that a security domain may be defined such that an external security service may be used. This permits too much leeway to the different container providers, and as a result, can cause confusion in a corporate system that uses a heterogeneous mixture of container providers.

The relevant portion of the EJB specification states that, "A security domain can be implemented, managed, and administered by the EJB server. For example, the EJB server may store X.509 certificates, or it might use an external security provider, such as Kerberos."

The important point for you, as a user of an EJB system, is that the containers that you purchase and use provide a clear definition of the security domains that they support, and that the containers supply tools to support interaction between the different domains that your corporation may use. The next section discusses one of the main differences between different security domains—principal naming.

Principal Naming

In a complex corporate environment, it is not unusual to find different security mechanisms being used, for example, Kerberos and SSL. These mechanisms have different ways of representing the same principal. Therefore, if your clients are deployed using different name mappings, you must map the different syntax representation of the same name. The EJB version 2.0 specification states that the EJB Container Provider should supply tools to aid you in completing this mapping.

Determine if your system uses different security mechanisms that use different naming syntaxes. If it does, be sure that your container provider furnishes the tools to translate between the representations of the principal name. If the tools are not provided, you will have to write code to make the transition. This can get tricky at times, so this may become an important criterion when choosing a container provider.

Another aspect of naming is passing the name of the appropriate principal between beans and between containers. Within a single container, the container provider is responsible for passing the correct name. The provider must furnish tools that the deployer can use to correctly configure the right principal to be passed between beans. The container provider should also provide tools to pass the correct principal between containers.

ejbContext

In our discussion about the bean providers' security coding, we stated that they could get the principal name or determine whether the principal was in a specific role. In order to obtain this information, they must first get the ejb context for the bean, javax.ejb.EJBContext. The ejb context object uses two methods to get this information:

- getCallerPrincipal()
- isCallerInRole(String role-Name)

The principal and role that are returned from these methods are related to the principal of the caller, that is, this information comes from the caller. The container does the work necessary to supply the principal information in the ejb context, so you don't have to worry about that part. However, there are some constraints on the EJB system so that the container can do its job.

Because these calls contain principal information that comes from the client, it means that clients must not change their principal information during a session with a server. A tricky situation can occur when a client is using a transaction. The client must keep the same calling principal during the transaction. Also, if multiple clients are involved in the same transaction, they must all use the same principal.

Security information is not available from the ejb context in all the potential method calls in the beans. In a stateless session bean, the security principal information is only available in business methods from a remote interface.

In a stateful session bean, the context security information is available from the following methods:

- ejbcreate
- ejbremove
- ejbactivate
- ejbpassivate
- Transactions (after begin before completion; after completion)
- Business methods from a remote interface

In an entity bean, the security principal information is available from the preceding methods and from the following methods:

- ejbFind
- ejbSelect
- ejbHome
- ejbPostCreate
- ejbLoad
- ejbStore

If you try to obtain the principal information from a method in a type of EJB not listed, the call will fail.

Auditing

The EJB security specification does not require auditing by the container provider. It only states that the container provider may supply auditing.

Auditing is an important security capability. When security is breached in your system, it is important to know who did what and when. This information can be used to find and fix security weaknesses in your system or to determine who is attempting to circumvent security either intentionally or unintentionally.

In some industries, like finance or health care, it is a legal responsibility to have an audit trail. There are even cases where auditing is more important than access control. One such case would be in allowing a doctor access to a patient's records. If a doctor is the only one available to someone who is not his patient, but is in critical condition, what is the correct course? Do you deny access to that doctor and thus cause the patient's death, or do you allow access but audit the event? We will assert that the latter course is the correct course.

The point at which auditing takes place is an important aspect of auditing. Two of the critical audit points are login and access decision. You will at least want an audit trail of failed logins and failed accesses. Because there are situations where you might not need an audit trail and because auditing can be expensive, it is important that the container provider provide you with a means of turning auditing off. CORBA has a very rich set of audit specifications, which we will cover in Chapter 3. Be sure to keep these in mind when evaluating the audit aspects of an application server.

We believe that auditing is a critical component that should be supplied by the container provider and should be an important item on your checklist for an acceptable EJB Container.

Using the Deployment Descriptor

We have talked a lot about the deployment descriptor. The deployment descriptor in version 2.0 is XML-based, which is a change from version 1.0 in which it was a serialized object. In fact, we have been using XML without having to provide a lot of explanation, and we bet you didn't have a hard time following it. We will now explain how the data types are enforced in a deployment descriptor and describe some XML constructs to give you a better understanding.

The deployment descriptor is used to pass information between the bean producer and the application assembler, and between the application assembler and the deployer. All this information is used by the container at runtime to ensure proper operation of an EJB application. The EJB specification version 2.0 defines two basic kinds of information in the deployment descriptor:

- Enterprise beans' structural information
- Application assembly information

The first type of information, structural information, is mandatory and includes such elements as the security roles and method permissions, which were discussed when we talked about the assembler's responsibilities. Another of the structural elements that we discussed was the security role references and which identity should be used in evaluating the permissions for accessing a particular method. This type of information should not be changed by deployers because they usually do not have any knowledge of the code and thus do not know the detailed security implications of this information. Changing it could inadvertently open security holes.

The second type of information, application assembly information, is optional. However, in a well-constructed EJB application, this information is important to guide you in deploying this particular bean so that it "plays well" with the other applications. Unless this is the only product that you are deploying, make sure that this information is included in any EJB products that you purchase, even if the information only states that there are no external dependencies. Although the lack of this information may not cause any serious problems with the particular bean, it may cause a group of beans making up an application to perform differently than intended.

In either case, it is best not to change any of the information supplied in the deployment descriptor by a predecessor. If you do, be sure that you understand all the consequences. When the deployment descriptor is verified by the container, you should get errors in those cases where you made inappropriate changes. This of course depends on how well the container provider finds and reports errors. Error checking is an important aspect of any container that you purchase. Next, we describe an attribute of XML that flags syntax errors.

An important detail in making XML work between different parties is a construct called the document type definition (DTD). The DTD defines the tags that can be in a particular XML file and describes their type and structure.

When an XML file is passed between two parties, the DTD should be made available to the receiving party so that the XML parser can determine whether the XML file is valid. An XML document has two levels of correct behavior; they can be well-formed, and they can be valid. Well-formed means that the XML document follows the rules of XML, such as nesting rules and closing elements with a closing tag. Valid means that they have followed the rules laid out in the DTD. Having a valid XML document is necessary to correctly parse and use the XML data. For example, suppose that a deployment descriptor has the tag <security-ident> instead of <security-identity>. How would the container know what is meant? This is the same as changing the spelling of a reserved word in a programming language except that in XML there are no reserved words. Well, that's not completely true, as you will see shortly, but in the example that we are using, it's true.

The DTD solves this problem by listing all the tags that a particular document uses. For example, a role is defined in a DTD as:

```
<!ELEMENT role (#PCDATA)>
```

where element is a reserved word defining role as a tag in the associated XML document. #PCDATA identifies the data type of the role as character data. Note that the elements in the DTD are case sensitive. Thus Role is not the same as role.

Another type that is used in the deployment descriptor is:

```
<!ELEMENT security-role-ref (description?, role-name, role-link?)>
```

In this type, we have the definition of the security-role-ref. This is an XML structure that contains an optional description, a role-name, and an optional role-link. The optional elements are identified by a trailing question mark (?). We have reproduced the security-role-ref defined by the bean provider earlier in the chapter:

```
<security-role-ref>
     <description>
          This role encompasses the administrators of
          the on-line shopping company.
     </description>
     <role-name>admin</role-name>
</security-role-ref>
```

This structure follows the definition in the DTD. The security-role-ref has nested in it a description element followed by a role-name element. However, notice that the role-link element is missing. The "?" following the role-link marked that term as optional. For the same reason, the description is optional and may be skipped.

You can write XML documents for a number of different purposes and each of the documents will have different semantics. For example, a medical report will have different terms than a billing document. Therefore, the way to tie the correct DTD to the correct document is by means of a header in the DTD, which in our case identifies it as a DTD for a deployment descriptor. This header is defined by the specification as:

```
<!DOCTYPE ejb-jar PUBLIC "-//Sun Microsystems, Inc.//DTD Enterprise
JavaBeans 2.0//EN" "http://java.sun.com/j2ee/dtds/ejb-jar_2_0.dtd">
```

The container includes parsers that can interpret the deployment descriptor's DTD and use that information to read the deployment descriptor, extract the information in a structured format, and use the information to programmatically perform the instructions contained in the XML document.

Sun plans to provide an ejb-jar file verifier that can be used by the bean provider and application assembler roles to ensure that an ejb-jar is valid. At present, all existing containers have their own validating parsers in order to be able to use XML and the corresponding DTD.

Recommended Permissions

The EJB version 2.0 specification has defined the access policy for certain permissions, which it recommends that container providers follow. It does not require that the support for these permissions be followed by containers, but those that do not follow these recommendations will not be portable.

Table 2.1 has been reproduced from the EJB version 2.0 specification. It defines the security permissions for which a container should either grant or deny.

The Beans Themselves

The purpose of the security aspects of EJB Containers is that the bean developers do not and should not concern themselves with security. Security is intended to be handled by the container using the directions contained in the deployment descriptor.

Table 2.1 Java 2 Platform Security Policy for a Standard EJB Container

PERMISSION NAME	EJB CONTAINER POLICY
java.security.AllPermission	deny
java.awt.AWTPermission	deny
java.io.FilePermission	deny
java.net.NetPermission	deny
java.util.PropertyPermission	grant "read", "*" deny all other
java.lang.reflect.ReflectPermission	deny
java.lang.RuntimePermission	grant "queuePrintJob", deny all other
java.lang.SecurityPermission	deny
java.io.SerializablePermission	deny
java.net.SocketPermission	grant "connect", "*" [Note A], deny all other

Note A: This permission is necessary, for example, to allow enterprise beans to use the client functionality of the Java IDL and RMI-IIOP packages that are part of the Java 2 platform.

In "The Bean Provider" section, we discussed the two calls available for coding security into the beans. Our advice is to avoid coding security into the bean code itself. You're really asking for trouble when you let the bean providers spread security throughout the applications. So unless you absolutely need a procedural instance of security, don't code any security into your beans. The reason that we emphasize this is that putting the security code in your beans seems to be the easy way out. Why bother with all the complexity of the deployment descriptors? If your EJB application system is a small, toy system, then this advice is not very pertinent. But, if your system is complex, then all the little bits of security coded in disparate places will inevitably result in conflicts and security holes.

Authentication

The EJB specification version 2.0 requires conformance to the Common Secure Interoperability v2 (CSIv2) specification. CSIv2 defines the methods of authentication, which includes username/password and SSL authentication. The more common method that people use is username/password. Unfortunately, although this is the easiest method to use, it is one of the weakest methods of authentication. Other means are public/private key and Kerberos. Public key, for example, SSL authentication, scales better than Kerberos, which is based on a symmetrical key.

There is some recent work going on to develop stronger username/password algorithms, such as the Simple Password Exponential Key Exchange (SPEKE) protocol. New security protocols are not accepted until they have gone through extensive trials of fire by cryptanalysis (they're the guys that try to break security algorithms) to try to find security holes in the algorithm. This can take years. Also, these algorithms need to have good performance characteristics. Part of the SPEKE protocol resembles the Diffie-Hellman protocol, which has been denigrated as being slow. Whether the SPEKE protocol will make it to the mainstream is unknown at this time, but keep your eyes on these developments as a strong username/password would be very popular.

Authentication is a specialized security process that is not unique to EJB. Therefore, we will not cover it in this book. There are a number of good books that explain authentication, ranging from the very technical, such as Schneier's *Applied Cryptography* (1996), which covers the underlying cryptography and authentication theory, to higher level treatises, such as Ghosh's, *E-Commerce Security* (1998). As usual, determine what type of authentication your container provider supports and how it interacts with the user.

One area of authentication that is important to EJB is the way the container interacts with the other portions of the end-to-end security system in your enterprise. EJB Containers and EJB clients are usually not the only systems used by your corporation. Today, a browser is the most common means used to securely access the perimeter firewall, and authentication is carried out by interaction with the browser. We cover this interoperable authentication problem in Chapter 5.

Authorization

Prior to version 2.0 of the EJB specification, authorization was based on access control lists (ACLs). An ACL simply states which EJB methods a principal or group can access. The approach is conceptually easy to grasp. Version 2.0 introduced the notion of method permissions, described earlier in this chapter. Method permissions expand on ACLs in allowing the use of a wild card to associate a role with all the methods in a bean. They also allow you to distinguish between overloaded methods by allowing the use of parameters in the method permission to distinguish between the overloaded methods.

Even with these extensions, every bean will have its own set of method permissions to determine which role can access its methods. If a new role is added to your system, this might mean changing the method permissions on hundreds or thousands of beans in multiple containers, depending on the size of your EJB system. Conversely, if a new method is added, this means tracking down all the principals and groups that can possibly interact with that method. If you miss one, it could leave a security hole in your system. It should be noted that the deployed form of authorization may not be in the form of method permissions.

Chapters 5 and 6 look at using other authorization schemes to interact with your EJB system to help with the scaling problem. In EJB, the container handles the authorization. It is up to you to maintain the method permissions.

Another aspect of authorization is to determine what level of granularity you need. Is it sufficient for a particular application to just control access to the application itself, or do you need to control access at the bean level, the method level, or even at the instance level? Note that EJB does not give you instance level control. We provide you with some ways to handle this in Chapters 5 and 6.

You will have to analyze each application to determine the granularity of authorization that is required. Different container providers support different levels of granularity, so be sure to find out what your candidate containers support and match that support with your present and future requirements.

Transport

When sensitive data is moved from container to another container, or in some cases, from bean to bean within a container, there is the possibility that the data might be read or modified by some outside party. Although there are other models for data protection, the most common means of protecting your data is the SSL protocol.

SSL provides integrity and encryption to messages moving between processes. It is the responsibility of the container providers to provide the integrity and encryption for your messages, which usually means that they have integrated SSL into their product or they have provided the hooks to run SSL. You should look for a container provider that incorporates the message protection directly. Bringing in a separate product and worrying about its integration is not a good idea. So be sure that message protection is incorporated into the container. In the next section, where we cover container to container interoperability, we talk about transport layer security and especially SSL.

Security with Container-to-Container Interoperability

The EJB specification version 2.0 requires support for the CORBA specification CSIv2. This gives EJB Containers the ability to securely interoperate between containers. This chapter discusses the security aspects of container to container interoperability, whereas Chapters 5 and 6 discuss the security aspects of end-to-end interoperability and EJB to CORBA interoperability.

A prerequisite for supporting CSIv2 is support for the CORBA transport protocol IIOP. EJB has accomplished this with its support of Remote Method Invocation (RMI) over IIOP. Before we go any further, let's make some sense out of this alphabet soup. CORBA is another object model, which is discussed in Chapter 3. CSIv2 is a wire level protocol that was jointly developed by the EJB and CORBA communities. It defines the format, means of transport, and interpretation of the security data that is passed between objects. This means that a receiving process that supports CSIv2 can get and interpret security information passed to it from a client that supports CSIv2.

There is one more piece to the puzzle. In order to transport the security data, it needs to be put some place in the message so that it doesn't interfere with the application message data. This is where IIOP comes in. The message format of IIOP defines a place in the request and reply headers, called the *service context*, where security data can be stored. This slot is completely separate from the application data and all the other header data, such as the TCP and IP headers. Previously, EJB only supported the RMI protocol. RMI, like IIOP, is a transport protocol, but it only supports Java and does not have a clean way to store the security data. Sun could have stayed with the RMI protocol, but IIOP, in addition to providing a means of transmitting security data, gives support to interoperability between EJB and CORBA. Recently, RMI and its transport, the Java Remote Method Protocol (JRMP), have been extended to support security.

Therefore, if the container you purchase supports the EJB version 2.0 or higher specification, it will be able to work with any other container that has this support. In addition, it will be able to interoperate with CORBA applications. There are some other decisions that you will have to make when mixing EJB and CORBA applications, but we cover these in Chapter 6.

Now we'll look at some of the flexibility that version 2.0 gives you. Version 2.0 supports the SSL protocol, which provides flexible support for encryption and integrity. The definition of integrity in this context is that the message is cryptographically signed—that is, SSL does a one-way hash of the message, and then encrypts the hash. If even one bit of the message is changed, the hash will not verify, and the recipient will know that the message has been modified. You can choose from a number of supported encryption algorithms, and these values can be negotiated between containers or between a client and a container if you are using an EJB or CORBA client. Each side of the transaction can set up the cryptographic algorithms that they will support in priority order. The negotiation will choose the highest priority that matches both sides.

Some of the reasons for negotiation include:

- Setting restrictions on the level of encryption that can be used depending on where the client and containers are located because many countries have restrictions on the strength of encryption
- The addition of new encryption algorithms
- The removal of algorithms that have been broken or are inefficient
- The cost of licensing patented algorithms versus unencumbered algorithms

Again, our usual caveat is: If you think that you will need to have some control over the encryption algorithms in your container for any of the preceding reasons, then check with your potential container vendors as to whether they support end user control of algorithm selection and how difficult they make it.

SSL handles authentication, either mutual authentication between the client and the server or server authentication only. In the SSL protocol, server authentication is optional, but most implementations treat server authentication as a requirement. Client authentication is optional in the protocol, although the server can require client authentication. SSL authentication normally requires X.509 certificates. An alternative to X.509 certificates is the Diffie-Hellman key exchange, but it is slow and rarely used.

The main problem with client certificates is the cost of the certificates and the hassle of distributing them to a potentially large employee or customer base. An alternative is to use password authentication for clients. However, password authentication is not as secure as certificate-based authentication. Passwords themselves are not maintenance free. One of the most common problems that help desks receive in password-based systems is forgotten passwords. The best solution is a system that supports a combination of password and certificate-based authentication, so that you can use certificates for access to sensitive data and passwords for less sensitive data. This will work if your client base has a large segment of people who only need access to less sensitive data. We discuss authentication further in Chapter 4.

The EJB specification refers to the CSIv2 specification for some of its details. CSIv2 specifies a lot of the low-level wire details that are necessary for interoperability, but are not necessary for you, the developer, to know how to effectively use the system. Some of the functionality of CSIv2 that is helpful for you to know are how implementations, such as an EJB Container, support algorithm negotiation and how the server can require certain security properties, called *association options*, of the client. We cover CSIv2 in Chapter 6.

Association Options

Servers create an object reference that the client uses to talk to the server. You should be familiar with object references from your work with EJB independent of any security work you may have done. These are the constructs that you get from a home interface and use to call a method in a distributed object. When the server container creates an object reference for a version 2.0 IIOP-based system, it puts security data in it. The client container reads this security data and takes some security actions based on the instructions that it receives from the server in this manner. The server can insert security requests that it requires the client to act upon as well as some security activity that it, the server, supports. Some of the options that affect the developer using containers are:

- Integrity
- Confidentiality
- EstablishTrustInTarget
- EstablishTrustInClient
- IdentityAssertion
- DelegationByClient

We have already defined the first two items: integrity and confidentiality. The server can require that the client use integrity or confidentiality by using SecRequires when setting the integrity or confidentiality association option, or the server can tell the client that it supports integrity and confidentiality by using SecSupports.

The third association option in the preceding list, EstablishTrustInTarget, is used by the client to require that the target authenticate itself (SecRequires) or by the target to say that it supports authenticating itself to the client (SecSupports). The fourth item, EstablishTrustInClient, is used by the target to require that the client authenticate itself to the target (SecRequires) or by the client to tell the target that it can authenticate itself (SecSupports).

When the target uses EstablishTrustInTarget, it is telling the client that it will be able to authenticate itself to the client if the client wants it to. It doesn't make sense for the target to require that it authenticate itself, so only the supports clause is used. The supports clause, when used by the target for EstablishTrustInClient, is the way the target tells the client that it can support client authentication if the client sends authentication data.

Before we get to the last two items in the list, you should know that in order to be able to use the cryptographic techniques, the EJB version 2.0 specification requires that container vendors support certain algorithms. The following cryptographic algorithms are required by the specification:

- SSL_RSA_EXPORT_WITH_RC4_40_MD5
- SSL_DHE_DSS_EXPORT_WITH_DES40_CBC_SHA
- TLS_RSA_EXPORT_WITH_RC4_40_MD5
- TLS_DHE_DSS_EXPORT_WITH_DES40_CBC_SHA
- SSL_RSA_ WITH_RC4_128_MD5
- SSL_DHE_DSS_ WITH_DES_CBC_SHA
- TLS_RSA_ WITH_RC4_128_MD5
- TLS_DHE_DSS_ WITH_DES_CBC_SHA

The way to interpret these representations of the cryptographic algorithms is that the last item in each algorithm pair is the one-way hash used for integrity, and the item that comes before it is the encryption algorithm followed by the number of bits used for confidentiality. For example, the first algorithm uses MD5 for integrity and RC4 with 40 bits for encryption. The first item in each algorithm refers to the protocol, either SSL or Transport Layer Security (TLS), which is a variant of SSL that is specified by the Internet Engineering Task Force (IETF). RSA are algorithms developed by RSA corporation. DHE represents Diffie-Hellman, which we have discussed earlier.

The most important points for you to determine are:

- When and where you need integrity or encryption.
- How strong it needs to be.
- What support your container vendor provides for letting you choose the strength of encryption.
- What flexibility the vendor gives you in choosing when and at what level of granularity the security of your messages can be turned on and off. For example, if a vendor does not give you a choice, besides not being specification compliant, the vendor might have chosen an algorithm that is totally inappropriate for your use.

IdentityAssertion and DelegationByClient have to do with delegation, which we cover in more detail in Chapters 6 and 8. At present, EJB does not use the last item, DelegationByClient. However, stay tuned to your favorite specification, and don't be surprised if this item shows up in the future.

Determine if any of the flexibility that is offered by these options is important to your system, either now or in the future. For those options that are important, determine how your potential container vendor handles them and how, or even if, the container allows you to assign them. For example, for confidentiality; does the container allow you to turn confidentiality on for some objects, but turn it off for other objects? If so, then the container supports the functionality of target_requires for confidentiality. The same holds true for each of the six options described in this section.

Who's Running the Show?

We discussed the ability to use the runAs technique to change the principal through the deployment descriptor. This can have a profound effect on the access permitted to different beans. For example, if you have a client that calls on a series of different containers before it reaches the final target, different principals may be used at each step in the chain. Figure 2.3 shows a client calling on an intermediate container, which in turn calls on a container where the resources that it needs reside.

Let's say the client uses the principal that started the process, which is the owner. When the client call reaches the intermediate container, that container can use the identity of the person that started the process, or it can runAs some other principal that was set in the deployment descriptor to call on the target container. The runAs method, as you remember from our earlier discussion, allows the use of two choices—use-caller-identity or run-as-specified-identity. This value is set by the application assembler. Use-caller-identity is a case of delegation, that is, the intermediate calls the target as if it were the client. When use-caller-identity is used, the access decisions at the target also utilize the identity of the client. This is called *user propagation*. We discuss delegation in more detail in Chapters 6 and 8.

This same process may take place within a series of beans in a single container, but it is not as significant as container-to-container calls. The security environment within a single container is well known. That is, the beans were chosen and deployed by one company. In the container-to-container situation,

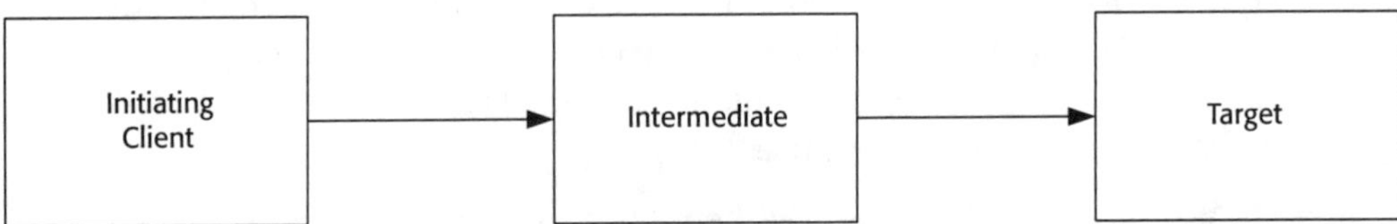

Figure 2.3 Delegation through a series of processes.

the target container may belong to an entirely different company. Additionally, the calls may go through a series of containers belonging to different companies. The ultimate target, to use a hackneyed example, may be the client's bank account. If one of the containers along the way was a rogue container that changed a deposit to a withdrawal and moved the money to another account, someone would not be happy.

EJB uses the principal of a trust relationship. This states that if a target container trusts an intermediate container, then the target container trusts all the containers that the intermediate trusts. This trust relationship propagates backward through all the containers. Container providers are required to supply a means of setting up a trust relationship between two containers. So, in the previous scenario of the waylaid bank account, the trust relationship between the target of the rogue and the rogue should have failed, and the internet bank heist should not have proceeded.

The consequences of mishandled delegation can be profound and complicated in a chain of intermediates. Not only do you have to worry about how delegation is handled within your own company, but you also have to worry about how it is handled within other companies into which your container makes calls. The list of actions you should take includes:

- Understand and evaluate the means of trust relationships that your containers provide.
- Understand and evaluate the means of trust relationships that the containers of other companies provide.
- Ensure that your application assembler evaluate the effect of runAs identities with respect to delegation.

One way that a trust relationship can be set up between containers is to use SSL mutual authentication, which in turn requires client certificates. The following is an overview of the SSL mutual authentication process. When the two containers first access each other, the SSL handshake protocol requires the server to pass its X.509 certificate. The client verifies the server certificate and uses the public key in the certificate to encode a secret. It passes the secret to the server, which decodes it with a private key that only the server knows. The server then modifies the secret in a known way. For example, it might increment a numerical value of the secret. The server sends the modified encrypted secret back to the client who can decrypt it with the public key and check that the proper modification was done. If the proper modification was done, the server is authenticated to the client. In mutual authentication, the inverse takes place with the client sending its certificate, and so on.

After the SSL authentication has been completed, the server knows that the intermediate is who it says it is. Next, the target container must determine whether that intermediate is a trusted entity. A simple method would be to use a list of trusted names that were set by the deployer in the deployment descriptor. The target container could then extract the Distinguished Name of the intermediate from its X.509 certificate, which was passed during the handshake and compare that name with the name from the trusted list.

The container provider could use other methods for determining trust, such as username/password, or it could use environmental conditions, such as when all the containers are in an isolated network with limited access. Password authentication is weaker than SSL authentication and should be suspect for sensitive transactions. Relying on a secure environment, although possible, is difficult with a widely distributed network. This also means that the use of the Internet is very difficult.

Once you have analyzed the trust methodology of your container provider, you then have to perform the same analysis on any other companies with which you will be interacting and on the companies that they may be interacting with. For example, your company might purchase an assembled part from company A. Company A might use a credit bureau to check your credit, and then it might use companies B, C, and D to complete your order. Company A might use your identity to check your credit and order the subassemblies. As a result, your identity is shipped all over the place. That being said, the expected use model of EJB does not include using identity assertion between businesses, that is, between security domains. Chapter 5 discusses the problem of interoperability between different tiers and security domains. Use the techniques described in Chapter 5 for company-to-company interaction, not identity assertion.

Of course you shouldn't get paranoid about this. As we stated in Chapter 1, security management is risk management. The extent of your design and usage model should be determined by the potential risk that can occur with your propagated identity, what your relationship is with the called company, and what their understanding of the process is including their controls and attention to details. When you finish this book, you will understand the principals of delegation, so you can use your business judgment to assess the risk and determine the amount of investigation you must do.

Summary

This chapter discussed the security aspects of EJB with emphasis on the EJB specification version 2.0. Version 2.0 of the specification has gone further than previous versions in specifying the security of EJB.

We followed the traditional EJB approach of describing the security duties of the bean provider, the application assembler, and the deployer. Because most of the security aspects of EJB are handled by the deployment descriptor, we paid particular attention to how security information was used and declared in the deployment descriptor and to the security consequences of these deployment descriptor values. This chapter used snippets of the deployment descriptor for eBusiness.com. Refer to Chapter 8 for the complete deployment descriptor of eBusiness.com.

Groups are an important scaling principle in EJB security, so we provided a thorough treatment of groups including what they are and how to use them. We introduced the concept of impersonation, which is when an intermediate bean in an application server assumes the identity of its caller. We showed how it should be used and cautioned against its misuse.

Throughout the chapter, we offered advice on which capabilities you should look for in EJB Containers. This is especially important in places where the EJB specification gives some leeway to the container providers. Even in cases where the specification is definitive, not all container providers will implement all provisions of the specification.

The next chapter discusses the security aspects of the other component model covered in this book, CORBA.

Securing CORBA Components

The CORBA Component Model (CCM) is a key feature of the CORBA 3 specification, and it is considered by some to be one of the most exciting developments to come out of the Object Management Group (OMG) since the IIOP protocol defined in CORBA 2. The three major parts of CCM are as follows:

- A container environment that packages transactions, security, and persistence, and provides interface and event resolution
- Integration with Enterprise JavaBeans
- A software distribution format that enables a CORBA Component software marketplace

Like EJB, CCM defines a persistent, transactional, and secure CORBA component container environment. Moreover, enterprise beans can be installed in a CCM container, which allows them to act as CORBA components. Unlike EJB, CORBA components can be written in different languages, including Java, C++, and many other languages for which OMG IDL mappings are defined.

For those who want to get a bit more information on CCM, the sidebar provides a brief introduction to the main concepts of the CCM architecture as found in the CCM specification (OMG 1999).

CORBA COMPONENT MODEL OVERVIEW

Ports

Components support a variety of surface features through which clients and other elements of an application environment may interact with a component. In general, these surface features are called ports. The component model supports five basic kinds of ports:

1. **Facets**, which are distinctly named interfaces provided by the component for client interaction
2. **Receptacles**, which are named connection points that describe the component's ability to use a reference supplied by some external agent
3. **Event sources**, which are named connection points that emit events of a specified type to one or more interested event consumers, or to an event channel
4. **Event sinks**, which are named connection points into which events of a specified type may be pushed
5. **Attributes**, which are named values exposed through accessor and mutator operations. Attributes are primarily intended to be used for component configuration, although they may be used in a variety of other ways.

Components and Facets

A component can provide multiple object references, called facets, which are capable of supporting distinct (i.e., unrelated by inheritance) CORBA interfaces. The component has a single distinguished reference whose interface conforms to the component definition. This reference supports an interface, called the component's equivalent interface, that manifests the component's surface features to clients. The equivalent interface allows clients to navigate among the component's facets and to connect to the component's ports. The other interfaces provided by the component are referred to as facets.

Component Identity

A component instance is identified primarily by its component reference, and secondarily by its set of facet references (if any). The component model provides operations to determine whether two references belong to the same component instance and (as mentioned above) operations to navigate among a component's references. The definition of *same* component instance is ultimately up to the component implementor in that they may provide a customized implementation of this operation. However, the component framework provides standard implementations that constitute de facto definitions of "sameness" when they are employed.

Components may also be associated with primary key values by a component home. Primary keys are data values exposed to the component's

clients that may be used in the context of a component home to identify component instances and obtain references for them. Primary keys are not features of components themselves; the association between a component instance and a particular primary key value is maintained by the home that manages the component.

Component Homes

CCM defines a component home meta-type that acts as a manager for instances of a specified component type. Component home interfaces provide operations to manage component life cycles, and optionally, to manage associations between component instances and primary key values. A component home may be thought of as a manager for the extent of a type (within the scope of a container).

Component types are defined in isolation, independent of home types. A home definition, however, must specify exactly one component type that it manages. Multiple different home types can manage the same component type, though they cannot manage the same set of component instances.

At execution time, a component instance is managed by a single home object of a particular type. The operations on the home are roughly equivalent to static or class methods in object-oriented programming languages.

This chapter explains CORBA security, which defines the security service for CORBA components as well as all other CORBA objects. (Because CORBA Security protects all CORBA objects, we'll use *objects* interchangeably with *components* for the remainder of the chapter.) Our brief description of CORBA security hopefully will mean you won't need to rummage through the 400-plus-page specification and related OMG documents. Although we'll do our best to familiarize you with CORBA security, it's not our intent to make you a master of the subject. Rather, we want to make sure that you have enough background information on CORBA and EJB security to understand the rest of the book. If you want to learn more about security in CORBA, we've provided additional sources of information at the end of this chapter.

This chapter does not teach the basics of security or the fundamentals of CORBA and EJB technologies and how to develop applications with them. We assume that you are familiar with CORBA technology and have written programs using it but have not necessarily done anything with CORBA security. If these assumptions are incorrect, you might want to wait until you gain more expertise in enterprise CORBA and Java before you proceed.

This chapter is almost exclusively devoted to CORBA security as a primary means of securing your valuable assets in the form of CORBA objects. However, keep in mind that as with any other software, there are many ways to make your managed and accessible assets via computer systems safe and secure. And CORBA-based systems are no exception. You can achieve safety by:

- Using physical security and enclosing the computer systems containing your CORBA objects in secluded rooms with impenetrable walls and unopenable massive doors
- Purchasing insurance for your computer-based assets so that in case of any damage, you will receive monetary compensation sizeable enough to make you happy

There are similar ways to secure your CORBA-based applications and corresponding resources, but due to their cost, most organizations try to find a suitable balance among physical security, insuring assets against possible damages, and mitigating the risks using conventional computer security. We assume that your company already knows how to take care of physical security—training its personnel and taking other necessary steps to manage security risks. Our role is to help you understand how you can employ CORBA security technology to increase the security of your CORBA-based applications, so that risk can be managed more efficiently.

We begin by concentrating on the concepts at the foundation of CORBA security as well as features and idiosyncrasies that are important for understanding the rest of this book. We will bring back the eBusiness.com example introduced in Chapter 1 to show you how to use CORBA security to protect this hypothetical storefront. Because you've already seen how to apply EJB security to achieve the same objective in Chapter 2, the example will also help you to appreciate the similarities and differences between the CORBA and EJB security models.

Benefits of CORBA Security

The CORBA security specification (CORBASec) defines a framework for providing security services to applications via the CORBA object request broker (ORB). The Security Service is one of several Common Object Services defined as part of the CORBA standard, which is shown in Figure 3.1. As with any other OMG CORBA specification, the security services are specified, but their implementation is deliberately not.

The following lists contain a summary of CORBASec merits.

- Defines standard interfaces for application security, which:
  - Simplifies security for developers and administrators
  - Hides infrastructure differences (public versus secret key, Secure Sockets Layer (SSL) versus Kerberos, Unix modes versus Windows NT access control lists (ACLs)

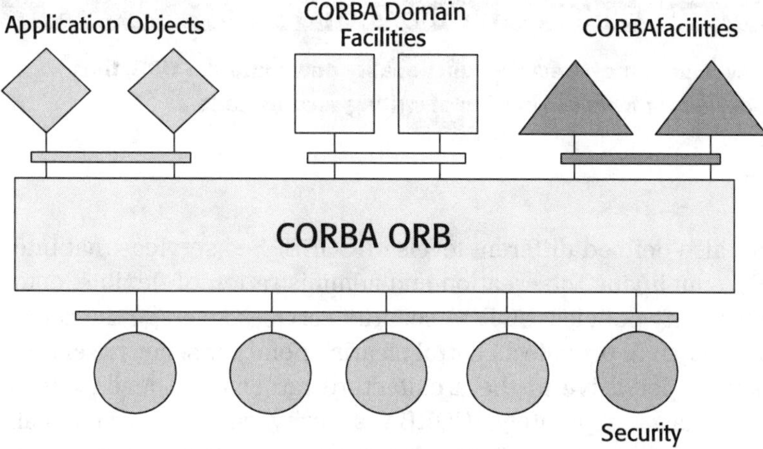

Figure 3.1 CORBASec defines the Security Service as one of the Common Object Services available to CORBA objects.

- Describes a common security platform across heterogeneous applications, ORBs, operating systems, and hardware
- Serves as an open extensible secure interoperability solution, which:
  - Builds on existing security mechanisms, such as SSL, Distributed Computing Environment (DCE), Simple Public-Key GSS-API Mechanism (SPKM), Kerberos, Secure European System for Applications in a Multi-vendor Environment (SESAME)
  - Allows replaceability of security services
  - Enables future interoperability among CORBASec implementations

CORBASec defines the following runtime functionalities visible to application developers and security administrators:

- Identification and authentication
- Authorization and access control
- Auditing
- Message integrity and confidentiality protection
- Authentication of clients and target objects
- Optional nonrepudiation
- Administration of security policies

ESI AUTHORIZATION PRINCIPLE: PUSH SECURITY DOWN

CORBA Security pushes most security functionality down into the ORB, thus relieving the developer from the burden of writing security code.

The OMG has also defined different levels of CORBASec services that interface with ORBs, simplifying the creation and administration of flexible, enterprise coherent security policies. CORBA security services leverage the central role played by the ORB to provide a central clearing point for security services. By making security pervasive in the architecture rather than needing to be enforced in each layer separately, CORBA security services dramatically reduce the need for developers to focus on low-level details to make applications secure.

Given that the CORBASec specification is over 400 pages long, you could ask, why not just use simple encryption, say with SSL, of Internet Inter-ORB Protocol (IIOP) messages going back and forth between CORBA ORBs? This would save developers and administrators from the trouble of implementing these complex standards. A simple security add-on for an ORB simply applies the SSL protocol to secure communications between the client and the server. SSL applies fixed security services for confidentiality and integrity to network communications. However, SSL alone is like a secure pipe. That pipe can be plastic, so no one can see inside (confidentiality), or steel, so no one can see or break in (confidentiality plus integrity), but both ends are open. It requires custom programming to extend control over the security sensitive operational environment in which communication takes place.

The main advantage of the OMG CORBASec over a simple SSL-based add-on is that it, when implemented in a compliant software product (commercial or public domain), makes systems less error-prone and also addresses other security challenges, such as:

- Dynamically managing access to resources based on an enterprise's security policy, the type and content of a transaction, and the credentials of the user.
- Preventing legitimate users of the system from gaining access to information that should be hidden from them.
- Stopping internal or external intruders from masquerading as someone else to obtain access to whatever that user was authorized to do or see. (In this scenario, security measures also must prevent actions and damage from being attributed to the wrong person.)

- Preventing internal or external intruders from bypassing security controls altogether.
- Tracing security breaches. This requires, among other capabilities, adequate identification of users.

More specifically, CORBASec defines two levels of ORB security. Any product compliant with CORBASec must support Level 1 or both Level 1 and Level 2:

- Level 1
  - Support *security-unaware* applications
  - ORB-enforced authentication, secure invocation, authorization, and auditing
  - Simple delegation
- Level 2
  - Support *security-aware* applications
  - Ability to select quality of protection, change credentials, select delegation options, and use audit services
  - Support administration interfaces using security policy domains

We discuss security-aware and security-unaware applications in later sections of the chapter. There are also the following optional functions:

- **Nonrepudiation.** Application interface for generating and checking evidence of claimed events.
- **Replaceability of security services.** Allows replacement of security services that are enforced by ORB.
  - **Security services.** Standard set of object security interfaces.
  - **ORB services.** Low-level interceptor interface within ORB to extend beyond security.
  - **Security ready.** ORB has security interfaces, but no implementation; designed for future extensions.

That pretty much summarizes the CORBASec highlights. The rest of the chapter describes in detail those parts of CORBASec that are necessary for understanding other chapters.

Although we assume that you know when we use the acronym CORBA that we don't mean "Concerned Off the Road Bicycle Association," and that you have some experience in programming and using CORBA, we'll refresh your memory with a brief summary of key CORBA concepts before we proceed with a detailed description of CORBASec. If you are very comfortable with the CORBA model and design or develop using this technology, you are welcome to skip the following section and go directly to the "Runtime CORBA Security" section.

A Brief Review of CORBA

CORBA technology, including the CORBA security service, defines a general-purpose infrastructure for developing and deploying distributed object-based systems in a broad range of specialized application domains. Application systems and the CORBA infrastructure, including the Security Service, are defined using standard CORBA declarative facilities.

Declarative Part

All entities in the CORBA computing model are identified with interfaces defined in the OMG Interface Definition Language (IDL). OMG IDL resembles C++, and it even allows the use of the C preprocessor macros, although today many believe that (heavy) use of such macros is not good practice. A CORBA interface is a collection of three elements: operations, attributes, and exceptions. The following IDL fragment from our eBuisness.com example shows the interface Product. The interface defines the following:

- Attribute ID of type ProductID, which is an alias for a native type string
- Operation getPrice(), which returns the price of the product associated with a particular instance of the interface
- Operation setPrice(), which allows the setting of the product price

If the price value is out of the supported range, for example, negative, the operation throws a user-defined exception InvalidPrice. The exception is defined right before the interface, so that it can be referenced, and has one data member called description, which when the exception is raised could contain a readable description for why the price is invalid. OMG IDL, as with most other programming languages, has several constructs, such as structs and enumerations as well as reserved keywords, which we put in bold font in the following code fragment.

```
typedef string ProductID;

exception InvalidPrice
{
     string description;
};

interface Product
{
     attribute ProductID ID;
     float getPrice();
     void  setPrice(in float NewPrice)
          raises InvalidPrice;
};
```

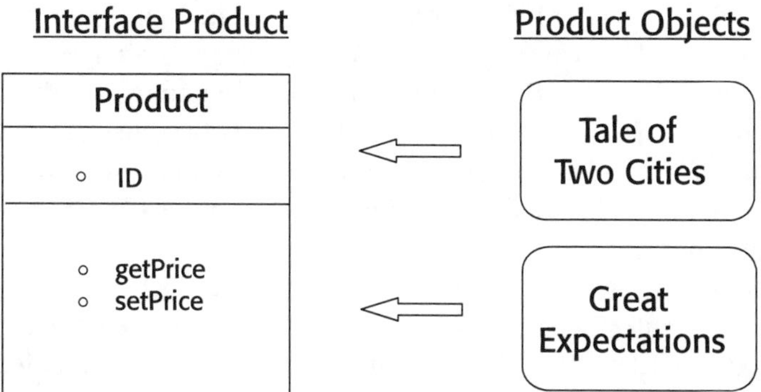

Figure 3.2 Objects are instances of interfaces.

An implementation of a CORBA interface is called a CORBA object. Hence, we use "CORBA object" or just "object" to mean "an implementation of a CORBA interface," where it does not cause confusion. In Figure 3.2, you can see that "Tale of Two Cities" and "Great Expectations" are both instances of the Product interface. The same application can implement more than one interface. This is critical for constructing complex and scalable distributed systems.

Interface definitions can inherit other interfaces. Interface inheritance allows smooth interface evolution and composition. The following IDL code shows how interface inheritance is employed to reuse the definition of operations defined in ShoppingCart in CustomerAccount. Because CustomerAccount inherits ShoppingCart, clients can invoke operations on the implementation of the former and as such, they invoke the operations of the latter. Interface inheritance is different from implementation inheritance, and you have to program all the operations of the CustomerAccount and ShoppingCart interfaces if you implement a CustomerAccount object. This capability is a necessary condition for the smooth evolution of complex software systems.

```
interface ShoppingCart
{
     void placeOrder  (in order new_order);
     void deleteOrder (in ProductID product_order_to_delete);
     OrderSeq listOrders ();
};

typedef string CreditCard;
typedef string CustomerID;

interface CustomerAccount : ShoppingCart
{
     readonly attribute CustomerID customer;
     void settleOrder (in CreditCard card);
};
```

The CORBA standard defines how IDL constructs are translated into various programming languages. It allows multiple language bindings, which means that CORBA objects can be coded in different programming languages and yet interoperate with clients and each other. Because of this, objects from different environments residing on different machines with different computing architectures can be integrated and shared among clients, which makes IDL-based objects inherently distributable.

Object functionality is exposed to other CORBA-based applications only through the corresponding interfaces by means of a CORBA runtime environment realized in CORBA ORBs. Thus, the runtime part is as important for understanding CORBA as the declarative part.

Runtime Part

When CORBA objects are deployed, they reside in OS processes and utilize CORBA middleware in the form of ORBs to make their functionality available to the clients as well as to receive and process invocations and return the results. Objects can act as clients as well, that is, making invocations on other objects, creating chains of invocations. Thus, in each invocation, there is a client making the invocation and a *target object* (or just "target") receiving the invocation. Clients and targets may reside in the same or different processes or in different hosts. Figure 3.3 illustrates this by showing a target object implementing the interface Product with ID "Tale of Two Cities" and a client customer, which invokes the getPrice() operation on the target and receives a return value. They are both in the same process, or process co-located, in this example.

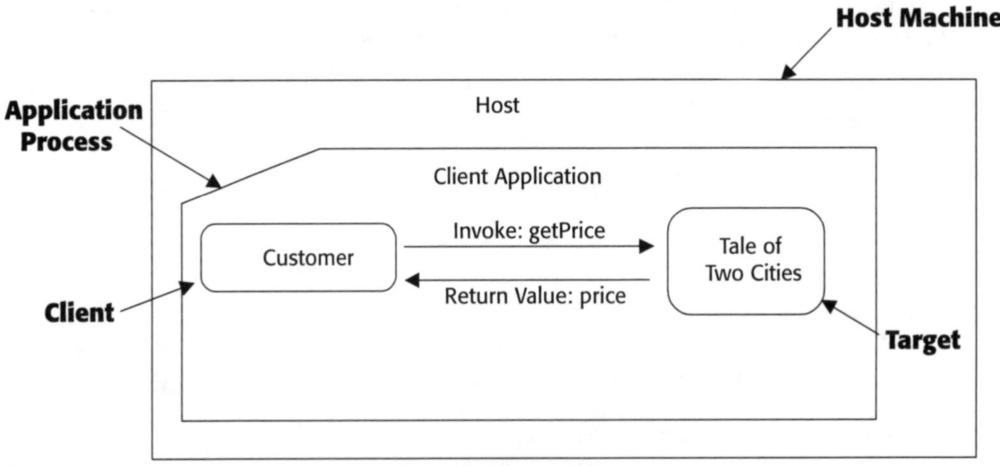

Figure 3.3 Object invocations—clients and targets.

The beauty of CORBA and EJB—as well as some other middleware technologies—is that they make object invocations transparent to the location of the client and target. Because CORBA defines the location independent runtime environment as ORBs for targets and clients to interact (see Figure 3.4), it makes many tasks (such as locating objects) much simpler for developers. The complexity of distributed communications doesn't disappear, but with CORBA, it becomes encapsulated in the ORB layer, which is developed and supplied by a middleware vendor.

A CORBA ORB is responsible for core middleware functions, such as:

- Register, keep track of, and find interface implementations
- Introduce clients to needed server objects
- Provide communication transport from a client to a target

Because an ORB provides all these functions, the only things a client needs to know are the definition of the interface on which it wants to make invocations and an object reference for the target that implements the interface. An

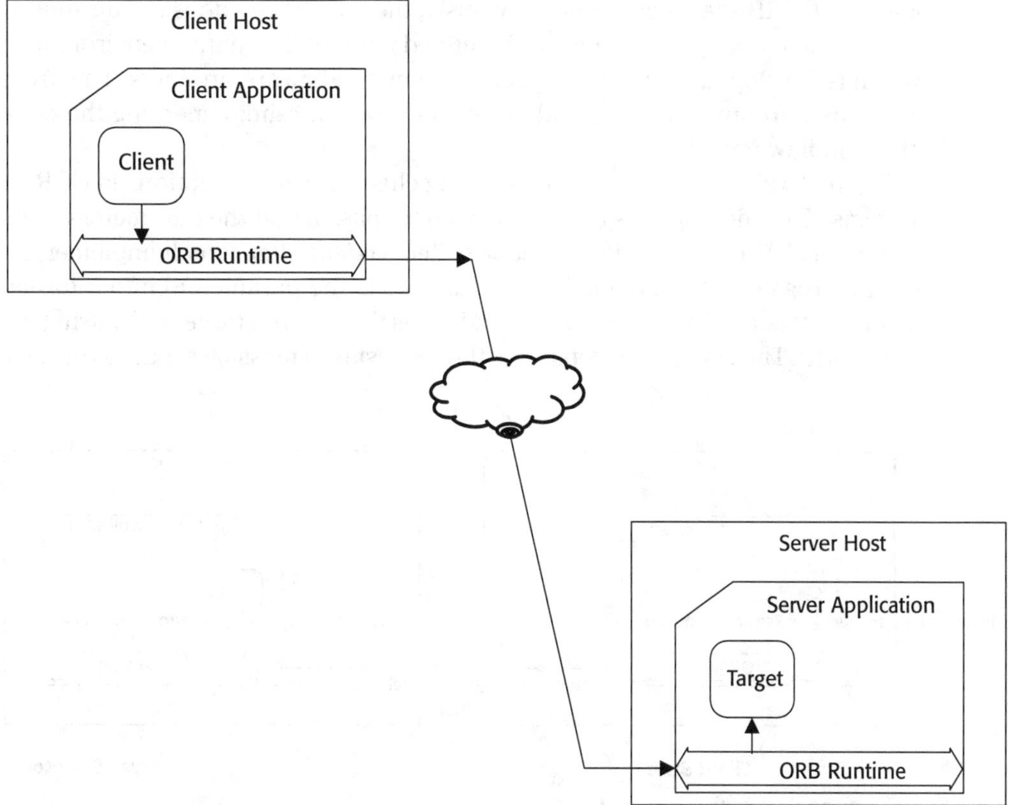

Figure 3.4 CORBA solution for distributed objects.

object reference is a handle through which a client requests operations on the corresponding object. CORBA defines a format for the interoperable object reference (IOR) that enables ORBs from different vendors to parse a reference and obtain enough information from it in order to ship the client's request to the target's ORB. This information includes the name (or IP address) of the machine hosting the ORB and the port number on which the ORB is listening for requests. There is also enough information for the target ORB to dispatch a request to the correct skeleton. The IOR format also allows for packing target security information into a reference that describes security characteristics of the target. We'll discuss what particular security related information can be found in an IOR later in section "Runtime CORBA Security." A client does not need to know about target implementation logic, nor about the language of implementation. It also doesn't need to know about the target host machine—where it is, whether the target object is in a currently running process, or how the target is instantiated and started. The underlying ORB infrastructure is left to take care of the details, locate the right target, and dispatch the invocation to it.

This brief description might sound too good to be true; however, there is no magic in CORBA. As mentioned previously, the complexity does not disappear, but instead is encapsulated into well-defined parts of the runtime environment, which is developed by vendors specializing in middleware products. This frees developers from reinventing and, most importantly, reimplementing the complex middleware layer.

Figure 3.5 shows the flow of data during client/target interactions in CORBA systems. The client makes a local invocation, passing all the parameters to an automatically generated piece of code called a *client stub*, which implements a local surrogate of the target. The stub marshals the parameters into a format that is understandable by the target and ships them to the target ORB using the client ORB. The client ORB separates the request into messages, packs the mes-

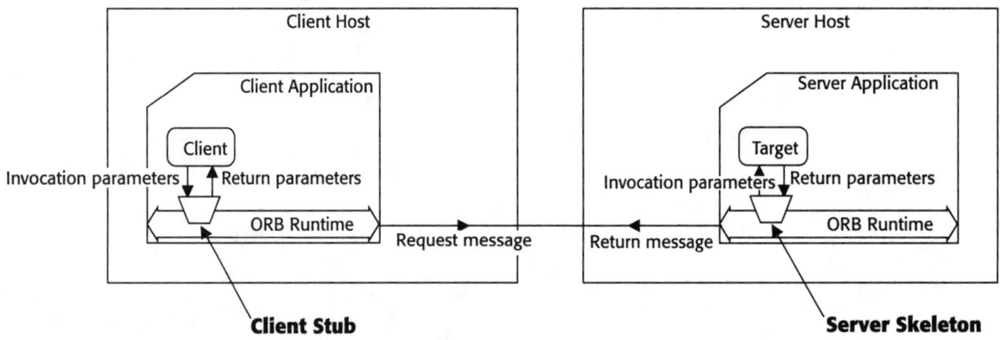

Figure 3.5 CORBA static invocation details.

sages, and sends them over wire to the target ORB. The latter unpacks the messages, reconstructs the request, and passes it on to the server counterpart of the client stub called the *server skeleton*. The skeleton performs the reverse task of the client stub. It unmarshalls the parameters, copies them into the address space of the target, and then informs the target implementation that a request is waiting to be processed. The stub (skeleton) code is automatically generated during compilation of the IDL code that defines the interface and is specific to the programming language of the client (target).

After the request is processed by the target, the results are passed back to the skeleton, which marshalls them into the form appropriate for the client, and then passes them on to the ORB to ship them to the client. Runtime security is enforced in CORBA some time between when the client makes an invocation on the target and when the invocation is dispatched to the target by its ORB.

Wire Protocol

CORBA ORBs communicate with each other, including sending object requests, using a special protocol for inter-ORB communications called Generic Inter-ORB Protocol (GIOP). Because GIOP is a connection-oriented protocol, requires reliable service and presentation of communicated data as a byte stream, GIOP messages are delivered over the Transport Control Protocol (TCP) in TCP/IP networks. Defined by the OMG, IIOP is a specialization of GIOP in TCP. GIOP messages sent between the sender and receiver ORBs are translations of request/response interactions between the corresponding CORBA client and server objects.

There are eight types of GIOP messages that can be exchanged between CORBA ORBs.

The following types of messages can be sent from client to server only:

- **Request.** For sending application requests
- **LocateRequest.** For finding:
  - If the object reference is valid
  - If the server can receive a request for the specified object
  - The address to which requests should be sent.
- **CancelRequest.** For canceling the prior (Request or LocalRequest) request

The following types of messages can be sent from server to client only:

- **Reply.** For returning results of the client request
- **LocateReply.** For responding to LocateRequest messages
- **CloseConnection.** For closing the connection

The following types of messages can be exchanged either way:

- **MessageError.** For sending a notification about an error condition on the client or on the server site
- **Fragment.** For sending fragmented messages

These messages are part of the state machine that defines communications between the CORBA clients and the servers at the wire level.

In order to give you a sense of what GIOP messages contain, we show a schema of a GIOP Request message in Figure 3.6. It consists of five parts: a GIOP message header, a Request message header, an object key of the target object, an operation name, and the operation body. GIOP message header formats are very similar to IP and TCP packet header formats. A GIOP message starts with a magic number that identifies the beginning of the message and is followed by the protocol version. Byte order field tells the receiver in what order (big or little endian) the rest of the message is in. The Message type field specifies that this is a Request message. The size of the message, not including the header, is then specified in bytes. Shown next is the most important field for our discussion—Service context, which we'll describe later. The ID of the

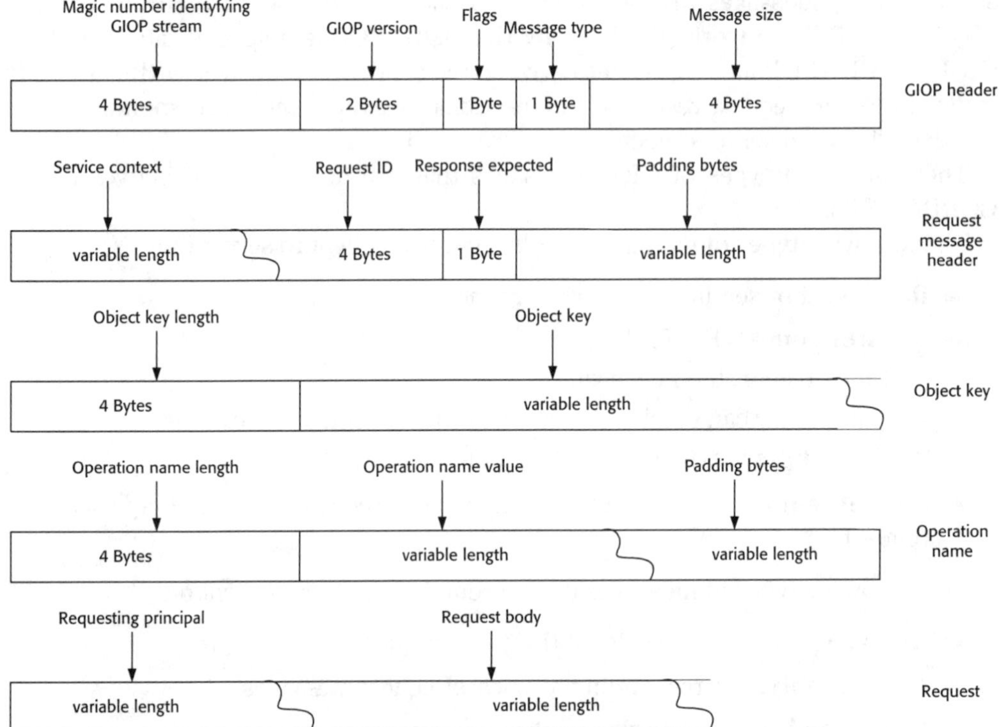

Figure 3.6 Structure of the byte stream representing a GIOP Request message.

request for matching replies follows, and is succeeded by an indication of whether a response is expected. Object key, which is opaque to the client, but managed by and needed for the server to dispatch the request to the right object, then follows. The operation name in string format comes after the object key. Finally, the name for the requesting principal (this field is obsolete) followed by the request body that includes marshalled arguments concludes a Request GIOP message.

You might wonder where the host address and the port number of the server are. They are missing from the message because Request messages are sent only after the connection between the client and the server is already established, making the entry point address unnecessary.

From a security point of view, it's important to note the following about GIOP Request messages:

- The server to identify the object uses an object key whose content is opaque to anybody except the hosting server. The client obtains the object key from the object reference. An object key is scoped by the hosting server and uniquely identifies the corresponding object only in the context of the server. That is, another object on another server may very well be identified with an object key of the same value, although the two objects could be completely unrelated. A server may include whatever information it seems to consider useful for the purpose of hosting its objects and dispatching requests to them. This is why the content of an object key is completely opaque to anybody but the object server.
- A list of Service contexts accompanies all request and reply messages; it's a place for passing request related data that different services, such as transaction and security, need to exchange.

Security Service passes all its data related to a particular request or reply in the form of a service context list element in GIOP Request and Reply messages. We'll discuss this in more detail later in the chapter when we discuss runtime CORBA security.

Object Reference

In order for a CORBA object to be accessible to its clients, it needs to have some equivalent of an address. Object addresses are presented in the form of object references. The ORB that hosts the object working together with the object adapter can create such references using the host IP address, the TCP port number, and other information essential for locating the object inside the ORB. Obviously, this information is specific to the TCP communication protocol because the IP address and the port number are part of the address. The information is also specific to the ORB that created the reference because object key is ORB-specific. In order to make such references understandable across ORBs from different vendors, the OMG defined a format for IORs.

The IOR structure is defined in a very generic way to support its future evolution and immediate extensibility: It's a sequence of object specific protocol profiles that follow the interface repository ID of the object in question. Any IOR must have at least one profile that identifies the object that is accessible via IIOP. All IIOP profiles put in an IOR have the following simple structure:

- IIOP version
- Host address
- Port number
- Object key
- A list of optional components

Again, from our point of view, the most interesting part of the IOR is the list of components, which allows additional information to be attached to the IOR so that it's available when the client establishes a connection with the server in order to make object invocations. Several standard components are specifically defined for supporting security, and we'll discuss them in the following sections.

When describing CORBASec, we'll use the same approach: We'll present it in two parts—runtime and declarative security.

Runtime CORBA Security

The runtime part of CORBA security service implementation is what performs the actual protection, as opposed to the declarative part, which allows security administrators to control the behavior of the runtime part.

One of the objectives of CORBASec runtime is to be totally unobtrusive to application developers. Most CORBA objects should be able to run securely on a secure ORB without any active involvement within the application code. In the meantime, it must be possible for an object to exercise stricter security policies than the ones enforced by CORBA security runtime. Even authentication is defined in such a way that the application developer programs as little as possible for a client application to authenticate a user.

Identification and Authentication

For treating different users and servers that initiate actions uniformly, CORBASec abstracts them into principals, which provide the basis for identification and authentication within CORBA. A *principal* is a human user or system entity

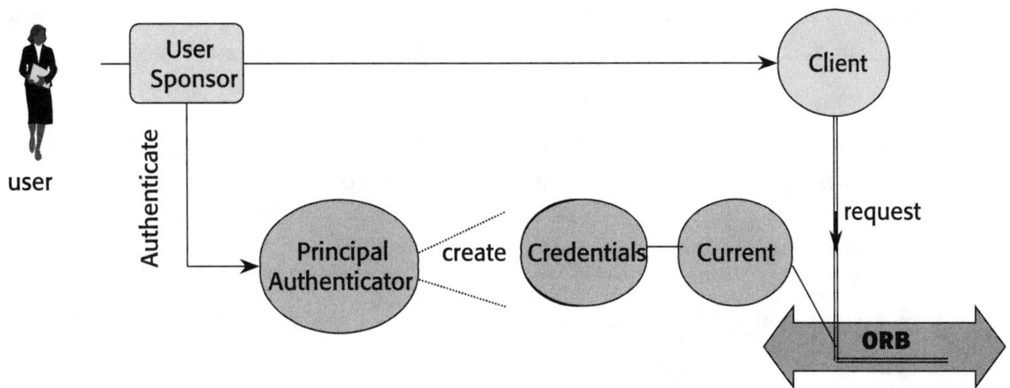

Figure 3.7 Authentication in CORBA.

that is registered with the system. When a principal is being authenticated to the system, it typically provides, via a *user sponsor*, its security name (such as a username), authentication information (e.g., password or cryptographic token information), and a set of requested privilege attributes (e.g., administrator role). A successful authentication results in an instance of *Credentials* interface, which holds a collection of the principal's security attributes that have been checked, approved, and certified by the CORBA security services. Security attributes may include several forms of principal identity as well as privilege attributes, which are used by the system to grant subsequent access to objects. CORBA security allows an extensible set of possible security attributes including access identity, audit identity, role, group, clearance, and capability. The main players involved in the identification and authentication in CORBA are shown in Figure 3.7.

Initiating principals are the ones that initiate activities. An initiating principal may be authenticated in a number of ways—the most common of which for human users is a password. For system entities, on the other hand, authentication data, such as a long-term key, must be associated with the corresponding

ESI AUTHENTICATION PRINCIPLE: TRUST NO ONE

CORBASec requires that both human users and application components authenticate. This approach secures each component that is part of a request chain and reduces the points of vulnerability. As a result protection against insider attacks can be very effective.

object. An initiating principal has at least one and possibly several identities, represented in the system by attributes, which may be used to:

- Make the principal accountable for its actions
- Obtain access to protected objects (though other privilege attributes of a principal may also be required for access control)
- Identify the originator of a message
- Identify whom to charge for use of the system

When a principal is being authenticated, it normally supplies:

- Its security name
- The authentication data needed by the particular authentication method used
- Requested privilege attributes (though the principal may change these later)

The principal may have privilege attributes that can be used to decide what it can access. A variety of privilege attributes may be available depending on access policies. The privilege attributes that a principal is permitted to take are known to the system. At any one time, the principal may be using only a subset of these permitted attributes, either chosen by the principal (or an application running on its behalf) or by using a default set specified for the principal. There may be limits on the duration for which these privilege attributes are valid and controls on where and when they can be used. Because CORBASec defines advanced concepts of privilege attributes, it enables access control policies based on roles, groups, clearance, and any other security-related attributes of principals.

Authenticated privilege and identity attributes, which are part of Credentials object, are used for the purpose of enforcing various security policies.

Policy Enforcement

CORBASec architecture achieves performance and administration scalability by means of policies and policy domains, where a security policy is associated with a policy domain (or just "domain"). Policies of more than one type can be associated with the same domain, and each object can belong to more than one policy domain. Domains can be organized in federations or hierarchies. We describe these compositions of policy domains and how to take advantage of them in more detail in Chapter 8. Policy decisions and enforcement can be object specific if each object is located in a separate domain, or a large group of objects can be associated with one policy domain. This means that the model scales (in terms of performance as well as administration) very well without losing fine granularity. Unlike EJB, CORBA objects residing on different computers can be protected with the same domains because CORBA security policy domains span multiple computers and therefore the same security policies.

ESI SECURITY ADMINISTRATION PRINCIPLE: COLLECTIONS FOR SCALE

CORBASec security policy domains provide support for administration scaling. Hierarchical security policy domains allow administrators to manage policies on very large numbers of resources independently of where those resources physically reside, and delegate security responsibilities across many administrators.

Similar to EJB, security policies are enforced completely outside of an application system at the ORB level. Everything, including obtaining information necessary for making policy decisions (such as access control), is done before the method invocation is dispatched to the target object. As Figure 3.8 shows, security enforcement code is executed inside of a CORBA security service when a message from a client application to a target object is passed through the ORB. Executed at the client ORB as well as at the target ORB, the security enforcement code uses the following three sources of information for making policy decisions to enforce:

- The security policy of the domain(s) to which the target belongs.
- The information from credentials of the client. In access control policy enforcement, these are client privilege attributes (such as access identity, group membership, role, and clearance), whereas for audit policy enforcement, security attribute of type AuditId is used.
- The message itself, which in the case of access control enforcement is a request to invoke an operation on the target object.

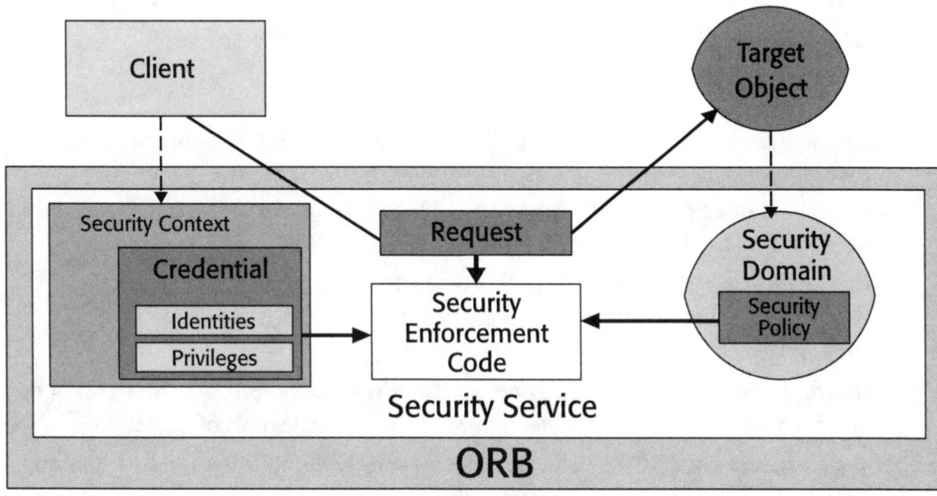

Figure 3.8 Enforcement of policies in CORBA security.

Although CORBASec specifies quite a few types of security policies, as described in the sidebar "Types of Security Policies in CORBA," we will concentrate mostly on invocation access (or just "access"), delegation, and audit policies. These are the milestone policies for any enterprise system, and we describe them later in the chapter. If you can master these three policies, then the rest will be significantly easier.

TYPES OF SECURITY POLICIES IN CORBA

CORBASec defines several types of security policies. The following descriptions are extracted from the specification:

- **Invocation access policy.** The object that implements the access control policy for invocations of objects.
- **Invocation audit policy.** This controls which types of events are audited during object invocation and the criteria controlling the auditing of these events.
- **Secure invocation policy.** This specifies security policies associated with security associations and message protection. For example, it specifies:
  - Whether mutual trust between client and target is needed (i.e., mutual authentication if the communications path between them is not trusted).
  - Quality of protection of messages (integrity and confidentiality).

There may be separate invocation policies for applications acting as the client and those acting as target objects. This applies to access, audit, and secure invocation policies. There may also be separate policies for different types of objects in the domain.

- **Invocation delegation policy.** This controls whether objects of the specified type in the policy domain, when acting as an intermediate in a chain, delegate the received credentials by default, use their own credentials, or pass both.
- **Application access policy.** This policy type can be used by applications to control whether application functions are permitted. Unlike invocation policies, it does not have to be managed via the domain structure, but may be managed by the application itself.
- **Application audit policy.** This policy type can be used by applications to control which types of application events should be audited under what circumstances.
- **Nonrepudiation policy.** Where nonrepudiation is supported, a nonrepudiation policy contains the rules for the generation and verification of evidence.
- **Construction policy.** This controls whether a new domain is created when an object of a specific type is created.

Another significant part of the CORBASec model is the security of IIOP messages traveling between ORBs. We explain this in the following section.

Wire Protocol

As described in the previous section on the runtime part of CORBA, any GIOP Request/Reply message contains a list of service context data, which is used by different services for inserting service specific information into the stream of communications between client and server. CORBASec defines a SecurityAttributeService element data type as an element of GIOP message service context, which may be used to associate security specific identity, authorization, and client authentication contexts with GIOP Request and Reply messages. This context element type is used for sending GIOP messages in order to exchange messages that are sent as part of security attribute service (SAS) context protocol between clients and servers. A key part of OMG's Common Secure Interoperability version 2 (CSIv2), SAS is very important for the secure CORBA and EJB interoperability protocol because it allows a client and a server to establish and maintain the security context they use to communicate securely. If the client and the server are capable, they can maintain a stateful security context, which is reused from request to request. Otherwise, the security context is established with every application request.

When the security context is being established, the client's authentication and authorization data are passed to the server, which the Security Service of the target server uses to decide if it trusts the authenticated identity of the client principal and to determine what operations on what objects the client is authorized to invoke. These attributes and the authentication data are passed over secure transport to guarantee the authenticity and integrity of the attributes. In order for the client and target ORBs to pass this data, they need to agree on a protocol for passing the data and a protocol for protecting the data. Defined by CSIv2, these sub-protocols comprise a three-layer architecture. We'll give a brief overview of CSIv2 here; Chapter 6 goes into further detail.

Figure 3.9 shows the three layers specified by the CSIv2 architecture. The transport layer provides protection of CORBA invocations and the returned

ESI SECURITY ASSOCIATION PRINCIPLE:
THINK END-TO-END, NOT POINT-TO-POINT

Transport security mechanisms such as SSL are inadequate in multitier environments because they cannot secure a chain of application requests—SSL only secures communication across a single client-server connection. CSIv2 builds on transport security to provide effective end-to-end security across a chain of applications.

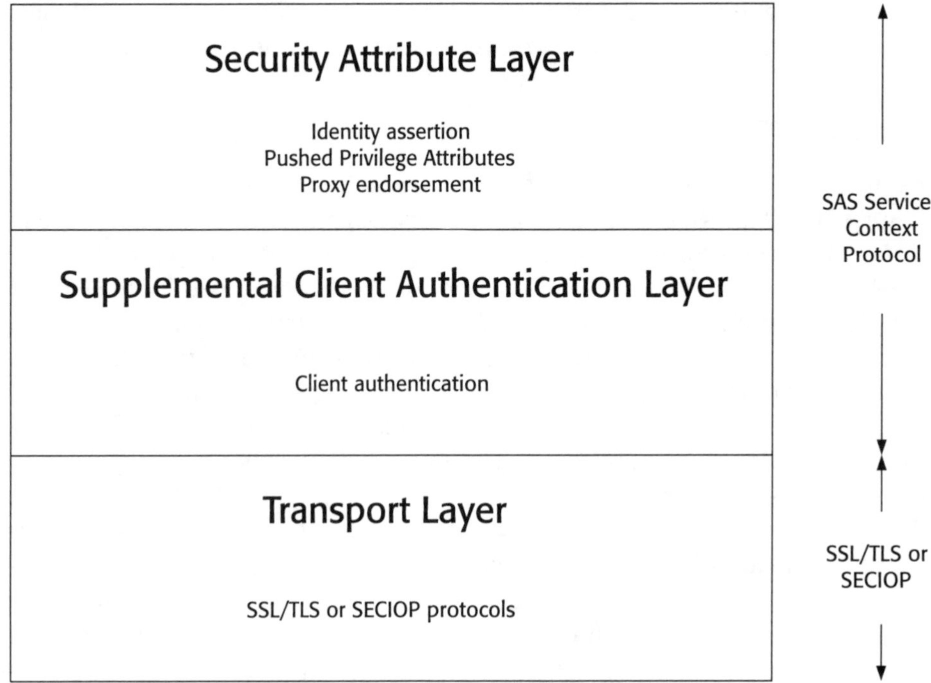

Figure 3.9 The three layers of the CSIv2 architecture.
Source: CSI, 2000.

results using either SSL/TLS or Secure Inter-ORB (SECIOP) protocols. It also provides target-to-client authentication. If the client can't authenticate itself using the transport layer, the authentication middle layer defines the format of the data exchanged between the client and the server in order for the client to authenticate. The highest layer is used to pass authorization attributes of the calling principal.

But how does the client know what security functionality and mechanisms the target server supports and requires for secure communications? The target server embeds this information into the IOR, which it passes to the client in some way, for example, via CORBA Naming or Trader services, or just writes it into a file accessible by the client. We described the content of IOR earlier. Each IOR for an object accessible through IIOP has a list of (tagged) components, which allows additional information to be attached to the IOR so that it's available even before the client establishes a connection with the server. This is where the client can find what security functionality and mechanisms the target supports and requires.

CSIv2 defines the following tagged components, which can be put in an IOR by the Security Service to describe what secure transport the object server supports:

- **TAG_CSI_SEC_MECH_LIST.** Contains a list of security mechanisms that the target object specified in the IOR can use at the transport layer to communicate with its clients. Each element of the list has a field that defines the transport layer security mechanism using one of the following values:
  - **TAG_NULL_TAG.** No security functionality at the transport layer is implemented.
  - **TAG_SSL_SEC_TRANS.** The target accepts SSL/TLS protected invocations.
  - **TAG_SECIOP_SEC_TRANS.** The target accepts protected invocations using SECIOP.

The client's Security Service uses this information to determine if the client and the target can communicate securely. Both security services need to support at least one common protocol defined by the transport layer. CSIv2 names SSL v3.0 and TLS v1.0 as mandatory. That is, any implementation of CORBASec must support secure inter-ORB communications using these protocols. A client might also choose to communicate with the target over an unprotected transport layer, and any compliant target must support this as well.

CSIv2 defines conformance levels for wire-level interoperability of CORBASec implementations, which we describe in detail in Chapter 6. The CSIv2 conformance levels are important for you to be aware of when you select your product because compliance to CSIv2 affects the level of interoperability between products.

Functionality Levels

Earlier, we briefly described the CORBASec functionality levels. As we pointed out, each level was designed to support a particular security type of application: security-aware and security-unaware. In this section, we explain what these terms mean.

CORBASec is designed in such a way that most applications can be secured via proper settings on the administrative security interfaces. This type of security control is called "declarative security" and such applications are called "security-unaware" to stress the fact that they don't exercise any protection explicitly and are secured by the external CORBA security environment. To support this type of application, a CORBA security product has to conform to Level 1. Those applications that, in addition to the protection provided by the external security environment, are in need of the enforcement of fine-grain or application specific security policies can access them via programming interfaces provided by any CORBA security implementation that conforms to Level 2. For this reason, they are called "security-aware" and are said to exercise "programmatic security."

After describing what is in conformance Levels 1 and 2, we'll explain in detail the capabilities of declarative and programmatic CORBA security in the following two sections.

Level 1: Security-Unaware Applications

A Level 1 compliant ORB enforces basic audit and access control functions for security-unaware applications, which are applications that possess no knowledge of the security functions applied to them.

In these applications, the system administrator defines the security context of network communications. Take the example of the operation getPrice(), invoked on an object implementing Product interface. With SSL alone, a fixed protocol for securing confidentiality and integrity is applied to the communication itself. With ORB level security, the system administrator can evaluate the operation being invoked and place constraints on how getPrice() is invoked, by whom, and under what circumstances. The administrator sets the policies for the type of security, such as confidentiality, that will apply to the communication. The application itself is security-unaware; it has no knowledge of the security functions applied to it.

Security-unaware applications are most appropriate when the security responses are not dependent on application specific data, such as the value of operation arguments or application specific security functions or policies. If the security policy depends on application data, the application necessarily becomes aware of security. In that case, Level 2 functionality is required to support such applications.

Level 2: Security-Aware Applications

Security-aware applications are more powerful, but are also more complex. They are endowed with the intelligence and authority to manage the security functions that apply to them.

CORBASec Level 2 includes application programming interfaces (APIs) that enable security-aware applications to manage their own security. This level is particularly important in enterprise environments where fine-grained, scalable approaches are needed.

Within the structure of overall enterprise policy, security-aware applications can possess intelligence about the communication and about the reason communication is being initiated. The applications can independently manage the user authentication, access control, confidentiality and integrity protection, and auditing of requests for the services and data they provide. At the same time, the application remains easy to analyze, and security administrators retain all the control they need to manage a secure environment.

Security-aware applications are useful when value judgments must be made about the security context of an invocation. For example, the application might need to recognize the difference in a medical record between a patient's blood type and AIDS status and apply content appropriate access controls.

Declarative CORBA Security

The three cornerstones of declarative CORBA security are rights, domains, and privilege attributes. Achieving a good understanding of them guarantees a 90 percent chance of succeeding in administering CORBA security. You should understand very clearly why you need them and how you can use them.

Why You Need Rights, Domains, and Attributes

What is all this fuss about granted and required rights and policy domains in CORBA? The objective of configuring access control mechanisms seems to be easy to achieve without sophisticated models. For example, you just grant user Johnson permission to invoke operation CustomerAccount::settleOrder() and you are done. Well, almost. If you do it this way, you also need to go through *all* of your users and do the same for each of them. Before long, you'll realize that instead of granting a permission explicitly to each user, which obviously takes a while not only to do it the first time but also to keep the "grantings" current, you can group all the users who should have permission to invoke settle() into some group, say Settlers, and grant the permission just to the group. By grouping users, things become easier for you as an administrator because you can remove the permission from the group or add another permission almost in one step. This is exactly what all the policy domains, attributes, and granted/required rights aim to give you—less hassle when administering large groups of users, objects, and operations.

It's obvious that domains, rights, and attributes introduce an additional level of indirection enabling more scalable administration, and this is how they make your life as a security and user administrator easier. But why do we need all three of them? Can't we just use user security attributes and object operations?

ESI SECURITY ADMINISTRATION PRINCIPLE: COLLECTIONS FOR SCALE

CORBASec rights, domains, and attributes provide a very powerful solution for administration scaling. These three collection mechanisms taken together provide one of the most general solutions for security policies defined by any computing standard.

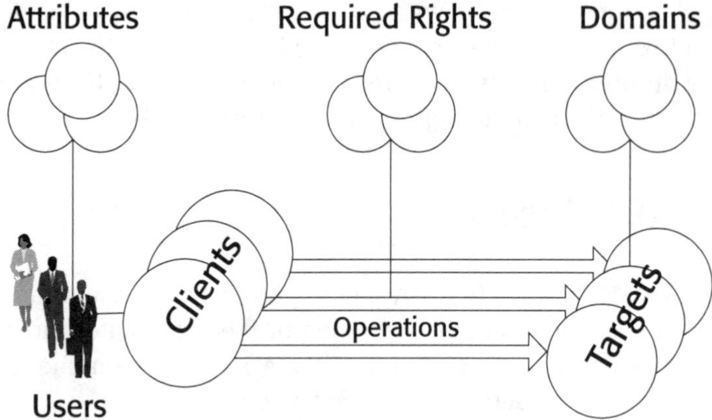

Figure 3.10 Users, operations, and server objects are grouped via attributes, rights, and domains.

To answer this question, let's go back to the basic invocation diagram for a distributed object-oriented (OO) system shown in Figure 3.10, and see why you need domains and rights in CORBA.

Ideally, we should be able to write policy statements that grant access to target objects for as many users as needed, no matter if there is one user or millions of them. The most common way to make the policies that flexible and expressive is to group users via user privilege attributes that specify such information as with what groups the user is affiliated, what roles he or she performs in the current session, and so on. This is exactly how the users and other active entities are grouped in the CORBA security model. The use of privilege attributes allows you to grant access to a collection of users who perform the same role in the organization, or have the same clearance, or are members of the same group, and so on. Users may have many kinds of privilege attributes and multiple values per attribute. In case you were wondering, privilege attributes are qualified as "privilege" because users are granted various privileges depending on what privilege attributes they have. Now that you understand the need for privilege attributes, let's talk about policy domains.

If it weren't for the security policy domains, you would have to explicitly specify access and other policies for each and every target object. The domains enable the scalability of policy management by allowing administrators to define collections of objects whose security is governed by a common policy. Such objects are assigned to a policy domain. In turn, the domain is associated with the policy that governs the security of all objects in the domain. This allows you to specify one policy per a potentially large group of objects belonging to one access policy domain. You can now see the importance of object domains from a security point of view. We explain the details about domains later in the chapter. At this point, let's move on to the last piece of the puzzle—required rights.

A very important capability needed for successful administration of access control is the grouping of methods (operations in CORBA terminology). You might not realize that the number of methods accessible on distributed objects in your enterprise is quite large. Just in our eBusiness.com example, we have 17 different operations. And you can easily imagine that in real enterprises there are hundreds of distinguished operations on distributed objects. Any security administrator can tell you that it's common to grant the same access to more than one resource in the enterprise. As a result, an administrator's job can be significantly eased if the operations that are alike in security requirements can somehow be grouped and administered at a group level instead of using individual operations. In addition, the use of such groups prevents security administrators from having to understand the semantics of methods. This is exactly what CORBA's required rights do.

Now that you understand why attributes, domains, and rights are needed, we will present a detailed discussion of what types of roles rights, domains, and attributes play.

The Role of Rights

In CORBA, every operation has a global set of associated RequiredRights, as shown in Figure 3.11. This set, together with a combinator *(all* or *any* rights), defines what rights a principal has to have in order to invoke the operation.

You might wonder what "global" means in the context of required rights. CORBASec defines required rights for a given operation on an interface to be the same no matter what domain or even organization the interface instance is located in. For example, if MemberAccountFactory::delete() requires both "set" and "manage" rights, then theses rights will always be the required rights for delete() on MemberAccountFactory anywhere in the world this interface is implemented. Of course, such a model is a bit beyond realistic assumptions, but you can always assume that the world ends at the exit gate of your company and not worry about the rest of the universe. For more complex cases with inter-company interactions, some implementations of CORBA security utilize the notion of required right domains, which has, although not standardized, proven to be very useful for architecting real-life solutions. You'll want to check with your CORBA security product vendor to see how it handles the scope of required rights.

In our required rights example, we used the "all" combinator, which makes a lot of sense because it means that all required rights should be "matched" in order for an access request to be authorized. Situations when required rights are combined with the "any" combinator, when any of the required rights should be "matched," are rare but not excluded. Throughout your work on modeling policies, you will find the use of the "any" combinator. We'll explain later what it means to "match" required rights.

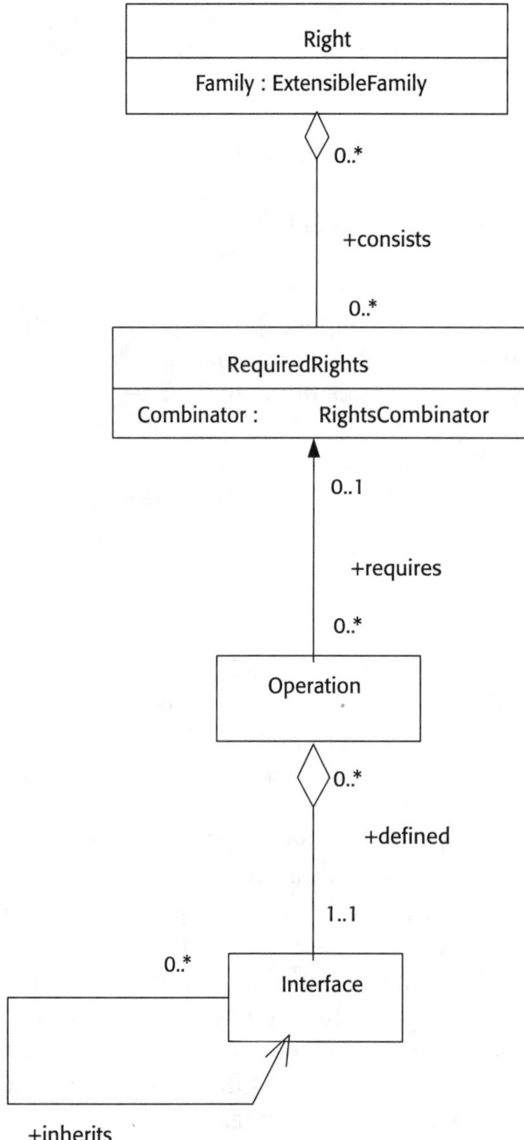

Figure 3.11 Required rights and operations.

Application designers and developers, supposedly the best people to know the effects of each operation, define and document required rights and their semantics for the objects they produce. However, required rights alone don't do much good because they merely state the requirements. How can we determine if the requirements are met and the invocation on the operation is permitted? CORBA security defines *granted rights* that have the same syntax as required rights but a different meaning, as you can see in Figure 3.12. This Unified

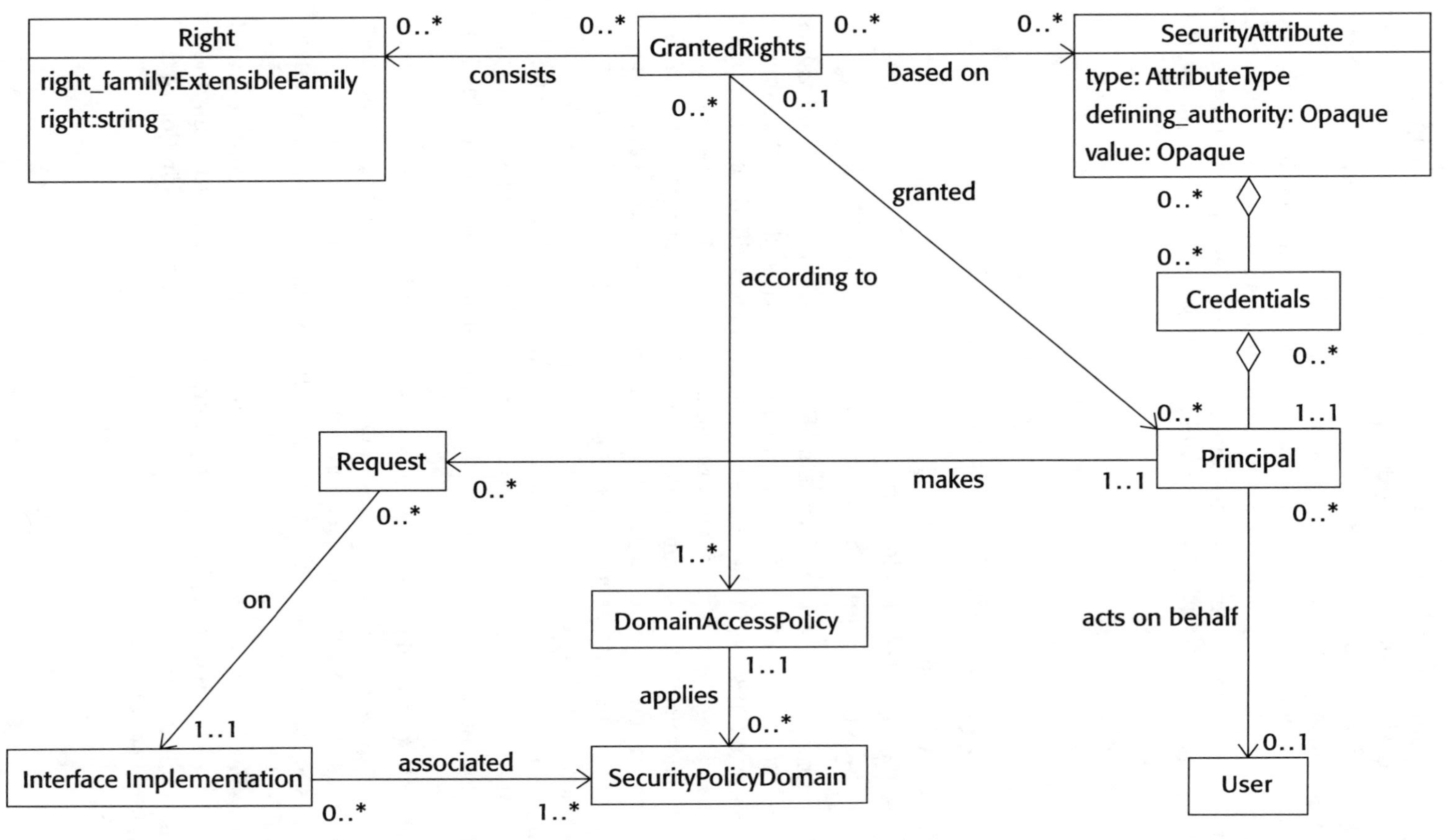

Figure 3.12 Relationships among the main elements of the CORBA authorization model.

Modeling Language (UML) diagram, which represents relationships among various important elements of CORBA security, should not scare you away because we've explained some of the elements, and we'll take care of the rest right now beginning with the rights, attributes, and domains.

First, a short note on the namespace of rights and security attributes. In order to avoid name pollution and to enable interoperability, CORBA security defines the scope of rights and attribute types, which are qualified using ExtensibleFamily members. The ExtensibleFamily struct is defined in the OMG IDL as follows:

```
struct ExtensibleFamily {
     unsigned short     family_definer;
     unsigned short     family;
}
```

The following ExtensibleFamily values are defined as:

- FamilyDefiner = 0 — OMG
  - Family = 0 — identity attributes
  - Family = 1 — privilege attributes

Using the mechanism of ExtensibleFamily, developers can add values as required to meet user specific security policies without fear of stepping into somebody's territory. In these cases, a family is identified, and then a set of types or values for this family is assigned. Family identifiers 0–7 are reserved for OMG defined families (family_definer=0) and therefore are standard values. We recommend you only use the OMG defined families if you can. This recommendation is made to keep things simple at the beginning and to aid in future interoperability. If, after a diligent effort is made to keep to the OMG defined family, you find it necessary to extend the family definition, be sure to clearly define the semantics of the extensions and where they should be used. It is also a very good idea to explicitly define the semantics of the OMG defined attributes because local usage of a standard term may vary.

CORBA security defines standard rights that are likely to be understood by administrators without requiring administrators to be aware of the detailed semantics of the corresponding operations.

The standard rights defined in the OMG IDL Security module are illustrated in Table 3.1.

However, these standard rights are not the only ones permitted by OMG. They may be extended using rights_family, which is defined using the same ExtensibleFamily type that was previously described. The definition of the IDL type Right is as follows:

```
struct Right {
     ExtensibleFamily     rights_family;
     String               right;
}
```

Table 3.1 CORBA Standard Rights

EXTENSIBLE FAMILY	RIGHT	PROSE NAME	DEFINITION
PRIVILEGE (0, 1)	s	Set	Used for any operation on the object that does not change its state
	g	Get	For operations on an object that changes its state
	m	Manage	For operations that manage the object
	u	Use	For operations on an object that may change the overall state of the system, but not the state of the object itself

Examples of required rights can be found in Table 3.2.

As you can see, we used a right ('a') that is not a standard right from the OMG Security module. We did it to show you how you can use new rights to

Table 3.2 Required Controls for the eBusiness.com Example

INTERFACE NAME	OPERATION NAME	REQUIRED RIGHTS
ProductFactory	getProducts	OPEN ACCESS
ProductFactory	lookup	OPEN ACCESS
Product	getPrice	g (all)
Product	setPrice	s m (all)
CustomerAccountFactory	create	OPEN ACCESS
CustomerAccountFactory	delete	s a (all)
CustomerAccountFactory	lookup	OPEN ACCESS
CustomerAccount	settleOrder	u (all)
CustomerAccount	placeOrder	s (all)
CustomerAccount	listOrders	s (all)
CustomerAccount	deleteOrder	s (all)
MemberAccountFactory	create	s m (all)
MemberAccountFactory	delete	s m (all)
MemberAccountFactory	lookup	OPEN ACCESS
MemberAccount	settleAccount	u (all)
MemberAccount	placeOrder	s (all)
MemberAccount	listOrders	s (all)
MemberAccount	deleteOrder	s (all)

accommodate your needs if the set of standard required rights does not suffice. We use special value OPEN ACCESS to denote those operations that don't require any right for invoking them. It's not a CORBASec standard notation or value; we employed it in our example to make this and other tables easier to understand.

Depending on the domain access policy *(DomainAccessPolicy* or DAP) enforced in a particular access policy domain, a principal (i.e., user or any other active system entity, such as service process) is granted different rights *(GrantedRights)* according to what privilege attributes it has. We show the granted rights for our eBusiness.com example in Table 3.3. For instance, if a principal is only granted right "s" (for "set") in an access policy domain, it can't invoke MemberAccountFactory::delete() because the operation requires "s" and "m" (for manage). However, if the same principal invokes delete() on a MemberAccountFactory implementation belonging to another domain where the principal is granted both "s" and "m" rights, then the invocation will go through. This is an example of how the matching of required and granted rights happens and what role access policy domains play. Let's describe a bit more of the mechanics behind attributes, domains, and granted rights.

CORBA access policy domains are encapsulated in DAP objects, one per domain, which define what rights are granted for each security attribute. Your CORBA security administrators are responsible for defining granted rights on a per domain basis. You can look at domain access policy as a prism, as in Figure 3.13. That is, privilege attributes are refracted by the corresponding DAP into granted rights. Which DAP is used depends on which domain the object belongs to. Whenever a principal attempts an operation invocation, the principal's granted rights are computed and matched with the rights required for the operation in question. If the match is successful, the invocation is dispatched. Otherwise, a security exception indicating that the client is not permitted to invoke the operation is sent back to the client.

Table 3.3 Granted Rights for Different Domains in eBusiness.com

PRIVILEGE ATTRIBUTE		DOMAINS AND GRANTED RIGHTS			
TYPE	VALUE	APPLICATION	ACCOUNTS	SPECIAL PRODUCTS	REGULAR PRODUCTS
AccessID	Parker	g	-	-	-
AccessID	Wilson	g	-	-	-
AccessID	Johnson	-	s, u	g	-
GroupID	Marketing	-	s, m	s	-
AccessID	Daly	-	s, u	-	g
Role	Administrator	-	s, a	-	s

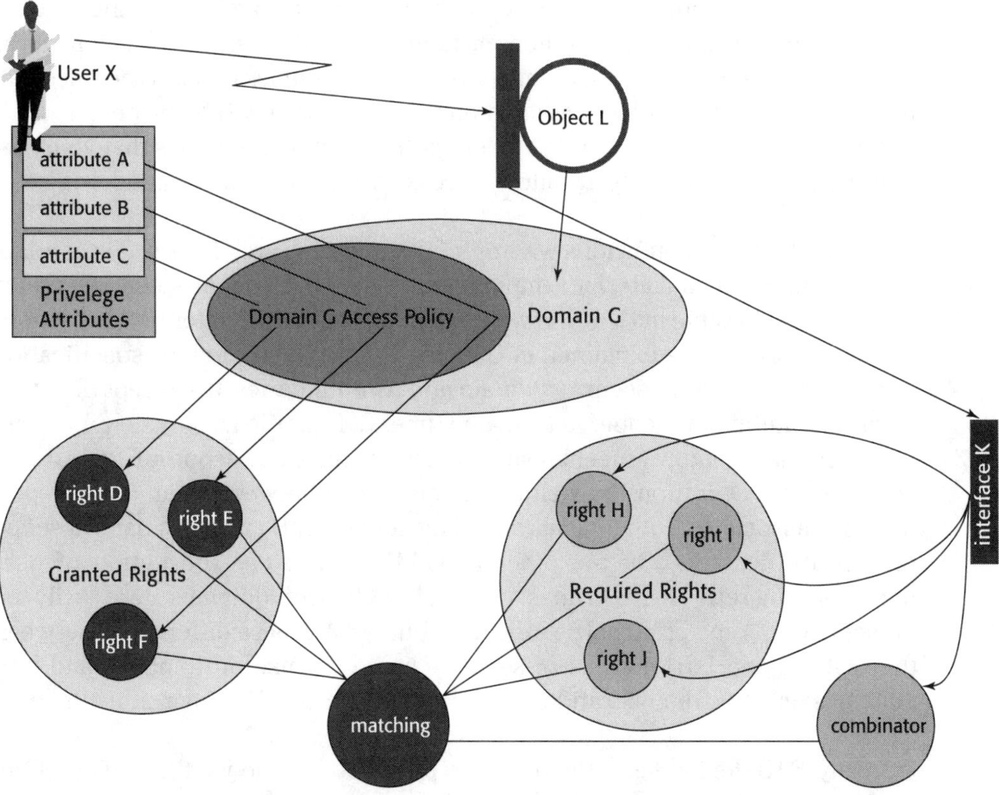

Figure 3.13 The role of access policy domains in CORBA authorization.

The matching is quite simple, but its semantics can be confusing. If the combinator is "all," then for every right from the set of interface's required rights there should be the same right in the set of the rights granted to the principal in the domain of the interface implementation. For example, if the principal has been granted rights "s" and "m" in a particular domain, it can invoke delete() on any instance of the MemberAccountFactory interface belonging to that domain. In order for the match to succeed in the case of an "any" combinator, the principal should be granted at least one right from the list of required rights. As a degenerate case, a principal with any granted rights is permitted to invoke an operation that has an empty set of required rights and the "all" combinator.

The Role of Domains

Domains, especially when it comes to security, are a very intriguing and at the same time vague subject. Different people have a different understanding of domains and their meaning. In this subsection, we'll elaborate more on domains to make sure we're all on the same page.

The concept of policy domains as we have said is a way of grouping objects. In addition to the grouping function, domains hold sets of policies, such as access policy, delegation policy, and so on. These policies contain the rules that determine the way an object associated with a domain will be protected. Let's use access policy as an example. Access policy contains the rules that your system administrator sets up to allow access to an object associated with that domain.

One of the usual confusions when security domains are discussed is overlapping domains. Can an interface implementation belong to more than one policy domain? It's possible in CORBA (we explain the semantics later in this section) but not in EJB, as we explained in Chapter 2. Moreover, the EJB specification does not define what a security domain and its boundaries are except that it's a means of limiting the scope. At the same time, EJB jar file Deployment Descriptors serve as a natural mechanism for determining the scope of logical and concrete role definitions as well as the mappings between them and the permissions associated with logical roles. This makes EJB jar files a natural scope of security domains. On the other hand, EJB does use the notion of user domains, whereas CORBA does not (although user domains can easily be implemented using principal security attributes). All these differences between the CORBA and EJB notions of security make the use of domains, and ultimately security administration, in mixed CORBA/EJB environments only harder.

In any EJB deployment, the object is provided by one jar file, which effectively excludes situations when it can belong to more than one security domain. This is not the case in CORBA security, in which policy domains are not bound to the physical location of the application objects associated with them.

So far, we've described in detail rights and domains, which are orthogonal and independent of each other. Principal security attributes, particularly privilege attributes, bring rights and domains together and complete the picture of declarative CORBA security.

The Role of Privilege Attributes

CORBASec generalizes the way users are aggregated using *security attributes*. As explained in Chapter 2, users in EJB are grouped via roles. Thus, even if you want to express user affiliation with a department from your company, you would still use EJB roles. CORBA uses the term security attributes, which is quite a bit more general than the EJB model.

The OMG Security module defines a set of standard security attributes. As we explained earlier in this chapter, security attributes are qualified using the ExtensibleFamily. The following code fragment is from the OMG IDL Security module, which defines the standard security attributes:

```
module Security {
        ...
        typedef unsigned long     SecurityAttributeType;

        // IDENTITY attributes; ExtensibleFamily = (0,0)
        const  SecurityAttributeType     AuditId=1;
        const  SecurityAttributeType     AccountingId=2;
        const  SecurityAttributeType     NonRepudiationId=3;

        // PRIVILEGE attributes; ExtensibleFamily = (0,1)
        const  SecurityAttributeType     Public=1;
        const  SecurityAttributeType     AccessId=2;
        const  SecurityAttributeType     PrimaryGroupId=3;
        const  SecurityAttributeType     GroupId=4;
        const  SecurityAttributeType     Role=5;
        const  SecurityAttributeType     AttributeSet=6;
        const  SecurityAttributeType     Clearance=7;
        const  SecurityAttributeType     Capability=8;

        struct AttributeType {
             ExtensibleFamily     attribute_family;
          SecurityAttributeType     attribute_type;
        }
        typedef sequence <AttributeType> AttributeTypeList;
        ...
}
```

The assignment of privilege attributes to users can be logically represented as a table that for each user ID enumerates a set of privilege attributes (their types and values) associated with the user. Table 3.4 illustrates an example of a user privilege attribute table.

In addition, CORBASec does not state how an implementation determines what attributes are automatically assigned to a principal at login, although it does mention that there may be a set of default attributes. Therefore, it is up to

Table 3.4 User Privilege Attributes

USERID	ATTRIBUTE TYPE	VALUE
Mparker	AccessID	Parker
	Role	administrator
Cdaly	AccessID	Daly
Psmith	AccessID	Smith
Mjohnson	AccessID	Johnson
Jwilson	AccessID GroupID	Wilson marketing

the implementation of a particular Security Service as to how the initial set of attributes is assigned to a principal. One method that could be used is, at login to the security system, the user is offered a choice of using the defaults assigned to them or choosing different attributes than they have been given permission to use. For example, user mparker could just accept the default attribute of AccessId=parker and Role=administrator, or he could choose to use only the AccessId=parker attribute. This set of attributes is Parker's base attribute set and is used for any applications run by user mparker unless the application takes further steps at runtime by using programmatic security available to it via a Level 2 security API.

Setting Audit Policies

CORBASec defines interfaces that allow administrators to specify audit policies. Particularly, administrators can define which security related events must be audited, that is, corresponding audit records generated by the ORB. However, the specification does not define the behavior, or the policies governing the behavior, of a CORBA ORB if an audit record cannot be recorded or otherwise processed by the audit subsystem, or another type of audit service failure occurs. CORBASec leaves this up to the implementation of the Security Service. Audit policies specify which events should be audited under what circumstances. The specification divides all events into two major classes: system and application security events.

Common to all applications, system events may occur in and must be recorded by the ORB, or security, or other subsystems. They include such events as:

- Authentication of principals
- Changing privileges
- Success or failure of object invocation
- Administration of security policies

ESI SECURITY ACCOUNTABILITY PRINCIPLE: AUDIT EARLY, NOT OFTEN

Auditing is expensive in distributed systems, so for performance reasons, it's better to do it as little as possible. By providing an audit service at the middleware layer, CORBASec allows auditing to be performed close to the application, resulting in more effective auditing.

Some application specific events may be relevant to security (e.g., transfers between bank accounts) and therefore could be subject to a security audit.

In order to accommodate these two major classes as well as other classes of audit events and different types of events within these classes, CORBASec defines a new type, AuditEventType:

```
module Security
{
  ...
  typedef unsigned short EventType;
  const EventType AuditAll = 0;
  const EventType AuditPrincipalAuth = 1;
  const EventType AuditSessionAuth = 2;
  const EventType AuditAuthorization = 3;
  const EventType AuditInvocation = 4;
  const EventType AuditSecEnvChange = 5;
  const EventType AuditPolicyChange = 6;
  const EventType AuditObjectCreation = 7;
  const EventType AuditObjectDestruction = 8;
  const EventType AuditNonRepudiation = 9;

  struct AuditEventType {
    ExtensibleFamily event_family;
    EventType event_type;
  };

  typedef sequence <AuditEventType> AuditEventTypeList;
  ...
};
```

A list of AuditEventType elements is passed as an argument to most operations defined on an AuditPolicy interface provided to audit administrative tools. The operations allow administrators to set, remove, replace, and examine audit selectors. The selectors specify what information should be used by the audit decision logic to determine if an audit record should be generated each time a security related event happens in the client or the target ORB. Similar to the rights required for invoking operations on an object, all or any selectors can be used for matching against the event in question. The following information can be used as a selector:

- Name of the interface the target object implements
- The value of the object reference used by the clients to get a hold of the object
- Name of the invoked operation
- Credentials of the client principal who is making the object invocation
- Time of the event in question
- Day of the week

Using Programmatic Security

No matter how accommodating the security policies are and how many application security requirements can be satisfied externally by CORBA security, there will be more applications that require—at least developers believe—more complex protection than what is guaranteed to security-unaware objects. CORBASec accommodates the needs of such applications by allowing them to use interfaces to CORBA security services for programming security enforcement code within applications. Such enforcement is called *programmatic security*. Even though we briefly describe what CORBASec has to offer for programmatic security, we strongly discourage you from programming any security logic into your applications because the complexity and the development, deployment, and administration costs become unreasonably high.

If an application has been written as a security-aware application, it may use the security infrastructure provided by CORBA security. It uses the security infrastructure via the Security Current object, which is a placeholder for the Security Service specific state information associated within the current execution context (i.e. thread). A CORBA client or target application obtains a reference to the object by making the following call:

```
ORB::resolve_initial_references ("SecurityCurrent");
```

Once a reference to Current is obtained, the application narrows it to either SecurityLevel1::Current or SecurityLevel2::Current depending on what functionality level is provided by a concrete implementation of CORBA security.

The SecurityLevel1::Current interface defines only one operation, namely get_attributes(), which is used for obtaining the client's security attributes. This operation is sufficient for making application specific access control decisions based on the privilege attributes of the client principal along with application specific factors. We devote all of Chapter 7 to the subject of protecting application resources via the enforcement of application specific authorization policies and using application specific factors.

The SecurityLevel2::Current interface inherits from Security:Level1::Current and defines the following additional operations and attributes:

```
module SecurityLevel2
{
  ...
 interface Current : SecurityLevel1::Current
 {

   // Thread specific
   readonly attribute ReceivedCredentials received_credentials;
```

```
    void set_credentials (
      in Security::CredentialType cred_type,
      in CredentialsList creds,
      in DelegationMode del
    );

    CredentialsList get_credentials (
      in Security::CredentialType cred_type
    );

    CORBA::Policy get_policy (
      in CORBA::PolicyType policy_type
    );

    void remove_own_credentials(
      in Credentials creds
    );

    // Process/Capsule/ORB Instance specific operations
    readonly attribute Security::MechandOptionsList supported_mechanisms;
    readonly attribute CredentialsList own_credentials;
    readonly attribute RequiredRights required_rights_object;
    readonly attribute PrincipalAuthenticator principal_authenticator;
    readonly attribute AccessDecision access_decision;
    readonly attribute AuditDecision audit_decision;

    // Security mechanism data for a given target
    Security::SecurityMechanismDataList get_security_mechanisms (
      in Object obj_ref
    );
  };
  };
```

The operations and attributes defined on the interface allow security-aware applications to:

- Manage their own and received (in the case of target or intermediate objects) credentials
- Obtain security policies configured administratively
- Look up security mechanisms supported by a particular server hosting a given object for communicating with clients
- Determine rights required for invoking a particular operation
- Authenticate to a CORBA security environment
- Obtain a decision of the access policy in regards to a principal with particular privilege attributes, a given object, and an operation on it

- Obtain an audit policy decision and write it into the corresponding audit channel

As you can see, this is quite an extensive list of functionalities that a security-aware application can use. We recommend that you don't exercise all of these functionalities in your CORBA applications unless you don't have any other choice.

Summary

This chapter provided background information on CORBA and securing CORBA objects, which is necessary for understanding the rest of this book. We limited descriptions to the material directly related to the issues of integrating EJB and CORBA security in an enterprise environment. As an example of securing CORBA objects, we showed the configuration of CORBASec compliant systems for our eBusiness.com system.

If you would like to learn more about CORBA security, we highly recommend Bob Blakley's "CORBA Security: An Introduction to Safe Computing with Objects" book (Blakley, 1999). It presents an excellent "big picture" on the subject by one of the authors of the specification. If you want to dive into all the details, nothing is more comprehensive than the specification itself (OMG, 2000a) and its complement, the final revision of the proposal for CSIv2 (CSI, 2000).

Now that you are familiar with the security architectures of the two major middleware technologies used for building enterprise systems, we will introduce other technologies essential for securing today's enterprises.

CHAPTER 4

Enterprise Security Technologies

There are a number of security technologies used by enterprises when they build a solution to meet end-to-end security requirements. This chapter provides an overview of security technologies that are currently available to developers to help secure their business application components. We discuss these common technologies, provide some general recommendations on their use, and describe where each of the technologies fit with respect to the perimeter, middle, and legacy tiers.

Because the purpose of this book is to discuss secure components that reside in the mid-tier, it's not our intention to give an exhaustive description of all of the other security technologies that are in use. However, it is important to understand how many of these technologies relate to components, and how they all fit together as part of a complete end-to-end solution. For each security topic, our brief survey tells you what you need to know about the technology and provides pointers to further information. The technologies introduced in this chapter are critical as we plan our secure component system, which we discuss in Chapter 9; and build the final integrated system, which we discuss in Chapter 10.

Figure 4.1 expands on the description of enterprise security technologies that were introduced in Chapter 1. As you may recall, perimeter security serves as the first line of defense and primarily protects against hostile attackers

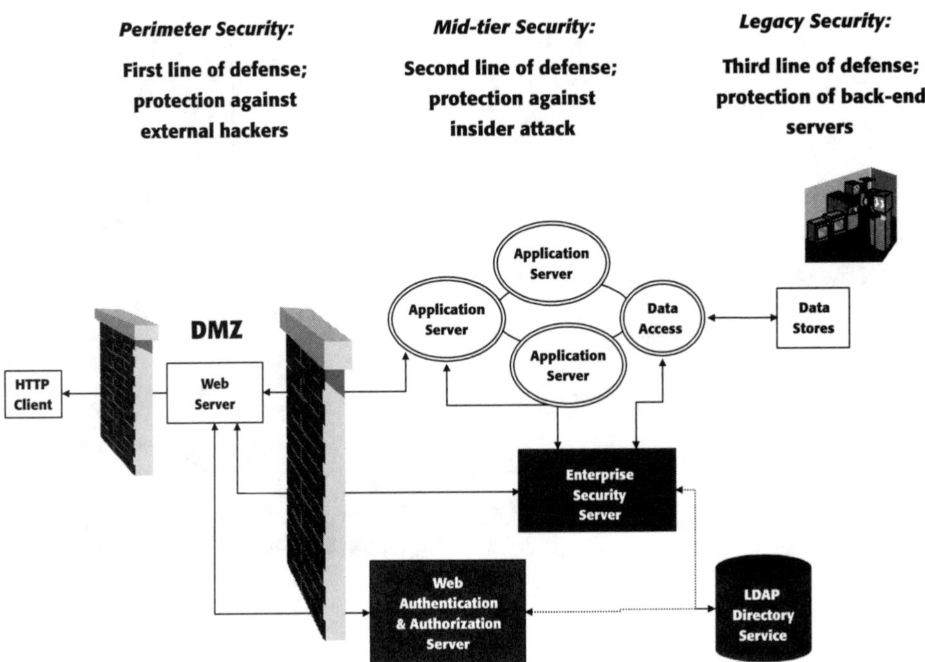

Figure 4.1 Enterprise security technologies.

outside of an organization. Mid-tier security serves as the second line of defense, providing another layer of protection against external attackers, and also protects against attackers that are within an organization. Legacy security provides the third layer of defense by protecting the back-end servers that contain an organization's most valuable resources. The combination of these three tiers of security makes it extremely difficult to mount an attack; even if one tier fails, the other tiers will still serve to defend against the vast majority of attacks.

Security technologies in the perimeter tier face outward toward an external network, which is typically the Internet. Because the perimeter may need to accommodate requests from virtually any client on the Internet, perimeter security mechanisms are designed for high performance and are usually coarse-grain. By coarse-grain, we mean that the decision of whether a client is authorized to perform a request is based on a simple criterion, such as whether the

ESI SECURITY ASSOCIATION PRINCIPLE: DESIGN FOR FAILURE

The security provided by each of three tiers intentionally has some redundancy. If one tier is compromised, the others will still provide protection and will limit the amount of damage that can be caused by an attacker.

client may use a protocol on a specified port. Perimeter security technologies include:

- **Authentication** of principals based on passwords, tokens, or public key certificates
- **Authorization** by filtering client packets or limiting client access to a specified Uniform Resource Locator (URL)
- **Cryptography** that protects messages transmitted between the client and Web server from disclosure or modification using encryption or digital signatures

Security technologies in the mid-tier provide a general set of protection mechanisms for the business logic. Mid-tier security technologies are effectively extensions to the underlying operating system because they provide similar security at the application layer to the security that operating systems provide to protect underlying platform resources (e.g., files and devices). Mid-tier security does not focus on protecting against outside attackers, as is the case in perimeter security. Instead, mid-tier security treats all business components as potentially suspicious and generally requires security checks as part of any component-to-component interaction. Mid-tier security technologies include:

- **Authentication** between component principals, which is usually based on public key certificates or secret keys
- **Authorization** of a client invoking on a target component interface/operation
- **Cryptography** to protect communication from disclosure or modification using encryption or digital signatures
- **Security Association** to establish trust between client and target components
- **Delegation** that allows a delegate principal to use the identity or privileges of an initiating principal so that the delegate may act on behalf of the initiating principal

Security technologies in the legacy tier protect the resources in back-end servers. The security mechanisms that protect legacy systems have been in place for a long time and are quite mature. In the past, these security mechanisms have been used to guard direct client/server access to sensitive legacy

ESI AUTHENTICATION PRINCIPLE: TRUST NO ONE

The most effective mid-tier security solutions require authentication of each component. This approach minimizes the damage that would be caused if an attacker attempts to insert a malicious component.

server resources. Today, enterprises are adapting the same mechanisms to guard legacy server access via the perimeter and middle tiers. Legacy tier security technologies include:

- **Authentication** of principals based on passwords, tokens, public key certificates, or secret keys
- **Authorization** of a client accessing a legacy resource (i.e., file or database record)
- **Cryptography** that protects messages transmitted between the client and legacy server from disclosure or modification using encryption or digital signatures

In addition to the preceding technologies, all tiers (perimeter, middle, and legacy) support various forms of accountability and security administration:

- **Accountability** provides a record of security relevant events to permit monitoring of a principal's actions.
- **Security Administration** maintains the security policy embodied in user profiles, access control lists (ACLs), passwords, and other data relevant to the security technology.

In the remainder of this chapter, we discuss the security technologies that are commonly used within the three tiers. For each technology, we describe how the approach addresses the relevant security services: authentication, authorization, cryptography, secure association, delegation, accountability, and security administration.

Perimeter Security Technologies

The common perimeter security technologies that are described in the following sections are:

- Firewalls/VPNs
- Cryptographic protocols
- Web-based security servers
- Intrusion detection

Firewalls/VPNs

A firewall protects one network from another. The benefits realized through the use of firewalls as the first line of defense include increased security assurance and intrusion alert capabilities. Examples of firewall products are Checkpoint

Firewall-1, Cisco PIX, and Raptor Eagle. The placement of firewalls on a network is critical to its ability to provide security. All network traffic must pass through a firewall before allowing any traffic onto a protected network. If network traffic is permitted to enter a protected network by any other means, the protection could be compromised.

Typically, a demilitarized zone (DMZ) is created to facilitate access from public networks to publicly available services (i.e., Web servers, public File Transfer Protocol (FTP) servers, etc.) without compromising the private internal corporate network. The basic configuration of the firewalls in a DMZ is a pair of firewalls with the publicly available services running on a subnetwork that is isolated between the firewalls. The pair of firewalls may be configured for redundancy so that a backup firewall can take over if a primary firewall fails. Firewalls may also be set up within an enterprise to separate groups of machines into *security enclaves*.

Virtual Private Networks (VPNs) allow a trusted network to communicate with another trusted network over open networks such as the Internet. VPN technology provides seamless and transparent communication between systems on the Internet while maintaining both the privacy and integrity of the communicated data. A VPN does this by creating a secure point-to-point tunnel between two network entities, such as enterprise gateways or from a client's desktop to a protected enterprise application. Data transmitted through this tunnel is both encrypted and authenticated. VPNs are useful for telecommuting employees and for communications with partners and business customers. Companies are frequently implementing VPNs to reduce network costs by allowing secure use of public networks.

Authentication

Firewalls provide coarse-grain authentication that is typically used to allow access to trusted networks based on IP or port addresses. Firewalls also support authentication mechanisms based on tokens (e.g., RSA SecurID). VPN technology provides a means of protecting and securing authentication data (such as passwords) as the data traverses over open networks.

Authorization

Firewalls/VPNs provide coarse-grain packet filtering based mainly on protocols and ports as well as other simple criteria, such as content-based filtering or protocol vectoring. The primary purpose of firewall authorization is to limit client access to specified servers and ports, for example, limiting a browser client to communicate only via Hypertext Transfer Protocol (HTTP) to a Web server within the DMZ.

Firewalls typically use a set of security proxies to initiate a connection; each security proxy is designed to listen for specific types of connection attempts. In addition to built-in application proxy services, firewalls may also support implementation of custom proxy-based services.

Firewalls are also designed to protect against a broad range of external attacks, such as IP address spoofing, Transmission Control Protocol (TCP) SYN flooding, Simple Mail Transfer Protocol (SMTP) weaknesses, port scanning, and downloaded Java applets, among many others.

Accountability

Firewalls/VPNs generally provide extensive logging capabilities for attempted accesses. Firewall audits should of course be used to provide logging of attempted hacker attacks.

Security Administration

Firewalls/VPNs provide administrative tools to define firewall policies that are stored within an internal database.

Cryptographic Protocols

For secure Web access, public key technology is commonly used as supported by the Secure Sockets Layer (SSL) protocol. SSL is a transport security protocol positioned above TCP but below the application layer of a communication protocol stack. It was originally developed by Netscape to provide security for Web-based HTTP transactions. In addition to HTTP, SSL is also used to provide secure transport for Telnet, FTP, and other application protocols. SSL is the basis of the Internet Engineering Task Force (IETF) Transport Layer Security (TLS) protocol version 1.0 [Dierks, Allen. *The TLS Protocol Version 1.0.* IETF Request for Comments 2246, January 1999].

SSL should be used to enforce end user confidentiality and integrity for Web access, which is usually based on 128 bit triple Data Encryption Standard (3DES) or RC4 session keys. For adequate protection, Web server certificates should be at least 1024 bit RSA keys.

Public key infrastructure (PKI) provides trusted key and certificate management. The public/private key pairs and certificates can be used to provide confidentiality, integrity, authentication, and nonrepudiation services. Users must be able to trust that the digital identity of the party that they are communicating with is valid. The PKI is responsible for providing this trust by establishing a system that correctly binds users with their digital identities.

Authentication

Certificates are a way for a trusted organization, known as a certificate authority (CA), to vouch for a user's (or server's) identity and public key. The CA accomplishes this by using its private key to sign a public key certificate, which is an electronic document that contains the user's name and public key. The CA's signature on the certificate indicates that the public key belongs to the named user. Depending on the CA's policy, the signature may also mean that the CA vouches for the trustworthiness of the user.

The signed certificate also prevents the undetected modification of the user's public key. If the holder of a public key certificate trusts the CA, and the CA signature on the certificate is valid, the holder can then be confident that the public key belongs to the person named in the certificate and that the public key is correct. The holder may then use the certificate to authenticate a message that was sent by the person named in the certificate and signed with his or her corresponding private key.

Verisign and Entrust are examples of popular CA products. Identrus, a global network of financial institutions, is an example of a consortium-sponsored CA. Identrus provides standards for banks to act as trusted third parties for e-commerce transactions. From a CA perspective, Verisign, Entrust, and Identrus provide the root CA; institutions often use a root CA certificate to issue their own certificates for their employees, customers, and applications.

The most common client authentication approach uses a digital signature to authenticate the server, complete the SSL handshake, establish an encrypted session, and use a conventional password protected by SSL encryption to authenticate the user. Although continued support for Web-based userID/password authentication is important, it's a good idea to begin planning for an evolution to PKI-based client authentication. Weaknesses of userID/password are well known, and they are even more vulnerable to attack in distributed systems.

When public key technology is used to authenticate the client, the client sends the server its public key certificate after server authentication is complete and the session key has been established. The client sends its signature on a combination of server and client provided information. The server verifies the signature on the client's public key certificate and verifies the client's signature on the combined data. If the signature is verified, the client is authenticated, and the encrypted session can begin. Smart cards are an effective means for securely carrying the client's private key. Technology for PC smart card readers is readily available and reasonably priced; in the future these readers are likely to be built into many Internet appliances.

The operation of SSL is normally transparent to the application that sits above it. However, once a user has been authenticated, the application can obtain information about the client's certificate through application programming interfaces (APIs) provided by the Web server.

Web-Based Security Servers

Products like Netegrity SiteMinder, Entrust getAccess, and Securant ClearTrust provide security for Web-based authentication and authorization. In this approach, each end user is defined in his or her own user profile in a user directory, and various authentication mechanisms are supported, such as password, RSA SecurID, Windows NT domain login, and certificate. End user authorization requirements for Web access are defined based on user access to URLs.

Authentication

Web-based security servers typically store user data in a Lightweight Directory Access Protocol (LDAP) directory service, which serves as the basis for user authentication. If the authentication check passes, the security server creates an encrypted cookie, which contains the username, IP address, browser, time, and expiration. The Web server returns the cookie to the client browser, which then uses the cookie for subsequent authenticated HTTP requests.

A variety of mechanisms are supported by Web-based authentication servers:

- **IDs and passwords.** Provide a simple to implement identity check. However, passwords can be forged, cracked, or spoofed if the password is poorly selected or if the password is not protected while in transit and in storage. This mechanism is appropriate for low risk applications
- **Tokens.** Provide stronger authentication. Examples of tokens include SecurID and CRYPTOCard. Tokens, however, are more costly and complex to implement than IDs and passwords. Tokens do not require special hardware on the client side and are frequently used for remote access to privileged services because they provide 2-factor authentication (physical possession of the token card and knowledge of the PIN).

ESI AUTHENTICATION PRINCIPLE: BALANCE COST AGAINST THREAT

Certificate-based authentication is very secure, but it may be expensive to deploy. Consequently, passwords are often the most appropriate form of authentication. As certificates and PKI become widely available and costs drop, certificates and other forms of strong authentication will naturally replace passwords for many applications.

- **Digital certificates.** Provide strong authentication as well. As discussed earlier, a reputable CA must issue the certificates, and the associated private keys must be protected while in storage. The CA must also support certificate verification and management services. These services allow a certificate's validity to be checked at the time of use and provide the capability to revoke certificates as needed. Web authentication servers use APIs to query for the user's identity and trust that the SSL authentication was correctly performed.
- **Biometrics.** Provide strong authentication. Biometrics include mechanisms such as retina scanners, voice recognition systems, and palm or finger print readers. These provide strong authentication, but can be costly and need to be evaluated with respect to false negatives as well as social acceptance. Biometrics are most common at controlled facilities or used for highly critical applications with limited users. For use with Web authentication servers, biometrics generally require custom integration.

Authorization

Web authorization servers focus on controlling users' access to Web pages (URLs), although authorization servers can support more general classes of access policy. The authorization policy supports user groups for scalability and is also extensible to allow customized access policies. Web authorization servers are usually based on a pull model, which means that the authorization server looks up the user's attributes for each access check rather than passing all attributes in a user credential.

Web authorization servers generally support access control at the directory and page level. This means that the entire page or a URL can be protected, but not a portion of it. To effectively provide personalized Web content or provide different levels of security to specific functions or information, a finer level of access control may be required. Fine-grain access control is supplied by mid-tier authorization products, which are described later in this chapter. Some issues of granularity can be addressed through careful security design of Web pages to ensure that information with different protection requirements are isolated and therefore reduce the number of authorization decisions.

Web authorization servers support application controlled, simple, unconstrained delegation. (Delegation is described in detail in Chapters 6 and 8.) Any intermediate application component that possesses a client's token is considered trustworthy to access any resources on behalf of that client. There appear to be few constraints on the transmission of tokens to prevent impersonation abuse. (This limitation is common to virtually all Web security products because they were not intended to handle multitier component security requirements.)

Accountability

Web server security products provide basic audit logs, automatically disable users, support alarms, and report client use of the Web policy server.

Security Administration

Web security products provide administrative tools to define the authentication and authorization policies. The policies are generally stored in an LDAP directory service.

Intrusion Detection

An intrusion detection system (IDS) monitors and potentially prevents attempts to break into or otherwise compromise a system component. Without an IDS in place, the likelihood of detecting an intrusion is greatly diminished. There are two basic models of intrusion detection: *anomaly detection* and *misuse detection*. Anomaly detection looks for activity that is different from a user's or system's normal behavior. Misuse detection looks for activity that corresponds to known intrusion techniques (signatures) or system vulnerabilities.

Intrusion detection systems typically provide:

- Monitoring and analysis of user and system activity
- Auditing of system configurations and vulnerabilities
- Assessment of the integrity of critical system and data files
- Recognition of activity patterns reflecting known attacks
- Statistical analysis for abnormal activity patterns
- Operating system audit trail management with recognition of user activity reflecting policy violations

An IDS may be either network- or host-based. A network-based IDS typically monitors the network for attempts to exploit known network security threats, whereas a host-based IDS monitors servers and their critical applications and data for abuse and misuse. Although a host-based IDS is not as fast as its network counterpart, it does offer advantages that a network-based system cannot match. These strengths include stronger forensic analysis, a closer focus on host specific event data, and lower entry-level costs.

There are two basic types of host-based monitoring:

A *network monitor* checks incoming network connections on a host by monitoring packets that attempt to access the host before the packets are passed to the networking layer of the host, which could represent a threat. (Note that a network monitor is different from network-based intrusion detection, as a network monitor only looks at network traffic coming to the host it is running on, and not all traffic passing through the network.) The IDS responds to network connections that represent some kind of intrusion attempt. An example of a product that performs this type of port monitoring includes the RealSecure Agent by ISS. The RealSecure engine runs on dedicated workstations to provide network intrusion detection and response.

A *host monitor* checks files, file systems, logs, or other parts of the host for suspicious activity that might represent an intrusion attempt (or a successful intrusion). Many host monitors come with the capability to alert systems administration staff regarding problems found. For Windows NT systems, the Event Log Monitor (ELM) displays a consolidated view of all the Windows NT event logs for the workstations and servers being monitored. It provides the capability to create custom views of grouped events, in which each view is dynamically updated as new events occur in the network. In addition to monitoring the Windows NT event logs, ELM monitors services, processes, and performance counters and generates alerts when things start to go wrong.

Mid-Tier Security Technologies

The common mid-tier security technologies described in the following sections are:

- Component-based security servers
- Cryptographic protocols
- Entitlements servers

Component-Based Security Servers

Where fine-grained access is required to support business security requirements, careful analysis and selection of products with fine-grained access control will allow customization of content down to the object level based on the user's identity and security attributes.

CORBA security products provide fine-grained access control down to the object interface and instance level. The CORBA security specification is part of the Object Management Group (OMG) Common Object Services Specification. Products that provide instance level fine-grained controls include Hitachi's TPBroker Security, Entegrity's NetCrusader, and IBM/Tivoli's Policy Director.

Chapter 3 describes CORBA security in detail, so we won't repeat the description in this chapter. Suffice it to say that security products that are compliant with the large CORBA security specification provide a sophisticated set of security functionality including authentication, authorization, cryptography, security association, delegation, accountability, and security administration.

Advanced Enterprise JavaBeans (EJB) security products that are based on the very recent EJB 2.0 specification are still under development. The previously listed products are migrating to the new EJB environment using some of the techniques that we describe in Chapters 5 and 6.

Cryptographic Protocols

Secret key (symmetric) cryptographic protocols have been commonly used in the middle tier within corporate networks. Secret key authentication using Kerberos and Distributed Computing Environment (DCE) security are known and proven technologies with good performance in corporate networks. However, it is generally accepted that secret key distribution and management is not tractable for very large numbers of users. Although public key technology is not used widely within corporate networks today due to performance concerns, there is some interest in moving in this direction. (See the "Perimeter Security Technologies" section for further details on public key technology, particularly SSL.)

CyberSafe Trustbroker is an example of a product that utilizes the Kerberos network security protocol. Kerberos is designed to provide strong authentication for client/server applications by using secret key cryptography. After a client and a server have used Kerberos to prove their identity, they can also encrypt all of their communications to assure privacy and data integrity.

DCE security has been used extensively in corporate networks in which its rich feature set and high-performance secret key authentication technology are critical requirements. DCE 1.1 security is a mature product that provides powerful and flexible support for all aspects of security: login, authentication, message protection, authorization, delegation, audit, and key management. DCE begins with Kerberos V5, which provides basic secret key (DES) authentication and message protection. DCE then adds Registration Servers and Privilege Servers to provide additional services.

Authentication

In the mid-tier, Kerberos provides application-to-application authentication. The client application provides a secret key that is derived from a password as the basis of authentication. The secret key may potentially be stored on a hardware token (DES card) for stronger authentication and may also be derived from a public key certificate.

A client authentication request to communicate to a specific server goes to the Kerberos Key Distribution Center (KDC). If the authentication check passes, Kerberos creates a ticket, which contains a secret session key and client identifier. The client uses this ticket to establish a secure authenticated TCP/IP session with the server.

Authorization

Kerberos does not directly support authorization; applications using Kerberos perform their own authorization checks.

In DCE security, the Registration Server contains a database of information on principal keys, universal unique IDs (UUIDs), and group memberships. The Privilege Server provides Privilege Attribute Certificates (PACs) that contain a principal and the groups to which the principal belongs. The PAC is protected by secret key encryption (DES) to prevent tampering and ensure authenticity.

Cryptography

Kerberos provides encryption and integrity services for messages exchanged between clients and server applications. Kerberos uses DES for encryption and RSA MD4/MD5 for integrity. Kerberos is capable of supporting 128-bit keys, which is the recommended key length for most applications.

Delegation

Kerberos supports simple unconstrained delegation. (Delegation is described in detail in Chapters 6 and 8.) In Kerberos, the delegation mode (proxiable and forwardable flags) may only be set in a ticket by the KDC, thus preventing untrustworthy intermediates from impersonating the original client. If the delegation mode is set in a ticket however, intermediates that possess the delegated credential may pass it on to other servers, potentially allowing client impersonation to be abused. Proxiable tickets can be restricted to a network address, but this constraint may not be very useful in a distributed component environment where application servers are common on many machines.

DCE security provides extended PACs, which have good support for delegation including traced delegation.

Accountability

The Kerberos KDC provides an activity log to support security audit.

Security Administration

Kerberos provides administrative tools to define new principals and update keys. The policies are stored in an internal database within the KDC. DCE extends security administration support for the Registration Servers and Privilege Servers.

Entitlements Servers

New *entitlements servers* are being introduced into the marketplace, which can provide fine-grained access controls for the middle tier. Indigo Elara and CrossLogix2 are examples of entitlements servers. These products are very new, so we recommend carefully evaluating this technology before performing any serious deployment.

An entitlement is a business access rule that describes the decision criteria applied when a user attempts to access an application resource. Entitlements management addresses administering and maintaining the various permissions, roles, privileges, and login rights for an organization's information systems users including suppliers, partners, customers, and employees. Resources include client/server applications, legacy applications, and Web pages.

Entitlements originated in the financial services world, and they may be best suited for that class of business applications. However, the basic entitlements model appears to be very general, and vendors believe that their approach is applicable to most other environments. Note that the concept of entitlements is closely related to the Resource Access Decision (RAD) facility described in Chapter 7.

Authentication

Entitlements servers emphasize authorization, so they generally rely on other products to support authentication. Elara has its own native username and password authentication mechanism and can be configured to accept different authentication credentials, such as smart card, SecureID, or Kerberos. CrossLogix2 does not provide any built-in authentication service, but instead relies on third-party authentication services, such as getAccess and SiteMinder.

Authorization

Entitlements servers identify three levels of entitlement that need to be managed: coarse-grain, fine-grain, and transactional entitlement.

- **Coarse-grain entitlement.** Controls access to broad categories of information resources, such as access to a client/server application. For Web servers, coarse-grain entitlement corresponds to access to a Web page.
- **Fine-grain entitlement.** Controls access to individual objects, such as buttons, links, menu choices, or other resources.
- **Transactional entitlement.** Controls access to a specific resource by examining specific parameter values that are being accessed. Transactional entitlement refers to dynamic processing that takes into account

the state values at the time of the transaction. Permission to perform a particular transaction may depend on the day of the week, the current balance of an account, or the current exchange rate of a currency.

Elara uses resources, privileges, principals, and roles to check for coarse-grain, fine-grain, and transactional entitlement. Resources are the tasks and procedures performed by application users, or they represent the business task that must be controlled in the application. Some resources correspond to a visual object on the user's screen, such as a button or a text entry field.

CrossLogix2 supports a business logic language that can express business relationships. A business rule grants or denies the availability of content for a particular individual or collection of related individuals (a role) provided certain conditions are satisfied. Conditions are logical expressions involving static and dynamic properties. An example of a static property is an office number; a dynamic property could be an account balance.

Legacy Security Technologies

The common legacy security technologies described in the following sections are:

- Mainframe security
- Database security

Mainframe Security

Several products may be used to secure resources on a mainframe. As a representative sample, we discuss the basic capabilities of Computer Associates ACF2. ACF2 can protect and control all security aspects of the IBM mainframe environment. ACF2 provides security to the OS/390 business transaction environment including Unix system services and applications as well as the IBM Websphere application server. ACF2 provides streamlined administration, single-point user sign-on, and platform/network level security and audit.

Authentication

ACF2 supports the basic authentication mechanism of userID/password and can also be integrated with many other authentication mechanisms including single use password substitutes, smart cards, LDAP, and PKI certificates. ACF2 supports *user exits* that may be tailored to provide custom authentication checks. User exits are points within the ACF2 product that permit calls to an external program, giving the security administrator control over the authentication and authorization processes.

Authorization

ACF2 provides very extensive and customizable authorization policies that focus on the mainframe environment. For example, datasets, CICS transactions, and terminal resources can all be under the direct control of the ACF2 security product.

ACF2 provides a role-based approach to mainframe security; a user can be associated with one or more roles. Administrators can be granted authority to maintain a limited number of users and resources and may be granted access to a limited set of administrative actions.

Cryptography

Using Kerberos and DCE, ACF2 provides the means to secure communications between OS/390 environments and open systems including MQSeries messages and TCP/IP.

Accountability

ACF2 provides extensive platform and network level security auditing facilities as well as external audit reduction and reporting tools.

Security Administration

ACF2 provides administrative tools to maintain security policies for the mainframe. The policies are stored within internal databases; user information can also be accessible via LDAP.

Database Security

All the major Relational Database Management System (RDBMS) products provide database security. They typically provide identification and authentication, access controls, auditing, integrity, encryption, and security management services. To reduce the need to implement database security, which can be tedious depending on the granularity of access controls, the database should be designed based on security requirements if at all possible. Database designs should isolate security relevant information and define records that match up role-based access control requirements.

Summary

In this chapter, we provided an overview to a variety of security technologies that are all part of a potential end-to-end security solution. We described the technologies and products in the context of the three tiers: perimeter, middle, and legacy. Perimeter security serves as the first line of defense and primarily protects against hostile attackers that are outside of an organization. For perimeter security technologies, we discussed firewalls/VPNs, cryptographic protocols, Web-based security servers, and intrusion detection. Mid-tier security serves as the second line of defense, providing another layer of protection against external attackers, and also protects against attackers that are within an organization. For mid-tier security technologies, we discussed component-based security servers, cryptographic protocols, and entitlements servers. Legacy security provides the third layer of defense by protecting the back-end servers, ensuring that an organization's most valuable resources are safe from unauthorized access. For legacy security technologies, we discussed mainframe security and database security.

All of these security technologies play an important role in securing the enterprise. No single security technology, however, could possibly address the variety of requirements necessary to provide an effective end-to-end security solution. Enterprises need to have the ability to integrate many different products into their Enterprise Security Integration (ESI) framework, and to evolve those products over time.

The next chapters explore ways to integrate these technologies to get you to the solution that you need. In Chapter 5, we discuss the general topic of interoperability of enterprise security technologies, and how EJB and CORBA security can help bridge the gaps. We present many of the enterprise security technologies again as we plan our example secure component system, which we discuss in Chapter 9; and we build the final integrated system, which we discuss in Chapter 10. By the time you finish this book you will see many techniques for integrating security technologies that will enable you to build an effective solution for enterprise security using EJB and CORBA.

Interoperability of Cross-Domain Components

Security challenges to modern corporations are rising with the dramatic increase in electronic data exchange between companies and their customers, partners, suppliers, distributors, and dealers. Most of this data exchange between companies is via legacy applications, and companies find that they cannot afford to replace these older applications in the short term. (Legacy applications not only include traditional ones such as relational databases and COBOL programs, but also more recent technology including security technology, which has been superceded by even newer technology.) The security challenge is to get the older technologies to interoperate across corporate boundaries.

No one security solution can solve a company's security requirements. As a result, you must face the interoperability issues of multiple security solutions. Within a company, differences in the underlying solutions pose their own difficulties including interoperability problems among:

- Products implementing nonstandard solutions for the same security functionality (e.g., varying proprietary user credential token formats)
- Products implementing the same security technology standard (e.g., varying support for certificate revocation lists for standard X.509 certificates)

- Products with the same security model but with differing cryptographic profiles (e.g. the Data Encryption Standard [DES] versus the Rivest, Shamir, Adleman [RSA] cryptographic algorithms)
- Products implementing differing semantics for similar security data (e.g., varying authorization policy semantics)

When the business requirements and practices of multiple companies must be considered, additional secure interoperability problems arise. These additional problems include:

- Differences in interpretation of security attributes between interacting companies
- Inability to create user credentials that can be used by a target company's applications

This chapter defines what secure interoperability means in an enterprise computing infrastructure. We introduce constructs to help architects and developers break the security problem into categories, and then use those categories to find solutions for the distributed security problem.

The starting point for our discussion includes the three security tiers that comprise any end-to-end enterprise security solution: the *perimeter tier*, the *mid-tier*, and the *legacy tier*. We expand on the concept of *security domains*, which fits within the context of the three security tiers. We show how a mixed model of security domains are used in architectures that reoccur in many companies that we have studied. After providing the rationale for using a mixed model of security, we show you how to bridge these models to get a best of breed solution. We finish the chapter with a discussion of how these security domains help us define an architecture for a distributed enterprise security system.

Be forewarned that we discuss a number of critical areas for which there are not yet standard solutions. We discuss the security principals and rationale behind these areas of interoperability and propose solutions that we, or others in the industry, have developed. We also discuss the ongoing security specification work that will solve some of the interoperability problems identified.

What Is Interoperability of EJB and CORBA?

Before describing the challenges associated with interoperability, we first need to understand what this term means to computing systems and how it affects both the level of security needed and the complexity of interaction between disparate software entities. In an ideal world, interoperability would mean that every application would work seamlessly with every other application regardless of differences in computing platforms, operating system, languages, or middleware. We believe we are on safe ground in saying that this will not happen in our lifetimes. The field of computer science, not just computer security, is too dynamic; new concepts are continually displacing existing theory and approaches.

Let's narrow the scope of interoperability to the subject at hand, namely, the ability of CORBA applications and Enterprise JavaBeans (EJB) to securely interoperate when running on the same or different machines. Because these technologies do not operate in a vacuum, we will also investigate how they interact with legacy systems within the enterprise and with perimeter technologies that enable secure access from outside the enterprise.

A prerequisite to secure interoperability is interoperability between CORBA and EJB independent of security. Let's look at two basic problems of interoperability that have an effect on secure interoperability. The first problem is moving data between a CORBA and a Java component. Java supports a transport protocol called Remote Method Invocation (RMI), whereas CORBA supports a transport protocol called Internet Inter-ORB Protocol (IIOP). (We provide an overview of both RMI and IIOP in Chapter 6. If you want a more detailed explanation of these transport mechanisms, there are a number of good books on this subject, for example, *Java in a Nutshell: A Desktop Quick Reference* (Flanagan, 1999) or *Mastering Enterprise Java Beans* (Roman, 2000). Both protocols define the way data is transferred from one module to another independent of whether the modules are in the same process, different processes, or even on different machines or networks. RMI can only be used between Java applications, whereas IIOP can be used between most combinations of languages including Java. The CORBA security protocol defines two main ways to transport security data from a client to the target—either in the Service Context or by means of specific messages at the transport layer. Both of these means of transporting security data depends on the IIOP CORBA protocol. Because the IIOP protocol does not exist in RMI and RMI uses a different model to pass different security information, it is impossible to pass CORBA security data using RMI alone.

EJB 1.1 and later specifications support running IIOP under RMI, which greatly simplifies the capability of CORBA and EJB to talk to each other. Because older software has a habit of never going away, be sure that you examine the capabilities of the application server that you purchase. For interoperability with an EJB application server that only supports native RMI, you have to build a nonstandard RMI to IIOP bridge and insert the bridge in your system at points of transfer between the CORBA and EJB components. In a new implementation, we strongly recommend that the EJB product that you choose supports RMI/IIOP. Even if your design does not currently include a mix of Java and CORBA, this product design provides future flexibility without imposing present constraints.

There are some constraints on the CORBA side as well. RMI has the ability to pass objects by value, that is, make an independent copy of the object on the remote system. Until recently, CORBA systems did not have this ability, and you could only pass objects by reference. A recent addition to the CORBA specification (CORBA 2.4 or later and IIOP 1.2 or later) added an "object by value" capability to CORBA. In CORBA, when you pass an object, you normally use a "pass by reference" because you pass an Interface Definition Language (IDL) interface. A CORBA IDL interface is a true interface; it only defines the methods associated with that object. When you pass an object by value, you also pass the state of the object. The object by value addition to the CORBA specification extended CORBA and the IDL to include a value type. Value types support the description of the state of the object. Value Types are always copied when passed as a parameter to a remote call. However, as with the RMI/IIOP specification, not all CORBA systems support pass by value. During the design phase, whether pass by value will be needed is important information in making your CORBA vendor choice. The pass by value choice is more esoteric than the IIOP/RMI choice and has a good chance of not being a requirement for your system. If pass by value will be used, you should talk to your potential or existing CORBA vendor about whether they support pass by value and if not, what their plans are to include this capability in the future.

Secure interoperability is a thornier problem than basic interoperability between CORBA and EJB. Secure interoperability between different implementations of CORBA object request brokers (ORBs) is not available because the initial CORBA security specification was not sufficiently defined. However, a modification to the CORBA specification known as Common Secure Interoperability version 2 (CSIv2), which defines a common wire protocol to permit interoperability, was approved in December 2000 (some of the authors were members of the team that worked on this modification). One of the key goals of CSIv2 is to incorporate interoperability between CORBA security and EJB security as well as interoperability between ORBs. Note that because the specification is very new, there will be a delay in the availability of supporting CSIv2 products. Some products may not update to CSIv2 because it will entail significant work on the vendor's part. CSIv2 and its relationship to EJB and CORBA is discussed in more depth in Chapter 6.

ESI SECURITY ASSOCIATION PRINCIPLE: THINK END-TO-END, NOT POINT-TO-POINT

Transparent interoperability requires a common end-to-end protocol to allow credentials to be passed among many different security technologies. Without a common secure interoperability protocol like CSIv2, interoperability must be achieved by implementing custom bridges between different mid-tier security technologies, which can be costly and time-consuming.

Until CSIv2-based products are widely available, the simplest approach for interoperability is to use a CORBA/EJB security service from one vendor throughout your enterprise. This same caveat holds for any potential interaction between companies. If you have suppliers or vendors you want to interact with through secure systems using CORBA or EJB, it's preferable for the interacting companies to use the same security service. Some of the solutions we propose in a later section on security domains provide alternative approaches.

The remainder of this chapter focuses on the general topic of interoperable security solutions and leaves the details of EJB and CORBA secure interoperability to Chapter 6.

Intracompany and Intercompany Security

Intracompany security involves the interactions that we discussed in the previous section as well as the basic problem of determining the optimal role of CORBA versus EJB in the internal architecture of a single enterprise. There is also the difficult problem of determining the middleware security policy for the enterprise as a whole, which is covered in Chapter 8. In the scope of this book, security policy may be thought of as the rules determining what entity—either human or computational—is permitted to access what software interfaces and methods in other distributed processes. In the days of a single monolithic mainframe, the operating system tightly controlled all access paths within a single machine. In the world of distributed components, there is no such single authority. As discussed in Chapter 1, distributed systems encourage enterprise connectivity across machines that may be located worldwide. As a result, access to enterprise resources can be controlled by disparate authorities.

One potential security problem is identifying a user. A user can be identified by a username similar to a login name, by an X.500 name, by a Kerberos name, or by some proprietary scheme used by the company. If one division of a company uses one type of name and another division uses another, the receiving division may not be able to interpret the name of the user in the division making a request. If the receiving division can't identify who is making a request, its only recourse is to deny access. Therefore, a mapping between different types of names, called a *principal mapping*, must be provided. At present, there is no standard specification for this mapping. Some of the name mapping problems, such as the mapping between X.500 and Kerberos names, have been addressed, but not all the differences have defined solutions. It is imperative that you analyze your system to identify the disjoint naming protocols and supply mappings between any different name types found. For example, a user might be identified in his browser as dflinn. This principal name is received by your system, which uses Kerberos. The Kerberos service wants the name in the form dflinn@realm. A message could then be passed on to a Secure Sockets Layer

(SSL) portion of your system that needs the name in the form of an X.500 Distinguished Name (DN): "CN=Donald Flinn, OU=programmer, C=US, O=Iona," and so on. Each of these boundaries needs to map the incoming name to the proper form for the next system. Look carefully at the systems that you intend to purchase to determine what name mapping they supply. If they don't supply the necessary name mappings, you will have to code them yourself or look at another security supplier.

User identification challenges go even further. Both EJB and CORBA support the concept of user roles, so the semantics of the same role name must be the same in two corporate divisions. CORBA provides more features than EJB in that CORBA supports more user attributes than just roles. However, EJB roles can be mapped in environment specific ways to security attributes including shared attributes, such as group memberships. A CORBA client calling on an EJB server must map the attributes it is using to the attributes supported by EJB. When designing your enterprise security, you must be alert not only to the different naming conventions that are used in different parts of your company, but you must also define differences between your own naming conventions and those of external customers and companies with which you will be doing e-commerce. When differences arise, unless a compromise between entities can be resolved, a name mapping protocol will have to be agreed upon between the companies.

Intercompany interoperability falls under the general topic of federation—or how the security policies and semantics of one company are understood and trusted by another company when they want to interoperate. (Federation is further discussed in Chapter 10.) Intercompany security problems are magnified because the security policies of the two or (in many cases) more companies will inevitably be different. A simple example:

> In Company A, a security administrator may have complete authority for all security, whereas in Company B, one security administrator may only be granted the authority to add new users and another administrator may only have the authority to grant attributes to a specific group of users. If a security administrator from Company B is allowed administrative access to Company A without any higher level intercompany policy, the administrator from B could add a new user to A and give that user complete freedom to do what he desired. This amount of authority is inconsistent with Company B's policy. This is a simplistic example, but it illustrates the potential problems added by automated intercompany interaction.

The following is one solution to this problem. The administrator from the outside company must apply for a Privilege Attribute Certificate (PAC) from the receiving company's registration server. PACs will be covered in detail in Chapter 6. At this point we will simply describe a PAC, which is specified in CSIv2, as a digitally signed certificate that associates specific security attributes with a person or machine. This means that the client must authenticate itself with the registration server of the company that is receiving the call from the client. The server of the target company must have attributes of the requesting company in its policy tables to allow access. This approach allows the server to distinguish between administrators in Companies A and B, and thus enforces different policies for the two different kinds of administrators.

The OMG recognizes the importance of the security federation problem, such as how do two or more unrelated companies securely interact with each other without proprietary means of understanding each others' semantics. There is work underway at the OMG to develop a standard method for two or more companies to exchange attribute data. This approach is along the lines discussed in the previous paragraph.

Another major problem is the interoperability of different security technology domains both within and between companies. The next few sections examine the problems of interacting security domains and propose solutions.

Security Technology Domains Relative to Security Tiers

A domain is a terribly overused concept in computer science. Security also overuses the word domain within its own scope. We will be careful to define the different uses of the term domain and define the context of these different uses.

The CORBA security specification defines a security domain as "a distinct scope within which certain common characteristics are exhibited and common rules observed." This CORBA definition of a domain defines domains as a way of grouping things. The things that are grouped together have to have a set of characteristics that are the same with respect to the security of the collection. For example, you might want to define a collection of server machines together because, from a security point of view, they share a common authorization policy.

The specification then goes on to define three types of security domains as:

- **Security environment domain.** The scope over which the enforcement of a policy may be achieved by some other means local to that environment (e.g., machines separated by a firewall), so it does not need to be enforced within the object system.
- **Security technology domain.** Where common security mechanisms (e.g., Web server security products) are used to enforce the policies.
- **Security policy domain.** The scope over which a security policy (e.g., authorization policy) is enforced. There may be subdomains for different aspects of this policy.

Security environment domains define types of security mechanisms other than the middleware security approaches that we are discussing. For example, the secure environment in a particular case might be applications running on a few machines that do not have any outside connections or access and in which all parts of the system including the users are completely trusted. These types of systems are not covered in this book.

The other two types of security domains are quite relevant to our discussion. For example, EJB and CORBA are two different security technology domains, and each uses a set of security mechanisms that are disjoint from the other. Beyond the two technologies themselves, it is necessary to consider the total security architecture in which these models operate. We will consider a number of different security technology domains. We'll use Figure 5.1 to help make these concepts clear.

There are three concepts depicted in the drawing: security domains, security policies, and security authorities. Security technology domains, depicted by the gray ovals, contain a collection of services that all use a common security technology. Examples of security technology domains are:

- Web server security products
- ORB/OTM/EJB security products
- Mainframe security products

All the services within a given technology domain can interoperate securely because they all use the same security technology. On the other hand, two services in different technology domains may not interoperate securely because they use different security mechanisms. For example, one domain may be using Kerberos and a second domain may be using SSL. In that case, you would have to build a security bridge between the different technology domains.

If you look closely at Figure 5.1, you will see an area where two technology domains overlap. In this area, a particular service may be using multiple security technologies, such as an EJB application server using data from a mainframe.

An obvious goal in dealing with security technology domains is to minimize the number of domains that you use. However, as you will see, different technology domains have capabilities that other domains lack, and some domains are better suited for protecting a given area of your enterprise than others. So the bottom line is that any enterprise, except for the smallest, will find itself using multiple security technology domains. This chapter explains the advantages and disadvantages of each and shows you ways to make them work together to use the best technologies of each.

The dark shaded area in Figure 5.1 depicts a security policy domain. A security policy domain defines a collection of services that obey a common enterprise security policy. For example, you might have a security policy specifying that all of the services in one policy are accessible by everyone, whereas in another policy domain access to the services is restricted to administrators.

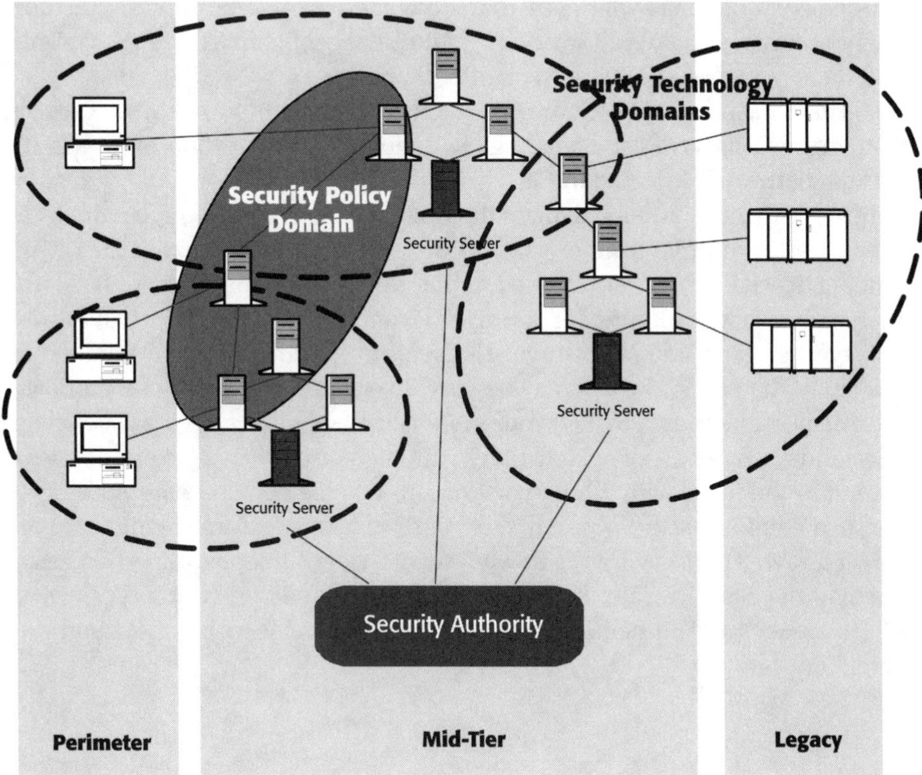

Figure 5.1 Domains, policies, and authorities.

Notice that a security policy domain can span multiple security technology domains.

In summary, security technology domains define the mechanism used to enforce the security policies defined by different security policy domains.

The third concept depicted in Figure 5.1 is that of a security authority. The security authority's job is to ensure consistent definition, interpretation and enforcement of policy domains. In EJB, the container takes on the role of security authority, whereas in an implementation of CORBA security, this job may be handled by a security server. To understand the need for a security authority, we should point out that the security authority handles the administration of security policy domains across multiple technology domains.

Before we leave Figure 5.1, notice that the domains straddle three different tiers: the perimeter tier, the mid-tier, and the legacy tier. Security tiers are used as a way of describing the different physical divisions of an enterprise's architecture. The perimeter is the area between the client and Web server. The mid-tier contains all your in-house applications that live on the internal enterprise network, and the legacy tier consists of those applications that have survived from the good old days when you didn't have to worry about distributed component security. We gave an overview of these concepts in Chapter 1; we'll discuss the tiers in more depth in the rest of this chapter.

In examining security technology domains, you should look at the ways various corporations have used existing technology to protect their enterprises. A common pattern is depicted in Figure 5.2.

The left side of Figure 5.2 depicts the first level of protection typically established by an enterprise, which walls off the corporate system from the outside world. A firewall is commonly used as the first level of protection. It is often accessed by a client running HTTPS (HTTP running over SSL). We call the area between the client and Web server the security perimeter tier or simply, the perimeter. The outside world may be very diverse and contain customers who desire access to certain parts of your systems and who have their own business information, a portion of which they want to share with your enterprise. In addition to the firms with whom you want to do electronic business, there are your own employees and possibly third-party data repositories, which are outside the firewall and to whom you want to allow certain constrained access.

Behind the first firewall, there is typically a Web server, which receives the HTTP messages and authenticates the various types of users to whom you want to grant access.

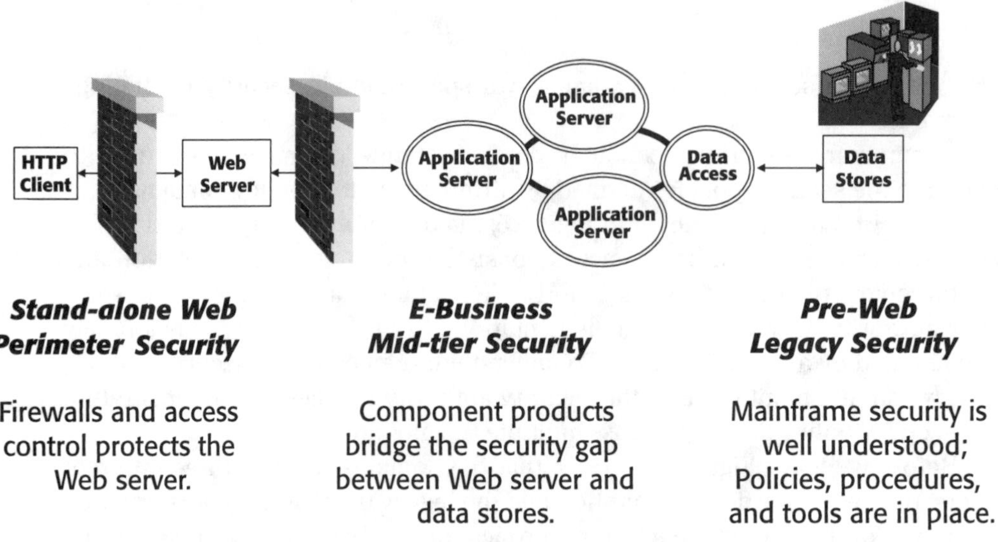
HTTP Client
Web Server
Application Server
Application Server
Application Server
Data Access
Data Stores
Stand-alone Web Perimeter Security
Firewalls and access control protects the Web server.
E-Business Mid-tier Security
Component products bridge the security gap between Web server and data stores.
Pre-Web Legacy Security
Mainframe security is well understood; Policies, procedures, and tools are in place.

Figure 5.2 Today's enterprise consists of a complex interplay of perimeter, mid-tier, and legacy systems.

After authentication, the incoming message is sent through a second firewall to what we call the mid-tier layer. In a growing number of cases, the incoming message is sent to an EJB application server. In the mid-tier, we also find what can amount to hundreds of a company's business applications, which are a mixture of EJB and CORBA applications.

In addition to these EJB and CORBA applications, there are usually a number of legacy applications. We will logically separate the legacy applications from the EJB and CORBA applications, which are in the mid-tier layer, because the security technology domains of legacy applications are different from the EJB and CORBA security technology in the mid-tier. It should be noted that in many cases legacy applications are separated from the mid-tier by another firewall. Thus, there may be a physical as well as a logical separation of these layers.

The mid-tier is treated as a zone where corporations think everything is under control. After all, this area contains the company's applications and is protected from those ruffians on the outside. Well, if you are feeling complacent about your mid-tier area, recall our discussion on this topic from Chapter 1.

Security break-ins by company insiders in the mid-tier layer can result in costly damage because this layer has minimal to no security in many cases. The security effort at many companies has been to allow only highly trusted entities such as employees and partner companies access to the mid-tier. With the advent of e-commerce, companies now permit access by less trusted entities such as suppliers, customers and other corporations. The result is that when these outside entities enter the mid-tier they, as well as insiders, have potential access to your sensitive data.

We present an overview of a flow of information across technology domains in the three security tiers in the next sections. The emphasis is on how these areas work together to pass security data. We then look at why these different security technology domains are commonly used. Once an understanding of this typical enterprise security architecture is gained, we can then describe methods of bridging the security between these domains.

ESI SECURITY ASSOCIATION PRINCIPLE: DESIGN FOR FAILURE

Because there is little distinction in e-business architectures between outsiders and insiders, it's increasingly likely that your enterprise network will be accessible by hostile attackers. Don't leave your internal network wide open by allowing application components to completely trust each other. If one component is compromised by a malicious attack, you don't want every other component to fail as well.

Security Domains in the Perimeter Tier

Today, a World Wide Web (WWW) browser is the most common means used to securely access the perimeter firewall. We are all familiar with browsers and how the browser asks the user to log in with a username and password to access a secure site. In the simplest, secure case, the browser supports HTTPS. This technology is used to access the firewall and to authenticate the user.

As discussed in Chapter 4, some firewall policies only allow an HTTP client access to the applications that the firewall is protecting. Others, such as TCP firewall policies, only allow access to predetermined addresses set in their internal tables. The basic problem with using CORBA with these older style firewall policies is that CORBA is very dynamic. The destination for a CORBA call is contained in the target object reference that the client uses to call on a particular object and thus, the address that the client wants to access is not necessarily known in advance or might change. Using dynamic addressing to firewalls that use an internal table to determine what internal processes can be accessed, potentially poses an impossible maintenance problem because it is not easy to know in advance what ports are to be addressed by the client. The inverse, larger problem, exists on the outgoing side, in which an internal client wants to call an external application. There is no practical way that the firewall can know in advance the addresses of all possible external targets.

A further problem is the existence of call-backs requested by an outside client. How can these be known in advance if a company has thousands of clients accessing the enterprise. Similar to CORBA, EJB also has dynamic flexibility and thus similar maintenance problems.

The OMG is working on a Firewall specification, which makes some changes to the representation of the object reference and will alleviate these problems. However, once again, we must wait for implementations of this specification before we can make practical use of these advances.

There are a number of steps that we can take today to work around these limitations. Basically, the solution is to provide a bridge between the existing technology domains—those that are in the perimeter and those that are in the mid-tier. The simplest solution is to make a connection from a browser that supports HTTPS to a Web server. The Web server authenticates the client in the simple case by requesting a username and password from the browser. In more secure cases, the client is authenticated using client SSL certificates. The authentication evidence is passed through the firewall protected by SSL to the Web server. The Web server uses the evidence presented to it to authenticate the client, and then calls into the mid-tier. The problem lies in whether the protocol in the mid-tier applications can interpret this evidence.

Security Domains in the Mid-Tier

An application server is the common recipient of a call from a Web server in the Demilitarized Zone (DMZ). The DMZ is the area between the external and internal firewalls and is not as well protected as the mid-tier. In this situation, a servlet in the application server gets a call from the Web server and receives the authentication evidence passed to it, usually in the form of a cookie, which contains encrypted authentication evidence. The servlet then verifies the evidence received in the cookie. The first step for the servlet is to assure the identity of the Web server. The servlet could have previously established an authenticated trust relationship with the Web server. Then the servlet could accept the evidence passed by the Web server without any further verification and retrieve the user ID from the HTTP header. Because of the previous trust relationship with the Web server, the servlet can treat the user as authenticated. If stronger security than a trust relationship is required the servlet may authenticate the evidence in each cookie itself.

EJB and CORBA in the Mid-Tier

We will cover the interoperability between EJB and CORBA in detail in Chapter 6. This section is intended to introduce EJB and CORBA interoperability.

At this point, if the application server supports RMI over IIOP and the intent is to use CORBA security applications in the mid-tier, the authentication evidence must be transformed into a form usable by CORBA. The CORBA format of the authentication evidence is encapsulated in an object called a *credential*, which is passed between processes in a token format standardized by the CORBA CSIv2 specification. The servlet has to transform the evidence received from the Web server to that specified by the credential.

An important point is that the format of the evidence specified in the CSIv2 CORBA specification is the same format that is specified in the EJB Java Security specification version 2.0. Although implementations that support this specification may not be released in time for your project, most EJB or CORBA security implementations from the major middleware vendors will support these specifications in the future and thus will interoperate. Therefore, you should investigate whether the application servers and CORBA ORBs that you are considering support CSIv2 or what their vendors' plans for such support are.

Once we have bridged authentication, we are then faced with differences in the authorization model between EJB and CORBA. EJB uses method-permissions to control access to server objects. Method-permissions can be either capabilities or permissions depending on how you write them as we discussed in Chapter 2. CORBA supports a richer and more scalable access decision model than EJB. In CORBA, broader attribute definitions are available to identify classes of users, such as groups, security clearance, and user-defined attributes. There is also a grouping model, called security policy domains, available on the server side.

Security Domains in the Legacy Tier

The last security technology domains to be addressed support legacy applications. The mid-tier applications will probably have a need for corporate data at some period in their lifetime. In many cases, this corporate data, such as accounting data, customer information, or employee information, has existed in your system long before any of the new technologies, such as CORBA or EJB, came on the scene. Normally, this legacy data is held in back-end relational databases on a mainframe. The protection scheme for such data will in all probability have a different format from the protection scheme used in the newer EJB or CORBA applications and may require authentication data that is disjoint from that used in the perimeter and the mid-tier.

CORBA has the advantage in that it defines well-known approaches to wrapping legacy applications. These approaches use the methods defined in the IDL wrapper to access the functions in the legacy application. Java 2 Enterprise Edition (J2EE) and EJB define connectors to aid in securely accessing legacy applications. Unfortunately, at this time, there is no standard means of bridging the security models between CORBA and legacy applications. In addition, the connector specification is recent, so there will be some lag time before implementations support this approach. We describe a nonstandard method to solve this problem later in this chapter.

Rationale for Mixed Security Technology Domains

The previous sections defined security technology domains in the three tiers and provided a brief outline of the ways in which the security between these technology domains could be bridged to interoperate. You are probably asking yourself—is this all worth the effort? Why not just use one security technology domain and bag the whole problem? The simplistic answer is that there is no single technology that offers the level of security needed for today's distributed architecture in a comprehensive and scaleable way. That's a pretty bold statement. Before going into the details of bridging these security technology domains, let's see if we can justify using multiple technology domains.

Mixed Domains in the Perimeter

Today, browsers are the most popular technology used in the perimeter. They follow established standards and have the advantage of lightweight and ubiquitous accessibility. A secure browser in conjunction with a firewall does a good job in protecting the host company from clients that it does not want to allow access. There does not appear to be a competing general solution at this time. This does not mean that there are not reasons to use other technologies where applicable, but a standard browser running SSL is the winner by far in the majority of cases in the perimeter security domain.

Competing technology will come along. In fact, the Simple Object Access Protocol (SOAP), which in its present incarnation is XML over HTTP, is becoming popular. To date, security considerations are not addressed in the SOAP submission to the World Wide Web Consortium (W3C). Because the only SOAP binding at present is to HTTP, from a security point of view, we can treat SOAP the way we treat HTTP or HTTPS. Given that, we will limit our discussion to HTTPS in the perimeter security domain.

There is ongoing work to define passing of security data in XML documents. The Internet Engineering Task Force (IETF) has put out a specification for digital signatures for XML and the World Wide Web Consortium (W3C) has released a specification to define Authentication Servers using XML and the digital signature specification. We expect that these and other standards will be important to consider in the future when securely integrating XML-based messaging.

In spite of all this activity the security bridging between the perimeter and the mid-tier technology domains is not standard. All this activity has to settle down into a coherent set of interacting specifications to say nothing of having middleware applications that support such a coherent approach. The next section "Bridging the Security Tiers" describes a non-standard approach to security bridging between these domains, which you can use while waiting for the coalescence and implementation of standards for perimeter to mid-tier secure interoperability.

Mixed Domains in the Mid-Tier

What about the mid-tier itself? Things get messier in this area. There are a number of contending programming languages, and more and more, new applications are based on distributed object models with a major emphasis on EJB and CORBA. Why not just pick one of these? It's not as clear cut as the case of HTTP in the perimeter. The two major contenders, EJB and CORBA, have differences in their security models. We discuss how to bridge these two domains in Chapter 6. Other mid-tier integration approaches such as Microsoft COM+, and messaging middleware such as IBM MQSeries complicate the interoperability picture even further. Although these other middleware approaches are important, we need to limit our scope to EJB and CORBA secure interoperability to avoid adding even more complexity to this book.

Independent of the mixed use of EJB and CORBA, there is the problem of bridging the differences between HTTPS and either of the two mid-tier object models. There is little use of HTTP in the mid-tier. It does not have the language constructs upon which to build the large scale, complex applications that are needed in the mid-tier. Therefore, if we are going to use HTTPS in the perimeter and full-bodied programming languages in the mid-tier, we have to contend with the differences between these two technologies. Some ideas and techniques to bridge these domains follow.

EJB is a server-side technology that can support access by Java clients. However, its security model at the present time does not readily support a scalable authorization model. Part of the scaling problem is that EJB uses method-permissions, which were described in Chapter 2. We will go into the discussion of the EJB Authorization model and method permissions further in the next chapter.

Note that the EJB specification does not say how a container should carry out access control nor how a principal is mapped to a group. Therefore, a particular implementation of container authorization may be limited in scale. Because access control lies at the heart of distributed security and is performed quite often, you should find out how your potential container provider does access control and get or preferably run performance numbers on potential application servers. Also, it is important that you determine what tools the container provider supplies to help you assign principals to roles and what kind of assignments you can have.

CORBA has a richer access decision model and can be used where security granularity and scalability are needed. In fact, as spelled out in Chapters 3 and 7, there are two access decision models in CORBA: the rights-based model and the Resource Access Decision (RAD) model. Although CORBA clients could be used in the perimeter through the mid-tier, this would mean heavyweight clients that are not readily amenable to the Internet. By heavyweight clients, we mean client applications written specifically for a particular task and that have a full implementation of CORBA security. This approach brings with it the problems of distributing and maintaining these applications for a large number of users—your customers and suppliers. Contrast this with a Web browser, which most users have on their systems. We could use a Java applet that supports CORBA, but this would mean transmitting the ORB to the client machine or storing the ORB on each client machine. Neither of these approaches meets today's requirement for clients using nothing but a standard browser.

In certain corporate situations, there may also be a requirement to use C or C++ for performance reasons. EJB does not support any language but Java, whereas CORBA supports a large number of languages. On the other hand, EJB does have a more rapid development environment with built-in transaction, persistent, and security services. Furthermore, Java is easier to learn than C or C++.

Mixed Domains in the Legacy Tier

CORBA does not support standard secure interactions with legacy applications. The J2EE Connector Architecture Specification has defined a new concept, which is that connectors describe a contract between a resource adapter and a container by which a container that supports connectors can establish a connection to a legacy application. By legacy applications, we mean standalone applications that were not written with a distributed paradigm in mind. An example would be the millions of lines of COBOL code that may have been written 10 to 20 years ago. These applications may exist on mainframes or mini computers and are accessed directly by the user through some batch process or through something like Job Control Language (JCL), which is used on IBM mainframes.

Although CORBA has been used for some time in wrapping legacy applications, there is no standard way of applying security between the wrapper and the legacy application. Distributed security can be used between the client and the wrapper; however, the security between the wrapper and the ultimate legacy target is more difficult. For example, if the target of the legacy application is a database that needs a password or it is a JCL script that needs a username and password combination to gain access, there is no standard way to pass that information. Some systems transmit the password from application to application using custom code in each application.

It can be stated with a high degree of confidence that few enterprises are ready to rewrite those millions of lines of legacy code. Because it is a given that the legacy technology domain will exist for the foreseeable future, this will dictate the use of a bridging technology between the mid-tier and the back-end.

Although J2EE has defined the connector specification as a solution to this problem, this specification is still new. As a result, there will be some lag time before containers supporting this specification are available. Check whether your container provider supports this application or what its plans are with respect to connectors. Most corporate computing implementations have existed for some time and have a number of legacy applications that corporations would be reluctant to replace.

Auditing

Somewhat orthogonal to the discussion of the different security technology domains is auditing. Auditing is an important aspect of security that is often downplayed or even ignored when a corporation is planning distributed security protection. Although auditing records after the fact activities, it is necessary if you are trying to find out if there were system break-ins or even failed security attempts. In the former case, you might say that it is closing the barn door after the horse has escaped, but without knowledge of break-ins, a corporation might not realize certain weaknesses and thus do nothing to correct them. Failed security breach attempts alert you to attacks on your system and help you to close the barn door before the horses escape.

There are some situations in which auditing is preferred over access decision. An example is a hospital that wants to limit the records a doctor is permitted to see, for example, only those of his or her patients. However, if in an emergency the doctor needs the records of another doctor's patient to save her life, you don't want the patient to die because access is denied. The proper approach is to give the doctor access to the records, but to audit the event. Auditing, as in the hospital case, is necessary to control random unauthorized access. Although the EJB specification states that the containers may implement auditing, it does not require auditing. CORBA, on the other hand, has a very detailed specification of auditing. Once again, it is up to you to closely inspect the documentation of the service that you are contemplating purchasing. A particular EJB container might have implemented a very extensive auditing capability, whereas a CORBA ORB vendor might not have implemented the full CORBA auditing specification. In normal situations, you might find that you need CORBA to supplement the weak or nonexistent auditing capabilities of your EJB container.

Security Administration

Last but not least is the area of security administration. In a large organization, especially one that is involved in e-commerce, there is a large amount of security data that has to be managed: hundreds of thousands or millions of users, hundreds or thousands of applications, and thousands of methods. Without some overall management by a security administration process, the task of managing all this data becomes nearly impossible. Neither EJB nor CORBA has a specification that fills the bill for administration. CORBA does require and supports security administration in its specification, but EJB avoids addressing this problem by stating that it is up to the container implementers to solve the problem of security administration.

Bridging the Security Tiers

Recently there has been significant activity to specify secure interoperability between EJB and CORBA, so the path to interoperability between these two security technology domains is becoming clearer. Yes, all the necessary specifications have not been released, but they are far enough along that implementers are beginning to write middleware that use the ideas from these emerging specifications. For the near-term, some nonstandard bridging between the two technology domains will have to be done. As upgraded tools and middleware are rolled out, these nonstandard bridges can be replaced in the near future as long as you understand what is coming and write your code with an eye toward future replacement.

In the previous sections, we described three security tiers:

- Perimeter security
- Mid-tier security
- Legacy security

Bridging is required between each of these security tiers due to differences in the technology domains specifically in the authentication models or differences in the authorization models. Additionally, in the mid-tier, EJB and CORBA represent two different security technology domains. EJB and CORBA bridging is covered in detail in Chapter 6.

Perimeter to Mid-Tier Interoperability

In order to understand the perimeter to mid-tier bridging, you first have to understand how security schemes work in browsers. There are a number of variations in the interaction between the browser and its target. We describe one of the general approaches.

In the perimeter security technology domain, a client is normally authenticated by means of a username and password or by an SSL certificate with the bulk of the authentication approaches employing the username and password method. Even though username and password is the weaker authentication method, its popularity is due to its simplicity and low cost. The following example concentrates on the username and password form of authentication.

ESI AUTHENTICATION PRINCIPLE: BALANCE COST AGAINST THREAT

As we've discussed before, certificate-based authentication is very secure, but it may be expensive to deploy. Consequently, passwords are often the most appropriate form of authentication. As certificates and PKI become widely available and costs drop, certificates and other forms of strong authentication will naturally replace passwords for many applications.

Browser to Web Server Interaction

To follow the explanation of the interaction between a browser and a Web server, refer to Figure 5.3. This example depicts the authentication of a user calling from the perimeter using a browser into a Web server in the mid-tier. Note that the method names in Figure 5.3 do not correspond to exact method names, but are intended to be descriptive.

The browser sends a request to its target, which is most likely a Web server (send_request). The Web server needs to retrieve authentication evidence to authenticate the user. The first time the browser makes a call, the Web server doesn't find any authentication data and sends an HTTP error message back to the browser (usually Error 403, no permission). Upon receiving this error message, the browser displays a Graphical User Interface (GUI) requesting a username and password. The browser retrieves this data from the information that

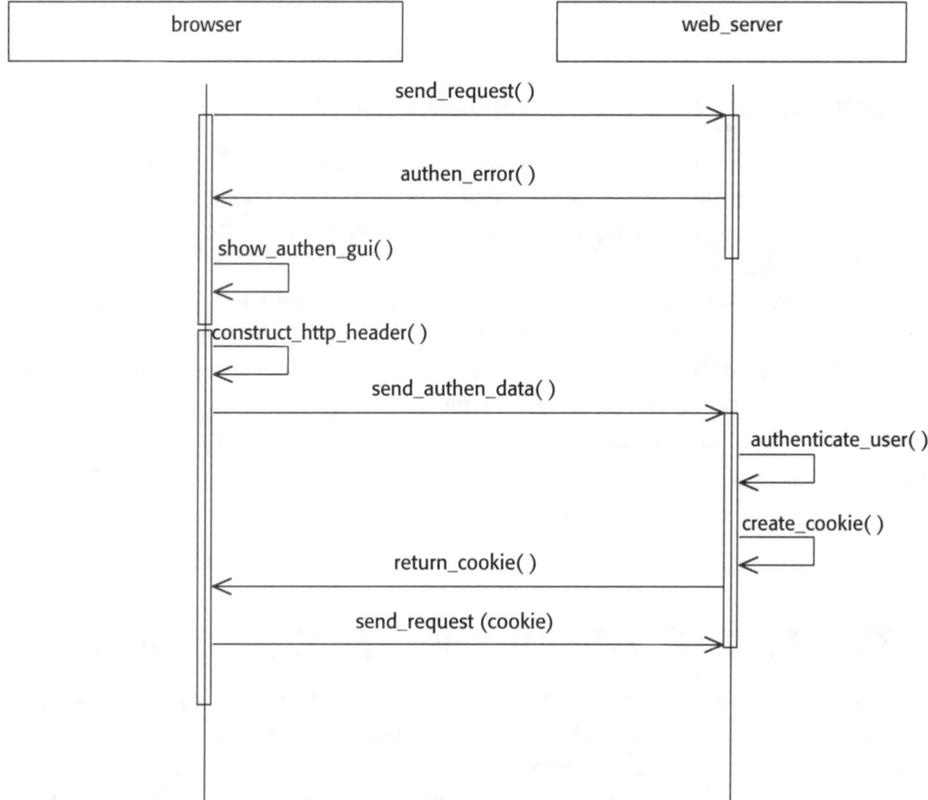

Figure 5.3 Browser to Web server authentication.

the user types into a GUI, constructs an HTTP header containing the username and password, and passes the message with this annotated header to the Web server (send_authen_data). The password is usually protected by SSL in its transport between the browser and the Web server.

When the Web server receives the message with authentication data in the header, it proceeds to authenticate the client (authenticate_user). If the authentication succeeds, the Web server usually constructs a cookie, which contains the username, the password, and a session ID. There are products that the Web server can use to carry out this authentication, or the Web server itself may contain code to authenticate the client. The Web server returns the cookie to the browser, which retains the cookie for future requests. If the browser makes a subsequent request, passing the cookie to the Web server, the Web server can use the information in the cookie (send_request) to identify the user without reauthentication.

A complication occurs if the user turns off cookies in the browser. In that case, the Web server may reject the call, or it may require that the browser send the password on every call. The latter case may be expensive, depending on the authentication computation required. Cookies are also used to pass a session ID, so that a session can be continued over many requests. HTTP is a stateless protocol, so without cookies, the session has to be reestablished on each request.

An alternate approach to the username and password method is to use SSL client certificates. These certificates have been standardized and contain the security name of the subject of the certificate, their public key, and additional information, such as the expiration time of the certificate, and version number. The certificates are cryptographically signed by a trusted third party called a certificate authority (CA). Cryptographic signing means that the CA constructs a one-way hash of the certificate and encrypts the hash with the CA's private key. This does two things: The hash ensures that the certificate cannot be changed after it has been signed and using the private key of the CA ensures that the CA vouched for the information in the certificate. The SSL protocol checks the latter by verifying the validity of the CA's signature. Specifically, this means that if you trust the CA, you can trust that the owner of the certificate is who the certificate says it is.

Whether the client employs a username and password or an SSL certificate type of authentication, the Web server will call on an application server and pass the username and password or SSL certificate. The message usually goes to a servlet in the application server, which has been coded to accept the authentication evidence and uses this evidence to authenticate the client. The servlet may do this itself, or it may use a commercial product to assist in the authentication process.

Passing Data from the Browser

Some of the commercial products that can be used for authentication using evidence from a browser are GetAccess from Entrust, SiteMinder from Netegrity, PolicyDirector from IBM and ClearTrust SecureControl from Securant. In the password case, these tools work by storing a username and password combination in their own database and compare the stored data with the username and password sent from the browser. For SSL certificates, they verify the certificate and ensure that the CA is a trusted one. These products have been integrated with some of the application servers. If you decide to use one of these products to bridge the two domains, it is important that you check the documentation of the commercial product to see if it has been integrated with the application server that you want to use. If the product has not been integrated with the application server that you are contemplating using, we suggest looking at another combination to avoid having to construct a custom bridge.

In CORBA, there is no standard way of using the data sent from a browser and converting that data to, for example, a credential in the CORBA world or a principal in the EJB world. The security data that comes from the browser is quite often contained in a cookie. Cookies are nonstandard; that is, the party that creates the cookie has its own format for encrypted data in its cookie. The Java servlet specification defines ways for the servlet to extract security information from an HTTP header as well as cookies that may be in the header. However, the servlet specification does not discuss interpreting the cookies nor give any standard format for cookies.

Recent specification work is leaning toward using XML to pass the security data in the perimeter and toward standardizing the security portion of the XML document. This work is in its early stages, but as it matures, it will become an important aspect of the security data transfer in the mid-tier. The emerging standards for XML security data transfers are incorporating work done by the IETF on a standard XML digital signature and combining this with the SOAP standard mentioned previously. This work has not yet addressed the problem of interoperability with the CORBA and EJB credential models in the mid-tier, but standardizing the wild and wooly security world in the perimeter is a necessary first step. The solution to perimeter to mid-tier interoperability will likely come in the form of a standard credential that is recognized by technologies in both the perimeter and middle tiers.

An Example of Perimeter to Mid-Tier Interoperability

Since neither CORBA nor EJB understands proprietary cookies, you will have to convert these cookies to something that they understand. The following piece of code gives you an idea of how to construct the bridging between a commercial authentication product and the servlet. This approach produces a CSIv2 token that can pass security data between CORBA and EJB applications.

The following example is C++ CORBA code. If your application server supports RMI over IIOP, the call verify_authentication_data can be made directly from the Java application server. In that case, because we are assuming that you are using an EJB container that supports RMI over IIOP, the Java container can make the call to a C++ CORBA object.

```
Security::AuthenticationStatus
SecServEJB_i::verify_authentication_data(
      const Security::Opaque& auth_data,
      Security::Opaque*& cert_data
)
{
  // This code snippet demonstrates one method of verifying
  // an HTTP cookie.

  // The first step is to bind to establish a connection to the
  // CORBA middleware.  In this CORBA security code this means
  // binding to the CORBA Services on the Security Server.

  BindToCORBAServices();

  //
  // When using a commercial cookie verifier bind to the
  // Server and modify the BindToCommercialCookieVerifier below
  // BindToCommercialCookieVerifier();
  //

  CORBA::Boolean pstatus = 0; // failure

  // Set up a CORBA data structure to hold the cookie

  Security::Opaque_ptr local_cert_data = new Security::Opaque(0);
  if (!CORBA::is_nill(local_cert_data))
  {
       THROW_CORBA_EXCEPTION ( CORBA::NO_MEMORY(NO_MEMORY_CODE,
                                          CORBA::COMPLETED_NO) );
  }

  cert_data  = local_cert_data;
  Security::AuthenticationStatus return_status =
      Security::SecAuthFailure;

  // get the authentication status from commercial cookie verifier
  // and catch the exception

  char *cookie = NULL;
  const char* user_id = NULL;
```

```
try
{
    //
    // you can change the type of the cookie
    // here, and then pass that to commercial cookie verifier
    //

    int len = auth_data.length();
    cookie = new char[len+1];
    if (cookie==NULL)
    {
      OpaqueRel(local_cert_data);
      THROW_CORBA_EXCEPTION (
           CORBA::NO_MEMORY(NO_MEMORY_CODE, CORBA::COMPLETED_NO)
           );
    }
    for(int i = 0; i < len; ++i)
      cookie[i] = auth_data[i];

    //
    // add code to the check_authentication_data method to
    // verify the cookie through a commercial cookie verifier:
    // - Add the real method name.
    // - Pass in the cookie.
    // - Return a user_id, which is a string
    // - Return true or false indicating success or failure
    // Note: you can add handling of specific exceptions below.
    //

     pstatus =
        mCommercialCookieVerifier->check_authentication_data(
                                            user_id, cookie);

      }  // end try

catch (const char *){
//
// add exception handling here
//
}

// Now that the cookie has been verified we want to convert
// the users name to a CORBA security name format.

if (pstatus == Security::SecAuthSuccess)
{
    // get the security name from the getPrivs
    char* security_name = 0;
    try
    {
      security_name = mgetPrivs->get_security_name(user_id);
```

```
    }
catch(const CORBA::Exception& excep)
{
  CORBA::string_free(security_name);
  OpaqueRel(local_cert_data);

  delete[] cookie;
  cookie = NULL;
  THROW_CORBA_EXCEPTION(
       SecServEJB_i::UnableToGetSecurityName(
       "Unable to Get Securityname"));
}
// Add calls to CORBA or EJB middleware to obtain user's
// attributes based on security_name.
// Using these attributes, construct a CSIv2 token and return
// via cert_data
    ...
```

Using the previous code as a guide, you can verify a cookie and retrieve the username using a commercial product that works in the perimeter. These products do not know how to interact with either CORBA or EJB in the mid-tier. However, using a simple bridge as described earlier, you can securely make a call from the perimeter to the mid-tier. After verifying the call, you can map the username into a security name, and use the normal CORBA or EJB middleware to retrieve the user's attributes and carry out CORBA authorization.

The J2EE specification leaves the means of mapping the security principal name up to the container provider. You should find out how your container provider accomplishes this. Understanding the intent of the preceding code snippet will help you understand the explanation of the container provider.

The Critical Web Server

From the previous discussion, you can see that the Web server is in a critical security position for the handoff from the perimeter to the mid-tier because it has the ultimate responsibility for verifying the client. Therefore, you must take care that the Web server is protected from insider attacks. It's not that the other components in the mid-tier aren't to be protected from attack, but the Web server is the component that determines whether the client is a legitimate entity who can come into your system. The firewall will assure that the incoming message is of the correct type, for example, HTTPS, and that it is directed to the correct Web server. However, the firewall does not authenticate the client. So be sure that the Web server machine is properly protected. Protecting computer systems and the processes running on them is outside the scope of this book. There are a number of books that cover this topic, such as *E-Commerce Security* (Ghosh, 1998).

Further, the authentication engine that the Web server uses should be in the mid-tier and not in the DMZ. Keeping the Web server's security tasks very simple enhances your chances of protecting the Web Server. If the model is simple then it lends itself to security analysis and thus to higher confidence in its protection. With the authentication engine and its security data tucked away in the mid-tier, the Web server only has to call on the authentication engine and ask for authentication of a user. If the authentication check passes, the Web server lets the request through; otherwise the request will be denied.

Another job of the Web server is to aid in the security scaling problems. Scaling capabilities are needed in systems that will be supporting a large number of users. This scaling is accomplished by aggregating the users in the system into named sets. Common sets are groups and roles, which were described in Chapters 2 and 3. Therefore, in addition to verifying the authentication evidence of the user, the Web server may be asked to assign a particular user to a group or role that is used by the rest of the system in place of the user's name. The commercial verification products mentioned earlier in this section support the use of groups, but it is up to you to determine what group each user should be assigned to. If you choose too broad a category, the group becomes somewhat useless in trying to determine what a user can do. An extreme case of defining too broad a group is that in which everybody fits into one group with the result that everybody is given the right to do everything. Too narrow a category can result in almost as many groups as people, so the scaling capability is lost. Chapter 8 covers this subject in more detail.

Mid-Tier to Legacy Interoperability

Unfortunately, there is no CORBA standard for mid-tier to legacy interoperability. There are a number of approaches to make this transition, and there are some products that help with some of the steps. Most solutions today wrap the legacy application with a CORBA wrapper.

The security problem in this case is the availability of authentication data required to open the legacy database that contains sensitive information. This authentication data required by the database, which may be a password, is not the client's password, but a completely different password that is applicable to the database. The application has to securely obtain this password or other authentication data to access the database.

As stated in Chapter 2, J2EE defines connectors to help in securely accessing a legacy application, but it does not address the need to store and get this orthogonal piece of data needed by the database. The connector specification does state that a facility is needed to pass authentication data needed by the legacy application but doesn't say how. One way to facilitate this transfer is for the servlet to pass the authentication data to the bean in its creation step, and then have the bean pass it through its series of bean-to-bean calls and in some cases, to beans in other application servers. A CORBA application can take a similar tack. There are two problems with this approach.

1. The developer must write security-aware code to handle passwords.
2. The authentication data must either be passed unencrypted or if it is encrypted, the bean developer is responsible for encryption and decryption code.

The first problem goes against one of our basic security principals—applications should be security-unaware; that is, developers should not have to write security code. The idea behind this recommendation is that making applications secure in a distributed environment is difficult and outside the expertise of most application developers. A common developer mistake, for example, is to hard-code into the application the passwords for database access, which is a terrible security practice. Another typical developer approach that is also bad practice is to store cleartext passwords in the filesystem. Also, in a distributed environment, the security of a particular application can depend on the string of applications used in the particular call. Therefore, not only do developers have to worry about their own application security, but they have to take into account the security processes in other applications, some of which may not yet be written.

The second problem is a specialization of the first. Passing the authentication data unencrypted can be quite dangerous, especially in light of our previous revelation of the high percentage of break-ins to corporate systems from insiders in the mid-tier. Network sniffers have become quite sophisticated and can even pick up data from outside a building. By the way, passing unencrypted authentication data is a poor security solution that we see in many EJB implementations. Using encryption adds the requirement that the developer understand the arcane world of encryption and decryption, public key infrastructure (PKI), and so on. In many cases, requiring this of the developer is a sure recipe for disaster as it takes special skills to handle this correctly.

Wrapping a legacy application in a CORBA wrapper bridge or using Java Connectors removes the constraint that the legacy application be able to

ESI AUTHORIZATION PRINCIPLE: PUSH SECURITY DOWN

It's difficult for a developer to write good security code if he or she is not experienced in security countermeasures. We recommend using an isolated security service developed by security professionals rather than embedding security in your application. The results are much more likely to be robust against malicious attacks. An example of such an isolated security service is the Unitary Login service that we describe below.

receive remote calls or even that it use a low-level remote call such as TCP/IP, which is difficult to program let alone secure.

Whether we use CORBA wrappers or EJB connectors, we still have the problem of securely passing the authentication data to the legacy application. The security service that is used as the sample CORBA security service for this book implements one solution called Unitary Login. Unitary Login is a CORBA object service that provides strong protection of legacy passwords and has a database containing a set of tuples for each registered owner of the tuple set. The tuples consist of a caller security name, primary key, a secondary key, a user ID, and authentication data (e.g., the password). Figure 5.4 shows the format of the data contained in Unitary Login. A similar approach could be used with EJB connectors.

Each registered owner is permitted access to only that set of tuples under his control. Referring to Figure 5.4, Owner 1 (typically the database wrapper bridge) and only Owner 1 has access to the user ID and authentication data identified by the caller security name, primary key, and secondary key indexing its data. The unitary login data, including all the owners and the data tuples assigned to them, are input into the Unitary Login system by the security administrator; that is, the owners do not add, modify, or delete the data assigned to them. All access to the Unitary Login system is controlled by CORBA security by means of the security policies assigned to the Unitary Login interfaces and methods. This is called *credential mapping* in J2EE terminology. This capability is not in the J2EE specification, but as we said the specification does discuss this as a necessary piece of a connector.

In the figure, if Owner 1 wants to retrieve authentication data from a mainframe, it would request data from the Unitary Login system by passing the caller's security name, the mainframe system name as the primary key, and the subsystem name (e.g., IBM's Customer Information Control System [CICS]), and would receive back through a secure SSL channel the user ID and password to be used to access that mainframe or subsystem. Note that this is a nonstandard approach for retrieving authentication data for the mid-tier or legacy interface, but it is typical of what is needed to solve this problem. This approach or something like it will need to be standardized in the future to solve this mid-tier to legacy data security problem.

J2EE talks about the necessity of having functionality like credential mapping. However, there are no details on its functionality. A Unitary Login approach could be used as the credential mapping service that J2EE talks about.

The following Java code sample illustrates how to use Unitary Login to retrieve the authentication data for a user requesting database access. The database wrapper bridge should call `getAuthenticationData` and supply the EJB session ID and the target mainframe system name. The call returns the mainframe user ID and password that the bridge should use to access the data-

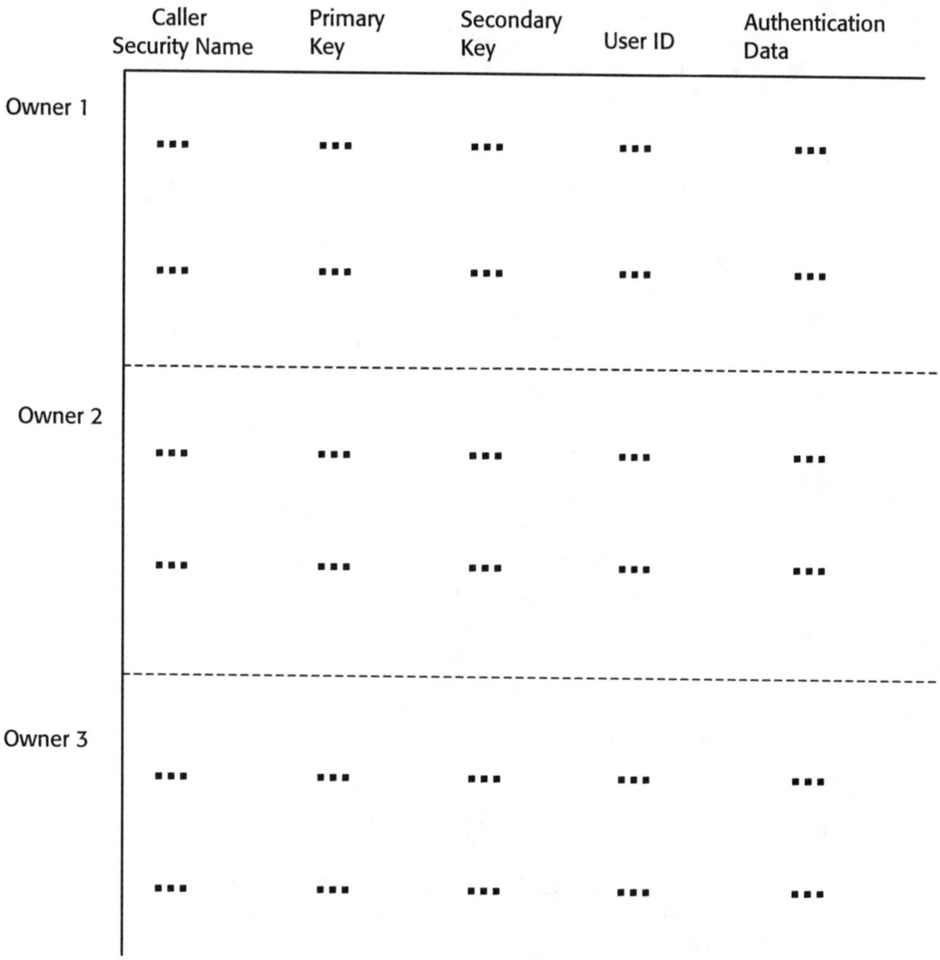

	Caller Security Name	Primary Key	Secondary Key	User ID	Authentication Data
Owner 1	...	...	...	...	...
	...	...	...	...	...
Owner 2	...	...	...	...	...
	...	...	...	...	...
Owner 3	...	...	...	...	...
	...	...	...	...	...

Figure 5.4 Unitary Login data layout.

base on behalf of the requesting user. The call should use SSL encryption and requires a secure association that only permits access by those owners defined by the security administrator according to the access policy.

```
public UloginData getAuthenticationData(String sessionID,
                                        String mfSysName)
        throws java.rmi.RemoteException
{
          // This code snippet shows how to securely transport the
          // password from the basic system, whether it be an
          // application or a Java Container to the legacy
          // application.
```

```
    // First we get the bridge's own credentials.
    // Once we have the bridge credentials
    // we can get the bridge user name from the
    // credentials object

org.omg.CORBA.SecurityLevel2.Credentials[] creds =
        bridge.getCredentialsForBridge();

if ((creds == null) || (creds.length == 0))
     throw new java.rmi.RemoteException(
                    "No credentials for bridge");
String bridgeuid = creds[0].GetSecurityName();

        // Next we get the
       // caller's credentials from the bridge

CredentialData userData =
                (CredentialData)bridge.lookup(sessionID);

org.omg.CORBA.SecurityLevel2.Credentials[] ucreds =
                userData.getCredentials();

if ((ucreds == null) || (ucreds.length == 0))
     throw new java.rmi.RemoteException(
                  "No user credentials from bridge");
       // Now that we have the user credentials we get the
       // security name of the user, sn

String sn = creds[0].GetSecurityName();

       // Set the holder for the output parameters;
       // password and the mainframe users id, mfuid,
       // required for database access.

org.omg.CORBA.Security.OpaqueHolder password =
       new org.omg.CORBA.Security.OpaqueHolder();
org.omg.CORBA.StringHolder mfuid =
       new org.omg.CORBA.StringHolder();

       // We will not use the subkey so it's not set.
String subkey = new String();

       // Lastly we call the getAuthData from the Unitary
       // Login to get the password associated with the user.
       // This call will use the credentials of the bridge to
       // authenticate the call to the Unitary Login process.

try {
         // We first bind to the security admin server
           com.acme.corba.security.idl.UloginAdmin
           admin_srv =
```

```
com.acme.corba.security.idl.ULoginAdminHelper.bind
              (orb, "/Corba/Security/MSS/AdminULogin:SecAdminSvr");

com.acme.corba.security.idl.ULoginAdminPackage.AuthDataStatus
               status = null;

           // Then call getAuthData on the admin server.
          status = admin_srv.getAuthData(
                                     Bridgeuid,
                                     sn,
                                     mfSysName,
                                     subkey,
                                     mfuid,
                                     password);

        } catch (... e) {
           // Exception Code not shown here
        }

    return new UloginData(mfuid,
                          new String(password.value));
    }
}
```

All of the over the wire connections should be protected by transport security, like SSL, which supports confidentiality and integrity on the wire.

Security Policy Domains

The second major type of security domain that we are interested in is the policy domain. CORBA has formalized several types of security policy. These types and a short explanation of each domain type as defined by the CORBA security specification(CORBASec) is included in the following list. A more detailed explanation is presented in Chapters 3 and 8.

Invocation Access Policy. Specifies rights that are granted to a client attribute and are used to determine access decision

Invocation Audit Policy. Specifies the events to be audited and the criteria to determine when and where to audit

Invocation Delegation Policy. Specifies whether and where to delegate and the type of delegation to be used

Secure Invocation Policy. Specifies a security association, which defines the security information that is passed from a client to a target and the level of security to use for the transfer of the message data.

Nonrepudiation Policy. Creates evidence related to the creation or receipt of a document. This evidence may be retrieved at a later date and used to prove the earlier creation or receipt of the document for whom the evidence was constructed.

Each of these policy domains identify an important subset of security. The first four are necessary for a distributed object system, whereas the fifth is an optional characteristic. The security model that is used in each of the three security tiers that we have described needs to satisfy the intent behind the first four policies. We will expand on this for the perimeter, middle, and legacy tiers. First, however, it is well known that the definitions given in specifications are not always clear, and the CORBA specification follows this tradition. Therefore, we'll describe in more detail the meaning of each of these policies.

When a security system tries to determine whether an entity has the right to access a resource, it uses the rules defined in an access policy. The definition of access policy uses the term client attribute as the alias for the entity to whom the rights are given. This promotes the concept of grouping things by their attributes.

In the perimeter, the security activity that takes place results in obtaining the principal's name and authentication evidence, such as a password or an SSL client certificate. This information is then sent to the Web Server where authentication and authorization are carried out. The component access policy is used in the mid-tier.

While all authorization could be carried out in the perimeter, we recommend that authorization also be enforced in the mid-tier. It is best to approach enterprise security from a viewpoint of multiple lines of defense. The first line of defense at the perimeter uses your perimeter firewall to direct incoming requests to a few entities, like your Web servers, which in turn authenticate the users and provide simple authorization checks. Web servers pass these users on to the mid-tier, where the middleware security in the application servers or CORBA applications carry out additional authorization of these authenticated users.

The Web server may have an access policy that states whether the client can or cannot be permitted to access the application server. The Web server only knows about a URL, so the access decision that the Web server uses at the granularity of the URL passed to it from the perimeter. Fine-grained access decision, i.e. at the method level, is usually made in the application server or in the CORBA security service. The topic of method level access decision is covered in Chapter 2 and 3. Access policy in the legacy domain mainly consists of username/password protection to a database or to a mainframe subsystem.

Audit policy is pretty straightforward: You want to record who has done what to your system. You especially want to record when someone tries to do something that they should not, such as unsuccessful logins or attempts to access methods for which they have no permission. However, when we look at what middleware implementers have done with respect to auditing, we find it inconsistent and lacking in many respects. Auditing is specific to a particular security product in the perimeter tier. In the mid-tier, CORBA has an extensive set of rules for auditing, whereas the EJB specification states that the container implementers may do auditing, but gives no guidance. On the other hand, legacy applications that are performed on mainframes have extensive auditing capabilities defined by the mainframe operating system. Databases also have specific auditing capabilities. You will have to examine the architecture and determine what level of auditing is appropriate for your system. After determining the appropriate level of auditing for your system, look at the audit policies available to you in each of the technology domains, and use the audit capabilities where appropriate. If there are not sufficient auditing capabilities in the system that you are considering, we would strongly suggest that you look at other middleware systems that provide the auditing capabilities you desire.

Delegation in a distributed system is a complex subject. Basically, it means that a person gives another person or system process the capability to act as their proxy in all ways, which is called *impersonation*, or puts certain restrictions on what the delegatee can do, which is called *restricted delegation*. In the perimeter, you can say that you are delegating your rights to the browser, to access a URL as you. This is pretty straightforward because you know where you want to go, that is, a particular URL, and you know what you want to do there. The mid-tier is where delegation can get complicated. Your original request may go through a number of applications, some of which may potentially be applications set up by someone trying to obtain unauthorized access to, say, your bank account. In a complex delegation scenario an authority, such as a system administrator, could delegate his rights to an application, which in turn could delegate the system administrator's identity to another application and so on. The complexity comes from determining who can act as a delegatee for whose rights. We will cover delegation in detail in the next chapter.

When a message is passed from a client to a server, many times there are security requirements on the level of encryption of the message, which is called *confidentiality*, and the ability to ensure that the data has not been altered, which is called *integrity*. In addition, it is necessary to pass certain security information from the target to the server, for example, the user's password. These two functions are handled by the secure invocation policy, which defines the setup of a secure association between a client and target. In the perimeter, you might want to pass a username and password. It is not a good idea to transmit the password without encrypting it. Also, if you are sending your credit card information, you want that encrypted also. Integrity checking is usually required by the mid-tier. Within the mid-tier, both aspects of secure association have to be decided as a message is passed from one application to another. The mid-tier secure invocation policy also decides what type of secure association is to be established when passing information to the legacy domain.

Nonrepudiation, as mentioned earlier, is not required in a secure distributed system, but is a function of security architectures that will be required as e-commerce becomes more pervasive. Nonrepudiation is analogous to a computerized Notary Public. A client sends a document to a trusted third party and that third party verifies that the document has originated from the client. Alternately, a target can send a document to a trusted third party with evidence of receiving it from the client. The third party verifies that the document has been sent by the client and has been received by the target. At a later time, the third party can be called upon to verify either of the previously described situations. Additional aspects of nonrepudiation defined in various specifications are the ability to securely store and retrieve a document on request. Nonrepudiation is included in the CORBA specification.

EJB supports some of these policies, such as access, simple delegation, and secure association, but not to the detail that is defined in CORBA. In addition, CORBA has defined a structure and an IDL definition for setting and using these policies. The CORBA specification, Security Domain Membership Management Service, details the structure and how to use each of these policy domains. The specification defines a hierarchical structure of policy domains; each of which contains a set of policies. There are also rules for walking the domain tree such that a corporation can mimic its organizational structure with the policy domain hierarchy and have aspects of policy control set by different levels in the organization. Set combinators are assigned to the edges between nodes, which can be used to widen the policies as the Security Service walks the tree (using the union combinator), or narrow the policies (using the intersection set combinator), or eliminate a policy (using the difference combinator).

In CORBA objects are dynamically assigned to a domain and take on the policies in the assigned domain. You can dynamically assign an object by overriding the security policy on a Portable Object Adapter (POA), which is *POA object assignment*, or assign the Object ID to a domain, which is *object instance assignment*. In addition, your security policy overrides can reference your object implementation, called the servant, at runtime and use runtime values from the servant to assign a POA or object instance to a domain. Alternately, a security administrator can statically assign security policy on the POA.

The EJB model does not presently support all these concepts. Therefore, there are two approaches for interoperability between the two policy models:

- Set the policy to the least common denominator.
- Use the CORBA policy models when using EJB.

The first approach can be used when the analysis of your enterprise security needs results in a simpler model for policy control. Some aspects that influence this decision are the lack of scaling requirements, the adequacy of using groups and roles for attributes, and the lack of a need for fine-grained access control.

As a warning, be sure to look not only at your corporation's present security needs, but also at its future needs as a distributed architecture becomes more important and more access from the outside will be required. An increased use of e-commerce will surely increase these needs. Designing an architecture that includes interoperability between the CORBA access decision and attribute models and the companion models in EJB allows you to use the best of both worlds. You can simplify the CORBA model by using one policy domain and only the role attribute, but an expansion to the CORBA access model is not standardized in the present EJB specification. In addition, as standards for integration and the implementation of these interoperability standards become available, the extended policy models may be incorporated into your architecture with increased security and efficiencies.

The use of policy domains is important in the interoperability between EJB and CORBA. Therefore, we provide more detail in Chapter 6.

Modifying Architectures for Security

The solutions that we have been discussing require a few high-level architectural modifications. These include the insertion of EJB to CORBA bridges, modules to handle conversion of authentication data from the perimeter to the mid-tier, and a means of securely passing authentication information from a mid-tier EJB or CORBA component to a legacy application. Figure 5.5 shows a complete sample architecture covering all three tiers with the most detail shown in the mid-tier.

Note that the example architecture assumes a container that supports RMI/IIOP and uses the Unitary Login Service previously discussed. A quick glance at this architecture illustrates the components that we have been talking about in this chapter.

Starting from the left side of the diagram in the perimeter tier, we have a client application, usually a browser, which makes a call on a Web server. The Web server then calls an application server in the mid-tier. In this architecture, the Web server needs to authenticate itself to the application server.

In the architecture shown, the Web server calls upon a servlet in the application server, passing the authentication information of the browser principal. In this case, the Web server must be authenticated to the application server as it has to be trusted to pass the correct client authentication evidence. For example, SSL certificates are publicly available, so without any further checks, a malicious user could obtain someone's SSL certificate and pose as the Web server, passing on the stolen certificate, which it claims belongs to the browser principal. The application server would then carry out an action and pass the stolen client's data back to the phony Web server. Unless the application server has formed some level of trust with the Web server, there is no way to stop a

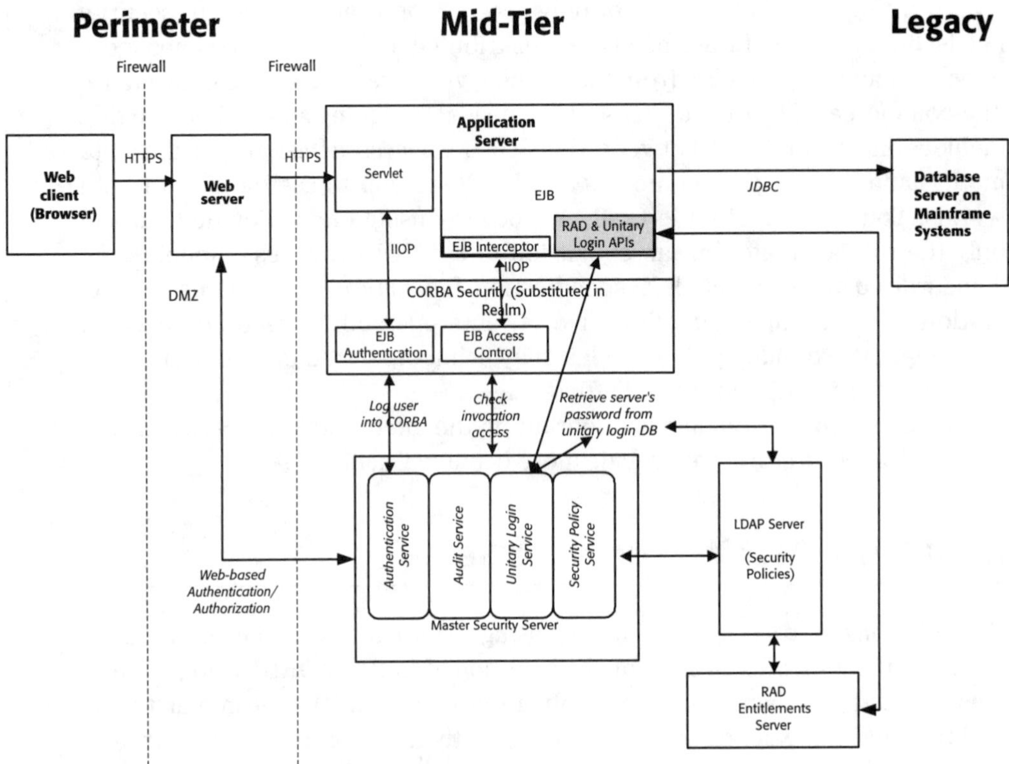

Figure 5.5 Sample multitier architecture.

bogus Web server. The case that we have just described is one of the target trusting the intermediate server, that is, the Web server. This situation is addressed in CSIv2 and is covered in more detail in Chapter 6.

Another architectural model would have the browser call directly to a servlet in the application server. The advantage of using the Web server is twofold. First, using the Web server separates the functional duties of the Web server and the servlet. The job of the Web server is to receive a call from the browser, authenticate the client, and pass the call to the appropriate application server. The job of the servlet in the Web server is to receive the authenticated call and determine the correct EJB to complete the task, call the bean passing the authentication information, and possibly call into a CORBA authentication model to create a CORBA credential if the architecture calls for the mix of object models for the reasons previously described. The second advantage to using the Web server is that the Web server can act as a proxy for the firewall, providing a single address or addresses depending on the number of Web servers used for incoming calls.

As discussed in Chapter 4, firewalls cannot handle dynamic addressing very well. What we mean by dynamic addressing is that both CORBA and EJB use object references to find their targets. Object references can point a client at one of a large number of servers. Because these servers cannot all be known to the firewall before the method call, there is no way that these addresses can be installed in the firewall. Therefore, firewalls are not well suited to either of these methodologies.

When the servlet in an application server is first called from the Web server, the container accesses the security realm to check permissions on whether a client can call an EJB. In the EJB and CORBA interoperability scenario, code to call CORBA security may be substituted in the realm. This code would call a CORBA Principal Authenticator, which would:

- Authenticate the cookie passed into the servlet from the Web server
- Create the CORBA credential for that client

Note that this is not the standard Principal Authenticator that you would find in a vanilla ORB. Therefore, this implies custom code. However, the CORBA security specification does not say what authentication data is used or how it is verified. This is an implementation decision. So, check with your security vendor, but don't be surprised if it has not implemented an advanced Principal Authenticator to handle interoperability as we have described.

It is worth noting that CORBA supports a newer type of access decision called RAD that is described in Chapter 8. RAD uses a policy engine or RAD entitlement server to make decisions based on rules related to resources rather than policies based on required and granted rights as in the more traditional access decision. The architectural diagram in Figure 5.5 shows both forms of access decision. Another point to observe in this diagram is that security policies are stored in the Lightweight Directory Access Protocol (LDAP). LDAP is becoming popular as a storage medium for corporate data that can be in the form of a key/value tuple stored in nodes that form a hierarchical structure. This format is a good match for security data, which consists of key/value pairs stored in hierarchies formed by X.500 type names.

The interoperability between the mid-tier and the legacy application is shown on the right side of the diagram. The EJB would make a call on a CORBA protected data store to retrieve the username and password for access to the legacy database. We have shown one such repository, Unitary Login, which we discussed previously. There is no standard yet for this type of service, but with recognition of the need, similar types of services and standards for this need should be available soon. J2EE has recognized the need for such a service with the use of connectors and resource-refs.

The basic architecture is that access to the legacy login service is controlled by the security access control. Each permitted entity has access to its own portion of the Unitary Login database, which consists of a key and a subkey, a user ID, and the authentication data for that user. The database server is a CORBA front-end to the mainframe database. If the legacy database that you are accessing supports Java Database Connectivity (JDBC), the database server is not needed. The security pattern that we have described protects the password to the legacy system, which should be different than the original browser password. In this scheme, as distributed calls are made through the system from the browser through the Web server, the servlet(s), and a probable series of session and entity beans, no legacy password is transmitted. Only the bean that makes a call to the legacy data has a connection to the Unitary Login and thus the use of the password to log into the legacy system.

In the architecture shown in Figure 5.5, we used only EJBs. There could just as easily be a mixture or EJB and CORBA components. The use of CORBA components makes the interfaces to the CORBA services simpler. There are no implementations of the CORBA component specification at this time, so we are not introducing CORBA components into this discussion.

Summary

This chapter concentrated on the problem of interoperability both within and between companies. The framework for this discussion was the dual concepts of security domains and security tiers. We described different security technologies and discussed the rationale for using these different technologies.

We used the definitions from the CORBA security specification, which defines three types of security domains:

- Security environment domain
- Security technology domain
- Security policy domain

The distributed application space was broken down into three security tiers:

- Perimeter
- Mid-tier
- Legacy

Investigating the characteristics of each of the three tiers in the context of a typical application architecture, we mapped the types of technology domains common to each of these categories. We found that the most complex and most neglected category from a security point of view was the mid-tier.

We introduced and discussed another concept taken from the CORBA specification—Security Policy Domains. This concept categorizes the security functionality that a distributed architecture must have. We described these policy domains and showed how they were satisfied in each of the tiers.

Our purpose in defining this architecture was to provide you with a model on which to design and build a distributed enterprise system that is flexible and scalable. We also offered reasons why you should use this architecture and these models to bridge some of the different object technologies and products that exist today to solve parts of the problems that are present.

In the mid-tier, we talked about two object models, CORBA and EJB, and made the argument that these models are, in truth, not competing but are complementary. The next chapter takes a closer look at the interoperability between CORBA and EJB and shows how to bridge the incompatibilities between the two to get the "best of the breed."

Interoperability of EJB and CORBA Components

If you examine large corporate computer systems, you will often find both EJB and CORBA in use. However, they are usually isolated from each other. Although you can get the two component models to communicate, it is more difficult to get the two security models to work together. The EJB and CORBA Security models have a number of similarities, but they also have differences that we have to worry about if we want them to interoperate.

You might ask—if there is an effort associated with making them work together, why bother? The simple answer that we touched upon in the last chapter is that each of the EJB and CORBA Security models have useful capabilities that the other doesn't have. Particularly in environments where Java components need to interact with non-Java legacy applications, interoperation between EJB and CORBA may be your only acceptable solution.

Both EJB and CORBA security (CORBASec) are used to solve a similar problem—protect user resources from unwanted access in a distributed environment. However, each model solves the problem from different angles. CORBASec—and for that matter CORBA itself—is the result of efforts by engineers from different companies to develop a set of specifications that work with different programming languages and platforms and that also provide the scaling and granularity that any enterprise might need. EJB resolves the problem by making the distributed system as simple as possible and works with one language—Java.

Ideally, you want both results, a simple to use security service and the ability to protect resources at as fine a level as you need in a particular case. Using CORBA and Java together and exploiting the best capabilities of each to solve the problem at hand allow you achieve these goals.

This chapter discusses practical approaches for making EJB and CORBA Security interoperate. The important points that are covered in this chapter are:

- The way that security is delivered to the developer of an EJB or a CORBA application by the security service provider, which is different in each model.
- The Common Secure Interoperability v2 (CSIv2) specification, which lays the ground work for interoperability between EJB and CORBA.
- The way that EJB and CORBA handle authentication and authorization, which is different in each model.

Making EJB and CORBA Work Together Securely

There are a number of challenges associated with attaining secure interoperability between EJB and CORBA, but we will show that they are not insurmountable. Like pesky children, they can play together, but they need some adult supervision. We'll provide you with the tools and ideas with which to make use of the best capabilities of the two security models.

The differences between the two models fall into the following, now familiar, security categories:

- **Authentication.** A process that deals with clients and servers supplying sufficient evidence to prove who they are.
- **Authorization.** A process that determines whether a client can access a particular method or resource.
- **Transport.** A means of securely transferring the necessary evidence and data from the client to the server.

Of the three categories, the transport layer has had the most advances in interoperability. These have come about because of the advent of Remote Method Invocation (RMI) over Internet Inter-ORB Protocol (IIOP) and the new CORBA specification CSIv2, which has been adopted by the EJB specification version 2.0. CSIv2 was introduced in Chapter 2 and in Chapter 5. This chapter digs deeper into the details of CSIv2 because it is an important technology in making EJB and CORBA interoperate.

RMI over IIOP technology is clearly laid out in the EJB version 1.1 and later specifications for EJB Container writers. The EJB version 2.0 specification requires container providers to support CSIv2 Level 0 functionality. As mentioned in Chapter 5, when purchasing an application server, you should be sure that it supports RMI over IIOP and that it supports CSIv2 for interoperability. Given that both your CORBA ORB and your EJB application server support CSIv2, the transport layer will not present any interoperability problems.

In the authentication layer, the difference between the two models lies in the type of authentication evidence that is sent from the client to the server. In the present EJB model, once you are in the container, the model assumes that one bean calling on another bean is a trusted relationship; that is, the called bean trusts the calling bean to pass on the correct authenticated identity. CORBA, on the other hand, goes to great pains to ensure that the authentication evidence is moved securely and assumes mutual distrust between the parties. We'll go into the nuances of this later.

The authorization layer is where there is the largest discrepancy between the two models. EJB explicitly declares the association between a client and the bean and its method that clients can access. The EJB model has a number of constructs that help in the scaling problem, such as:

- The use of roles and the ability to allow common access to all methods in a bean.
- Role membership is scoped to the application.
- Roles and permissions are logical; thus, the deployer has the freedom to map them to a specific set of principals.

The EJB specification does not state how a container provider should implement access control nor how the logical roles should be mapped to principals. For any specific container, it is your responsibility to investigate that container's authorization model for your specific implementation requirements.

In this chapter, we point out the particular advantages and disadvantages of each model and show you ways to take advantage of the strengths of each

ESI AUTHENTICATION PRINCIPLE: TRUST NO ONE

CORBASec assumes a mutual suspicion model that requires authentication of both human users and application components, while EJB security generally trusts bean-to-bean communication. Because CORBASec requires component authentication, CORBASec provides a stronger means to protect against malicious components than the EJB security standard. To address this need, EJB container providers may supply additional security functionality, which enforces stronger, but nonstandard, authentication of components.

model. We give you concrete paradigms and approaches to help you get EJB security and CORBASec to interoperate in each of the security layers. We also give you sufficient background in the existing and new technologies in this area to aid you in choosing the best parts of each technology.

Advantages of Combined Technologies

We talked about the advantages of using different technologies in Chapter 5. As e-commerce becomes more extensive, a large majority of architectures will be allowing external clients to access their enterprise using an external browser. EJB application servers are prepared to receive this kind of access. The servlets in a typical application server can be derived from an HTTP servlet base class supplied by the container, which contains methods for extracting usernames and cookies from the incoming HTTP header. This information can then be used to authenticate the user who is attempting to access the system.

Although CORBA-based applications can also be written to interact with and extract information from the HTTP message, this is not as easily done as it is in an EJB Container. You have to write specific code in the CORBA server to capture and parse an HTTP call. This is not an easy programming task. More importantly, it also contradicts our advice of not putting your security code in the application, but instead putting it into the middleware layer.

On the other hand, CORBASec has the capability of giving you finer grained control over who can access what by means of its richer set of attributes and security policy domains. At the same time, CORBASec gives you the ability to handle large numbers of users as well as the ability to dynamically assign policies to objects at runtime. Security policy can be specified down to the object instance in CORBASec.

The most straightforward way for an EJB Container to implement its access control is to use the information from the method-permissions; that is, ascertain what role can access what method to determine access control. However, method-permissions are on a per-bean basis, which can cause administrative problems when the enterprise has thousands of beans and the organization has to add another role or change an access rule.

ESI AUTHORIZATION PRINCIPLE: PUSH SECURITY DOWN

Because EJB has built-in support for HTTP requests from Web servers, it is easier (and thus more secure) to use EJB application servers rather than CORBA components to secure HTTP requests. Once an EJB component has processed the HTTP request and made subsequent calls to components using RMI over IIOP, CORBASec can provide fine-grain authorization of the IIOP requests.

CORBASec also improves administrative scalability by providing an additional layer of indirection between the user's attributes and the resource that you are trying to protect. The CORBASec model establishes this level of indirection by assigning required rights to interfaces and methods and assigning effective rights to the client's attributes. Using rights as an additional level of indirection, you can dramatically reduce the number of permission entries, which simplifies administration. Assigning rights is described further in Chapter 8.

There can be a large amount of security data to be administered if fine-grain control is demanded by your situation. CORBA has an administrative advantage over EJB in that it does not require the redundancy of security data that EJB does. As stated in Chapter 2, EJB requires that each bean have its own method-permission list in the deployment descriptor, whereas in CORBASec, each attribute, domain, and right is separately managed. These separate policies are brought together at runtime and evaluated to arrive at an access decision. In EJB, the container provider possess flexibility in how it uses information from the deployment descriptor. Therefore, a particular container provider can mitigate much of the scaling problems depending on the type of scaling support it builds into the container. This is an important aspect of security that you must investigate when choosing a container provider. Consequently, if you have a large installation, be sure to ask your container provider what scaling capabilities it provides.

Generally, EJB is simpler to program because the EJB Container takes care of a number of the more difficult programming constructs, such as transactions, security, and distributed interaction. Wouldn't it be great if we could select the best parts of each security model and use them where they are needed in building an enterprise system? This is just what we are going to do—give you the ideas and concrete approaches to let you use EJB security and CORBASec where they are best suited.

Packaging Security for the Component Developer

CORBASec is contained in libraries, which developers link into their application, and executables, which supply external security services, such as administration. Chapter 3 described the CORBASec services that are provided by the libraries. The EJB Container, on the other hand, provides the security. This is a different paradigm from the more familiar model of linking in functionality contained in a library. Therefore, in this section, we take some time to explain how you should work with an EJB Container.

In Chapter 2, we described how to code security into an EJB Container using for the most part the deployment descriptor. In this section, we look at how the container handles security. As we have stated a number of times, security code is best handled by the middleware and not by the programmer. EJB Containers follow this principle. Quoting from as far back as the EJB version 1.1 specification:

> The Enterprise JavaBeans architecture will make it easy to write applications: Application developers will not have to understand low-level transaction and state management details, multi-threading, connection pooling, and other complex low-level APIs.

One of these low-level details is our favorite topic, security. As long as the security provided by the container meets the requirements of your organization, your security needs are solved. However, life is usually not that accommodating. If you are a small company that is not involved in e-commerce, then the default security in an EJB Container might suffice. For all others, the latter part of this chapter provides you with the tools to choose the "best of the breed" between CORBA and EJB. In this section, we drill down into the security aspects of a container, so that you can judge whether the container provided security is sufficient for your needs. We'll start at the beginning with a call from a client to an EJB.

JNDI Security

As you know from your work with EJB, when a client wants to call a method in an EJB, it first gets the home interface by calling on the Java Naming and Directory Interface (JNDI). It then gets the object reference to the remote interface from the home interface. Finally, it calls a business method using the object reference for the remote interface. As you will see, each of these calls can be protected by the container, especially with the incorporation of CSIv2 into version 2.0 of the EJB specification.

In order to secure the JNDI calls to retrieve the home interface, the naming server must be secured. This means that the call from the container to the naming interface has to support a secure transport between the two. In addition, the naming service has to authorize the caller for the method called. A more important requirement is that the naming service must authenticate itself to the container. These requirements can be satisfied if the container provider secures the naming service and performs the required authentication and authorization checks. If the container calls on a rogue naming service without any security checks, the container can be fed bogus home interfaces, which can result in potentially disastrous consequences. Although this mutual authentication can be done, it is not common practice in many implementations.

Another sensitive activity occurs when a server registers a home interface with the naming service. The naming service requires the server to authenticate itself, and then does an authorization check on the server's authentication evidence sent to the naming service. Conversely, the naming service itself should be authenticated to the server that wants to register the home interface. This activity is also not commonly done.

A malicious attacker could install a hostile application that masquerades as a legitimate service in a system that has not secured its naming service. For example, in a banking application, clients could innocently pass sensitive information, such as credit card numbers and personal identification numbers (PINs), expecting that the information is going to the bank. In reality, however, the masquerading application could collect the sensitive client data for fraudulent use. In order to avoid these attacks, you should examine your infrastructure, not just your applications, and assure that those pieces that are sensitive have been properly secured.

We provide you with a deeper understanding of what is going on during mutual authentication and secure transport when we discuss CSIv2 in detail later in this chapter.

We would be remiss in not pointing out that the EJB security specification version 2.0 does instruct the container provider to do just what we described in securing the naming service. To secure the naming service, the specification tells the container provider to use the CORBA specified naming service (CosNaming), and establish a secure connection with the naming server. The question is, does the system that you are using secure the naming service? Once again, be sure to determine whether your container provider or your system supplies this capability.

Even though we are beating up on the poor container writers, we can't let CORBA off without also taking it to task. CORBA implementations have the same problem. The calls to the naming server may not be secure in CORBA installations because, in many cases, the CORBA middleware vendor does not secure the naming service. In both EJB and CORBA, the middleware says "trust me." Don't. It's up to you to take the knowledge that we give you in this book and check the security aspects of the middleware that you are using.

Container Security

Let's now look at the security in the container itself. In a series of calls from bean to bean within a container, the specification states that the principal is propagated from one bean to another; that is, bean 2 does not authenticate the principal that has been propagated from bean 1. As we discussed in Chapter 2, the deployer enables this propagation by configuring runAs-specified-identity or use-caller-identity, which are used on inter- or intra- container calls. Is this a problem? Well, it depends on the specific situation. As stated in Chapter 1, security is basically risk management. This means that you should assess the value of the information that you are trying to protect, and then trade off the value of that information against the system constraints imposed by different levels of security. System constraints, as a result of differing levels of security, can be measured in terms of performance, cost, and user inconvenience.

What are the types of problems that you should look for when the caller's identity is propagated from one entity to another? For one thing, be sure that the calling principal is not one that has authority or capabilities beyond what you expect the bean to be allowed to do. When you are using externally purchased beans, assess the reputation of the bean provider because you are essentially sending data to a black box that you purchased from that bean provider. Are the deployment descriptors for the container reviewed before a .jar file containing the new set of EJBs is allowed into the container? Have you reviewed the principals that would be enabled by the runAs call? Remember that as the number of interactions increases, the security assessment becomes harder.

Should you be paranoid? When the degree of your paranoia matches the sensitivity of the data, that is what risk management is all about. Therefore, understand the type of data the called bean is being sent or may return and depending on the sensitivity of that data, carry out an appropriate investigation of a new bean. This investigation of a new bean or beans may go as far as developing and running your own series of test cases on the new bean commensurate with what is at risk.

Security between Containers

Today, the bulk of the protection is at the boundary between the perimeter and the mid-tier, and it should be noted that this boundary transition to EJB or CORBA is not standardized. However, we've pointed out in previous chapters that insiders acting in the mid-tier commit many of the reported security violations. With the popularity of e-commerce, you may be permitting customers or other businesses inside your firewall, which vastly increases the number of insiders. Given these facts, determine the risk factor for an insider to substitute a malicious or badly written bean into a container that would let a customer or others gain access to your internal network.

When you are making calls between containers, especially if the call is to a container in another company or to a container supplied by a provider that you have not dealt with before, the risk level increases. The EJB security, in either case, depends on the security provided by CSIv2. This is the same interoperability standard that controls the security in CORBA and by extension the security between a CORBA application and an EJB container.

EJB and CORBA Transport Protocols

Before we can dive into CSIv2, we need to provide you with an overview of the two transport protocols used by EJB and CORBA: RMI and IIOP. You'll need to understand IIOP in order to understand CSIv2 because CSIv2 is built on IIOP.

You'll also need to understand RMI because EJB talks directly to RMI, and since EJB specification version 1.1, RMI has been layered over IIOP. CORBA objects themselves talk directly to IIOP. Therefore, the lingua franca of EJB and CORBA is IIOP. The illustration in Figure 6.1 helps to disambiguate this mouthful of acronyms.

Figure 6.1 contains a simplified picture of data passing from a client to a server using the RMI over IIOP stack. In this diagram, you see that the client transport stack on the left consists of the application at the top, which passes data to the RMI layer, which then passes data to the IIOP layer. The data is then passed over to the server using the IIOP protocol. The IIOP layer on the server side passes the data up to the RMI layer, which passes the data to the application.

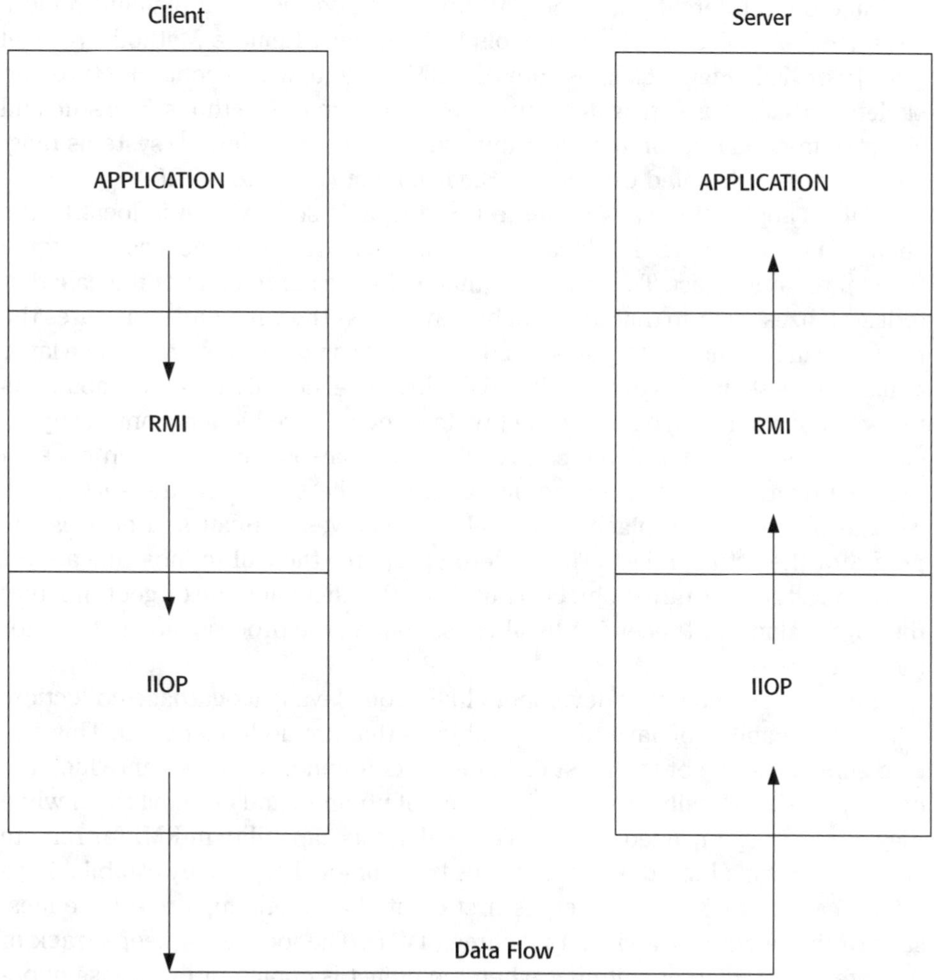

Figure 6.1 Data flow through EJB and CORBA stacks.

With this introduction, let's look at the various protocols involved in moving data from one process to another in more depth. We start by providing an overview of the Java mechanism, RMI. We then follow this overview with a description of the CORBA IIOP protocol. Finally, we look at the first attempt at interoperability between EJB and CORBA, namely RMI over IIOP.

RMI

RMI is a Java transport architecture and set of APIs that makes it possible for remote Java objects talk to each other. A goal of RMI is to conceal the low-level details of accessing a remote object for the developer. By using the APIs of the RMI architecture, developers can write their code as though they are calling a local method when they are actually calling an object in a different virtual machine on a different platform. RMI makes it possible to implement remote calls using a choice of wire protocols like the Java Remote Method Protocol (JRMP) or IIOP. Figure 6.2 illustrates the RMI system, which contains stubs and skeletons that act as surrogates or proxies to the remote methods. The stub and skeleton method is a common method used by most middleware systems ranging from the Distributed Computing Environment (DCE) to CORBA.

A client application calls a method on the RMI stub, which is local to the client. To the client, this is a local method call. The stub code acts as a proxy to the real remote object. The stub code marshalls the parameters of the call; that is, it serializes them so that they can be sent across the wire, and it prepares the method call for transfer to the target. It then calls on the remote reference layer to handle the semantics of the call and the low-level details. This layer abstracts the way the call is made so that the low-level details are hidden from the application developer. Finally, the call reaches the transport layer, which does all the dirty work of setting up the actual call to the server. At the server, the reverse process takes place. The skeleton receives the call and acts as the proxy for the actual object. The skeleton prepares the call to look like a local call and calls on the target object. Thus, both the client and the target think that they are making and receiving local calls, making the process much easier for the developer.

One of the features that developers like about Java is its garbage collection, which is the ability of Java to delete objects that are no longer used. This feature eliminates one of the most difficult tasks found in C or C++ in which the developer is responsible for keeping track of pointers and deleting them when they are no longer needed. Java has extended this capability in RMI for remote calls. When using RMI, the system keeps track of local objects by establishing a reference count when the object is first created and sending a reference message to the remote Java virtual machine (JVM). The local JVM keeps track of the reference by incrementing it when the object is copied or otherwise duplicated and decrementing it when an object duplicate is deleted. When the last

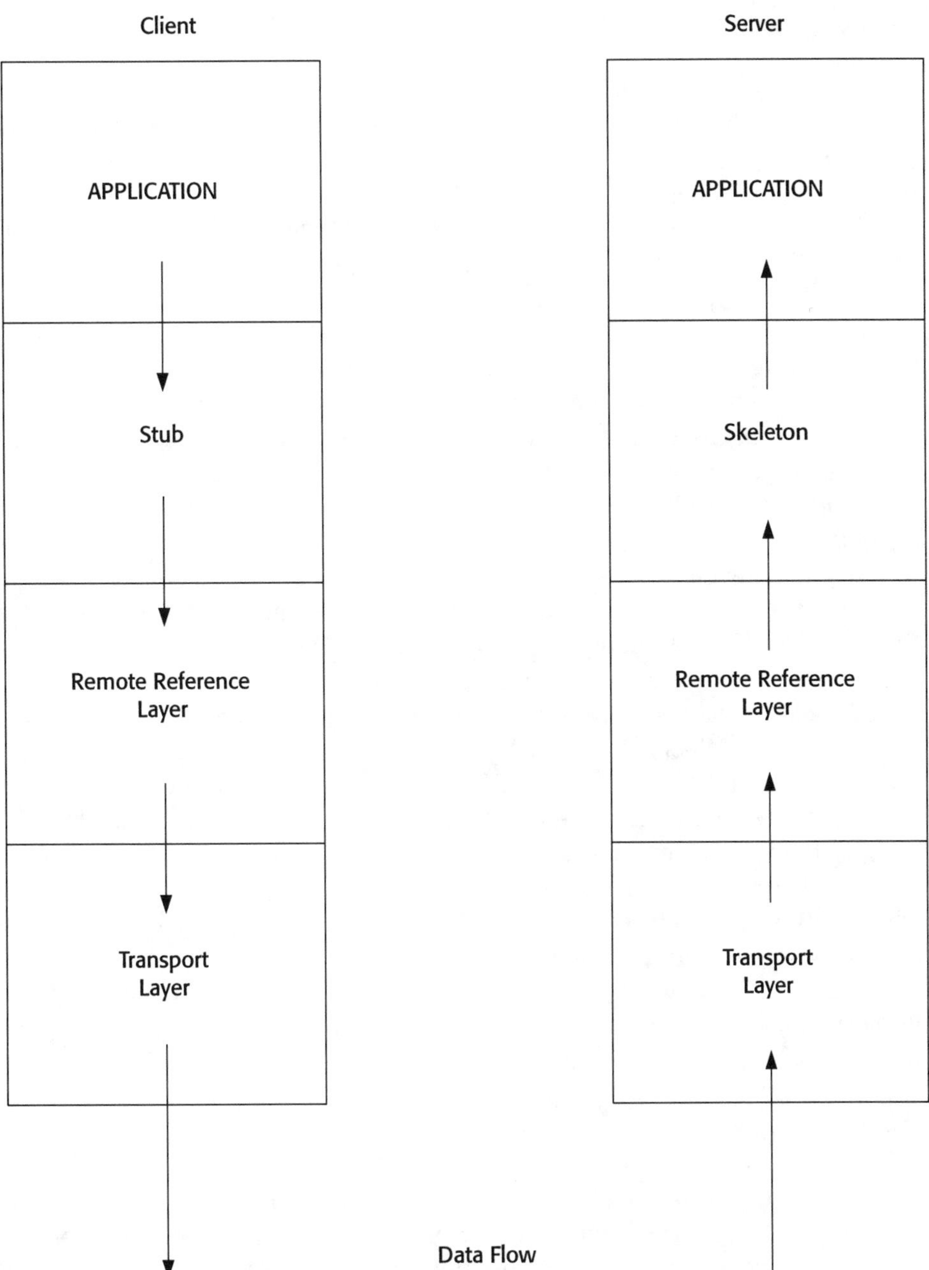

Figure 6.2 RMI transport stack.

local reference to an object is deleted, an unreference message is sent to the remote machine. When no other local references to the object exist, the JVM garbage collector deletes the object. The actual implementation of remote garbage collection has subtleties that we will not go into in this brief overview of RMI.

There are some limitations to RMI. RMI is a Java only transport. That is, it only works with Java clients and servers. These limitations allowed the RMI designers the freedom to hide the complexity of the transport code behind familiar Java interfaces. In addition to being limited to Java remote calls, RMI has its own, unique transport protocol JRMP.When using JRMP, an RMI enabled client can only talk to an RMI enabled server. As you will soon see, RMI capabilities have been expanded with the extension of RMI over IIOP.

As with all remote calls, the calling object needs to locate its target. It does this by getting a remote reference to the target object. RMI supports a simple naming mechanism called the *rmiregistry*. Target objects register their object references with the rmiregistry keyed by a name. The client can then call on the registry, passing it the object's name, and receive an object reference to the remote object. The client can use this object reference to make a remote call on the object.

The remaining mystery is, where do the stubs and skeletons come from? The creation of stubs and skeletons is handled by running the Java code through the RMI compiler. The RMI compiler inspects the Java code and wherever it finds a remote call, it creates stub and skeleton methods to handle the transport work.

As far as security goes, RMI relies on the security of the underlying transport, generally Secure Sockets Layer (SSL), to provide authentication and protect remote calls and replies. Unlike IIOP, which we discuss in the next section, security is essentially transparent to RMI. The RMI team is actively working on security extensions for the RMI JRMP transport layer. The Java Community Process (JCP) program has approved the Java Specification Request (JSR) 76, which defines a high-level set of APIs for RMI. JSR 76 covers basic security mechanisms, including delegation, confidentiality, and integrity. We should see a specification in answer to JSR 76 that will facilitate service providers in making authentication services available to container providers. Stay tuned to your favorite specifications for security in RMI.

IIOP

IIOP is the CORBA remote invocation protocol that does similar work to that done by RMI. The IIOP protocol consists of the General Inter-ORB Protocol (GIOP) message structures, Interoperable Object Requests (IOR), and a means of encoding requests/replies for over the wire transport called the Common Data Representation (CDR). This protocol uses TCP/IP as the underlying transport.

The IOR is constructed by the target and contains information necessary for a client to find the target, such as hostname and port, and information on how to find the correct method in the target process. The IOR also contains a list of what the CORBA specification calls *tagged profiles*. A profile can be broken down into multiple components. The components that we are interested in are the *security components*. These components have an identifier, assigned by OMG, to distinguish the different security mechanisms that a target supports. The detailed security data for a particular security mechanism is contained in its component. One of the jobs of CSIv2 is to define the security data and format of the data that is placed in the respective security components.

The IOR structure is reduced to a bit stream, which can be transported over the wire. This bit stream representation of the IOR is called the *object reference*. A client can read an object reference to find the target and, for our interest, determine what security information the target supports and requires. The object reference can be transmitted to the client in a number of different ways. It can be passed as a parameter in a call to a client, retrieved from a naming service, placed in a mutually accessible file, or even written on a piece of paper and passed around as in a 1950s spy movie. The most popular way to transmit the object reference to the client is for the target to register its object reference in a naming service and have the client retrieve it from the naming service.

Once a client acquires an object reference, it can determine what security mechanisms the target supports and what the target requires of the client. For example, the target might require that the messages that the client sends be encrypted and that the client authenticate itself to the target. This way the client can set up its security in such a way that the target will accept its messages. It might be that the client cannot meet the requirements of the target, and it might drop its request, try a different request, or try to negotiate some lesser requirements with the target.

IIOP uses TCP/IP as its basic transport mechanism. What IIOP does is describe how to use GIOP with TCP/IP. Figure 6.3 illustrates what the IIOP stack looks like.

GIOP defines all the nitty-gritty transfer syntax. For example, it defines how all the data types are constructed for wire transfer. It also defines the message formats that are passed between the client and the target. For security, we are especially interested in the definition of the request and reply headers. GIOP defines a slot in these headers, called the Service Context, which CSIv2 uses to pass security data.

Because CORBA and thus IIOP were designed to work with multiple languages, a new specification language was developed by the OMG, which is used to map to the traditional languages like C, C++, and so on. This specification language, which is called the Interface Definition Language (IDL), is used to define all the remote interfaces that a given CORBA program uses.

Once you have defined your remote interfaces in IDL, the next step is to compile them using an IDL compiler. There are IDL compilers written for all the popular programming languages. If the target language is C, C++, COBOL, Java, ADA, or any one of the supported languages, you use the IDL compiler for that

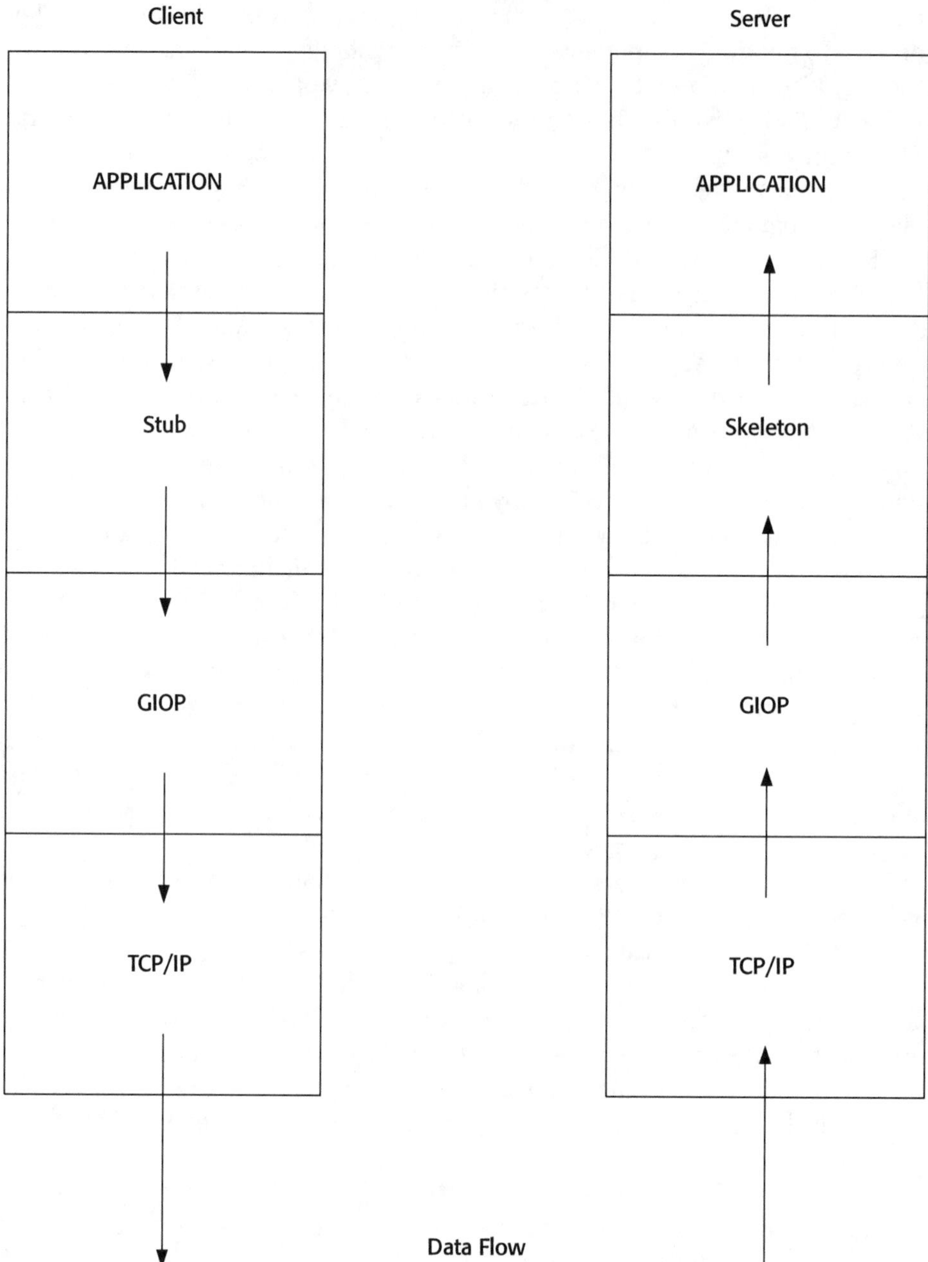

Figure 6.3 IIOP transport stack.

language. Similar to the RMI compiler, the IDL compiler creates a stub and a skeleton. In this case, the stubs and skeletons are written in the target language of your choice and support the IIOP protocol for remote transport. The practical result of this is that you can write a distributed program in the language of your choice and your program will be able to talk to another CORBA program written in the same or a different language.

The advantage of GIOP over TCP/IP, or IIOP, is that it is designed to accept requests directly from an object and send replies to the object without any specific ORB architecture requirements. It is also general enough to be used with EJB components. Sun and IBM, recognizing this advantage and desiring to enhance the interoperability of Java, led the development of a specification for RMI over IIOP that was adapted for use with Java. This approach is discussed in the next section.

RMI over IIOP

RMI was incorporated into Java with the Java 1.1 release. As stated earlier, RMI makes coding remote calls from Java easy in that all the developer has to do is run his or her Java code through a compiler to produce the stubs and skeletons. In the CORBA world, the developer has to write the remote interfaces in a language neutral way using IDL, and then compile this code to produce the stubs and skeletons. This means that the developer has to learn another language, IDL. The use of IDL is necessary to permit CORBA to support a number of different languages.

Recognizing the relative simplicity of RMI and the interoperability and robustness of IIOP, IBM and Sun teamed up to write the RMI over IIOP specification. Using RMI over IIOP, Java developers can run their Java code through the RMI compiler to produce the stubs and skeletons without learning the IDL language. The resultant code can interoperate with CORBA programs written in different languages.

To get RMI and IIOP to work together, OMG wrote two additional specifications: Object by Value and the Java to IDL mapping. CORBA objects that are passed using the Object by Value specification pass additional information about an object such as its state and language level operations. In this way an object can be reconstructed at the target; Java/RMI uses pass by value in many instances. The second specification, Java to IDL mapping, worked out the low-level inconsistencies between Java and IDL and defined a mapping between the two languages. These two extensions to CORBA allowed the construction of compilers to take Java code and produce stubs and skeletons consistent with those produced from IDL and thus consistent with IIOP. On the RMI side, a few slight changes to the RMI APIs allowed RMI to work with both its native transport JRMP and IIOP.

RMI over IIOP supports interoperability between CORBA and Java. However, although RMI over IIOP is a prerequisite to secure interoperability, this protocol alone does not support interoperability between the security services of EJB and CORBA. This is where CSIv2 comes in.

Common Secure Interoperability Version 2

In this section, we will finally describe the CSIv2 specification. The purpose of this CSIv2 description is to help you understand the technology, so that you can use it effectively in making EJB and CORBA work together and make intelligent choices in implementations that use the technology. After you finish this chapter, you will have enough information to make the choices with respect to the variations that CSIv2 supplies to satisfy your distributed requirements.

CSIv2 addresses the problem of defining a wire format to transfer security data between CORBA to CORBA objects, J2EE to J2EE objects, and between CORBA and J2EE objects. You might wonder; what is a wire security format? It is the detailed specification of the bits that the security data must conform to when being passed from one process to another process. It also defines where in the message the security data must be placed as well as the protocol that the security data must follow. If a target knows that the security data must follow these specifications, then it can unambiguously interpret the security data and make judgements on how to use the security data that it receives from a client.

There was a previous Common Secure Interoperability (CSI) specification written into the original CORBASec specification. However, the previous CSI portion of the security specification was too loosely written for CORBASec for one vendor to interpret the data from another vendor. Not only does CSIv2 solve the secure interoperability problem between CORBA implementations from different vendors, but also with the cooperation and hard work of Sun Microsystems representing the EJB specification, CSIv2 went a long way to solving the secure interoperability issues between CORBA and EJB. The CSIv2 specification is a significant step for developers working on systems that use distributed objects, which we would venture to say, is the majority of developers working on large projects.

The objective of the CSIv2 specification is to define the wire protocol of CORBA objects, that is, the format and rules to send the security information from a client to a server in order to support the secure interoperability between that client and server. A second important objective is to support secure interoperability between EJB and CORBA. The team that wrote this specification did a lot of low-level work to create an effective interoperability solution.

Because this book is aimed at the user of security services rather than those who build the security services, we will skip the low-level details and only describe what is required for you to be able to take advantage of the CSIv2 standard. You will be able to use this knowledge to understand how the EJB and CORBA products that you use can interoperate and determine for yourself how to best use the capabilities of CSIv2 in your enterprise.

CSIv2 defines three logical layers that are used to transfer the security credentials from a client to a target. The designers of the protocol chose these three layers because they needed a security protocol that would transfer these fundamental, conceptual pieces of security information. The layers are as follows:

- Authorization layer (or Attribute layer)
- Authentication layer
- Transport layer

The first two layers are the subject of a new protocol defined by CSIv2: the secure attribute service (SAS). The transport layer supports the security mechanism that you choose—for example, Transport Layer Security (TLS) or the Secure Inter-ORB Protocol (SECIOP). All three layers work together to support passing the security data, so that the target can satisfy all of its security requirements. The system supports a great deal of flexibility in the way you can set up different types of security between the client and the target. This flexibility is important because you will have different requirements for securing different resources and different activities. For example, if you have a client that wants to purchase an item and the purchase request has to pass through a different service to check the purchaser's purchasing power, then you will need one of the forms of delegation supported by CSIv2. Another example is the option to trade off performance for complexity in the client. We show you how to use the flexibility of CSIv2 in this section. But first, let's start with a client that wants to securely pass some information to a target.

The first part of the protocol, which passes the authorization security information, is not as straightforward as it may seem. SAS uses the service context in the request or reply header as defined by the GIOP protocol to pass most of the security data. The SAS protocol defines how authorization data is passed from the client to the target. We'll use the term attribute layer as defined by the CSIv2 specification as the name of the layer used to pass the principal attributes. The attribute layer uses a Privilege Attribute Certificate (PAC) to pass the privilege attribute data. The PAC's main purpose is to standardize the structure used to securely pass the privilege attributes. The CSIv2 authors preferred to use existing standards wherever they could, so they chose an existing PAC standard defined by the Internet Engineering Task Force (IETF). We provide a detailed description of a PAC later in this section.

The second layer of CSIv2 supports authentication. In some cases, the security mechanism in the transport layer handles authentication. For example, SSL supports client authentication when the target requires that the client provide authentication based on a public key certificate (PKC). In cases in which the underlying security transport does not support authentication, the CSIv2 authentication layer will do the job. However, CSIv2-supported authentication may not be as strong as cryptographically based transport layer authentication because the most common method supported by the CSIv2 authentication layer is username and password. Corporations can get the added security of authentication at the transport layer for some of their clients, while allowing CSIv2 to support the simpler username and password authentication for less critical clients. The CSIv2 authentication layer also includes support for any Generic Security Service Application Program Interface (GSSAPI) request/reply mechanism so an implementation could use a strong authentication mechanism, such as Kerberos GSSAPI.

The third layer defined by CSIv2 is the transport layer. In this layer, CSIv2 uses the Transport Layer Security (TLS) as the security mechanism, which all conforming security services must support. TLS is a security mechanism standardized by the IETF and is based on SSL. The first release of TLS contains only minor changes from SSL and is backward compatible with SSL. The main advantage of TLS is that it is an updated version of SSL that is supported by a standards body. Practically speaking, the name TLS is synonymous with SSL because SSL is the commonly accepted name for this technology. We will use the terms TLS and SSL interchangeably in this chapter.

A CSIv2 security service can work with other secure transports, such as the Secure Inter-ORB Protocol (SECIOP), but it must support TLS/SSL so that there is at least one security mechanism that a client and target have in common.

Therefore, in CSIv2, we have three layers that support the basic trio of security: authorization, authentication, and message protection. This may sound all neat and tidy, but once again, things are not so simple. People want more flexibility in using security. We already mentioned one example of flexibility: SSL can supply authentication in the transport layer through the use of SSL client and server certificates negating the need for the CSIv2 authentication layer. Another situation in which flexibility is required in using these layers is when we want to use delegation. We'll introduce and explain the rationale for these complicating factors one by one in the remainder of this section.

Another element of flexibility that CSIv2 supports and one that you will find useful is *stateless* and *stateful* connections. A stateful connection is when the target retains information about a particular security connection so that verification of the client only has to be done the first time the connection is made. In a stateless connection, the client verification is carried out on every request because the server retains no knowledge of the security of the request. The CSIv2 protocol defines security information that is passed between the client and server so that they can negotiate transfer of security information either by stateless or stateful means.

The advantage of a stateless connection is that it results in a lightweight target; that is, it does not have to retain any information from one call to the next. The downside is that a stateless connection incurs a performance penalty. Because the target does not keep the security state of all its clients, its performance is degraded by the need to verify the authentication evidence on every call from the client to the target. The performance penalty can be heavy if you are using an expensive authentication method, a large number of attributes, or delegation. In these cases, you might want to use a stateful connection. On the other hand, the performance penalty can be negligible if you are using propagation from a trusted intermediate. We'll provide you with the details on propagation and trust a little later. Note that CSIv2 only requires stateless connections and does not mandate stateful connections, so not all middleware suppliers will give you the choice of stateful connections. In fact, the EJB version 2.0 specification only supports the stateless protocol.

The important point for you in choosing stateless or stateful security is whether you will need a stateful transfer for performance reasons and if so, whether your security service supports it. If you determine that you want a stateful transfer and your security service supports it, then you have to determine how your security service lets you set a stateful mode.

In the following sections, we discuss other flexibility items in CSIv2 in each of the three layers defined by the specification: the authorization (attribute), the authentication, and the transport layers. Through no accident, these layers match the fundamental divisions of security. CSIv2 specifies what security information is passed between a client and a target in each of these layers. As you have seen, there is a lot of flexibility in the type of security data that is passed in each of the CSIv2 layers. Consequently, the CSIv2 protocol provides an architecture that supports several different security solutions.

CSIv2 Attribute Layer

In CSIv2, the attribute layer can carry two types of information:

- A set of client privilege attributes defined in an *authorization token*
- A client identity defined in an *identity token*

These tokens are both optional, and their use depends on the level of CSIv2 support provided by the security service, as we'll explain in a later section. Roles are a familiar type of client privilege attribute, which we discussed in Chapter 2. The CSIv2 authorization token supports the privilege attributes defined by the IETF specification in "An Internet Attribute Certificate Profile for Authorization" (S. Farrell and R. Housley, draft-ietf-pkix-ac509prof-05.txt).In addition to roles, the attributes specified in this specification include groups, access identity, charging identity, and clearance.

The Authorization Token

As defined by the IETF Attribute Certificate specification previously mentioned, privilege attributes are contained in an *authorization token* called a PAC. PACs provide a standard way for a client to pass its attributes to a target; the target may then make an access control decision based on the client's attributes (e.g., a client acting in the role of an administrator). PACs are similar to identity certificates in that they are issued and digitally signed by a trusted authority. When an authorization token is implemented carefully, it is difficult for an attacker to steal a PAC and use its attributes. Unlike identity certificates, PACs may be issued for specific applications and are usually short-lived, having a validity period of a few hours or less.

PACs are encoded using the Abstract Syntax Notation Number One (ASN.1) structure. ASN.1 is an international standard supported by the International Telecommunications Union (ITU), which defines a format for encoding data types that can be transferred easily over the wire. (By the way, this is one of the few standards for which you have to pay! The price is about 22 Swiss Francs.) We're not going to go into an explanation of ASN.1 except to discuss using it as an aid for reading the PAC notation. ASN.1 has a format for the binary representation of an element, each of which is composed of a tuple of type, length, and value. It also has a human readable form that is used to describe ASN.1 structures.

The top level definition of a PAC in the human readable form of the ASN.1 notation is:

```
AttributeCertificate ::= SEQUENCE {
     acinfo               AttributeCertificateInfo,
     signatureAlgorithm   AlgorithmIdentifier,
     signatureValue       BIT STRING
}

AttributeCertificateInfo ::= SEQUENCE {
     version              AttCertVersion DEFAULT v1,
     holder               Holder,
     issuer               AttCertIssuer,
     signature            AlgorithmIdentifier,
     serialNumber         CertificateSerialNumber,
     attrCertValidityPeriod   AttCertValidityPeriod,
     attributes           SEQUENCE OF Attribute,
     issuerUniqueID       UniqueIdentifier OPTIONAL,
     extensions           Extensions OPTIONAL
}
```

SEQUENCE is an ASN.1 structure that can roughly be compared to a list of heterogeneous elements. As you can see, SEQUENCEs can be nested; for example, the AttributeCertificateInfo is nested within the AttributeCertificate. A PAC's first element is a version number field. Each of the elements are broken down further. For example, the version is an integer, which in ASN.1 can be of any size and not limited to a machine size.

The holder field defines the owner of the PAC, that is, the identity for whom or what the PAC represents. The holder can take one of three forms. The most common form used when the transport security is SSL is represented by a pointer to the definition of the owner in the SSL certificate, which is passed in the transport layer. The pointer consists of the name of the Certificate Authority (CA) that issued the certificate and the serial number of that particular certificate. The CA name and serial number are contained in the SSL certificate;

thus, the PAC is tied to that particular SSL certificate because the combination of CA name and serial number uniquely defines a certificate. Therefore, the pointer in the PAC defines the identity in the accompanying SSL certificate. In this way, PACs for a particular owner are tightly bound to the authentication evidence of that owner.

The holder can alternately be represented by the owner's name or by the third option, an ObjectDigestInfo. The latter representation incorporates in the Holder field a hash of a link to the owner, for example, its public key.

The issuer is the name of the Attribute Authority (AA) that issued the PAC. The signature field identifies the cryptographic algorithm that is used to sign the PAC. The serialNumber is a unique number for that AA; that is, the combination of the AA name and the serialNumber must be unique in the PAC.

The attrCertValidityPeriod is the time period for which this PAC is valid.

The attributes field is a list of the attributes that have been assigned to the holder of the PAC by the issuing AA. These attributes are the information that the security service is interested in transferring from the client to the server. The PAC binds the attributes to the owner and provides evidence to verify the integrity of that binding.

The issuerUniqueID is a field that is usually not used.

The extensions fields are additional fields that may be used in a PAC. CSIv2 uses one of the extension fields; we will cover this later

The last two items in the PAC, the signatureAlgorithm and the signatureValue, are used to cryptographically sign the PAC. The signatureAlgorithm is the name of the cryptographic algorithm used. The signatureValue is the actual digital signature of the PAC. A digital signature is formed by computing a one-way hash of what is to be signed, in this case the PAC, and then encrypting the hash with the private key of the AA. The hash of the PAC results in a unique value. If even one bit of the document is changed, there is an extremely high probability that the computation will result in a different hash value.

The target security service verifies the PAC signature by decrypting the hash value with the AA's public key, and then rehashing the PAC and comparing the two hash values. If the hash values match, then the target knows that the PAC has not been modified since the AA signed it. Because the AA's public key could decrypt the correct hash value, the target knows that the PAC was signed by the AA for which the target has the public key, and that public key must be that of the issuer of the PAC. Thus, the target can trust the PAC if the target trusts the AA. Next, you will see what is needed to trust the AA.

CSIv2 specifies that the client may pass a list of one or more X.509 PKCs that identify the AA. Each PKC is used as verification evidence of the previous certificate in the chain. The PKC that follows the PAC is used by the target security service to verify the AA that signed the PAC. The target verifies the PKC by using the signature in the same way that the target used the signature in the PAC to verify the PAC. The reason that there may be a list of PKCs is to support a certificate hierarchy; the target might not directly trust the AA that signed the PAC.

In that case, the target would move down the chain until the target finds a PKC from an entity that the target trusts. At that point, the target has the public key of the trusted entity and uses that public key to verify the PKC. The public key is usually contained in a PKC from the trusted authority that the target obtained in some out-of-band method. For example, you might have received the PKC from the authority in person, by certified mail, or by some other means.

Figure 6.4 shows a chain of X.509 PKCs that verify the user's PAC. The user's PAC is verified by the X.509 PKC of the AA that issued the PAC. The AA in turn is verified by the Certificate Authority (CA) that issued the X.509 certificate to

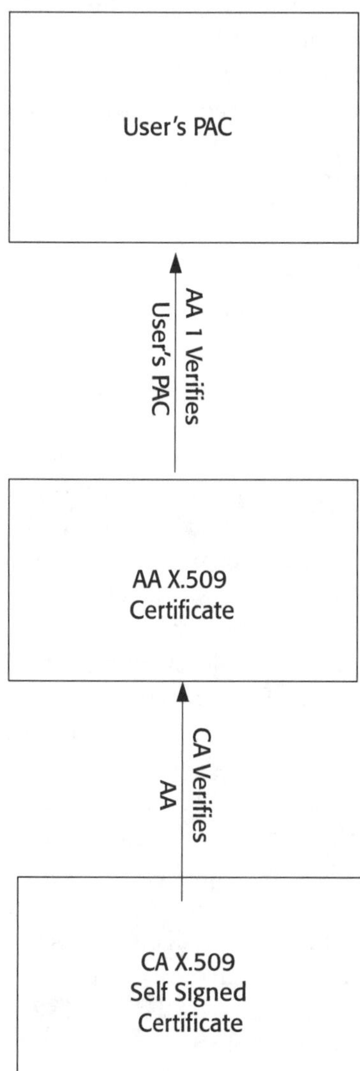

Figure 6.4 Certificate chain.

ESI SECURITY ASSOCIATION PRINCIPLE: DESIGN FOR FAILURE

PACs are digitally signed and bound to an underlying authentication identity. These countermeasures reduce an attacker's ability to tamper with the PAC contents or masquerade as the client. As a result, PACs are effective at preventing a successful insider attack from propagating through a corporate network. If a malicious attacker obtains a PAC that does not permit impersonation, it is very difficult for the attacker to exploit the PAC to get access to other mid-tier applications.

the AA. The CA's certificate is a self-signed certificate. That is, the CA's certificate is not verified by any higher authority. This certificate, called the *root certificate*, is a certificate that the target security service trusts, although the target may stop at the AA's certificate if it trusts the AA. If the target does not trust any of the certificates in the chain, the PAC is not valid and the target will deny the client's request. This chain of certificates may be arbitrarily long. It may consist of a PAC and the AA's authentication certificate, or it may have a chain of three, four, or more certificates.

Normally, PACs have a short lifetime, usually just days or weeks, and authentication evidence whether in the form of a PKC or a password have a much longer lifetime. PKCs usually have a lifetime of a year or more. This is because a CA who issues the PKC, for instance, an SSL certificate, has to carry out an investigation of the principal to ensure that principals are who they say they are. This takes time, effort, and money. On the other hand, an AA who issues PACs can verify the principal by verifying their PKCs, and then issue a PAC using the previously stored attributes of that principal.

Other reasons for the short life of a PAC are to reduce the probability of spoofing of the PAC, to let a principal change its attributes when making requests to different targets, and to support the issuance of PACs by AAs tied to the target.

Now that we've defined the authorization token, we move on to the other token in the CSIv2 attribute layer, namely the identity token.

The Identity Token

The *identity token*, which can be a list of PKCs or simply a name, is a new concept introduced in CSIv2. This token is used to represent the identity of the issuing client, that is, the "spoken for" principal. Using the information from the three layers—attribute, authentication, and transport—the target can determine if some form of delegation is being used. In the identity assertion case, the intermediate merely asserts that the target should use the principal defined by the identity token. We'll discuss delegation further in a later section.

The CSIv2 attribute layer may be thought of as one of the ways that a target discovers the identity and other characteristics of the initiating caller. In CSIv2 there are other ways for a client to send evidence of who it represents. The next section introduces the authentication layer in which the username and password is passed, followed by a section on the transport layer in which security mechanism evidence can be passed.

CSIv2 Authentication Layer

If you want to use a username and password combination for authentication rather than or in addition to SSL certificates, then the username and password authentication evidence is passed in the CSIv2 authentication layer using a *client authentication token.* When a username and password is used, it is not necessary to pass authentication data in the transport layer. CSIv2 defines a mechanism for the username and password called GSSUP. The CSIv2 specification uses the Generic Security Service (GSS) specification as a model in a number of its internal structure definitions because its writers wanted to stay as close to existing specifications as possible, and also because they wanted to allow for the use of other GSSAPI mechanisms, such as Kerberos. The structure of GSSUP as defined in the CSIv2 specification is as follows:

```
typedef sequence <octet> GSSToken;
sequence <octet> UTF8String;

// GSSUP::InitialContextToken
struct InitialContextToken {
        Security::UTF8String username;
        Security::UTF8String password;
        CSI::GSS_NT_ExportedName target_name;
};
```

The target_name field of the GSSUP:: IntialContext contains the name of the authentication domain in which the client is authenticating.

You might have noticed that all the values are UTF8Strings. UTF8 is an encoding that supports character sets that cannot be contained within the limited 127 ASCII character set, such as many of the languages that use characters that are not in the English character set. For example, the Chinese language contains thousands of characters. UTF8 can use more than one byte to define a character and thus can handle the thousands of Chinese characters as well as other non-ASCII characters. UTF8 characters that are in the ASCII set reduce to the one byte ASCII representation of those characters.

One reason that CSIv2 uses GSSUP is to integrate with authentication systems that require you to provide an unencrypted password. The password

ESI SECURITY ASSOCIATION PRINCIPLE: DESIGN FOR FAILURE

Transmitting passwords in the clear, even on an internal corporate network behind firewalls, is poor security practice. If your network is accessible by a hostile insider, all of your passwords will be exposed and your entire system will be compromised. Better practice is to use transport security to protect password transmissions. This approach is still dangerous, however, because the receiving application must be trusted to protect passwords. If a single application that handles passwords is compromised, the attacker will have broad system access. Best of all is not to transmit passwords at all and to rely on cryptographic authentication methods, which eliminates vulnerability to this class of attack.

contained in the client authentication token is transported in the clear (unencrypted). What? Did I hear you say "in the clear"? Remember that CSIv2 is predicated on a transport layer security, such as SSL, to protect the messages. If you have chosen to have messages encrypted by SSL (which you should!), the SSL handshake that sets up the SSL protection takes place before any messages are transmitted, so that the password is encrypted during transmission by SSL. In that case, your password is safely sent to the server. An important warning: *If you do not choose transport encryption, then your password is available to any hacker who can sniff your wires.* Intercepting packets containing passwords is fairly straightforward for an attacker. If you are sending unencrypted messages over the Internet, your password is obviously at risk. If for some reason you can't use SSL to protect your password, you can encrypt the password yourself. This requires a prior arrangement with the target identifying the encryption algorithm so that the target can decrypt the password. It is a lot easier to use SSL encryption and let the system do the work.

Part of the system might be using Kerberos names and another part might be using X.500 names. The receiving system uses the target name to determine the name type it should use to interpret the username.

CSIv2 Transport Layer

The transport layer in CSIv2 is conceptually the simplest of the three layers if you are using the required SSL protocol. SSL can supply encryption, integrity, target authentication, and if required by the target, client authentication.

CSIv2 requires that an implementation supports SSL and optionally can support the SECIOP mechanism defined in the preceding CSI specification.

You have seen the three security layers—namely attribute, authentication, and transport—defined by CSIv2. The next section shows how the three layers work together to transmit and delegate credentials from client to server.

Credentials and Privilege Delegation in CSIv2

Privilege delegation occurs when a client (the initiator) gives some intermediate server the right to use the client's credentials to do work on the client's behalf. On the surface, this sounds simple enough, but as we dig deeper into delegation, we will see that it can get very complex. In this section, we describe delegation support in CSIv2. We describe delegation in general and advise you on the use of delegation in Chapter 8.

The simplest type of delegation is when a client gives an intermediate server the right to act as the client in all situations; that is, the intermediate server impersonates the client. This can be pretty dangerous unless the client trusts that server not to do anything harmful to the client, such as withdraw all your money from your bank account. A delegation model called *unconstrained delegation* (or *impersonation*) permits any intermediate to act on the client's behalf.* As you can imagine, this could become quite dangerous as your delegated identity is passed from intermediate to intermediate. You wouldn't give this intermediate program the right to impersonate you unless you trusted the total environment in which your client, all intermediates, and the final target of the delegated call were running. In any case, be very careful about where you permit others to impersonate your client.

Let's look at a common example in which you might use impersonation that relies on trust. When you deal with your bank, you trust that the bank will assume the responsibility of treating your electronic banking activities securely, so that no harm comes to your monies. The bank itself may be using delegation as it moves your requests from department computer to department computer to satisfy your request. Therefore, the bank has to assure itself that there are no rogue programs or back doors into its programs, which might allow a delegated identity to be stolen. You have established a trust relationship with your bank, and you expect the bank to rectify any mistakes that its system might cause. This trust relationship is supported by banking laws and the government banking authorities. So in terms of risk management, you probably feel that the risk is commensurate with your need for banking facilities as long as the bank has been authenticated as your bank. In this case, unconstrained delegation within the bank is probably acceptable.

CSIv2 supports more than impersonation. A second form of supported delegation is *restricted (or constrained) delegation*. In constrained delegation, the client names the intermediates that it trusts. From a security standpoint, restricted delegation is a major improvement over impersonation. Restricted delegation significantly limits the number of intermediate servers that are trusted to use a client's credentials, and as a result is less risky than impersonation.

---

*There is still debate over the precise definition of "impersonation." For consistency, we use the definition from CORBASec (OMG, 2000a).

In CSIv2, restricted delegation is accomplished by using one of the extension fields in the PAC—the *proxy attributes* field called ProxyInfo. The proxy attributes field identifies proxies that are endorsed by the AA to proxy for the owner of the PAC. ProxyInfo is defined as:

```
ProxyInfo ::= SEQUENCE OF Targets where
Targets ::= SEQUENCE OF Target
```

The target is the name of an intermediate that can act as a delegate for the owner of the PAC. An honest intermediate can refuse to delegate if it is not listed in the named proxy attributes. Of course, a dishonest intermediate can ignore the proxy attributes and try to delegate anyway. The important check is for the next process in line. That is, the target of the intermediate checks the validity of the calling intermediate and rejects the delegated call if the target cannot validate that the intermediate is in the list of proxy attributes. If the target in the proxy attributes consists of the value "Any," then the type of delegation is unconstrained delegation, and any intermediate may use the PAC.

To give you an idea of the different ways that credentials and delegation may be supported in CSIv2, we'll walk through some examples. Figure 6.5 shows the general scenario of an initiating client object named P1 invoking on an intermediate object named P2. The intermediate P2 then invokes on a target object.

Figure 6.5 also shows the CSIv2 credentials tokens that may be passed from intermediate P2 to the target object as part of the SAS Service Context Protocol. The SAS protocol supports transmission of the authorization token (PAC) and identity token at the SAS security attribute layer, and the client authentication token at the SAS authentication layer. In addition, an identity may be transmitted by the underlying secure transport, such as an X.509 certificate via SSL.

For any particular use of CSIv2, the intermediate will typically transmit only some of these tokens. Table 6.1 provides examples of CSIv2 credentials that may be passed from intermediate P2 to the target object, and the validation checks made by the target object.

In all of the examples, the identity of intermediate object P2 is transmitted as the authentication identity of the calling principal. The identity of P2 may either

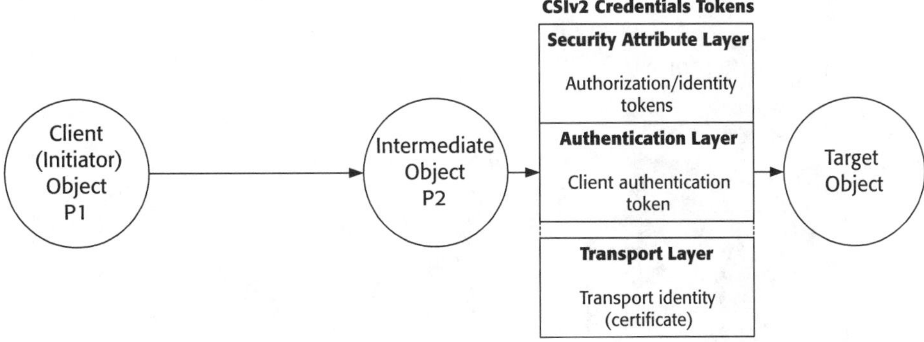

Figure 6.5 CSIv2 invocation scenario.

Table 6.1 Examples of CSIv2 Credentials Passed from Intermediate to Target

SECURITY LAYERS	1 NO DELEGATION	2 NO DELEGATION, PUSH PRIVILEGE ATTRIBUTES	3 IDENTITY ASSERTION-BASED DELEGATION, BACKWARD TRUST EVALUATION	4 AUTHORIZATION TOKEN-BASED DELEGATION, FORWARD TRUST EVALUATION	5 AUTHORIZATION TOKEN-BASED DELEGATION (RESTRICTED), FORWARD TRUST EVALUATION
Security Attribute Layer Authorization/ Identity tokens	—	P2 PAC	P1 identity token	P1 PAC, "Any" proxy attribute; P1 identity token	P1 PAC, P2 identity proxy attribute; P1 identity token
Authentication Identity Client authen-tication token or transport identity	P2 identity	P2 identity	P2 identity	P2 identity	P2 identity
Target Validation Checks	—	P2 PAC belongs to P2 identity	P2 permitted to speak for P1 identity based on rules on the target; presumed trust if target has no rules (impersonation)	P1 PAC belongs to P1 identity; "Any" proxy attribute permits any intermediate to use P1 PAC (unrestricted delegation/ impersonation)	P1 PAC belongs to P1 identity; P2 identity proxy attribute permits P2 to use P1 PAC (restricted delegation)

be transmitted by the CSIv2 SAS protocol as a client authentication token or by the underlying security transport layer (e.g., X.509 identity certificate using SSL). In either case, the target object first checks the validity of this authenticated identity to make sure that the caller really is P2. Note that the intermediate P2 never passes any authentication evidence for the client P1. The target trusts the intermediate to have authenticated the client. This trust must be established before the target can accept an invocation from the intermediate.

Example 1 shows the case of no delegation, in which intermediate P2 invokes on the target object with P2's own identity. In this case, there is no need for any attribute layer tokens to be transmitted. The target will make any subsequent authorization checks for the invocation using P2's identity. If the target needs to use security attributes associated with P2 (say, P2's roles), the target will pull (i.e., look up) the attributes from a security service.

Example 2 also shows the case of no delegation, but this time intermediate P2 also pushes along its privilege attributes in a PAC. Because the target receives P2's attributes in a PAC, there is no need for the target to look up the attributes. The target checks that the PAC it receives from P2 is bound to P2's authentication identity (i.e., the P2 PAC holder field matches P2's identity) to ensure that an attacker is not attempting to spoof using P2's PAC.

Example 3 is our first case of delegation. The intermediate P2 passes an identity token for the client P1 as well as its own authentication identity P2 as the calling principal. This example illustrates *identity assertion-based delegation* because the intermediate is asserting only P1's identity rather than any of P1's privilege attributes. If the target wants to check on additional attributes for P1 it has to pull them from a security service. The target uses its own rules to establish whether intermediate authentication identity P2 is trusted to speak for P1. CSIv2 defines validation of an identity assertion based on target rules as *backward trust evaluation.* CSIv2 defines target acceptance of an identity assertion without considering the authentication identity (i.e., transport or physical architecture ensures that only trustworthy intermediates can assert an identity) as *presumed trust.* Because the initiating client cannot impose restrictions on the use of its delegated identity, this is also an example of *impersonation.*

Example 4 is another case of delegation, in which the intermediate P2 passes P1's PAC, P1's identity token, and P2's own authentication identity as the calling principal. This example illustrates *authorization token-based delegation* because the intermediate is asserting P1's privilege attributes in the PAC. The target first checks that the P1 PAC it receives is bound to P1's identity token to ensure the basic integrity of the PAC. In this case, the check of the PAC owner uses the attribute layer identity token rather than the authentication identity as in example 2. The target detects delegation based on this comparison: if the PAC owner matches the authentication identity, delegation is *not* in effect; if the PAC owner matches the attribute layer identity token, delegation *is* in effect; if PAC owner matches *neither* identity, the target rejects the request and returns an exception. Finally, the target uses the information in the PAC proxy attributes to confirm that the authentication identity P2 is permitted to proxy for the PAC owner P1. Remember that the target trusts the intermediate so this check also depends on that trust since PACs may be publicly available. CSIv2 defines validation of delegation based on rules provided by the caller (the PAC proxy attributes) as *forward trust evaluation*. Since "Any" is the P1 PAC proxy attribute, any intermediate is permitted to proxy for this PAC. In this case delegation is *unrestricted*, which is also known as *impersonation*.

Our final example 5 is the last case of delegation, and is a variation of the authorization token-based delegation of example 4. As in the preceding example, the intermediate P2 passes P1's PAC, P1's identity token, and P2's own authentication identity as the calling principal. The target check of the P1 PAC against the P1 identity token is also the same. In this case, however, the P1 PAC has a proxy attribute that contains the P2 identity. This proxy attribute allows only P2 to proxy for this PAC, which illustrates *restricted delegation*.

The overarching principal in delegation is that when the intermediate asserts the identity or PAC of the spoken for principal the target needs to trust the intermediate to properly handle the identity of the initiating client. This trust can be established by some out-of-band method (presumed trust) or by using the normal authentication between the intermediate and target prior to the series of assertions by the intermediate.

In summary, we have the following variations on delegation and means to establish trustworthiness in CSIv2:

- **Authorization token-based delegation.** The intermediate passes authentication evidence and a PAC, which may contain a list of accessible intermediates, to some intermediate or target.
  - **Forward trust evaluation.** The target validates the delegation based on endorsement rules provided by the caller.
- **Identity assertion-based delegation.** The intermediate asserts the identity of a client by means of an identity token. The target trusts the intermediate to be truthful in its assertion.
  - **Backward trust evaluation.** The target applies its own rules to the client authentication identity and the asserted identity.
  - **Presumed trust.** The communication environment is such that only trusted intermediates can assert an identity. The target does not need to consider the authentication of the intermediate.

CSIv2 Association Options in the IOR

Security information about the target is transmitted to the client in the IOR. An important piece of information that the IOR contains is which security mechanisms the target supports—for example, SSL or SECIOP.

Another important type of information in the form of a bit field in the IOR is what security traits the target supports or requires. These are called the *association options*, many of which relate to our previous section on delegation and trust. Some of the more relevant association options are:

- **Integrity.** Target supports or requires integrity protected messages.
- **Confidentiality.** Target supports or requires encryption protected messages.
- **EstablishTrustInTarget.** Only "supports" is applicable. Supports means that the target can authenticate itself to the client.
- **EstablishTrustInClient.** Support means that the target can authenticate the client. Requires means that the target requires that the client authenticate itself.
- **IdentityAssertion.** Only supports is applicable. Supports means that the target can accept an asserted identity based on trust.
- **DelegationByClient.** Supports means that the target can evaluate trust in the intermediate based on information in the ProxyInfo field in the PAC, that is, a delegation token in conjunction with the supported IdentityAssertion bit. Requires means that the client must provide a delegation token permitting the intermediate to be a proxy for the client.

Conformance to CSIv2

An implementation can choose to support any of three levels of conformance to be CSIv2 compliant, namely conformance Level 0, Level 1, or Level 2. Each higher level includes the required functionality of the levels below it. The following list contains the conformance level requirements taken from the CSIv2 specification. It paraphrases some of the more exacting language in the specification to make the conformance easier to understand.

The EJB version 2.0 specification requires conformance with Level 0 only. Conformance Level 0 is the lowest or base level that an implementation can follow and be compliant. This level requires supporting:

- SSL/TLS and username and password authentication
- Identity assertion using the service context protocol
- SAS protocol over secure and unsecured connections
- SSL 3.0 and TLS 1.0 mandatory cipher suites
- Stateless mode of operation
- Association options (the DelegationByClient association option is not required)

Conformance Level 1 adds additional requirements for a conforming implementation beyond those of Level 0:

- Client support for including an authorization token in the SAS Establish-Context messages, that is, a push model for privilege attributes.
- A target will recognize the attributes and extensions defined in the IETF PKIXAC protocol.
- A target that supports pushed privilege attributes must include the names of privilege authorities in its IOR.

Level 2 adds the following requirements to Level 1:

- Implementations support authorization token-based delegation.
- Target is capable of evaluating the proxy rules in the PAC to determine if an intermediate can assert the attributes of the initiating client.
- Targets that accept identity assertions based on ProxyInfo in the PAC and states this in its IOR.
- Targets that require an endorsement to act as an intermediate must represent this requirement in its IOR.

In addition to the preceding conformance requirements, there is an orthogonal conformance that implementations can support, that is, the use of a stateful or stateless transfer of security data. All implementations are required to support the stateless mode of transfer, whereas stateful transfer is optional.

Interoperable Security Layers

Now that you understand the important pieces of security technology underlying the interoperability between EJB and CORBA, we will look at each of the security layers, authentication, authorization, and transport, with an eye to understanding the remaining differences and how to use the best features of EJB and CORBA.

Authentication

When your EJB Containers and CORBA applications implement CSIv2 authentication, CORBA and EJB processes pass compatible security tokens that either object model can interpret and use. Therefore, authentication is no longer a problem for EJB and CORBA interoperability when both models use CSIv2.

If your EJB Containers or your CORBA applications do not support CSIv2, then you will have to build your own bridge between the two security systems. We realize that older technology is never completely replaced by the newer technology, so we will not leave you hanging. The next section describes how to bridge authentication between EJB and CORBA for systems that do not support CSIv2.

Extending EJB to CORBA Authentication

Your situation is as follows: You have a container that receives an HTTP message at its built-in HTTP servlet. You want to make a call on a CORBA application, and neither system supports CSIv2. The solution entails building a CORBA Principal Authenticator (PA) object that knows how to verify a cookie and build a CORBA credential. You might have to build the PA yourself or have a professional service organization that specializes in interoperability build a PA object that will do the job. The following example describes a form of a credential mapping service. This is not a standardized service.

Recalling our discussion in Chapter 5, there is also an interoperability problem between tiers. So, even if the EJB and CORBA that you are using support CSIv2, there is still the incompatibility between the perimeter tier and the mid-tier. Therefore, a similar technique will have to be delivered by the container provider, or you will have to construct the transformation between the tiers yourself.

In the following example, a servlet in the container receives a cookie from the perimeter tier. The servlet could validate the cookie itself, but unless the servlet already has a secure authenticated means to send the cookie to the CORBA client, the servlet should get past the cookie and the username to the PA in the bridging software and obtain a CORBA credential for the user. Later, CORBASec will securely transmit this credential as part of the secure association when the servlet invokes on the CORBA client.

The CORBA PA authenticate method is defined as follows:

```
Security::AuthenticationStatus authenticate (
        in Security::AuthenticationMethod method,
        in Security::MechanismType mechanism,
        in Security::SecurityName security_name,
        in Security::Opaque auth_data,
        in Security::AttributeList privileges,
        out Credentials creds,
        out Security::Opaque continuation_data,
        out Security::Opaque auth_specific_data
);
```

We are interested in three parameters in this method, `auth_data`, `security_name`, and `creds`. The cookie is passed in through the `auth_data` parameter, and the username is passed in through the `security_name` parameter. The CORBA credential that is created in the PA implementation is returned in the `creds` out parameter.

The new `PrincipalAuthenticator::authenticate` method validates the cookie. The validated username is then used to construct a CORBA credential using the standard security library provided by your middleware vendor.

There are no standards to make the transformation from EJB authentication evidence to a CORBASec credential. As an example, we define `Principal-`

Authenticator::authenticate as a wrapper for the SecServEJB_i::verify_authentication_data, which we presented in the Chapter 5 section entitled "An Example of Perimeter to Mid-Tier Interoperability." A CORBA call, verify_authentication_data, is made on the C++ CORBA object in our example. Note that calls between languages, Java to C++ in this case, are handled transparently by CORBA. C++ is used to verify the authentication data for performance reasons because cryptographic calculations can be expensive.

The call to verify_authentication_data passes the cookie in the auth_data parameter, and the call returns the CORBASec certificate in the cert_data in_out parameter:

```
Security::AuthenticationStatus
SecServEJB_i::verify_authentication_data(
        const Security::Opaque& auth_data,
        Security::Opaque*& cert_data
)
{
...
}
```

Some of the commercial products that can be used for cookie-based authentication evidence from a browser are GetAccess from Entrust, SiteMinder from Netegrity, and ClearTrust SecureControl from Securant. Using one of these commercial products, we can pass it the cookie, and the product will return a boolean result indicating whether the user has supplied the correct password in the cookie. Once the cookie has been verified, the security service uses the username to retrieve the CORBASec name.

A problem can arise with respect to naming. If an X.500 format is used as the security name and the browser uses a short string, for example, a login username, there is a name syntax incompatibility. Note that this is one example in which name mapping is required, which is a very common security bridging requirement. One solution is to store the security name in a Lightweight Directory Access Protocol (LDAP) directory, and store the browser login username as an LDAP attribute of the Common Name (CN) node of the LDAP hierarchy. A secondary index of the username attribute is constructed in LDAP to facilitate rapid lookup by username using one of the LDAP APIs, such ldap_search, to retrieve the name.

Using the security name, verify_authentication_data creates an X.509 certificate and a PAC. CORBA implementations that support CSIv2 will have credentials that contain both a user certificate and a PAC. If you were using a security service that doesn't support PACs then you would simply create a credential using only the user name. The next code snippet illustrates how these certificates are created.

```
Security::Opaque* cert;

try
{
```

```
  cert = mcertGenerator->create_certificate(security_name);
}
catch (const CORBA::Exception& excep)
     ...
     // create the Personal Attribute Certificate
  pac = mpacGen->create_pac(*attrList,
                            *cert,
                            delMode,
                            *authDomList,
                            controlValue);
     ...
```

Once you have created a credential, you can leave the bridge code and use the standard security code supplied by your middleware vendor to set these certificates into the credentials object. The servlet can then use the CORBA credential as authentication evidence during invocations to supply authentication attributes for CORBA applications. Because the preceding code is nonstandard, you have to know the attribute data format for the security service that you are using.

CSIv2 does not solve the discontinuities at the tier boundaries. You still have to use a credential mapping service similar to the one mentioned previously as well as the methods that were discussed in Chapter 5 to overcome the tier discontinuity problem. However, CSIv2 does solve authentication interoperability between EJB and CORBA. For systems using CSIv2, authentication interoperability between EJB and CORBA is no longer a problem.

Authorization

Authorization between EJB and CORBA is not as simple as the authentication situation. The first area in which the two authorization models differ is in the privilege attributes that are supported. EJB only supports a username and roles, whereas CORBA supports a username and roles as well as a number of additional attribute types. Another difference is that the deployer in EJB assigns roles to a principal in some platform specific way. The deployment descriptor tells deployers the roles for which they must set assignments. The information in the deployment descriptor also tells the deployer what capabilities are expected to be conferred based on role membership. In CORBA applications that support CSIv2 conformance level 1 or higher, attributes are assigned to a client principal by an AA and are transmitted to the target in the PAC. Note that because EJB only supports Level 0 of CSIv2, container suppliers are not required to support PACs. However, nothing stops a container supplier from providing support for authorization tokens. In the narrow or minimum adherence to the specification, the only attribute that is passed between a client and a target in EJB is the username. It is up to the deployer to assign roles, as you learned in Chapter 2.

In making a call from CORBA to EJB, any additional attributes types used in CORBA will be lost. Compatibility between attributes in each model must be done by an out-of-band means. The deployer must decide who can access the EJB resources. Because most containers will not have the ability to look at pushed authorization tokens, the deployer's decision must be based on the identity attribute. A more sophisticated container could use information from a pulled authorization token or in the future from a pushed authorization token. The pull model as defined by CSIv2 simply means that the server uses the authenticated security name of the client, goes to an AA that it trusts, and requests the PAC of the named client. The server has to authenticate itself to the AA or have a trust relationship with the AA. If these conditions are met, the AA returns the PAC to the server.

On the other hand, when a call is made from EJB to CORBA, the CORBA implementation can use a pull model to get a PAC related to the username passed from EJB as described above.

If you recall from Chapter 2, EJB uses method protection for authorization. From Chapter 3, you learned that CORBA uses a level of indirection based on required rights and security policy domains to make its access decision. It assigns required rights to the methods and interfaces, and through the use of policy domains and the granting of rights to principal attributes in the domains, CORBA generates a list of effective rights for a principal. A CORBA access decision is made by evaluating the set of rights required against the set of rights assigned to an attribute of a principal. Furthermore, in Chapter 7, you will learn about another CORBA access decision model called Resource Access Decision (RAD). RAD permits runtime information to be used in the access decision.

The access decision models of EJB and CORBA are obviously different. There are two important results of their differences:

- Scaling
- Granularity

On the surface, method-permissions, which are used by EJB, do not scale well to large numbers of beans and user groups. Because each bean has a list of method-permissions, which contains the resources that each role can access, a change or addition to the roles can mean a change to each of the method-permissions that the role is in. This can result in a severe maintenance problem. As we stated earlier, the EJB specification does not say how a container provider should implement access control. Therefore, it is up to the container provider to determine how to use the information in the method-permissions available to it to make an access decision. The scaling capability is thus highly dependent on the implementation of the container. This is a critical area that you should thoroughly investigate if you have a large installation.

CORBA's use of rights breaks the direct dependence between the resource (methods or interfaces) and the user attributes (groups, roles, etc.). Additionally, CORBA's use of policy domains separates the dependence of the rights granted to the user from the code and makes it an administrative task to set policy in domains.

With respect to granularity, both CORBA and EJB support setting access decisions down to the method level. However, CORBA's use of domains allows making access decisions down to the object instance level. Specifically, different instances of the same interface may be dynamically assigned to a different domain, which can have different access policies. This results in the possibility of different access policies being used by the different instances of the same interface. There is some recent effort in the EJB community to specify object instance control for the EJB Container.

Another aspect of domains is that they can be hierarchical. You can take advantage of this if the CORBASec provider has implemented the new CORBA specification—Security Domain Membership, which is working its way through the OMG approval process. This specification defines the hierarchical structure of domains and defines a way of walking the domain tree to combine rights using the set properties of union, intersection, or subtraction. If your security provider has implemented this capability, then one way you can take advantage of this is by modeling the domain hierarchy to your corporate structure. Then using, say, the union combinator, you can set a few corporate policies at the root node, which would represent your corporate requirements, and then set more specific policies as you move down the tree to nodes that represent your divisions, sections, and workgroups. The access decision would then be the combined result of the rules set by each level of your corporation.

CORBA also provides privilege attribute types, which go as far as letting you define your own attribute types. For example, you could define an attribute type of Sales, and then have attribute values for U.S., European, and Asian. EJB, on the other hand, supports the concept of logical privileges, or roles. Although you could get the same effect using just the logical roles of EJB by having a US_Sales role, a European_Sales role, and an Asian_Sales role, the granularity of having types such as Sales, Manufacturing, and Accounting in CORBA, more directly supports the modularity of your attributes.

How Rich Does It Need to Be?

Do you really need all the flexibility that the CORBA model permits? That depends on where you are in modeling your security. When you are first designing the security for your corporation, we strongly urge you to keep it simple. Don't use all the power that the security models offer you because the modeling can very quickly become so complicated that you will have a very difficult time assessing the security effects as a transaction ripples through your system. We cover this topic in more detail in Chapter 8.

There is also a good chance that you will be using EJB as well as CORBA. In your first pass at your architecture, determine whether the EJB authorization model is sufficient for your needs. If you find areas that you determine need more granularity, then plan to bridge into the CORBA authorization model, which is discussed in the next section.

When there is an existing distributed system using CORBA and EJB or one or the other object models alone, study the architecture in areas in which security administration is giving you trouble to determine if you need more or less granularity or scale. Use your knowledge of the best points of CORBA and EJB to redo parts of the system in the best object security model for the job. If there is a part of the system that uses EJB and has become a security administration bottleneck, think about substituting a CORBA security model. For example, using the previous example, you might have originally used just two roles, Sales and Manufacturing, for your whole organization. You might now see the need for developing attribute types of US_Sales and so on, or you might have started out with all your policies in one domain and now want to model your corporate structure with a hierarchy of domains to better enforce your corporate security policy.

Conversely, if there is a part of the system in which the business logic is changed frequently, think about substituting EJB for CORBA because the EJB model was designed to explicitly use a paradigm to support the inclusion of business logic.

When examining your architecture, determine what resources you are trying to protect and who needs access. This means that you will need to have a thorough knowledge of your system and what the various computer programs are designed to accomplish. Only when you have this complete understanding can you make judgements on the balance of EJB and CORBA. Obviously, security is not the only criteria, but it is an important part of the picture. Too little security and you put your resources at risk, too much security and it can be the cause of unnecessary performance penalties. Our mantra bears repeating again: Security is risk management. The rationale and details of these propositions are presented in Chapter 8.

Extending EJB to CORBA Authorization

Authorization is the one aspect of security in which there is not yet a standard for interoperability between EJB and CORBA, even if the systems are based on CSIv2. As we explained earlier, EJB authorization is simpler than CORBA authorization. EJB uses a different protection model, which is method-permissions, whereas CORBA uses a combination of rights and domains.

The one common item between the two object models is the use of a user identity. Even with user identity, there may still be a need to map between two forms of a username. However, because the underlying entity is the same, this is just a matter of the form it takes, although it might mean an explicit listing of each form of the username. For example, we discussed earlier an implementation that stores the user login name in the LDAP tree.. The login name, in this case, is the same name used in the EJB implementation, so the mapping can be done by an LDAP lookup.

Now, let's say that you need to use the more extensive authorization of CORBA at some point in your EJB system. You can pass the username from your EJB implementation to your CORBA implementation and map between the two name representations if necessary. Because we are predicating the use of CSIv2, this information can be passed in the service context between the two processes. Whether your EJB is using username and password or SSL certificates, the name of the calling identity is passed if you use one of the forms of delegation described in the section on CSIv2. The CORBA process uses the username as the AccessId attribute to carry out the authorization using rights and domains, or it can obtain the attributes using the pull method described earlier to get the user's PAC.

The following code shows you how to set the extended attributes of the user and make the CORBA program aware of these attributes. Use the following standard CORBASec calls to retrieve the attributes from the Security System, and then set these attributes on the principal.

```
SecurityLevel1::Current curr =
        orb->resolve_initial_references ("SecurityCurrent");

Security::AttributeTypeList attributes_type;

Security::AttributeList requested_privileges =
        curr->get_attributes (
           attributes_type
);
```

You first get the Security Current from the ORB by using the resolve_initial_references call. Then, you declare a list of attribute types and pass the list of the type of attributes that you want into the get_attributes call. This returns the list of requested privilege attributes that belong to the principal who is the owner of the process making the call. Using this list of privileges, make the set_privileges call to associate the privilege attributes returned from the get_attributes call as shown next.

```
boolean succeeded;
boolean force_commit = true;
SecurityLevel2::Credentials creds;
Security::AttributeList actual_privileges;

succeeded = creds->set_privileges (
     force_commit,
     requested_privileges,
     actual_privileges
);
```

The boolean force_commit tells the security system to make the change immediately. You pass in the requested_privileges that you obtained from the previous requested_privileges call. If the attributes are associated with the owner of the process, the call returns true in the succeeding boolean. The actual_privileges that the security system set on the principal are returned as an out parameter. You should check these against the privileges that you requested to be set on the principal because the system may not have set all the privileges that you requested. This may be because you did not have the required authorization to set all the privileges.

In the previous `verify_authentication_data` example, the credentials were those associated with the principal that was used in the EJB application, which was then passed into the CORBA application. This association is made using the code that we introduced in Chapter 5. In the CORBA application, you get the credentials for the EJB principal by calling:

```
creds = curr->own_credentials();
```

The own_credentials and set_privileges calls are standard CORBA security service calls, which are available to the application if the Security Service supports Security Level 2 functionality. The other calls that we used are Security Level 1 calls.

Summary

This chapter looked at the two object security models, EJB and CORBA, and pointed out that there are reasons to use both models in a corporate system. The goal of EJB is to use a simple distributed model based on one language—Java—and an authorization model that uses a single attribute type, roles, and authorization rules based on method-permissions. The EJB specification does not describe the authorization mechanism, which is left up to the container provider. CORBA, on the other hand, supports most popular programming languages, a large number of attributes including user defined attributes, and a scalable fine-grained authorization model based on rights and domains as well as a second authorization model, RAD. This flexibility necessitates a more complex security model for CORBA than for EJB.

We pointed out that there are reasons to use both security models. You'll want to select the best points in each model in order to design an optimum security model that best suits your enterprise. In some parts of your system, the easier development model of EJB may be preferred. In other parts of your system, you may want the flexibility, finer granularity, and scaling capabilities of CORBA.

Given that there are reasons to use both models, it quickly becomes apparent that due to their different goals the two models do not inherently work together. Therefore, we went into some detail in these areas of incompatibility and discussed the approaches that the standards bodies are working on to make EJB and CORBA work together. In those areas in which standard solutions have not yet been established, we described techniques to overcome the remaining incompatibilities.

From a standards point of view, the most significant advance in moving the interoperability of EJB and CORBA forward has been the CSIv2 specification. Many companies representing CORBA and EJB implementations have worked on this specification. The companies that worked on the CSIv2 specification were also EJB Container suppliers and had a strong desire for interoperability.

In order to describe the CSIv2 specification, we provided you with a brief overview of the technologies underlying the specification. These technologies are RMI, which originated in the EJB model, and IIOP, which originated in the CORBA model. These were combined to produce RMI over IIOP, which is used by both models. Once these technologies were described, we then moved to a description of CSIv2. We discussed how CSIv2 addresses the three major divisions of distributed security, authentication, authorization, and secure transport.

We then discussed some areas of interoperability that were not completely solved by CSIv2 and uncovered the fact that authorization was the layer that had the largest differences between the two object models. We presented you with some solutions that were not yet standardized but would allow you to bridge the differences between the two models.

The access decision model that we've discussed so far has emphasized container enforced access control, which allows applications to be completely security-unaware and does not put any security code in the application level. However, there are times when the traditional access decision model is not sufficient for your needs, and for which you should consider using the RAD model, which we discuss in the next chapter.

CHAPTER 7

Protecting Application Resources

This chapter explains how you can employ the CORBA Resource Access Decision (RAD) facility to protect application resources when the capabilities of middleware security are not enough. We begin by discussing how fine-grain access control can be implemented using different approaches, and we show the benefits of using RAD. We then explain what RAD is and how you can take advantage of it. Finally, we walk you through the eBusiness.com example to demonstrate how to use RAD in your applications.

The RAD facility is a new specification, so there are few commercial implementations currently available. However, vendors are working on RAD products—check our Web site for new developments in this area.

Beyond Middleware Access Control

You will find security, and particularly access control, functions provided by middleware to be best suited for your needs in securing the mid-tier layer. However, there are particular classes of applications that require fine-grained control of access to enterprise resources, or enforcement of application specific policies, or both. In such cases, by just using middleware security, you would not achieve all your objectives.

In the following section, we use the eBusiness.com example to illustrate the alternatives you have for engineering fine-grain or application specific access control, discuss their pros and cons, and ultimately concentrate on the choice we recommend for your solutions—RAD.

Refining Access Control in the Example

As you recall from the eBusiness.com example described in Chapter 3, users may access information about accounts and products. In the version of the eBusiness.com security policy described in Tables 3.2 and 3.3, you may have noticed that any user who can access his or her instance of the MemberAccount interface in the Accounts domain is also permitted to access other users' accounts in the domain. eBusiness.com does not intend to define such a permissive policy. The company wants to separate users' account information, so the specified policy is inadequate. This limitation exists because we put all of these objects in the same access policy domain Accounts. On the other hand, the security policies of storefront eBusiness.com require that Customers and Members have access only to their accounts. How can we prevent Customers and Members from accessing accounts they don't own? We can achieve this goal in several ways. Let's briefly examine what these approaches are as well as their pros and cons.

One approach is to create a separate domain for each distinguished CustomerID or MemberID, and place each account object in the corresponding domain (e.g., "Account 1234") as illustrated in Figure 7.1. As you can see, there are as many Account domains as there are unique IDs of Customers and Members. We put these domains under domain Accounts, which allows security administrators to apply common access policy to all account objects at the level of this domain. Then, for each individual Account domain, we grant necessary rights to Customers and Members so that only owners can access their account objects. Let's configure the access policy tables using a short example

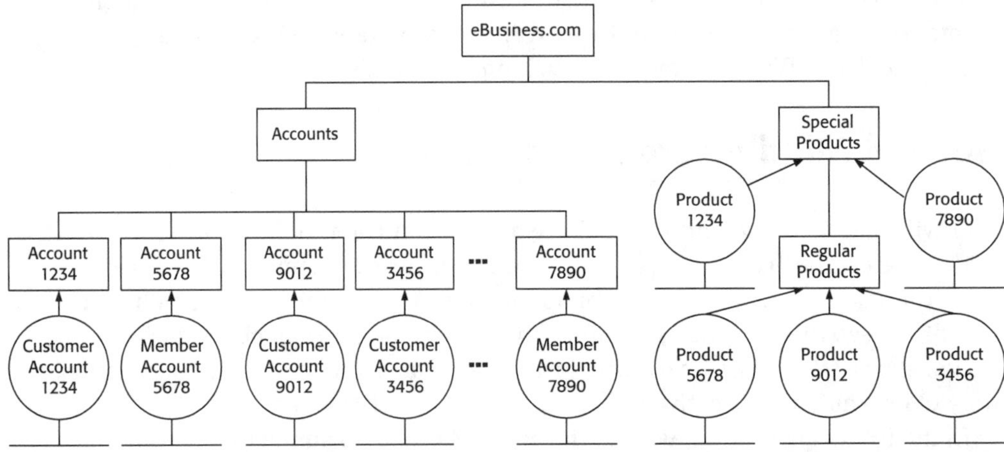

Figure 7.1 The domain and object outline for the solution with separate access policy domains per account object.

Table 7.1 Granted Rights in Each of the Account Domains in eBusiness.com

	GRANTED RIGHTS IN EACH DOMAIN		
ATTRIBUTES	APPLICATION	ACCOUNT 1234	ACCOUNT 5648
AccessID=Daly		su	
AccessID=Johnson			su
Role=staff	s		

with only two accounts. Table 7.1 shows that the principal with AccessID Daly is granted rights *su* when it's accessing objects in domain "Account 1234." The user is granted these rights because the account is owned by this user. The same story applies to user Johnson and domain "Account 5648." Users performing role "staff" are granted right *s* when they access any object located in domain "Accounts" or in its subdomains. Note that right *u* is not granted to staff, so that only the owner of the account can settle the corresponding orders.

What is the advantage of this approach? We fully achieve our policy objective: The access to the accounts is completely controlled by CORBA Security (CORBASec), and the implementations of account objects are totally unaware of the enforced policies. But how many domains would have to be created, and how many changes would have to be done? Obviously, we would have at least as many policy domains as user accounts, which may be disadvantageous from the point of view of runtime performance scalability. And, if the company changes the policies at a later time, which is inevitable in today's enterprises, the changes would have to be made to every other domain. Depending on the policy change, your security administrator may need to tinker with thousands (and maybe even millions) of domains just to implement one change in the policy. Also, each time an account is created or deleted, the corresponding domain would have to be created or deleted, increasing the burden of security administration and the chances of human error. You have probably realized that this way, although correct, can be cumbersome.

Alternatively, we could change the logic of CustomerAccount and MemberAccount interface implementations and make them check whether the accessing user is the owner of the corresponding account. Because this allows us to get back to only one policy domain containing all account objects, we would avoid performance scalability problems, and most importantly, make the life of the security administrators in eBusiness.com much easier. However, the burden is now shifted onto application developers, who need to code the authorization logic and its changes inside the TCustomerAccount and TmemberAccount implementations. For example, if eBusiness.com changes its policy to allow customer service representatives to access accounts in order to provide better service, then all implementations of account objects have to be recoded. In this simple example, it may appear that the coupling of application and authorization logic does not seem to be that dangerous. But think about your

ESI AUTHORIZATION PRINCIPLES: PUSH SECURITY DOWN VS. APPLICATION DRIVEN

This scenario demonstrates the fundamental tension between infrastructure-enforced security and application-enforced security. We've looked at eBusiness.com's business objectives, so we know the security requirements we need to address. We want to push security down into the middleware, but this approach doesn't completely satisfy eBusiness.com's needs. We could fix this problem by adding security to the application code, but application-enforced security will result in a weaker security solution.

own company and count the number of different applications there are and how often the authorization logic has to be adjusted. You soon realize that embedding authorization logic in your applications is not a good idea.

So far, we have two extreme approaches:

- We completely separate the access control and business functions by implementing the former in the middleware security and make the life of the security administrators difficult because the number of policy domains (and the amount of administrative work) becomes proportional to the number of customer accounts.
- We couple access control and application functionalities and thus avoid the excessive number of domains, but shift the complexity over to the shoulders of the application developers.

Authorization Server

Can we find a solution that allows scalable security administration and yet avoid coupling of access control and application logic? Yes. Our third approach avoids the undesirable side effects of the two previous approaches. Using it, we make account objects delegate the checks determining whether the user is the owner to an outside application level authorization service. Such a service is logically one per policy domain, even though its instances can be replicated in order to achieve the desired level of availability, fault tolerance, performance, and scalability. Authorization decisions are made by an instance of the service—the authorization server. An application system enforces decisions made by an authorization service without knowing how they have been made, as shown in Figure 7.2. Thus, both the application and the authorization server are part of what the security gurus call a *reference monitor*. Let's see how we can use an authorization server to achieve the objectives of the eBusiness.com example.

As in the second approach, we employ only one policy domain in which all account objects (MemberAccount and CustomerAccount) are placed; their implementations limit access to owners only. Although the objects enforce

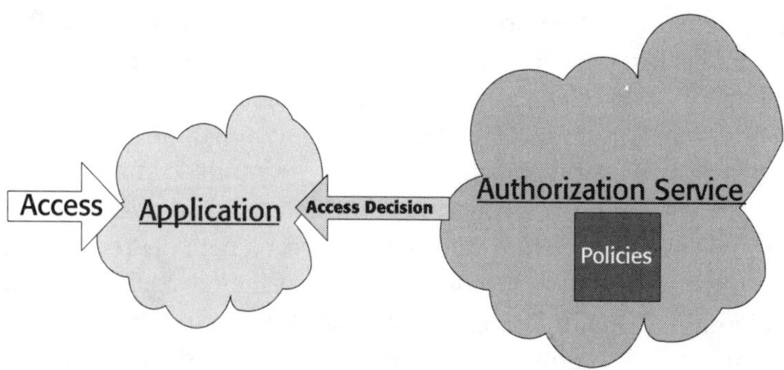

Figure 7.2 The idea behind the use of authorization servers is very simple.

authorization policies, they do not make authorization decisions. Instead, they delegate the decisions to an authorization server, which encapsulates access control logic. This approach liberates the developers from implementing authorization logic inside their applications. Moreover, the approach allows security administrators to have a single place for making changes to authorization policies, which further reduces the cost of security administration.

Once you've grasped the simple idea of using authorization servers, you can easily see the following main advantages:

- **Logical centralization of authorization rules**. Provides inherent consistency and coherency of authorization policies enforced throughout a policy domain.
- **Ease of policy change and update.** Authorization is made in a logically single place.
- **Security administrators can replace a policy.** Authorization logic is centralized and de-coupled from the application logic, which allows your security administrators to replace a policy with a new one of a different type without affecting application systems.
- **Single point of administration.** Centralization of authorization rules naturally features a single point of administration for all systems belonging to one authorization policy domain, significantly lowering the cost of administration.
- **Timely decision making.** An application system can decide when to obtain an authorization decision from the server; therefore, it can do so right at the time when such a decision is needed.
- **Resources of any level of granularity.** Authorization decisions on resources of any level of granularity can be obtained from the server because an application uses the server while it is processing a request. This lifts the limitation of the other approaches in which the granularity can be only as fine as a method on an interface instance.

But there is no free lunch with this approach either. For this approach to be feasible, several important issues must be addressed, or it will fail miserably. First, it is much more challenging to design an implementation of such a server so that it does not become a bottleneck in terms of performance. Second, if the server fails, all application systems served by it will have to resort to a simplistic and very limiting policy such as "always deny" or "always grant," which would render systems unoperational. Thus, you need to provide such servers with a high degree of fault tolerance. And this is when the separation of concerns principle kicks in. Now authorization is "outsourced" to a full-blown enterprise service in which design, implementation, integration, and configuration have to be done with performance, availability, and scalability in mind. Actually, this is true for any other critical distributed enterprise service. Because we explain the security aspects of enterprise integration in this chapter, we will only slightly touch on the general issues of distributed systems engineering and refer you to many excellent books about this topic (Emmerich, 2000; Rauch, 1996; Tanenbaum, 1995; Coulouris, 1995).

Using our eBusiness.com online store, we have shown you a typical case in which middleware access control is just not enough for implementing a company's security policies. We've revealed several methods, and their pros and cons, of implementing the goal policies. Having read about the most promising approach, application authorization services, you are now ready to look more closely at one of its representatives—RAD—and dive into the details of its architecture in order to understand how to employ it.

Resource Access Decision Facility

In the rest of this chapter, we describe the latest technology for application-level authorization servers—the RAD facility standardized by the OMG, which is a representative of authorization services. We illustrate the very simple yet extremely powerful idea behind RAD by showing how eBusiness.com can efficiently employ an authorization server for implementing the policy of restricting access to account objects by owners only. The flow of interactions between application client, application system, and an instance of the authorization service is depicted in Figure 7.3.

The sequence of the interaction is as follows:

1. A client of the application system invokes an operation on the application.
2. While processing the invocation, the application requires an authorization decision from the authorization service.
3. The service makes a decision, which is returned to the application.
4. The application enforces the decision. If access was granted by the authorization service, the application returns the expected results of the invocation. Otherwise, it either returns partial results or raises an exception.

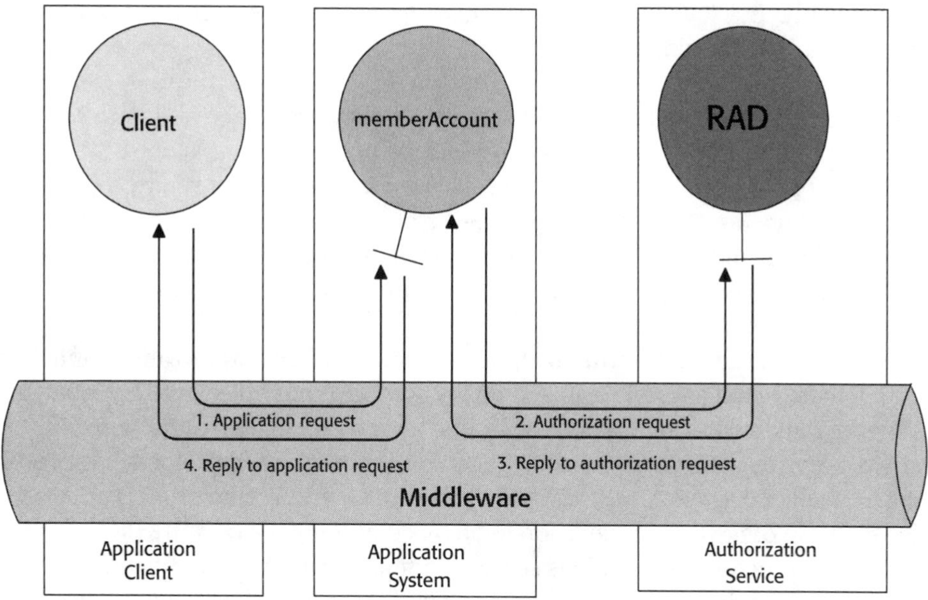

Figure 7.3 The role of RAD.

Pros and Cons of Using RAD

Besides addressing the requirements for fine-grain access control, RAD has several other important benefits. Let's discuss them in detail.

The architecture allows the use of information obtained from workflow systems and other sources, thus supporting policies specific to the application domain. This is important for many enterprises in which authorization is based on what function(s) and on what stage of the overall workflow a particular user performs. This also permits the workflow enforcement. For example, eBusiness.com could have a policy rule that allows for the shipment of an order only after the order is paid, which depends on the status of the order processing. With RAD, the order status information could be, for example, provided by the DynamicAttributeService (DAS) in the form of a dynamic attribute of special type order status with a value indicating its status. Appropriate policy evaluators (PEs) could use the attribute to evaluate their rules.

In eBusiness.com, full access is granted only to the owners of their accounts, that is, those users whose CustomerID is the same as the ID of the account. To realize this, the PE is developed to compare the account ID and the user's CustomerID, which is either inserted in the list of user privileges during the authentication phase or looked up by the PE or DAS each time an authorization request is served by RAD. If these two IDs are the same, full access is granted. Otherwise, access is limited to some degree. This is an example of one more feature of RAD. That is, it enables the use of application specific information in access control decisions.

Due to the encapsulation of authorization logic into a separate service, which can be implemented as a network server, consistency of access control policy enforcement across applications can easily be achieved. This is one of the most important benefits of authorization services in addition to the removal of authorization logic (and consequently code) from the application. As you know, many modern enterprises suffer severely from the enforcement of inconsistent policies across their applications, and there are many human resources put into the administration of disparate applications.

In addition, the architecture supports the multipolicy authorization model, in which there could be more than one policy source or multiple authorities responsible for making a verdict. This may not be a very valuable asset for you, but this could be critical for large in which where authorization decisions need to be made at several levels. Later, you will also see that this feature of RAD allows for the creation of new policy decision logic by combining the existing PEs.

The architecture also enables security administrators and application developers to maintain a clear separation of responsibilities. The former define the policies, and the latter implement policy enforcement. Developers are isolated from coding the authorization logic inside of their applications, which makes the development and maintenance cycles shorter and requires less effort to design, implement, debug, test, and evolve an application. Administrators don't have to learn how to configure each and every system. They have one logical point of administration, which makes their job easier and more productive.

Finally, factors specific to the application domain can be supported by authorization systems using, as an underlying implementation, traditional *Lampson's access matrix*. The matrix contains a row for each subject and a column for each resource, and each cell specifies access rights granted to the subject for the corresponding resource.

Note that RAD is by no means a replacement or substitution for EJB and CORBA security because they provide more than just access control: They also provide several other security services such as user security administration (group membership, role assignment, etc.), authentication, communication integrity and confidentiality, audit, and nonrepudiation. EJB and CORBA security even control invocations on RAD interfaces. Moreover, an application server obtains privilege attributes of the client principal through EJB or CORBA security interfaces before it passes them to the RAD server.

Before we continue with more details on RAD architecture and usage, we would like to warn you that it is not a panacea for every possible case. The use of an application-level authorization server does not come for free. It has its own problems and faces its own restrictions. To achieve the previously mentioned benefits, RAD design requires application-level enforcement of authorization decisions and assumes agreement on the semantics of resource names between the application developer and the owner. We discuss this further in the section "RAD Interfaces and Data." In addition, RAD might be not suitable for some application domains or enterprises. Particularly, existing applications may have to be rewritten (or wrapped) in order to use the service, which can be expensive or even impossible. One other significant obstacle is system performance. Our experience shows that if an application requires an access control decision every 10 ms or even more frequently and its owner cannot afford performance degradation of more than 5 percent, then the use of a separate authorization server is a difficult implementation challenge. In some cases, it requires various tricks, such as a local cache, to be implemented in order to cope with performance penalties.

Middleware or RAD Authorization?

A more important question is what is the trade-off between generic access control enforcement outside of an application, such as CORBA and EJB security, in which an application is completely security-unaware, and fine-grain application specific access control that requires the application to make a call to an authorization server. One of this book's guiding principles is to eliminate security code from applications, but RAD conflicts with this goal in order to achieve fine-grain application specific control. One issue, for example, is that bypassability is straightforward in RAD—you need to ensure that the developer remembers to call RAD at every relevant place. Interceptor-based middleware security is less likely to have such an issue. How should you resolve this trade-off? When is interceptor-based middleware security better to use, and when is RAD better?

As a rule of thumb, we recommend that you architect application security in such a way that interceptor-based middleware protection is used as much as possible, and you resort to RAD and other similar techniques mandating application security awareness only when the requirements can't otherwise be met. For example, you would use middleware security to protect access to the interfaces of your application services, and use RAD for authorizations on fine-grain resources that the services access on behalf of users while processing their requests. The best practice is to use RAD in conjunction with middleware security mechanisms rather than one or the other.

RAD Standard

In this section, you learn what the RAD specification is about and how to take advantage of it. The OMG RAD standard (OMG, 2000) defines a conceptual architecture that encapsulates authorization logic in a service external to the application and is independent of the specific security models and policies. It relies on and uses the CORBASec environment for secure authenticated communications (i.e., message authenticity, confidentiality and integrity protection) between the service and the applications as well as among the service components. RAD also assumes that the underlying security infrastructure provides a means for an application to obtain security attributes of the accessing principal. Such an architecture not only significantly simplifies both application and security system development, but also allows organizations to uniformly manage and enforce their security policies.

Although the RAD specification, as any other CORBA standard, defines only IDL interfaces, data structures in OMG IDL, and their semantics in English prose, the use of EJB is not precluded. A RAD server can either have an EJB interface, or a bridge for EJB clients can be provided. When you choose an implementation of RAD, you should make sure that your EJB applications can use the RAD server.

RAD Interfaces and Data

Let's go back to Figure 7.3 and describe the simple interface between an application system and RAD, which an application developer uses to obtain a decision. The interface defines two operations, access_allowed() and multiple_access_allowed(), which are different only in the number of authorization requests. The first argument passed in each operation is a list of security attributes of the client principal. They are syntactically and semantically the same as CORBASec attributes. The attributes are obtained by the application server from the middleware security infrastructure. Besides the attributes, access_allowed() receives a resource names and operation, and multiple_access_allowed() receives a list of resource name and operation pairs. The application is expected to compute the resource names and operations as part of its application logic. An application obtains a binary (yes/no) authorization decision from an instance of RAD service.

It is the contract between the application and its enterprise environment to ask for an authorization decision and enforce the decision. Of the parameters passed by the client, the first two (resource name and access operation) are most worthy of discussion.

RAD introduces an abstraction called *protected resource name* or just *resource name*, which is used to abstract application dependent semantics of entities—the access to which is controlled by the application. A resource name can be associated with any valuable asset of the application owner; the access to which is controlled according to the owner's interests. In the eBusiness.com example, the account information is a protected resource uniquely identified by account ID. Thus, a resource could have the form {"eBusiness.com", "account id" = "1234"}, where the first part is the name of the authority that named the resource, and the second part ("account id" = "1234") specifies the ID of the Customer and Member accounts.

```
//*****************************************************
//   Types that identify a secured resource
//*****************************************************
struct ResourceNameComponent {
     string       name_string;
     string       value_string;
};
typedef sequence<ResourceNameComponent> ResourceNameComponentList;

typedef string ResourceNamingAuthority;

struct ResourceName {
     ResourceNamingAuthority       resource_naming_authority;
     ResourceNameComponentList     resource_name_component_list;
};
```

In order for an application and a RAD server to work in concert, the owner of the application and its developer need to either agree on the semantics of the resource names or use standard names, which is equivalent to agreeing to the semantics defined by a third-party, standard organization. Depending on the application domain of your company, the naming can be very straightforward (each resource name consists of only one element uniquely identifying the resource) or can be complicated (multi-element names of the resource). This is because, when you have millions of resources, you want to come up with naming schemes that allow scalable resource-to-policy mapping. Mapping resources to policies can be done by grouping resource names in hierarchies or by matching them with regular expressions. PolicyEvaluatorLocator and PEs can then be implemented with efficient algorithms for determining what PE(s) and policies inside each PE should be used for a given resource name.

If your vendor-supplied application has its own naming schema that is incompatible with yours, one option you have is to implement a complex and probably inefficient algorithm for mapping resource names into PEs and their policies. Alternatively, you could have a separate instance of RAD (at least an AccessDecision object [ADO] and a PolicyEvaluatorLocator [PEL]) serving applications of that particular vendor. As you can see, no choice is perfect if your naming schema is incompatible with that of your vendor. This is why it is important to think about a resource naming schema beforehand and make it scalable and consistent across all applications in your company. As for applications purchased from vendors, your best bet is to require that the resource naming schemata of their applications be reconfigurable via meta data, so that the applications can adopt your naming schema. But this is not always possible, which means some mapping from one schema to another could be required.

```
//*******************************************************
//Types that identify an operation and an operation list
//*******************************************************
typedef string                     Operation;
typedef sequence<Operation>        OperationList;
```

An *access operation* (e.g., create, read, write, use, delete) abstracts the semantics of access to resource(s) associated with a resource name. An application may manipulate account and order information or may provide different hierarchies of menus to different eBusiness.com staff. In either case, it is up to the application system developers and the enterprise security administrators to agree on the semantics of the operation name used for each access. RAD does not interpret the semantics of access operations. For our example, we can just use the operation name "access" when we want to check whether a user should have access to the Customer's account object. Simple yet very generic data structures for operations (an arbitrary string) and resource names (a list of string name-value pairs) have good expressive capabilities for this task. Before an application requests an authorization decision from a RAD server, it should identify the resource name and the access operation name associated with serving the client request.

RAD Architecture

The RAD approach is very similar to most solutions based on authorization services in the way the client, application, and the RAD server interact, but it is different in the internal composition of its elements, which we discuss in this section.

The aim of the RAD architecture is to enable implementation of its components by various vendors due to the diversity in the requirements of access control policies, performance, scalability, and other system properties from different government and commercial markets. Five types of components comprise a RAD service: Access Decision Object, Policy Evaluator, Decision Combinator, Policy Evaluator Locator, Dynamic Attribute Service. We describe them in the following sections.

Access Decision Object

The ADO serves as the front end (or proxy, in the terms of software design patterns) to RAD clients. That is, RAD clients don't know that any other RAD interface but the ADO exists. It also coordinates the interactions between other RAD components. So, you can look at the ADO as a hub through which the majority of the interactions in the RAD service occur.

The following listing illustrates the ADO runtime interface and the supplemental data structures used by application servers as defined in OMG IDL:

```
struct AccessDefinition {
     ResourceName      resource_name;
     Operation         operation;
};
typedef sequence<AccessDefinition> AccessDefinitionList;
```

```
enum InternalErrorType {
     Fatal,
     NotFatal
};

exception InternalError{
     InternalErrorType ed;
};

typedef sequence<boolean> BooleanList;
typedef Security::AttributeList AttributeList;

//**************************************************
//     interface AccessDecision
//**************************************************
interface AccessDecision {

     boolean access_allowed(
          in  ResourceName     resource_name,
          in  Operation        operation,
          in  AttributeList    attribute_list
     )
     raises (InternalError);

     BooleanList multiple_access_allowed(
          in  AccessDefinitionList  access_requests,
          in  AttributeList         attribute_list
     )
     raises (InternalError);

};
```

When an application server invokes access_allowed(), it passes the name of the resource and access operation for which it wants to get an authorization decision from the RAD server. The application also passes a list of privilege attributes of the principal that is requesting access to the resource. The attributes are exactly the same as the ones defined in CORBASec. As a result, the application server gets back either a yes/no authorization decision or, if something goes unexpectedly wrong, an exception InternalError. The following is a sample fragment of Java code illustrating how an application server programmer would obtain an authorization decision from RAD.

```
//Get a reference to AccessDecision object and store it in obj
Object obj = ...

// Narrow obj to AccessDecision
AccessDecision ado = AccessDecisionExtHelper.narrow(obj);

try
{
           boolean decision = ado.access_allowed(
           resourceName, operationName, attributeList);
```

```
}
catch (InternalError ex)
{
     // Handle the exception
}

if( decision == False )
{
     // Deny access to the client
     ...
}
// Access the resource on behalf of the client
...
```

If an application wants to save time and obtain several authorization decisions regarding access to more than one resource for the same principal, it invokes multiple_access_allowed(), which differs only in passing a list of resource and operation name pairs, and receiving a list of yes/no decisions back.

By now, you are probably wondering what resource names look like. A resource name is a list of name-value pairs with a naming authority prefixed as shown at the top of Figure 7.4.

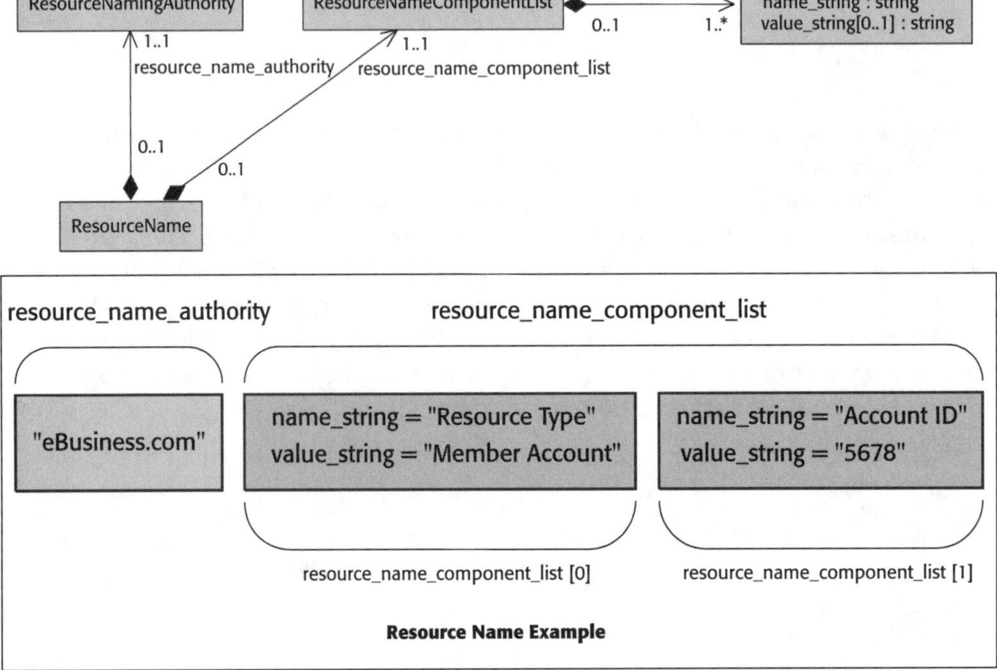

Figure 7.4 Format and example of a resource name.

The structure of a resource name is very generic, so that different types of resources for diverse application domains can be accommodated. A data member resource_naming_authority is used to scope each and every resource name in order to avoid the usual problem of name space conflicts. The bottom part of the figure shows an example of a resource name for the eBusiness.com storefront. We used the domain name of the company as a naming authority to scope its resource names. This particular resource refers to a member account with account ID=5678.

To help you understand the big picture, we show a hypothetical sequence of invocations between a client, the MemberAccount object for account 5678, and the ADO in Figure 7.5. The client, acting on behalf of user Johnson, invokes method MemberAccount::settleAccount() on the object for account #5678. Because all the account objects are in the same access policy domain, CORBA access control mechanisms can't discriminate access requests on a per object basis. They can either allow or deny invocation of settleAccount() on *all* the MemberAccount objects in the domain. Therefore, the job of the RAD authorization service is to authorize only the account owner to settle an account. In order to make an access decision, RAD needs to know the account number for the accessed MemberAccount object. This information is passed to RAD as an element of the resource name. The operation on the resource has the name "settle" to reflect the nature of the access, although it does not have to correlate with the name of the invoked operation on the object interface. In your organizational environment, you might find that operation names should correlate with, for example, the stages of the workflow process. In the eBusiness.com example, most principals don't have any privilege attributes other than AccessID, which is what is passed to ADO.

Now let's look at other RAD components.

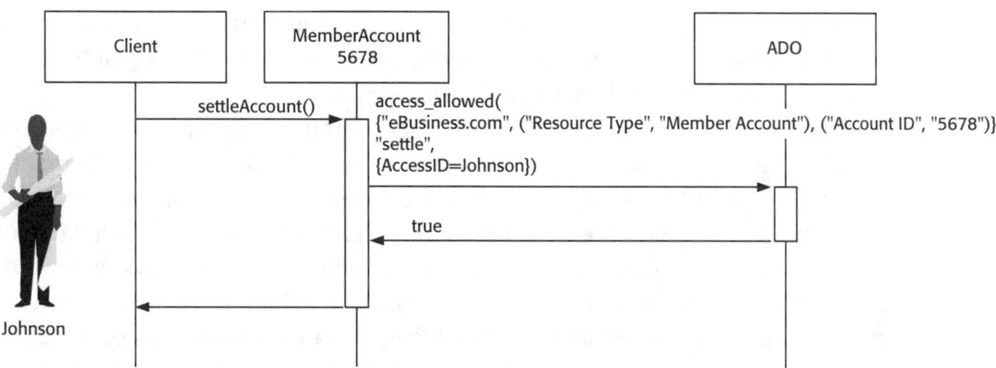

Figure 7.5 Invocations between a client, the MemberAccount object for account 5678, and the ADO.

Policy Evaluator

Zero or more PEs perform evaluation decisions based on the policies governing the access to protected resources. All PEs, no matter what evaluation policy engine is used, have the following runtime interface:

```
enum DecisionResult {
 ACCESS_DECISION_ALLOWED,
 ACCESS_DECISION_NOT_ALLOWED,
 ACCESS_DECISION_UNKNOWN
};

struct ExceptionData {
     short      error_code;
     string     reason;
};

exception ComponentError{
     ExceptionData ed;
     InternalErrorType it;
};

interface PolicyEvaluator {
     DecisionResult evaluate(
      in ResourceName      resource_name,
      in Operation         operation,
      in AttributeList     attribute_list
     )
     raises (ComponentError);
};
```

As you saw in the previous IDL code, each PE can return a result that means "grant," "deny," or "unknown." Why would a PE return "unknown," which means that it could not determine the decision? In some cases, because of reasons such as misconfiguration, a PE does not have a clue as to what policy from its set of policies it should use to evaluate an authorization request. As we will discuss next, a decision combinator filters the results from each PE, so the "unknown" case is never seen by the application that called ADO. Applications always see either yes/no decisions or an exception.

You or your vendor can implement the PE itself in many different ways. You can make it as simple as one that always, let's say, denies access, which actually could be useful for temporarily blocking access to a set of resources. Or, you can make it very complex, for example, a distributed and hierarchical decision system that includes some AI and other intelligence. As you know, you can "hide" anything behind an interface, and this is the beauty (and the devil) of encapsulation. One reasonable and most frequent implementation of a PE you will encounter is some decision logic "on top" of a rule database. How complex the logic and how fancy the database schema are depends on the particular requirements for authorization policy capabilities. In our eBusiness.com store-

Table 7.2 Account Numbers Information for eBusiness.com

ACCOUNT NUMBER	OWNER
1234	Diana
5678	Johnson
9012	Sheridan
3456	Graffiti
7890	McArthur

front example, we want to allow only account owners to settle their accounts. Consequently, the database schema could be as simple as a two-column table consisting of account numbers in one column and their owners in the other, as shown in Table 7.2. Moreover, this information is probably already stored somewhere else in the company, so the PE does not have to replicate this data as long as it is readily available to the PE.

Decision Combinator

In our simple example, we don't need more than one PE. But what if, because of some other reason (such as politics in your company), you need to use two or even more decision engines? How do you combine the results? This is when a *decision combinator* (DC) becomes handy. The DC combines the results of the evaluations made by potentially multiple PEs into a final "yes/no" authorization decision by applying a certain combination policy. The ADO invokes the DC using the following interface, which delegates the combinator to make a verdict. The ADO then blindly passes the verdict back to the RAD client who made the original invocation on the ADO.

```
//********************************************************
// interface DecisionCombinator
//********************************************************
interface DecisionCombinator{
     boolean combine_decisions(
          in ResourceName resource_name,
          in Operation operation,
          in AttributeList attribute_list,
          in PolicyEvaluatorList policy_evaluator_list
     )
     raises (ComponentError);
};
```

A simple and yet useful combination policy could be a logical union of the results received from the PE, so that if at least one of them grants access, the

DC (which means the RAD server too) grants the access. For instance, if one PE grants access only if the accessing user is the owner of the account in eBusiness.com and the other grants access if the user is a senior staff member at eBusiness.com, then the DC performing a logical "OR" operation on the results from the PEs could be used in our storefront example. The second PE makes authorization decisions based on roles of users using the role-based access control (RBAC) model, which we will call "RBAC PE."

Another example of a combination policy is one with priorities. Let's say you want to implement the capability to block access to the accounts during maintenance time. A possible way for you to do this would be to have a PE that denies access only during maintenance periods (or to those accounts that are undergoing maintenance procedures at the time of the access request). Then, you configure the combining logic in your DC to treat this PE ("Maintenance PE") as the highest authority. That is, if the PE denies access, then the DC returns "no," no matter what other PEs return. The logic in the DC can even perform a shortcut and return "no" right away if the Maintenance PE did so. This setup is illustrated in Figure 7.6.

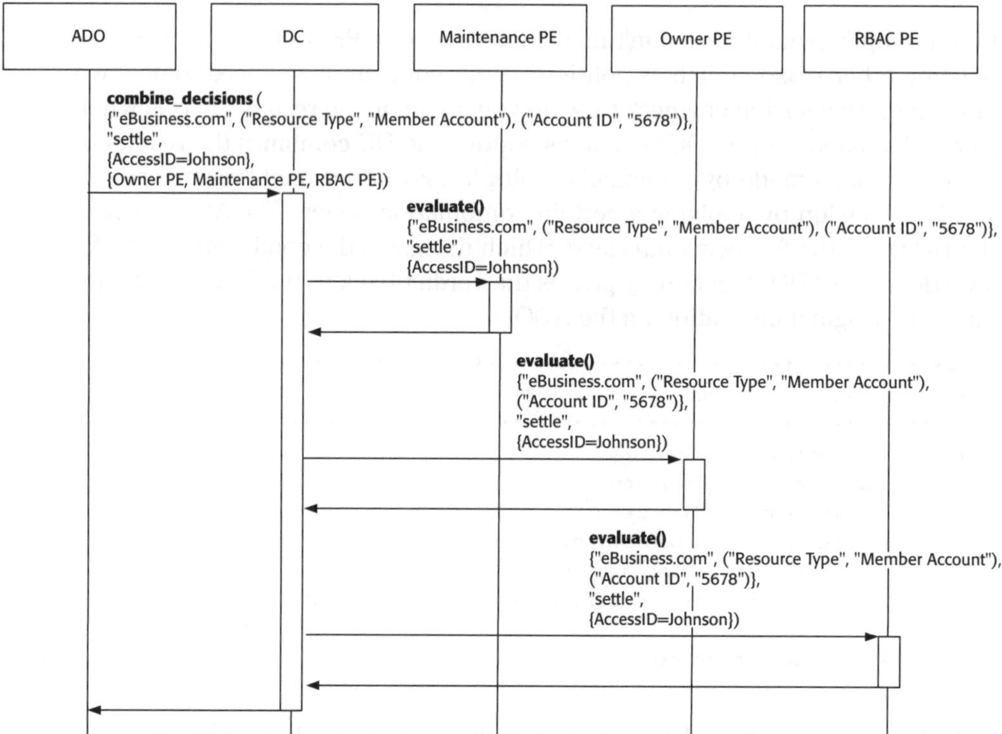

Figure 7.6 Example of a sequence of invocations among the DC and instances of PEs for eBusiness.com.

As you can see in the figure, the DC receives the same arguments as evaluators plus a list of PEs so that it knows what PEs should be used for making an authorization decision. The invocation on the DC in the Figure 7.6 only lists symbolic names of the PEs. In fact, as shown in the following IDL code, a PE is actually identified by both the PE's interoperable object reference (IOR) and its name.

```
struct NamedPolicyEvaluator {
     string                    evaluator_name;
     PolicyEvaluator      policy_evaluator;
};
typedef sequence<NamedPolicyEvaluator> PolicyEvaluatorList;
```

The IOR allows the DC to invoke evaluate() on a PE, whereas the name can be used by the combinator for policy based on selection of a PE, such as the one in our example, when the Maintenance PE has the highest authority. A PE name is used because an IOR does not carry any semantics of a PE, and our DC is not able to guess which IOR corresponds to the Maintenance PE. And even if it could, in your combining policies, we are sure you would not want to use the values of IORs because they depend on many, sometimes uncontrollable things, such as the object location on the network. This means that almost any change in the distributed environment (a port or host interface's IP address for an object) would result in changing the IOR value.

Having explained how a DC invokes PEs and makes a binary yes/no decision based on ternary results received from one or more PEs, we should now explain who determines which PEs should be used for an authorization decision and how they are determined. And this is exactly what we are going to do next.

Policy Evaluator Locator (PEL)

The PEL determines which of the PEs should be used for a resource name. For a given access request to a protected resource, a PEL keeps track of and provides references to potentially several PEs and a DC (yes, a different DC can be used for different authorization requests!) that are collectively responsible for making an authorization decision. The following is the interface definition for a PEL.

```
struct PolicyDecisionEvaluators {
     PolicyEvaluatorList    policy_evaluator_list;
     DecisionCombinator     decision_combinator;
};

//*****************************************************
//     interface PolicyEvaluatorLocator
//*****************************************************
interface PolicyEvaluatorLocator {
     PolicyDecisionEvaluators get_policy_decision_evaluators(
          in ResourceName      resource_name
     )
     raises (ComponentError);
};
```

The ADO calls a PEL's get_policy_decision_evaluators() to obtain the list before it delegates an appropriate DC for the evaluation task. A PEL uses only the name of the resource for determining the PEs and the DC. You configure a PEL using its administrative interface, which allows the assignment of PEs and a DC to resource names in several different ways. You can define a default DC and a list of evaluators that will be used whenever no assignment is found for a given resource name. Then, all authorization requests will be evaluated with the same PEs and a DC. However, you may need to use different PEs or a decision combinator for different groups of resources. For this, the RAD specification defines the notion of *resource patterns*.

Patterns are used to group resource names without requiring the PEL administrator to enumerate all the resource names individually; this is accomplished by associating lists of PEs with resource name patterns and checking whether a supplied resource name matches any of the patterns with which it has associated PEs. Next, we briefly describe how a PEL decides whether a pattern matches a resource name.

Patterns are syntactically the same as resource names except that there are some rules about the format of patterns. Every pattern must have a resource naming authority, and a regular expression cannot be used to specify the authority. The list of resource name components should have at least one element. Regular expressions can be used in two different ways in patterns. First, you can use them in the value_string of a resource name component in the pattern, and the component will be called a value pattern. For value patterns, the matching rule states that "a resource name component matches a component value pattern only if its name_string exactly matches the pattern's name_string, and its value_string matches the component value pattern's value_string regular expression."

The second kind of resource name component that can occur in a pattern is a component wild card pattern; elements of which have the following values:

name_string is "*"
value_string is "*"

Every resource name component matches a component wild card pattern. You will find component wild card patterns useful for specifying groups of resources that are organized in hierarchies. For such resources, a resource name pattern with a component wild card pattern can specify all the resource names that have the same first elements as the ones in the pattern. We know this sounds a bit confusing, so let's illustrate the patterns using our eBusiness.com example. We use one set of PEs for authorizing access to accounts, and another set of PEs for all other company resources. We then set up our PEL to use a Maintenance PE, an Owner PE, an RBAC PE, and the corresponding DC for accounts by using the resource pattern shown in Figure 7.7. We use a default list of PEs and a default DC for all other company resources.

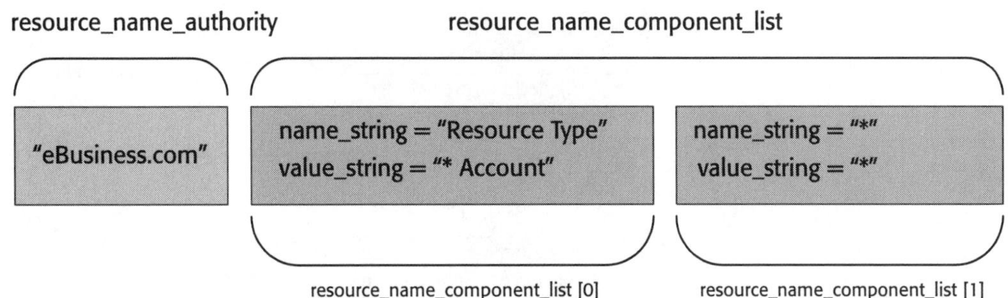

Figure 7.7 All resource names for Customer and Member accounts will match this pattern.

We utilize value patterns because we want Customer and Member accounts to be served by the same set of PEs and DC. Wild card patterns allow us to specify that all account resources, no matter what they are and as long as they fall under "* Account" should be evaluated using the same PEs and DC. In order to use patterns, you need to make sure that your RAD vendor's product is compliant with the conforms class "RAD with Patterns."

If you want to specify different PEs and a different DC for individual resource names, you can do so with patterns, which can be kind of clumsy of course, or use a separate PEL administrative interface called PolicyEvaluatorLocatorNameAdmin. To help you better understand which administrative capabilities for PEL are defined by the RAD specification, we show all the PEL related interfaces in Figure 7.8.

The figure shows one runtime and three administrative interfaces because each administrative interface only defines operations for the corresponding type of association between resource names and sets of PEs and combinators. Operations on PolicyEvaluatorLocatorBasicAdmin allow you to manage a default set of PEs and a combinator, PolicyEvaluatorLocatorNameAdmin defines operations to assign individual resource names to PEs and combinators, and PolicyEvaluatorLocatorPatternAdmin defines operations to assign resource patterns to PEs and combinators. For you to appreciate the interfaces, in Figure 7.9 we show a sequence of calls on PEL administrative interfaces that would result in its correct configuration for our eBusiness.com example.

First, the administrator using an administrative tool sets the default list of PEs and the DC. From then on all authorizations for all resource names that are not explicitly assigned to PEs and a DC will be evaluated using the default combinator and evaluators. The administrator then registers a resource name pattern for handling all resources related to Customer and Member accounts of the eBusiness.com storefront. After the registration, the resource name pattern is used to assign a list of specific PEs and the corresponding DC to this resource name pattern. The registration is necessary; otherwise some ghost patterns could live forever due to misconfiguration and there would no way to find out about them.

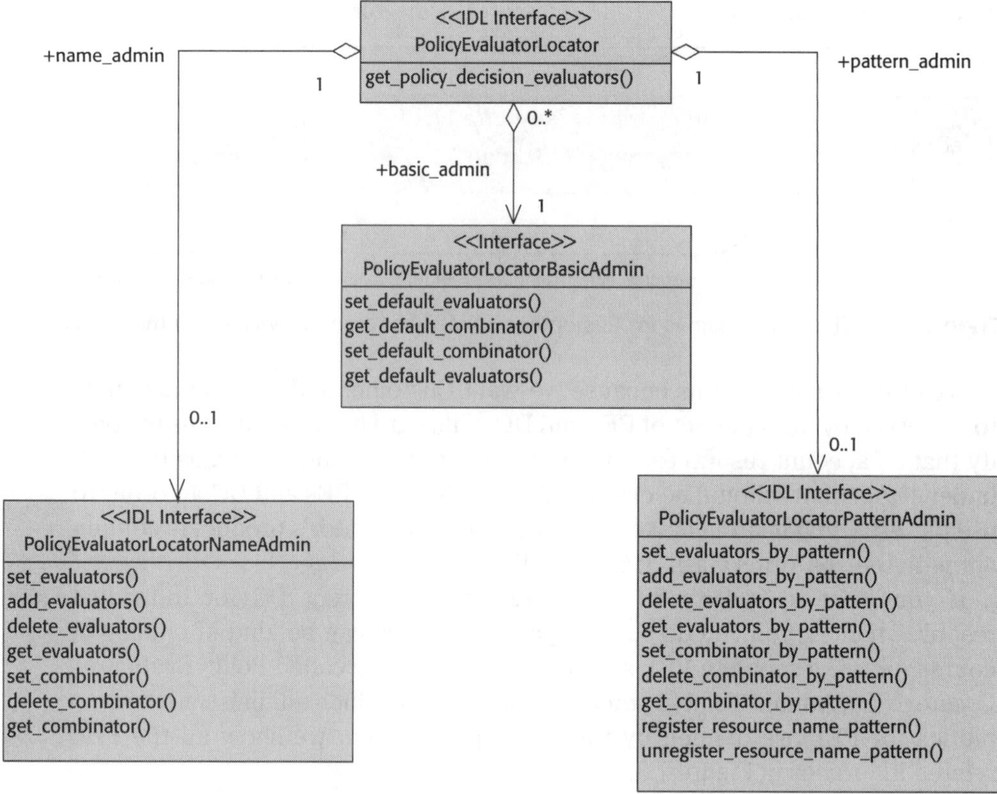

Figure 7.8 Runtime and administrative interfaces for a PEL.

We have one more note about patterns before we move on to the next RAD component. The semantics of the pattern interface for PEL is such that you can overlap patterns provided that the underlying implementation of your PEL can handle this feature (check with your vendor). This gives you the unlimited power of dynamically composing evaluation policies. This feature can be very helpful and dangerous at the same time because it might result in unexpected combinations of PEs. Our advice in regard to patterns is to get comfortable with the basics of using patterns before you attempt to use the pattern overlapping feature.

Dynamic Attribute Service

One of RAD's distinguishing architectural elements is the use of DAS. It enables the support of policies based on values that can change from request to request or be determined by the state of an organizational workflow. These factors are furnished by DAS in the form of dynamic attributes, syntactically equivalent to principal security attributes. The ADO obtains the dynamic attributes from DAS

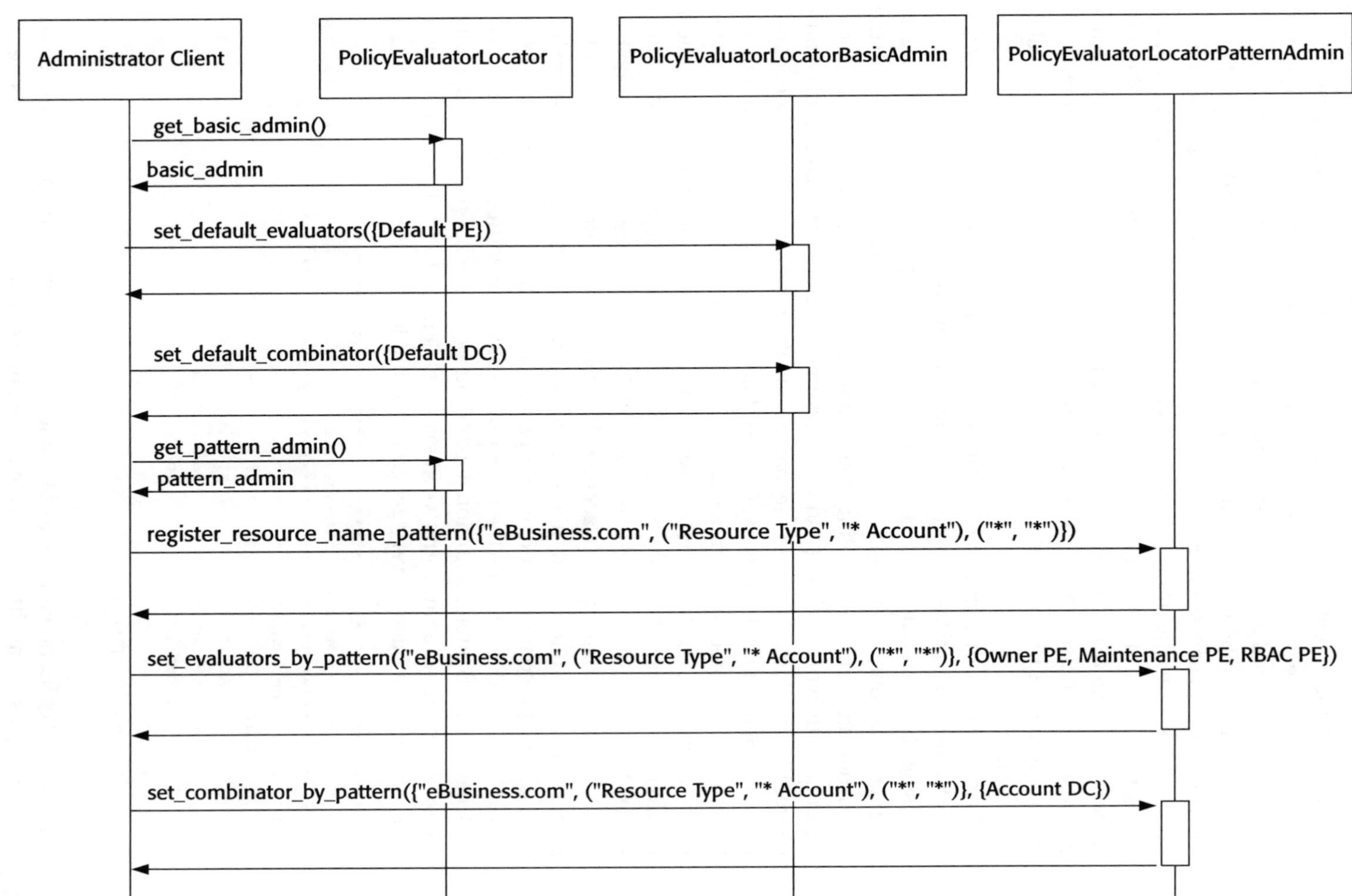

Figure 7.9 Sequence of calls on PEL administrative interfaces for configuring a PEL to support the eBusiness.com example.

before it passes the request to the corresponding DC and PEs. The values of dynamic attributes can be determined only at the time that a request for an authorization decision takes place. Thus, they are specific to the request in question. The introduction of DAS in the RAD architecture increases the variety of information available for making authorization decisions and enables the use of the traditional access matrix to support complex and dynamic access control policies. For example, if eBusiness.com changes its business model and introduces the notion of a customer "friend" who can settle an order for the customer, then DAS would determine the relationship between an account owner and a user. If the user were a "friend," DAS would add a security attribute indicating this fact. A PE would then make a decision based on the attribute's value of "friend."

To give you another example of using dynamic attributes, let's slightly change the scenario with eBusiness.com and add a new feature—a VIP option. By choosing this option at the time of creating the account or later by upgrading the regular account to this option, a customer can open a debit account with the storefront and, after depositing some money, use this money to settle the account instead of providing and verifying credit card information on each purchase. We omit details of the mechanics enabling such functionality because they are not essential for this example. But now we allow each customer to use the money deposited in his or her account to make purchases, that is, settle his or her account. In order to authorize a settlement of an account, RAD is now required to check whether the debit account of the customer has enough money to pay for the purchase. As you have probably guessed by now, the balance on the customer's debit account is a dynamic factor that could change from request to request. And this is when DAS becomes useful because the balance can be presented as a dynamic privilege attribute whose value is determined by the DAS each time the owner of the account settles the account.

Because a DAS implementation depends heavily on what particular dynamic factors it serves, no administrative interface is defined for it. The runtime interface, on the other hand, is very generic and simple:

```
//*******************************************************
// interface DynamicAttributeService
//*******************************************************
interface DynamicAttributeService {
     AttributeList get_dynamic_attributes(
          in AttributeList      attribute_list,
          in ResourceName       resource_name,
          in Operation          operation
     )
     raises (ComponentError);
};
```

Its implementation can use as much as all the information about the authorization request or as little as nothing. The component can return the same list of attributes, add new attributes to the list, or even delete some attributes from the original list. As you can see, there is a lot of freedom in what can be implemented as DAS. Another consideration that you may want to keep in mind is that the use of dynamic factors can be very expensive performance-wise because some of them may have to be mined out of corporate databases, which is not a trivial or speedy task.

Putting It All Together

Now that we have discussed all five types of RAD components separately, we will describe how interactions happen among all of them. The following interactions among components of the authorization service are shown in Figure 7.10.

1. The authorization service receives a request via the ADO interface.
2. The ADO obtains object references to those PEs and DC that are associated with the resource name in question.

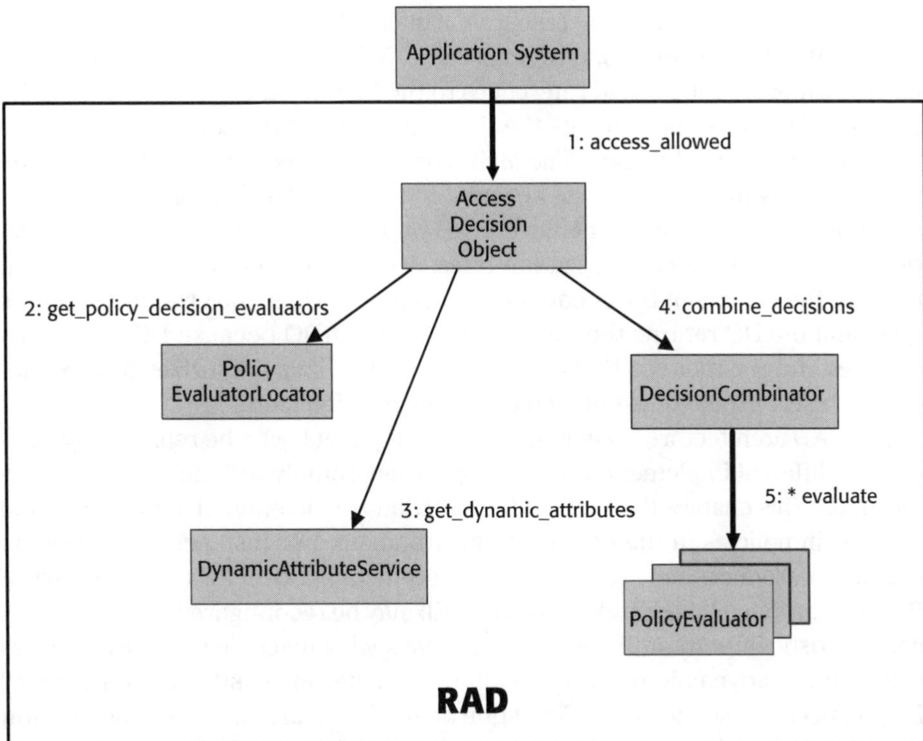

Figure 7.10 Interactions among RAD components.

3. The ADO obtains dynamic attributes of the principal (client) in the context of the resource name and the intended access operation to be performed.
4. The ADO delegates a DC instance for polling the PEs (selected in Step 2) and combining multiple results of evaluations made by PEs into a final decision.
5. The DC obtains decisions from PEs and combines them according to the combination policy. The decision is forwarded to the ADO, which in turn returns the decision to the application.

Let's look at an example of all the interactions that happen among RAD components when they serve an authorization request. We'll use our eBusiness.com example, pieces of which we have already described in this chapter. In Figure 7.11, all of the pieces are put together into one diagram.

The authorization policy contains a statement that an account can be settled by its owner. In this example, the account object is requesting authorization to perform the operation "settle" on a resource named {"eBusiness.com", ("Resource Type", "Member Account"), ("Account ID", "5678")}. Access is to be performed for a principal with AccessID=Johnson. The ADO obtains from the PEL a list of references to PEs and the DC, which should be used for making an authorization decision on a resource named {"Ebusiness.com", ("Resource Type", "Member Account"), ("Account ID", "5678")}. The PEL returns a reference to the Account DC and references to the Maintenance, Owner, and RBAC PEs. The DAS does not change the list of security attributes, which specifies that the AccessID is Johnson. The Maintenance PE checks to see if any maintenance work is occurring on the account and returns "yes" because no work is going on at this moment. The Owner PE implements owner-based authorization. According to the authorization rules, users have access to the accounts if they are the owners of the account to be accessed. Thus, the Owner PE returns "yes" and the DC returns the same answer to the ADO because DC needs only one "yes" from either the RBAC or the Owner PE. This authorizes the account object to serve the request on behalf of principal Johnson.

The RAD architecture is such that all its components can be replaced dynamically by different implementations as long as they comply with the interface specifications. This enables the support for insertion and deletion of applications and changes in policies in the computing environment. For instance, if application insertion introduces new resources to be protected, a new PE (or even a set of PEs) can be dynamically added, and the PEL may be reconfigured to use it. Is this characteristic important to you? Do you have such a dynamic workflow process that mandates dynamic reconfiguration of the enterprise authorization service? Do you need the service reconfiguration at all? These are the questions that you want to answer before going through the trouble of developing or buying a fancy implementation of RAD that performs all these reconfigurations on the fly.

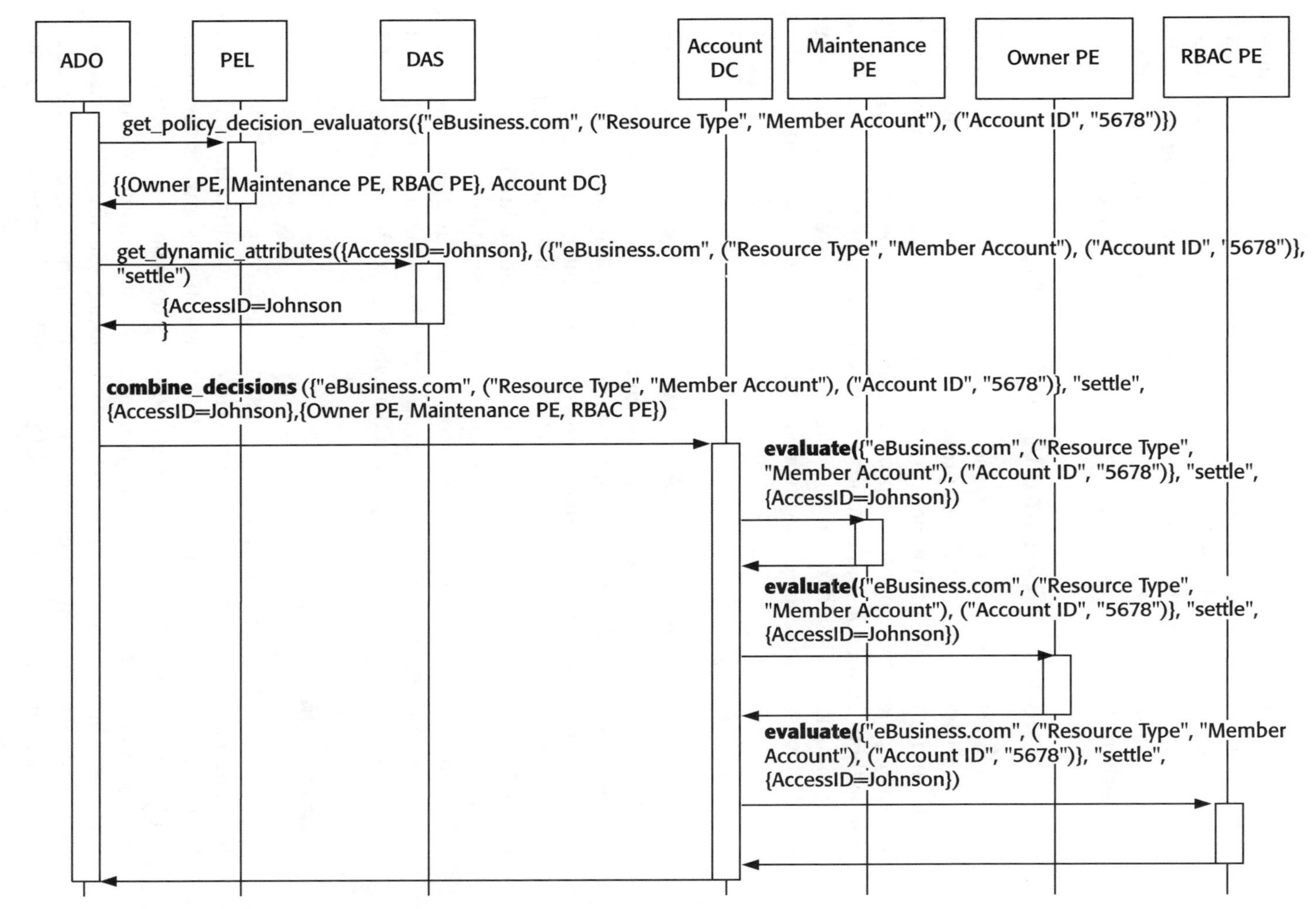

Figure 7.11 A complete interaction diagram for the eBusiness.com example.

Although we presented RAD components as logically disjointed, in practice, they can be co-located in the same process or host. CORBA's intrinsic freedom of object co-location allows you and your RAD vendors to further the support for dynamic composition and reconfiguration as well as for high availability and fault tolerance of the services based on RAD architecture. Again, arbitrary location of RAD objects can be unaffordable from performance and implementation points of view, which is something you should think about before committing to a particular RAD product or designing a home-grown implementation.

What Belongs to RAD and What Does Not

RAD architecture does not encompass all possible data and functions needed for authorization services to work properly based on the architecture. It leaves some out for the sake of simplicity, or because other services in your computing environment are supposed to provide them, or even because the specification authors could not find a good enough yet sufficiently generic design in order to make it a standard. In the following sections, we help you to understand what is in the scope of RAD specification and what is beyond.

Runtime Model

Unlike most authorization services, the RAD architecture does not restrict its implementations in the type of supported authorization policies. This was done purposefully to avoid mandating any particular policy language because today there is no such language that could be accepted as a universal "one size fits all" language for authorization policies. This is why the scope of authorization policy representation is beyond the RAD standard, as shown in Figure 7.12. The definition of authorization policies and the corresponding languages are expected to be evaluator specific. You too will probably find that authorization policies in your organization are best represented in a language specific to the application domain of your company and maybe even to the company itself.

Administrative Model

All RAD components, in addition to the runtime interfaces previously described, have interfaces to administer them. Those interfaces constitute the RAD administrative model; the scope and main elements of which are shown in Figure 7.13.

Even though the RAD architecture purposefully does not provide a means of specifying authorization policies and their representation, it allows RAD administrators to apply policies defined via implementation specific PE interfaces to protected resources. This is carried through with the notion of a policy name and with administrative interfaces for PE and PEL. A policy name is employed to associate the policy with a resource name for those PEs that can evaluate

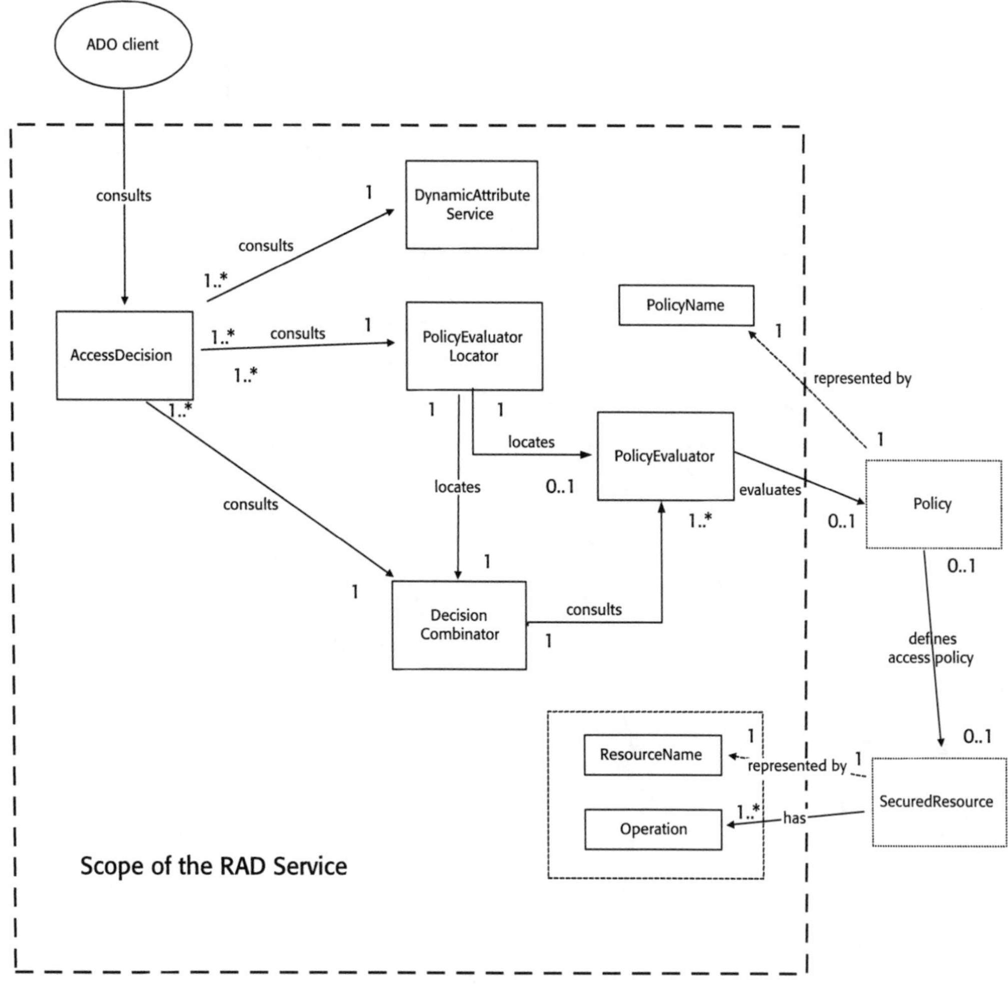

Figure 7.12 Main runtime elements and their relationship to the architecture scope (OMG, 2000).

more than one policy. By naming a policy and avoiding a definition of policy representation, we keep the RAD architecture open to the multitude of existing and future authorization policy languages.

Another reason for allowing each PE to be administered using a different interface and access control rules written in a different language is that such a design enables the use of existing policy engines, which were not originally developed to be PEs (e.g., Resource Access Control Facility, or RACF), and the support for future ones.

Runtime and administrative interfaces and the supporting data structures defined in OMG IDL, along with prose description of their semantics, constitute the RAD architecture. Its computational view is shown in Figure 7.14.

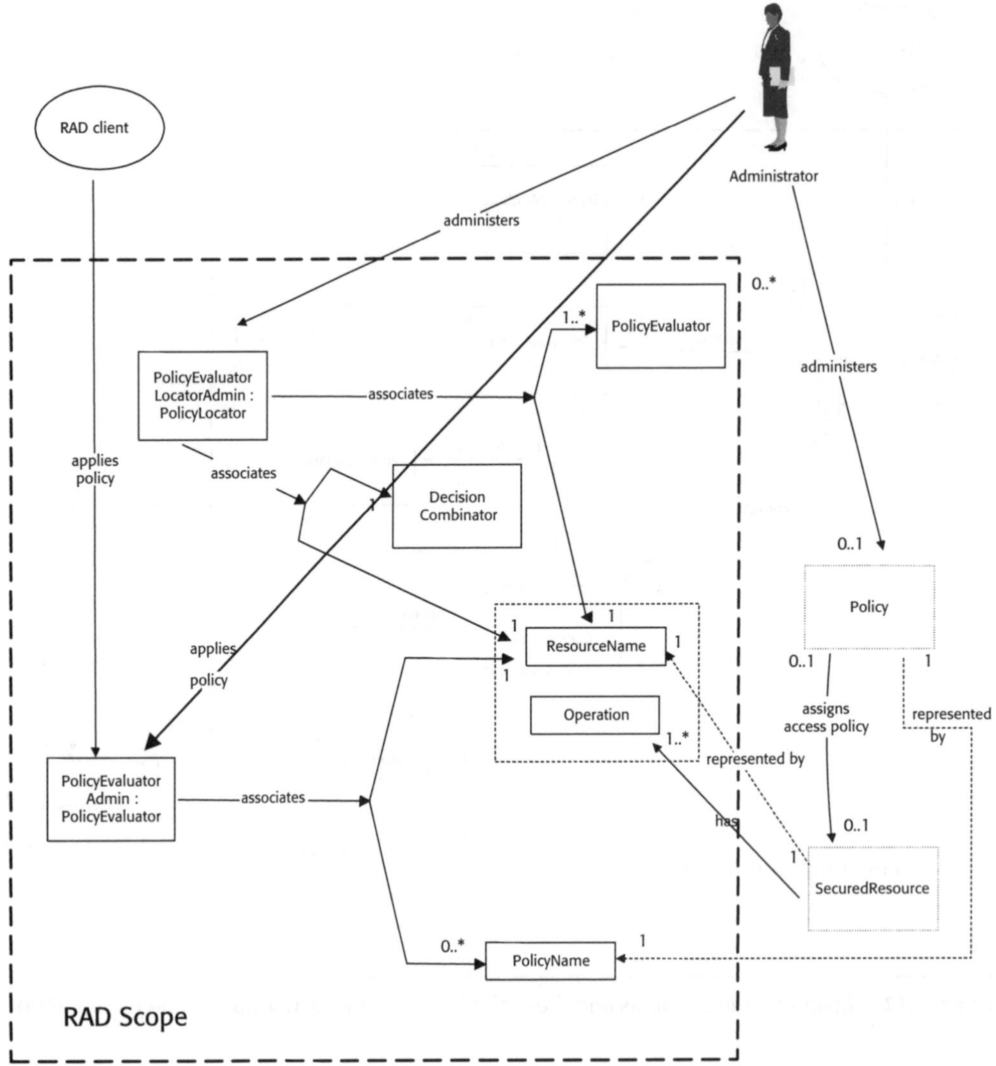

Figure 7.13 Administrative elements and their relationship to the architecture scope (OMG, 2000).

We have already described the semantics of operations on the AccessDecision interface. Let's walk through the rest of the runtime interfaces and briefly see what they do. PolicyEvaluatorLocator::get_policy_decision_evaluators() returns a list of PEs, each coupled with its name as a string and a reference to a DC, which will invoke the evaluators and combine received results into a single yes/no decision. ADO delegates this work through operation combine_decisions() on the DC interface. Before ADO does the delegation, though, it obtains

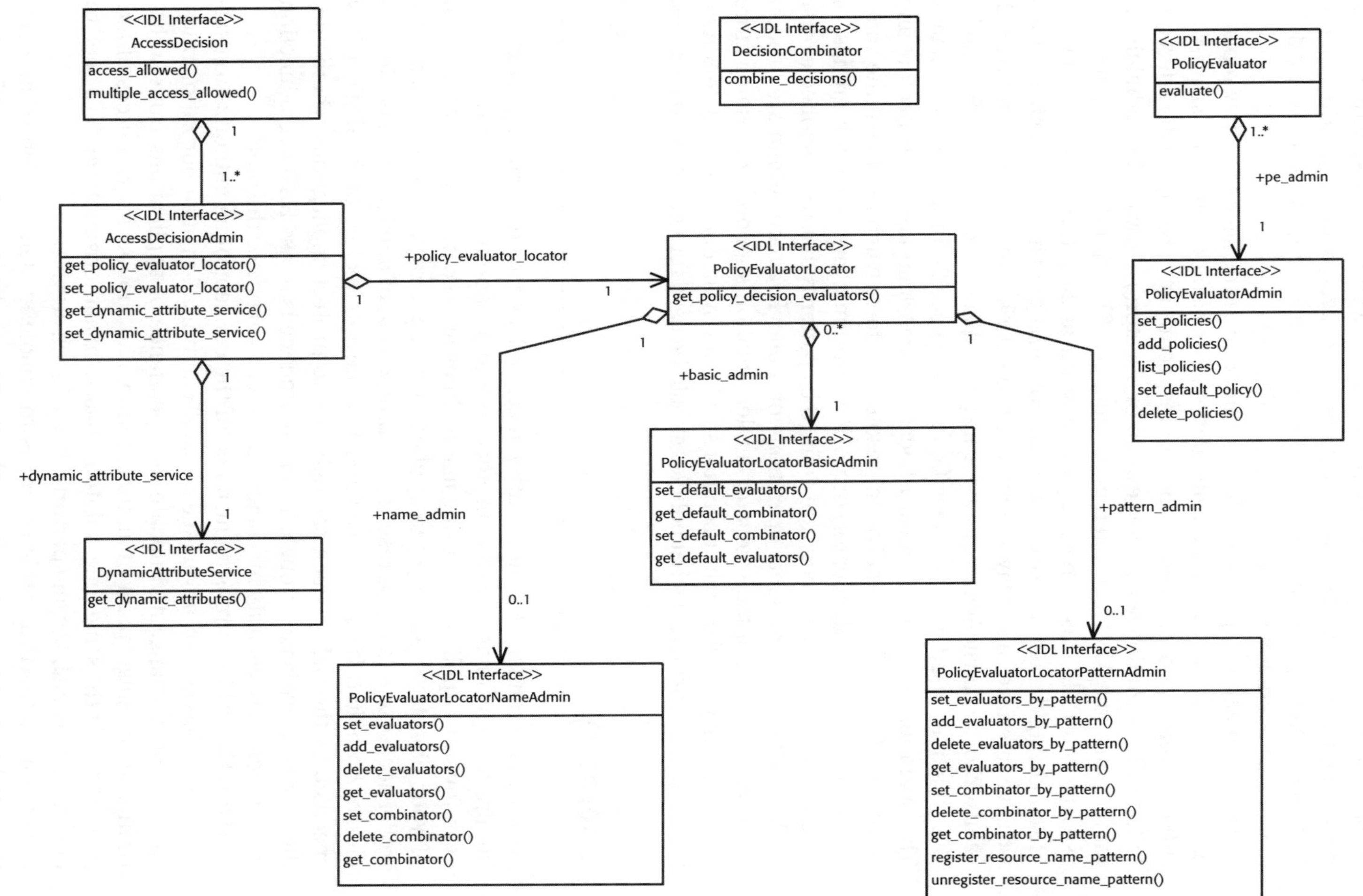

Figure 7.14 Computational part of the RAD architecture.

a list of privilege attributes for the principal in question updated with dynamic attributes by invoking DynamicAttributeService::get_dynamic_attributes(). A DC polls each Policy Evaluator, or as many of them as it needs to make the decision, using operation PolicyEvaluator::evaluate().

The administrative part of the RAD architecture is designed to allow replaceable RAD objects within an implementation. For instance, the *AccessDecisionAdmin* interface contains operations for inspecting and specifying the reference to the PEL. Operation set_policy_evaluator_locator() allows a RAD administrator to "point" the ADO to a different instance of PEL. After the change, the ADO uses the new PEL. This is an example of how the architecture addresses the goal of supporting changes in policies and the computing environment. Other administrative interfaces also play an important role. Operations defined on PolicyEvaluatorLocatorBasicAdmin allow for inspecting and setting default PEs and a DC, which are used when no specific ones are specified for a resource name. The operations on PolicyEvaluatorLocatorNameAdmin are for inspecting and setting a DC and PEs on individual resource names, whereas almost the same operations on PolicyEvaluatorLocatorPatternAdmin are used for groups of resource names. These groups are defined by patterns that we described earlier in this chapter. The optional operations on PolicyEvaluatorAdmin are used in those cases in which the evaluator implementation supports the use of more then one policy. Similar to the operations on PolicyEvaluatorLocatorNameAdmin, they allow for specifying what policies should be used for what resource names.

Summary

We always recommend using security in general, and access control in particular, provided by middleware to protect your applications and resources. However, for some applications, using just middleware security would not meet all of your objectives because the applications might require fine-grained control of access to enterprise resources, enforcement of application specific policies, or both. In this chapter, we described the architecture of the RAD facility specified by the OMG, which can help you to protect applications where middleware security is not enough. The best practice is to use RAD in conjunction with middleware security mechanisms rather than one or the other.

The RAD architecture is an instance of the concept of an authorization service, which has several advantages: logical centralization of authorization rules, ease of policy change and update, independence of applications from authorization logic, single point of administration, and support for resources of any granularity. At the same time, solutions based on authorization services need to ensure high availability and performance of such services.

The aim of the RAD architecture is to enable implementation of its components by various vendors due to the diversity in the requirements of access control policies, performance, scalability, and other system properties from different government and commercial markets. We described the RAD architecture and explained the role and the semantics of each of its components.

The ADO serves as the front end (or proxy) to RAD clients and coordinates the interactions between other RAD components. PEs perform evaluation decisions based on the policies governing the access to protected resources. The DC combines the results of the evaluations made by potentially multiple PEs into a final "yes/no" authorization decision by applying a certain combination policy. Which PEs should be used and how many is determined by a PolicyEvaluatorLocator, which keeps track of and provides references to potentially several PEs and a DC that are collectively responsible for making an authorization decision for a given access request. DAS enables the support of policies based on values that can change from request to request or be determined by the state of an organizational workflow.

RAD is by no means a replacement or substitution for EJB and CORBA security services, which typically provide security services such as user security administration, authentication, communication integrity and confidentiality, audit and nonrepudiation, and even controls invocations on RAD interfaces. You should view RAD as a service at the application layer that has to be protected by a general security infrastructure as does any other application.

Before you resort to solutions based on RAD or a similar technology, you need to get the most out of your CORBA and EJB security services. Thus, you should thoroughly understand the capabilities of their security policies, what you can and can't do, and what you'd rather not do when using middleware security. The next chapter, which describes advanced authorization and delegation policy topics, will help you get a deeper understanding of the capabilities of EJB and CORBA security policies.

Scaleable Security Policies

When you begin to model policies that are large and complex, you soon realize that it's not easy. You need to set up CORBA policy domains, required rights, and privilege attributes to satisfy business security requirements. You are probably wondering how you are going to translate your high-level organizational security policies into the language of logical roles as well as methods in EJB, and rights, attributes, and policy domains in CORBA. This chapter is intended to help you with exactly these issues.

This chapter helps you write manageable, scalable, and easy-to-understand authorization policies for CORBA and EJB. You will also learn how to take advantage of delegation for supporting complex invocation chains without jeopardizing the security of your company. All discussions in the chapter actively use the descriptions of EJB and CORBA security from Chapters 2 and 3.

We provide guidance on a variety of security policy issues for dealing with large-scale applications. Most important are the three mechanisms that define collections for scale: access rights, security attributes, and security policy domains. Together they form a powerful foundation for authorization policies. We begin by discussing the use of access rights, which create collections of interfaces and operations. Because access rights are not supported in the EJB standard, this discussion focuses on CORBA security (CORBASec), although the basic principles apply to many other authorization solutions. Next, we

ESI SECURITY ADMINISTRATION PRINCIPLE: COLLECTIONS FOR SCALE

Access rights, security attributes (e.g., roles and groups), and security policy domains are all grouping mechanisms that provide support for administration scaling. This chapter explores how these approaches fit together, particularly in the context of RBAC.

discuss security attributes, which are used by EJB and CORBA to create collections of users. We then present several models for role-based access control (RBAC) that show how access rights and security attributes can be used to define hierarchical access using organizational roles. To complete the topic of authorization policy, we move on to security policy domains, which define common security policies for collections of components. Credential delegation is the last large-scale application policy that we discuss in this chapter. Delegation is commonly required for chains of invocations across many components, but we recommend avoiding it if possible.

Using Rights Wisely

As we described in Chapter 3, every operation in CORBA has a global set of associated required rights. This set, together with a combinator (*all* or *any* rights), defines what rights a principal must have in order to invoke the operation. Required rights are a way of grouping operations in CORBASec. An important part of designing required rights is the definition of the rights. Similar to privilege attributes, these definitions should be consistent over the whole organization and should be understood and used by the administrators when they are assigning the set of required rights for the interfaces and methods that are to be controlled. In defining the set of required rights, you should take into account how they will be used by the objects in a domain and what attributes of a principal will be assigned what effective rights in a given domain. Another important point to keep in mind is that required rights need to apply across the inheritance hierarchy unless overridden by a derived interface.

The CORBASec runtime environment is not aware of interface inheritance. Given the following interface definition, when the placeOrder() operation is invoked on the CustomerAccount interface, the security service doesn't recognize the fact that this method is derived from the ShoppingCart interface.

```
interface ShoppingCart
{
     void placeOrder  (in Order theOrder);
     void deleteOrder (in ProductID  ProductOrderToDelete);
     OrderSeq listOrders ();
}
```

```
interface CustomerAccount : ShoppingCart
{
     readonly attribute CustomerID Customer;
     void settleOrder (in CreditCard theCreditCard);
};
```

As a result, you must set required rights on the two instances of the placeOrder() operation, one for each interface that uses it. Even the describe_interface() operation defined on CORBA::Object, which uses the Interface Repository, reports back all operations in derived classes without indicating their inheritance status.

In order to resolve this shortcoming, we suggest you make sure that the administrative part of the CORBASec product you buy has the capability of browsing interfaces that have required rights set on them and a definition of interface inheritances. These will allow your administrators to cope with the lack of required rights inheritance.

Because required and granted rights—as opposed to principal security attributes—never get outside of your enterprise, you have more flexibility with respect to designing and modeling your security policies with rights and domains. Later in this chapter, we provide examples of designing rights to support role-based policies with role hierarchies. This discussion will give you an idea of how to take advantage of having complete control over rights when modeling security policies with CORBA.

Although your organization has complete control over required and granted rights, be very careful in defining the rights and their semantics. First, you must take into account how rights will be used by the objects in the authorization policy domains and what attributes of a principal will be assigned to what rights in a given domain. For this, you need to have a very good understanding of the security policies you are implementing.

Second, definitions of required rights must be consistent over the whole organization and must be understood and used by the administrators when they are assigning them to the methods to be controlled. It is important to use the same rights families across all divisions of the company because even if the divisions don't communicate with each other today, they probably will in the future.

For large systems and enterprises, it is not a trivial task to determine the implications of assigning particular required rights to interface methods and granting rights to privilege attributes. Ideally, you want to have a means to model your policies with required and granted rights, privilege attributes, and policy domains. You shouldn't expect that every CORBASec product comes with modeling capabilities. If your product does, consider it a nice bonus and take advantage of the tools.

Privilege attributes, required rights assigned to interface methods, the rights granted to attributes in a domain, and the assignment of object instances to domains are interdependent, although this interdependence is not particularly obvious when each is analyzed in isolation. Having said this, we discuss privilege attributes next.

Using Attributes Wisely

Security attributes allow grouping of principals and applying the same security policies to such groups. You need to consider a number of points in order to use privilege attributes to your advantage. One is that care and thought must be put into choosing what attributes are assigned and allowed to which individuals because this determines how these individuals, acting through applications, will be controlled by the security services. This further emphasizes the need for your organization to explicitly define the semantics assigned to a particular attribute. For example, what does the term *supervisor* mean in your organization? Is it any supervisor or are there meaningful gradations of supervisor as that attribute applies to the security of the system. Furthermore, what are the semantics of a combination of attributes? Is a "clerk" in the insurance division semantically equivalent to a "clerk" in the complaints department, and so on?

In addition to assigning attributes to individuals, it may also be important to assign attributes to application entities that can control server applications. For example, you might have an application that automatically forwards certain forms. In that case, the forwarding application might need certain attributes to access the servers to which the forms are forwarded. One approach might be to create an entity for that purpose, give it specific attributes, and use these attributes to determine access to that server.

When discussing attributes in Chapter 3, we stated that it is preferred to adhere to the OMG set of defined rights. One of the reasons for this is to reduce complexity and another reason is to make interoperability easier. Because attributes are used on both the client side, which may be from one company, and on the server side, which may be from another company, interoperability dictates that both companies have a common set of attributes. Rights, on the other hand, are within the purview of the company that controls the access to the server implementation; therefore, you can have more flexibility defining those rights.

If you asked us to choose between using only a few privilege attributes or using many, we would recommend somewhere in the middle. Too few groups, roles, and other attributes do not provide enough granularity in authorization policies. Too many attributes, and each attribute will be easy to understand, but the overall authorization policy will be very complex. You will need to find your own happy medium in your particular environment. The number of attributes used for modeling security policies will also depend on the administration tools you are using and the training of your security administrators.

We recommend you follow this list of rules for managing security attributes:

- Because enterprises are dynamic, the security constraints represented in attributes and policy domains have to be continually modified and updated.
- The semantics of each attribute value must be clearly defined between any two disparate entities, so that all of them agree on the meaning of attribute values.
- Your organization needs to explicitly define the semantics assigned to a particular attribute (e.g., "administrator") and a combination of attributes (e.g., a "clerk" in the Insurance division and a "clerk" in the Complaints department).
- It may be important to assign attributes to entities that can control server applications (e.g., applications that automatically forward certain forms).
- Strive to find an optimum balance for your company between using too many attributes and too few, so as not to lose the required level of granularity and be able to manage the complexity.

An Argument for Roles

Although (as we discussed in Chapter 7) CORBA and EJB access control mechanisms are sometimes inadequate for addressing all security requirements, they allow the enforcement of authorization policies outside of applications. In addition, they are very well integrated with the corresponding services. These two factors make the use of CORBA and EJB access control mechanisms, when they are sufficient, more favorable than programmatic application level control with the OMG RAD and similar authorization models. The latter are used when the built-in mechanisms are functionally inadequate. Before you opt to employ application level access control, it is important to take maximum advantage of middleware access control. This is why a good understanding of CORBA and EJB access control capabilities is crucial for engineering the protection of application resources.

In the next sections, we help you to take one more step toward mastering CORBA and EJB access control by showing how role-based access control (RBAC) models can be supported using CORBA and EJB security services. First, we explain different RBAC models so that RBAC becomes for you not just another buzzword, but instead a meaningful access control concept. We also describe what is required from an implementation of the CORBA and EJB security services in order to support various RBAC models. These sections will advance your understanding of the CORBA and EJB authorization mechanisms' capabilities, which are vital to the use of middleware in protecting enterprise application resources.

Overview of RBAC

RBAC (Sandhu et al., 1996) is a family of reference models in which permissions are associated with roles, and users are assigned to appropriate roles. Although groups and roles are closely related, and RBAC may be implemented in group-only systems such as Unix and MS Windows, the concepts of roles and groups are different. If used properly, a group usually represents organizational affiliation (e.g., department, laboratory, division, or group of workers) or geographical location (company branch, building, floor, and even room). Examples of groups are marketing department, nuclear physics laboratory, computer support group, Dallas office, east building, and intensive care floor. A role can represent competency, authority, responsibility, or specific duty assignments. Role examples are clerk, VP, financial officer, and shift manager.

Some variations of RBAC include the capability to establish relations between roles, between permissions and roles, and between users and roles. There are four established RBAC reference models: unrelated roles ($RBAC_0$), role-hierarchies ($RBAC_1$), user and role assignment constraints ($RBAC_2$), and both hierarchies and constraints ($RBAC_3$). The RBAC models support three security principles in varying degrees:

Least privilege. Requires users to operate with the minimum set of privileges necessary to do their jobs.

Separation of duties. Requires that for particular sets of transactions, no single individual be allowed to execute all transactions within the set. A commonly used example is the separation of a transaction needed to initiate a payment with a transaction needed to authorize a payment.

Data abstraction. Requires security policies to be independent of the concrete representation and form of data and other valuable resources. In other words, RBAC models abstract the access to system-specific resources into system-independent access permissions. The permissions can represent anything you want. For example, they could mean the use of CPU time, modification of patient records, and even eating candies.

RBAC is an important concept for handling large-scale authorization policies: Most of the security community believes that eventually RBAC will prove to be more effective in security administration than other mainstream models, such as lattice-based *mandatory access control* (MAC) and owner-based *discretionary access control* (DAC), which are explained in the following sidebar. Access control based on roles has become so popular in the industry that today almost all security products claim to support the role paradigm; however, not everyone can explain what it means. Therefore, we'll give you a brief introduction into each of the RBAC models before we describe how a CORBA or EJB security implementation can support them. You can then judge and decide for yourself which RBAC model(s) you want to use in order to get your job done.

DAC AND MAC IN NUTSHELL

There are several widely accepted access control models. Besides RBAC, two others are owner-based discretionary access control (DAC) (NCSC, 1987) and lattice-based mandatory access control (MAC) (Bell and LaPadula, 1975) models. Brief explanations of each are as follows.

The main premise of DAC is that individual users are owners of resources and because of this they have complete discretion over who should be granted what access permissions for their resources. This is why DAC is often referred to as owner-based. In order for a user to access a resource, its owner should explicitly permit access to the resource by that user. Usually, DAC policies are implemented in the form of access control lists (ACLs), where each resource has an ACL administered by its owner. Because discretionary models are so generic and flexible, they easily suit access control requirements for any system. However, if the number of resources is large, then DAC administration becomes too expensive and burdensome for the resource owners. Another problem with the DAC model is that it's almost impossible to enforce consistent policies and determine what access is granted to a user. To do either of these tasks, you have to go through all the resources and read the information in their ACLs.

In MAC, each user and resource is assigned a security level (e.g., "confidential," "secret", or "top secret"). Security levels are usually partially ordered, thereby creating a "lattice." For instance, "secret" is higher than "confidential" and lower than "top secret." The sensitivity of the resource is reflected in its security level. The security level of a user, sometimes called "clearance," reflects the user's trustworthiness not to disclose sensitive information to users not cleared to do so. In MAC-based systems, a user is usually allowed to read only those resources that have a lower security or the same security level as the user. For example, a "secret" cleared user can read "confidential" and "secret" information but not "top secret" information. In addition, a user may write into a resource if the resource's security level is higher than the security level of the user. Thus, the information can only flow up from lower levels to higher levels. This model is better at ensuring consistency of organizational policies than owner-based DAC, as long as the security levels are assigned properly to the resources and users. However, it is not flexible and thus not very supportive of dynamic business workflow. Also, it's only concerned with information flow, which does not make it very suitable for service-based systems, such as today's businesses, in which services as well as information have to be protected.

Among the four RBAC reference models known in the security community, $RBAC_0$ is the base model. It only requires that a system have the notions of users, roles, permissions, and sessions. There are no constraints on the assignment of permissions to roles and users to roles or any relations among roles in $RBAC_0$. $RBAC_1$ has hierarchies of roles in addition to all the features of $RBAC_0$. $RBAC_2$

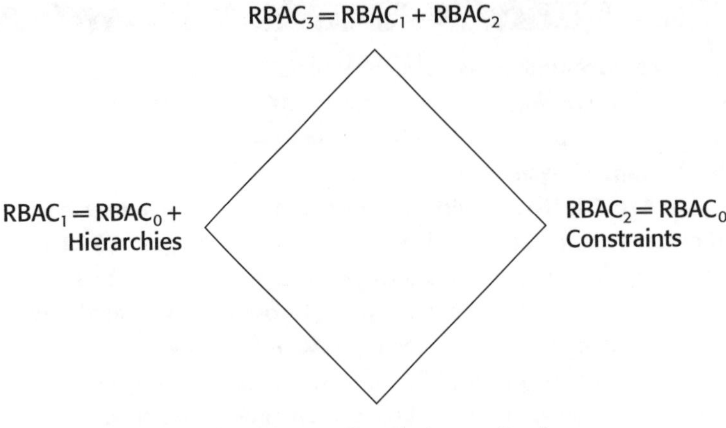

Figure 8.1 Relationships among RBAC models.

has constraints on the assignment of users to roles and permissions to roles in addition to all the features of $RBAC_0$. $RBAC_3$ combines $RBAC_1$ and $RBAC_2$ and has both role hierarchies and constraints. See Figure 8.1.

According to the RBAC family of models, each session is a mapping of one user to possibly many roles. When a user establishes a session, logging into the system and authenticating activates a subset of roles assigned to the user by the user's administrator(s). The permissions available to the user are the union of permissions from all roles activated in that session. RBAC treats permissions as uninterpreted symbols because their semantics is dependent on the implementation and system, which enables data abstraction.

In the upcoming sections, we walk you through all four RBAC models, describe them, and explain how you can implement them in CORBA and EJB security.

$RBAC_0$: Just Roles

A system implementing the $RBAC_0$ model can be described using the following simple and ordinary elements:

- Sets of users, roles, permissions, and sessions as described in the previous section.
- Assignment of permissions to roles, which you can picture as a table as shown in Table 8.1, with rows representing roles, columns representing permissions, and cells marked if the corresponding permission is assigned to the corresponding role and unmarked otherwise.
- Assignment of users to roles, which you can picture as a table as shown in Table 8.2, with rows representing roles, columns representing users, and

Table 8.1 Assignment of Permissions to Roles for eBusiness.com Example

	PERMISSIONS																			
	ProductFactory		Regular Product		Special Product		CustomerAccount				MemberAccount				CustomerAccountFactory			MemberAccountFactory		
ROLE	getProducts	lookup	getPrice	setPrice	getPrice	setPrice	placeOrder	deleteOrder	listOrders	settleOrder	placeOrder	deleteOrder	listOrders	settleAccount	create	delete	lookup	create	delete	lookup
Visitor	X	X													X		X			X
Customer	X	X	X				X	X	X	X					X		X			X
Member	X	X	X		X						X	X	X	X	X		X			X
Staff	X	X	X	X	X	X	X	X	X		X	X	X		X	X	X	X	X	X

cells marked if the corresponding user is assigned to the corresponding role and unmarked otherwise.

- A way of determining which user runs a given session (this is abstracted in RBAC using the hypothetical function *user(s)*, which receives the session ID as an argument and returns the user ID).
- A way of mapping a given session into a set of roles (this is abstracted in RBAC using the hypothetical function *roles(s)*, which receives the session ID as an argument and returns a set of roles activated for that session).

Table 8.2 $RBAC_0$ Assignment of Users to Roles for eBusiness.com Example

	USERS			
ROLES	PARKER	WILSON	JOHNSON	DALY
Visitor				
Customer				X
Member			X	
Staff	X	X		

If we use roles to model the security requirements for our eBusiness.com example listed in Chapter 1, we would get the permission-to-role assignments shown in Table 8.1. You can see in the table that everyone can invoke all the operations of a visitor. Although we introduce the role "visitor," we could just make the visitor permissions open to everyone and drop the role "visitor" altogether.

The user-to-role assignment relation for our example is shown in Table 8.2. For simplicity sake, we only have two users that are staff members as well as one customer and one member.

That's it. The basic model is very simple and is based on simple and natural concepts that we use in security every day: users, roles, sessions, and permissions. In the next section, we explain how $RBAC_0$ is mapped into CORBA access control.

$RBAC_0$ Using CORBA

The correlation between $RBAC_0$ and CORBA main elements is shown in Table 8.3.

Because we can group operations using rights in CORBASec, the permission-to-role assignment table will be different than Table 8.1. Instead of one table, we'll have two tables that express the same permission-to-role assignment as the original one (i.e., Table 8.1). The first table groups operations by means of required rights, and the second table determines what rights are granted to what roles.

Table 8.4 illustrates the rights required for accessing operations on objects. We used the right combinator "all" for all the sets of required rights. As stated in the discussion on rights in Chapter 3, if a principal has, for example, right "g" in its set of granted rights, then that principal is allowed to invoke any operation from rights set "g." We created five rights sets and placed each operation into one of the sets. All operations available to any visitor went into the "OPEN ACCESS" set. All other operations went into one of the four other sets.

After looking at the table, you might ask, "Why on earth have they chosen these particular rights to group the methods?" We could very well have used some other rights, but we decided to adhere to the standard rights predefined in the CORBA security specification where possible. This is why we used stan-

Table 8.3 Correspondents between RBACO and CORBA Elements

RBAC	CORBA
Users	Users
Roles	Privilege attributes of type "role"
Permissions	Sets of rights
Sessions	Principals, which are nothing but authenticated sets of security attributes from the CORBA access control point of view

Table 8.4 Grouping Operations Using Required Rights in CORBA

	OPERATIONS																			
	ProductFactory		Regular Product		Special Product		CustomerAccount				MemberAccount				CustomerAccountFactory			MemberAccountFactory		
REQUIRED RIGHTS SET	getProducts	lookup	getPrice	setPrice	getPrice	setPrice	placeOrder	deleteOrder	listOrders	settleOrder	placeOrder	deleteOrder	listOrders	settleAccount	create	delete	lookup	create	delete	lookup
OPEN ACCESS	X	X													X		X			X
g			X		X															
s							X	X	X											
su										X										
p											X	X	X							
pu														X						
m				X		X										X		X	X	

dard rights from the "CORBA" family *g, s, m, u*. As previously mentioned, it's a good idea to use standard rights unless there is a justified reason not to.

One such reason might be the inability or difficulty to only use the four standard rights and their combinations to group all the methods. For instance, four rights were not enough to model the security policies for the eBusiness.com example because we used only one domain, "Accounts," to place all account objects instances of CustomerAccount and MemberAccount interfaces. We didn't want customers to access accounts of members, so we needed to use different required rights for operations on CustomerAccount and MemberAccount interfaces. However, because we already used all four standard rights, we had to resort to introducing one more right "p" of the family "other." This is also a good example of the inherent interdependency between rights and domains. If we had located CustomerAccount and MemberAccount objects in separate domains, the four standard rights would have been sufficient. Keep in mind that in order to maintain the complexity, you must be judicious about creating new rights.

Table 8.5 Granting Rights to Roles $RBAC_0$ for Domain Accounts

DOMAIN ACCOUNTS				
	GRANTED RIGHTS			
ROLE	**u**	**s**	**p**	**m**
Visitor				
Customer	X	X		
Member	X		X	
Staff		X	X	X

Another rule of thumb is to use rights according to their semantics as much as possible. For example, in Table 8.4, we located only inspector (get*) methods in rights set "g," which represents "get." However, this rule is difficult to follow if you try to limit yourself to standard rights only. As you can see, there is an inspector method listOrders() in the "s" (representing "set") rights set.

After we group methods using required rights, we can use required rights as permissions in RBAC. We can then operate with the five sets "g," "s," "su," "p," "pu," and "m" as first class permissions instead of 19 methods, which results in nearly a four-fold reduction in the amount of administration data.

The other table determines which rights are granted to which role. This table is not necessary for defining a generic RBAC system, but is essential for configuring each access policy domain in CORBASec. An example of such a table for domain Accounts is shown in Table 8.5. According to the table, for instance, staff gets rights *spm*, and visitors don't get any rights because they only have access to publicly available operations. Customers, on the other hand, are assigned to rights *us* and members—to rights *up*. Right *g* is not granted to any role because it is only required for invoking operations on the Product interface (see Table 8.4), and instances of the Product interface are not in domain Accounts as you may remember from Chapter 3.

Once we've grouped methods using required rights and have assigned granted rights to roles, we can make the $RBAC_0$ assignment of permissions to roles in CORBA. Table 8.6 provides an example of the assignment for domain Accounts. A complete permission-to-role assignment for the eBusiness.com system would be a collection of such tables for all the domains—Application, Accounts, SpecialProducts, and RegularProducts.

An $RBAC_0$ system in the language of CORBA is described as follows:

- Users, attributes of type "role," rights, and principals
- Assignment of granted rights to role attributes (or just roles) as exemplified in Table 8.5
- Assignment of users to roles as in Table 8.2 for example

Table 8.6 Assignment of Permissions to Roles in CORBA Using Groups of Required Rights for Domain Accounts

	PERMISSIONS				
ROLE	s	su	p	pu	m
Customer	X	X			
Member			X	X	
Staff	X		X		X

- Hypothetical function *user(s)*, which receives session *s* as an argument and returns the user ID
- Hypothetical function *role(s)*, which receives session *s* as an argument and returns a set of roles activated for that session

The granted rights are the union of rights granted to every role the principal is in. The preceding description of $RBAC_0$ in the language of CORBA and the one in the beginning of the section on $RBAC_0$ are identical except for the terms, which are different in RBAC and CORBA terminology.

As a practitioner, you are definitely more interested in specific requirements for a security product than in somewhat theoretical descriptions of $RBAC_0$ models and their translation into the language of CORBASec. Anticipating your practical interests, we list the requirements in the form of a checklist. In order for a CORBASec product to support $RBAC_0$, it should:

- Comply with the specification
- Provide a means to administrate a user-to-role assignment
- Provide a means for users to select, through a user sponsor, a set of roles with which they would like to activate the new principal
- Implement *PrincipalAuthenticator*, which creates principal credentials containing privilege attributes of type role according to a user-to-role assignment
- Implement *PrincipalAuthenticator*, which creates principal credentials containing one and only one privilege attribute of type *AccessId*

If you only need $RBAC_0$ functionality, then the preceding list tells you exactly what you need to watch for when you select a CORBASec product. Now, let's see how EJB can support $RBAC_0$.

$RBAC_0$ Using EJB

The representation of main $RBAC_0$ elements in EJB is shown in Table 8.7.

An $RBAC_0$ system in the language of EJB is described as follows:

Table 8.7 Correspondence between $RBAC_0$ and EJB Elements

RBAC	EJB
Users	Users
Roles	Roles
Permissions	Methods, as specified in <method-permission> elements of deployment descriptors
Sessions	User authenticated identity, used for "pulling" all roles the user is assigned to

- Users, roles, methods, and user identities
- Assignment of methods to roles in <method-permission> elements of the bean deployment descriptor
- Assignment of users to roles in the security environment of the bean container
- Hypothetical function *user*(s), which receives user authenticated identity s as an argument and returns the user ID
- Hypothetical function *roles*(s), which receives user authenticated identity s as an argument and returns a set of roles activated for that identity

As discussed in Chapter 2, the assignment of permissions to roles is done in EJB by the Application Assembler in the deployment descriptor using the <method-permission> elements. For every group of methods and roles in Table 8.1 for which the assignment is the same, the Assembler writes a separate <method-permission> element. After examining Table 8.1, eight such groups are formed and are shown in Table 8.8, which is different from Table 8.1 only in the way the methods are sorted. Now the methods are put together in groups with the same roles having access to the methods.

Let's take a look at how the <method-permission> elements of the deployment descriptor look for the eBusiness.com example in the case of $RBAC_0$. Table 8.8 is rewritten in the language of <method-permission> elements.

```
<!--
Everybody can invoke the following methods
-->
<method-permission>
        <role-name>visitor</role-name>
        <role-name>customer</role-name>
        <role-name>member</role-name>
        <role-name>staff</role-name>
        <method>
             <ejb-name>ProductFactory</ejb-name>
             <method-name>*</method-name>
```

Table 8.8 Grouping of Methods and Roles into Groups with the Same Permissions

ROLE	ProductFactory		CustomerAccountFactory		MemberAccountFactory	Regular Product	CustomerAccount				MemberAccount				Special Product	CustomerAccountFactory	Regular Product	MemberAccountFactory		Special Product
	getProducts	lookup	create	lookup	lookup	getPrice	placeOrder	deleteOrder	listOrders	settleOrder	placeOrder	deleteOrder	listOrders	settleAccount	getPrice	delete	setPrice	create	delete	setPrice
Visitor	X	X	X	X	X															
Customer	X	X	X	X	X	X	X	X	X	X										
Member	X	X	X	X	X	X					X	X	X	X	X					
Staff	X	X	X	X	X	X	X	X	X		X	X	X		X	X	X	X	X	X

```
        </method>
        <method>
             <ejb-name>CustomerAccountFactory</ejb-name>
             <method-name>create</method-name>
             <method-name>lookup</method-name>
        </method>
        <method>
             <ejb-name>MemberAccountFactory</ejb-name>
             <method-name>lookup</method-name>
        </method>
</method-permission>

<!--
Permissions for regular products
-->
<method-permission>
        <role-name>customer</role-name>
        <role-name>member</role-name>
        <role-name>staff</role-name>
        <method>
             <ejb-name>Product</ejb-name>
             <method-name>getPrice</method-name>
        </method>
</method-permission>
```

```
<!--
Permissions for special products
-->
<method-permission>
        <role-name>member</role-name>
        <role-name>staff</role-name>
        <method>
             <ejb-name>Product</ejb-name>
             <method-name>getPrice</method-name>
        </method>
</method-permission>

<!--
What customers and staff on their behalf can do
-->
<method-permission>
        <role-name>customer</role-name>
        <role-name>staff</role-name>
        <method>
             <ejb-name>CustomerAccount</ejb-name>
             <method-name>placeOrder</method-name>
             <method-name>deleteOrder</method-name>
             <method-name>listOrders</method-name>
        </method>
</method-permission>

<!--
What only customers can do
-->
<method-permission>
        <role-name>customer</role-name>
        <method>
             <ejb-name>CustomerAccount</ejb-name>
             <method-name>settleOrder</method-name>
        </method>
</method-permission>

<!--
What members and staff on their behalf can do
-->
<method-permission>
        <role-name>member</role-name>
        <role-name>staff</role-name>
        <method>
             <ejb-name>MemberAccount</ejb-name>
             <method-name>placeOrder</method-name>
             <method-name>deleteOrder</method-name>
             <method-name>listOrders</method-name>
        </method>
</method-permission>
```

```
<!--
What only members can do
-->
<method-permission>
        <role-name>member</role-name>
        <method>
              <ejb-name>MemberAccount</ejb-name>
              <method-name>settleAccount</method-name>
        </method>
</method-permission>

<!--
What only staff can do
-->
<method-permission>
        <role-name>staff</role-name>
        <method>
              <ejb-name>CustomerAccountFactory</ejb-name>
              <method-name>delete</method-name>
        </method>
        <method>
              <ejb-name>MemberAccountFactory</ejb-name>
              <method-name>create</method-name>
              <method-name>delete</method-name>
        </method>
        <method>
              <ejb-name>Product</ejb-name>
              <method-name>setPrice</method-name>
        </method>
</method-permission>
```

Although the descriptor fragment is long, it becomes quite obvious once Tables 8.1 and 8.8 are understood.

If you only need $RBAC_0$ functionality, the following list provides you with exactly what you need to watch for when you select an EJB Container product. In order for an EJB Container to support $RBAC_0$, it should:

- Comply with EJB 2.0 or higher specification
- Provide a means to administer user-to-role assignments or use a client-side authentication infrastructure that supports the assignment
- Provide a means for users to select a set of roles with which they would like to log on or use a client-side authentication infrastructure that supports such means

When security professionals talk about roles, they often mention role hierarchies, which is exactly what $RBAC_1$ defines. Let's look at how CORBA and EJB security can support $RBAC_1$.

$RBAC_1$: Role Hierarchies

$RBAC_1$ is actually $RBAC_0$ with role hierarchies, which is as powerful a concept as inheritance in object oriented (OO) systems. We'll explain why.

After working with roles for a while, you will find, if you haven't already, that some roles share responsibilities and privileges. By this, we mean that users assigned to different roles often need to perform the same operations. Moreover, a number of general operations within your company are usually performed by all employees. For example, in the case of eBusiness.com, everybody can look up all products and create a customer object, and staff members can do everything customers and members can except settle orders and accounts. As such, you can improve the efficiency and provide for the natural structure of the company by utilizing the concept of role hierarchies defined in $RBAC_1$. A role hierarchy defines roles that have unique attributes and may be senior to other roles, that is, one role may be implicitly associated with the permissions that are associated with another "junior" role. If used appropriately, role hierarchies are a natural way of organizing roles to reflect authority, responsibility, and competency.

An example of a role hierarchy is shown in Figure 8.2. As you can see, the role "customer" is senior to role "visitor." This means that members of the role "customer" are implicitly granted permissions of the role "visitor" without the administrator having to explicitly assign all the permissions of visitors to customers. The most powerful roles are represented at the top of the diagram, and the less powerful roles are represented at the bottom. The roles at the top of the diagram are associated with the greatest number of permissions.

If your security environment supports $RBAC_1$, you can reuse assignment of permissions to roles so that senior roles "inherit" permissions assigned to

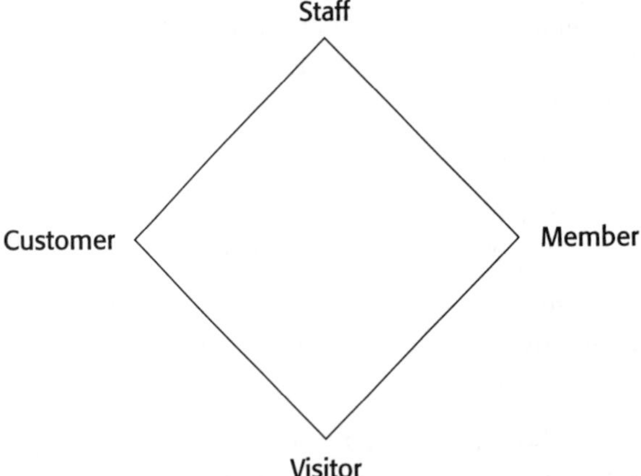

Figure 8.2 Initial role hierarchy for the eBusiness.com example.

junior roles. Keep in mind that assignment of a user to a role implies implicit assignment of that user to all the roles junior to that role. For example, because we assigned user Parker to role "staff" (see Table 8.2), that user is explicitly assigned to roles "customer," "member," and "visitor" and can activate any of these roles when he logs into the eBusiness.com computing environment.

In the following sections, we'll briefly describe how $RBAC_1$ is expressed in terms of CORBA and EJB and also explain what functionality needs to be in place in order to support $RBAC_1$ in CORBA and EJB.

$RBAC_1$ in CORBA

An $RBAC_1$ system in the language of CORBASec is described as follows:

- Users, attributes of type "role," rights, principals, granted rights to attributes assignment, and user to attributes assignment as well as function *user()* are exactly the same as in $RBAC_0$.
- A role hierarchy is introduced in which some roles inherit from others so that there is the notion of seniority.
- The calculation of which roles are activated for a given principal is different from $RBAC_0$. Function *roles()* not only returns the active roles, but also all the roles junior to the activated one.

The granted rights are the union of rights granted to every role as well as its juniors that the principal is in.

Function *roles()* is implemented and enforced by a *PrincipalAuthenticator*, which was described in Chapter 3. A user provides to a *UserSponsor* a set of roles with which he or she wants the principal to be activated. The *PrincipalAuthenticator*, during the authentication with the UserSponsor, creates new credentials of the principal. The credentials have roles, which are requested by the user, provided that the requested roles satisfy the definition of function roles for $RBAC_1$.

Figure 8.3 illustrates $RBAC_1$ using the eBusiness.com example. In this figure, we have slightly reworked what we did for $RBAC_0$ and have shown the changes. We also had to improve the role hierarchy because the hierarchy shown in Figure 8.2 had the following drawback: If we granted access to method settleOrder() for customers and settleAccount() for members, then staff members would also be permitted to invoke these operations because they were senior to members and customers. To solve this problem, we employed "private" roles. Two new roles "private customer" and "private member" are now senior to customer and member respectively, although they are not junior to role "staff," which is exactly what we need.

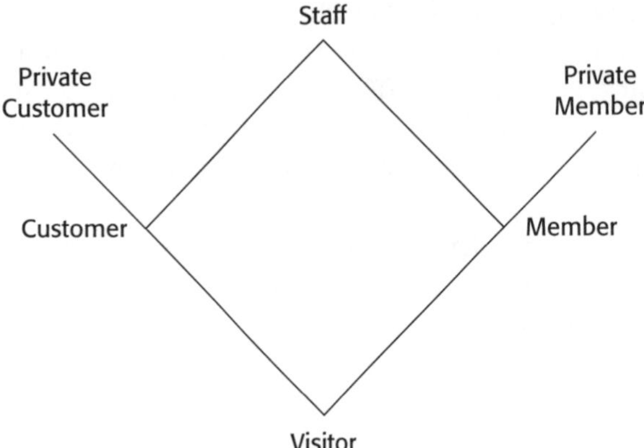

Figure 8.3 Improved role hierarchy for the eBusiness.com example.

With the new hierarchy, we have a new assignment of granted rights to role, which is shown in Table 8.9 for Domain Accounts. Because we are using role inheritance, we only grant those rights that are necessary for the role and are not assigned to any junior role. This is why role "staff" only gets right "m."

Because we introduced two new roles, we need to assign users to them. Table 8.10 shows the new user-to-role relation. Now roles "customer" and "member" become auxiliary roles that are only used for holding permissions, and no users are associated with them.

Let us recap the main difference between the implementations of $RBAC_1$ and $RBAC_0$ in CORBA.

- Introduction of role hierarchy in $RBAC_1$, which changes the assignment of rights to roles, and
- Different implementation of hypothetical function *roles()*, which returns only explicitly activated roles in the case of $RBAC_0$, and activated roles along with the junior ones in the case of $RBAC_1$.

Table 8.9 Assigning Rights to Roles for $RBAC_1$ for Domain Accounts

DOMAIN ACCOUNTS				
	GRANTED RIGHTS			
ROLE	u	s	p	m
Visitor				
Customer		X		
Private customer	X			
Member			X	
Private member	X			
Staff				X

Table 8.10 $RBAC_1$ Assignment of Users to Roles for eBusiness.com Example

	USERS			
ROLES	PARKER	WILSON	JOHNSON	DALY
visitor				
customer				
private customer				X
member				
private member			X	
staff	X	X		

A valid implementation of $RBAC_1$ could be one that allows a user to specify any role junior to those in which the user is a member. In this case, an implementation of *PrincipalAuthenticator* activates all roles that are junior to the specified role. For example, when user Parker logs into the system, he can activate role "staff" or any of the roles junior to it. If, for example, she activates the "staff" role, the list of privilege attributes contained in the credentials of her principal contains the following roles: visitor, customer, member, and staff.

So, what do you need to look for if you decide to utilize CORBASec implementation and enforce access control based on the $RBAC_1$ model? In order for a CORBASec implementation to support $RBAC_1$, it should:

- Implement $RBAC_0$
- Provide a means to administer the role hierarchy
- Implement *PrincipalAuthenticator*, which creates principal credentials containing privilege attributes of the type role according to the role hierarchy and the assignment of users to roles as well as function *roles()*

$RBAC_1$ in EJB

An $RBAC_1$ system in the language of EJB is described as follows:

- Users, roles, methods, user identities, assignment of methods to roles in <method-permission> elements, and user to roles assignment as well as function *user()* are exactly the same as in $RBAC_0$.
- A role hierarchy is introduced in which some roles inherit from others so that there is the notion of seniority.
- The calculation of which roles are activated for a given principal is different from $RBAC_0$. Function *roles()* not only returns the active roles, but also all the roles junior to the activated role.

Although the section of the deployment descriptor <method-permissions> is not noticeably shorter, there are fewer repetitions in it compared to the case of $RBAC_0$ because of the role hierarchy.

```
<!--
Every visitor can invoke the following methods
-->
<method-permission>
        <role-name>visitor</role-name>
        <method>
             <ejb-name>ProductFactory</ejb-name>
             <method-name>*</method-name>
        </method>
        <method>
             <ejb-name>CustomerAccountFactory</ejb-name>
             <method-name>create</method-name>
             <method-name>lookup</method-name>
        </method>
        <method>
             <ejb-name>MemberAccountFactory</ejb-name>
             <method-name>lookup</method-name>
        </method>
</method-permission>

<!--
Permissions for regular products
-->
<method-permission>
        <role-name>customer</role-name>
        <role-name>member</role-name>
        <method>
             <ejb-name>RegularProduct</ejb-name>
             <method-name>getPrice</method-name>
        </method>
</method-permission>

<!--
Permissions for special products
-->
<method-permission>
        <role-name>member</role-name>
        <method>
             <ejb-name>SpecialProduct</ejb-name>
             <method-name>getPrice</method-name>
        </method>
</method-permission>

<!--
What customers and staff on their behalf can do
-->
```

```
<method-permission>
        <role-name>customer</role-name>
        <method>
             <ejb-name>CustomerAccount</ejb-name>
             <method-name>placeOrder</method-name>
             <method-name>deleteOrder</method-name>
             <method-name>listOrders</method-name>
        </method>
</method-permission>

<!--
What only customers can do
-->
<method-permission>
        <role-name>private customer</role-name>
        <method>
             <ejb-name>CustomerAccount</ejb-name>
             <method-name>settleOrder</method-name>
        </method>
</method-permission>

<!--
What members and staff on their behalf can do
-->
<method-permission>
        <role-name>member</role-name>
        <method>
             <ejb-name>MemberAccount</ejb-name>
             <method-name>placeOrder</method-name>
             <method-name>deleteOrder</method-name>
             <method-name>listOrders</method-name>
        </method>
</method-permission>

<!--
What only members can do
-->
<method-permission>
        <role-name>private member</role-name>
        <method>
             <ejb-name>MemberAccount</ejb-name>
             <method-name>settleAccount</method-name>
        </method>
</method-permission>

<!--
What only staff can do
-->
<method-permission>
        <role-name>staff</role-name>
        <method>
```

```
            <ejb-name>CustomerAccountFactory</ejb-name>
            <method-name>delete</method-name>
        </method>
        <method>
            <ejb-name>MemberAccountFactory</ejb-name>
            <method-name>create</method-name>
            <method-name>delete</method-name>
        </method>
        <method>
            <ejb-name>Product</ejb-name>
            <method-name>setPrice</method-name>
        </method>
</method-permission>
```

If you decide to use the functionality of $RBAC_1$, which we recommend, then the following list tells you exactly what you need to look for when you select an EJB Container product. In order for an EJB Container to support $RBAC_1$, it should:

- Implement $RBAC_0$
- Provide a means to administer the role hierarchy or be integrated with an authentication environment that administers a role hierarchy
- Implement authentication mechanisms or be integrated with an authentication environment that can set a list of active roles according to what role the user has activated during the log on process

Implementing a *least privilege principle* also requires users to operate with the minimum set of privileges necessary to do their jobs (for example, when a user is assigned to role "staff" but wants to act in role "member," which is junior to "staff"). The requirement is not always obvious, and you may run into a situation where no product available on the market implements such a feature. However, for some enterprises this could be a necessity.

$RBAC_2$: Constraints

Constraints in RBAC are predicates that apply to user-to-role and permission-to-role relations as well as to hypothetical functions *user()* and *roles()*. They enable an implementation of the *separation of duties* principle, which requires that for particular sets of transactions, no single individual be allowed to execute all transactions within the set. A good example of separation of duties in the case of eBusiness.com is prohibiting staff members to settle orders or accounts for customers and members. Because staff can add products to orders for customers and members, they could potentially abuse their rights by shipping unwanted products to customers and members, and then charge their credit cards. In order to protect customers from such situations, staff members in eBusiness.com are prevented from activating roles "private customer" or "private member."

There are two types of separation of duties: static separation of duties (SSD) and dynamic separation of duties (DSD). An example of a static separation was provided in the preceding paragraph. DSD relaxes some of the limitations of SSD. For example, with DSD, a user can be assigned to both "administrator" and "auditor" roles, which are by nature conflicting roles because auditors inspect the work of administrators; however, only one role can be activated in each session. Thus, the user can act either as an administrator or an auditor, but not as both. $RBAC_2$ enables SSD and DSD via constraints on various relations and functions.

Constraints on user-to-role relations are enforced by an implementation of user administrator tools. Constraints on functions *user()* and *roles()* are the responsibility of authentication environments. For example, in CORBASec, that would be the task of *PrincipalAuthenticator* interface implementation. Constraints on privilege-to-role relations are enforced by an implementation of security administrator tools.

To configure your CORBA or EJB security services to support $RBAC_2$, you'll need to make sure that they:

- Implement $RBAC_0$
- Support constraints on user-to-role relations by user administrator tools
- Implement authentication functions with the support of constraints on functions *user()* and *roles()*
- Enable the enforcement of constraints on privilege-to-role relations by security administrator tools

$RBAC_3$: $RBAC_1$ + $RBAC_2$

$RBAC_3$ is a combination of $RBAC_1$ and $RBAC_2$ as well as any additional constraints on the role hierarchy. It can be implemented in CORBA as well as EJB security. In order for an implementation of CORBA or EJB security to support $RBAC_3$, it should:

- Implement $RBAC_1$
- Implement $RBAC_2$
- Implement possible additional constraints on the role hierarchy

We've already discussed the requirements for the support of $RBAC_1$ and $RBAC_2$ by CORBA and EJB security service implementation. The implementation of additional static constraints on the $RBAC_1$ role hierarchy is to be done by user administrator tools. For the support of dynamic constraints, additional functionality in the implementation of authentication functionality is required in addition to the administrator tools.

Concluding Remarks on RBAC

Understanding middleware access control mechanisms is critical for protecting resources of enterprise applications. In the previous sections, we defined $RBAC_0$ and $RBAC_1$ models in the languages of CORBA and EJB security and described how $RBAC_0$ through $RBAC_3$ could be implemented using these two middleware technologies. We showed you what functionality needs to be implemented to comply with the CORBA or EJB security standard in order to support RBAC. We also illustrated the discussion with examples for eBusiness.com.

As discussed earlier, implementations compliant with the CORBA and EJB specifications can support $RBAC_0$, $RBAC_1$, $RBAC_2$, or $RBAC_3$. However, additional unspecified functionality is required. Your authentication services need to support roles and their hierarchies ($RBAC_1$). To support constraints ($RBAC_2$), the authentication infrastructure has to enforce them. You also need tools to administer user-to-role and role-to-permissions assignments.

We provided you with a framework for assessing implementations of RBAC models by CORBA and EJB security products. The framework described in the previous sections provides directions for CORBA and EJB security developers to realize RBAC in their systems and also provides criteria for selecting implementations that support models from the RBAC families. We provided information to advance your understanding of the CORBA access control mechanism's capabilities and maximize your ability to utilize them, which is vital to the use of CORBA and EJB middleware in protecting your application assets.

To learn more about RBAC, go to:

- The RBAC Web site at the National Institute of Standards and Technology (NIST) at http://hissa.ncsl.nist.gov/rbac where the concept originated
- The Laboratory for Information Security Technology Web site at www.list.gmu.edu, which is actively progressing the model
- The Association for Computing Machinery (ACM) Web site at www.acm.org/pubs/contents/proceedings/series/rbac, which contains the proceedings on the RBAC workshop

Now that we have discussed access rights, security attributes, and how they are used to support RBAC, we move on to the final authorization policy topic: domains. As you will see, all of these concepts work together to define collections that support scaleable authorization policies.

Using Domains Wisely

Security policy domains were introduced in Chapter 3. As discussed, security policy domains are used to group resources (i.e., components) so that security policies can scale to very large systems. Security policy domains are used indirectly in EJB and extensively in CORBA.

EJB does not directly define security domains. Instead, the specification leaves the implementation, management, and administration of security domains up to the container provider. As a result, there is little we can say in general about security domains in EJB because the implementations vary widely in each vendor's product. Consequently, our discussion on domains concentrates on CORBA rather than EJB. Although the EJB standard does not address security domains, the principles introduced in this chapter are still generally applicable to commercial vendors' EJB products. Our discussion of security policy domains focuses on grouping components in hierarchical collections, which is similar to the proprietary solutions of several EJB products.

The CORBASec specification uses security policy domains extensively. CORBASec defines a policy domain as a set of objects to which a security policy applies for security related activities. A security authority administers the security policy domain. Because security policy domains are sets of arbitrary objects, it's possible to define very complex interrelations of domains. Figure 8.4 shows some basic types out of which all possible domain compositions are created. Domains may be defined as a proper hierarchy, or they can be federated, which we explain a little bit later, or any combination thereof.

In a proper hierarchical tree (one parent and many children), one domain completely encloses another domain, and all objects associated with a subdomain are associated with the superdomain as well. This makes understanding and using domain composition in a hierarchy easier than the federated domain example shown in Figure 8.4(b) because hierarchies are simpler for human beings to understand. In Figure 8.4(a), Domain A has two subdomains B and C. Domain B, in turn, encloses Domain D, which has one object F. Domain C has objects G and H. But objects don't only have to be at the bottom of domain hierarchies. As you can see in the figure, Domain A contains object J, which is governed by the policies of Domain A only. On the other hand, object F is controlled by the policies of Domains A, B, and D. Another way of looking at the domain hierarchy is as sets of nested scopes. How can, for example, authorization decisions be derived from the policies of Domains A, B, and D? There could be several ways (and you want to make sure you understand which way is supported by the product of the vendor of your choice). One way is similar to file systems, in which access rules to the root of the hierarchy are more permissive than to the lower levels, and more restrictive rules override more permissive ones. But this is not the only way to combine policies in the domain hierarchy. Another way could be one in which more specific rules (the rules that define the policies of the immediate domain containing the object) supersede the generic rules. Depending on your application domain and the ways security policies are modeled and implemented in your organization, the case can be made for any way of combining the policies in the domain hierarchy.

Your CORBASec implementation can support compositions in which there are some objects belonging to more than one domain directly, as in Figure 8.4(b). Because the security of such objects is governed by the policies of all the domains

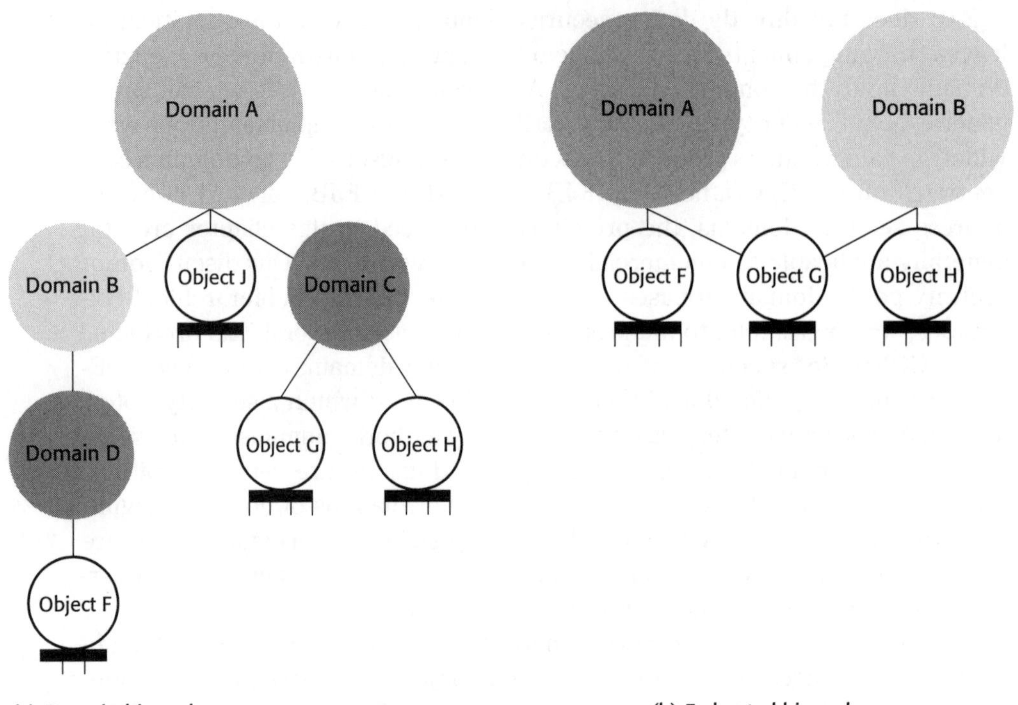

Figure 8.4 Different ways to compose CORBA security domains.

containing the objects and there is no predefined relationship among domains—as is the case with domain hierarchies—there have to be rules that specify how to resolve disagreements between the policies (i.e., when some polices grant and others deny access). Compositions of such domains are called federations.

Although the CORBASec specification allows complex domain interrelations to be supported, the specification does not describe a standard way to compose policies across domains. This means that you need to completely understand which domain compositions are supported by a CORBASec product before you buy it. Otherwise, you could find it very difficult to implement your authorization policies if you use multiple domain compositions and your CORBASec product does not support the required compositions. But there is hope for you and for CORBASec vendors in regard to this problem.

To aid end users in administering the security of CORBA environments, the Object Management Group (OMG) security community requested a proposal (RFP) for a specification that would define services for:

- Managing the lifecycle and operation of CORBASec domain managers
- Providing more comprehensive management of the objects assigned to CORBASec domains than those present in the existing CORBASec specification

The specification response to the RFP, submitted by Concept Five Technologies, Inc. and Hitachi, Ltd., and supported by several other companies, is called Security Domain Membership Management (SDMM) Service. The specification, which is still under development as of this publication, is summarized in the sidebar.

SECURITY DOMAIN MEMBERSHIP MANAGEMENT SERVICE SPECIFICATION FROM THE OMG

What should you expect from this Security Domain Membership Management Service specification? Most likely, the following three sections will be part of it:

- **Object Domain Mapping (ODM).** Will describe how objects are mapped to domain managers
- **Security Domain Management.** Will describe how graphs of domain managers are related to each other.
- **Security Policies Using Domain Hierarchies.** Will describe how existing CORBASec interfaces interpret policies when they are defined in a hierarchy of domain managers

The ODM will map objects to one or more security policy domains, which will be defined as collections of object references; each of which will have a common set of security policies and be managed by a certain Domain Manager object.

The ODM will map objects to security policy domains in terms of domain names. Each security policy domain will have a name; security policy domain names will have the same structure as names defined by the Naming Service.

Security domain management will be provided via the DomainAuthority and DomainAuthorityAdmin interfaces. Given a security policy domain name supplied by the ODM, the DomainAuthority will supply the associated domain manager. DomainAuthority will also define operations to traverse the graph of security policy domains. DomainAuthorityAdmin will define operations to set relationships between domains.

The ODM and Security Domain Management interfaces will permit overlapping domains. That is, objects may belong to multiple domains, and domains may have multiple parent domains. However, compliant implementations will not be required to support overlapping domains. Compliant implementations may support a hierarchical model of domains by requiring each object to belong to a single domain and each domain to have a single parent domain.

The specification will also define standard policy composition semantics for domain hierarchies. Semantics for policy composition with overlapping domains won't be defined and will remain implementation dependent.

We expect the specification to become a formal OMG standard or become a part of CORBASec specification some time in late 2001.

Using Domain Structures for Composing Security Policies

SDMM access policy is the most complicated of the policies because the security system traverses the tree from the domain containing an object to the root, applying combinators at each level. SDMM defines a default combinator, called "union," that we will use to compose granted rights in multiple domains in the hierarchy.

The domain hierarchy for the eBusiness.com application, as shown in Figure 8.5, consists of four domains: Application, Accounts, SpecialProducts, and RegularProducts. We assign eBusiness.com object instances into these domains as follows:

- **Application.** ProductFactory object.
- **Accounts.** CustomerAccountFactory, CustomerAccount objects, MemberAccountFactory, and MemberAccount objects.
- **SpecialProducts.** Product objects that are special (offered only to members).
- **RegularProducts.** Product objects that are regular (offered to both customers and members).

Consider how rights were granted to different roles earlier in Table 8.5, when a user made invocations on the objects located in domain Accounts in the case of $RBAC_0$. Table 8.11 extends this definition and shows granted rights for all the domains used.

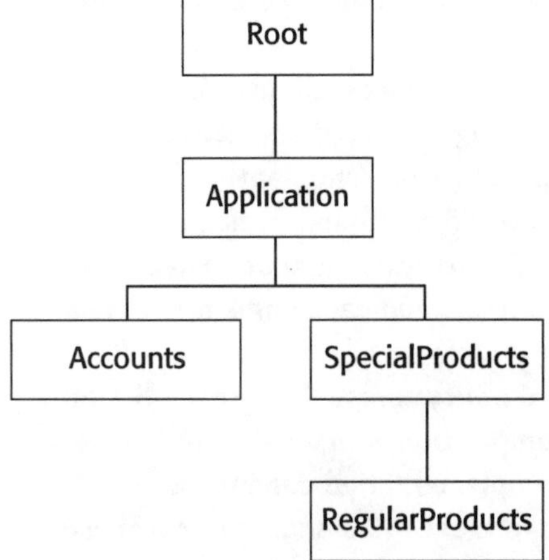

Figure 8.5 Policy domain hierarchy for eBusiness.com.

Table 8.11 Granted Rights to Roles in Each of the Domains in the eBusiness.com System for $RBAC_0$

	GRANTED RIGHTS IN EACH DOMAIN			
ROLES	APPLICATION	ACCOUNTS	SPECIALPRODUCTS	REGULARPRODUCTS
Visitor				
Customer		su		g
Member		pu	g	
Staff		msp	gmsp	

To get a feeling of how SDMM specifies the use of domain hierarchies in access control, let's calculate which rights are granted to user Daly, who is acting in role "customer" and attempting to invoke an operation on an instance of Product located in domain SpecialProducts. According to Table 8.11, customers are granted no rights in domain SpecialProducts. The domain is a subdomain of Application, which is a subdomain of the root domain. However, customers are not granted any rights in either Application or root domains. Thus, Daly is denied access to obtain or set prices for Products in the SpecialProducts domain.

However, if Daly attempts to invoke operation getPrice() on a Product object located in the RegularProducts domain, which is a subdomain of SpecialProducts, a user is granted right "g" in RegularProducts and no other right in any higher levels of the hierarchy. Thus, Daly's effective rights for accessing objects in RegularProducts consist of "g," which is sufficient for invoking Product::getPrice(). As you can see, authorization decisions can be very straightforward when the number of rights is small and compositions of policy domains are simple. But we can assure you that the decisions can quickly become incomprehensible for an average person if the prudence is lost. Table 8.11 was provided to you for $RBAC_0$. We leave the creation of a similar table for $RBAC_1$ and the hierarchies of roles for you as an exercise.

A given distributed system may contain hundreds of thousands of objects that must be associated with various security policies, such as access and delegation policies. As stated earlier, trying to administer these objects on an individual basis is an impossible task. Therefore, CORBA uses the concept of Security Domains to supply a measure of scale to control these object instances. The policies are associated with a domain, and sets of objects for which the policies are appropriate are assigned to a domain.

One of the first steps in setting up the security for your systems is identifying the set of domains and determining whether they are adequate for your security requirements. In order to do this, you have to determine, in more detail, how the other parts of the security system that you have defined interact with the domains and whether the full set of interacting parts make up the whole that you need. This might take several iterations. We hope that the previous sections, which described the rights, attributes, and domains in more detail, will help you to accomplish this task. The next step is to set up your distributed systems so that all the objects end up being in the proper domains. For this, you need to have a means of assigning objects to domains.

Assigning Object Instances to Policy Domains

The CORBA specification does not specify how the CORBASec service implementers should map object instances to domains. As we described earlier in this chapter, the SDMM service specification defines this implementation. Until the major products on the market implement the specification, this area will remain implementation-specific. Therefore, it is important that you examine the means that a particular implementation uses to map object instances to security policy domains. Every object should be assigned to a domain when it is created. In many aspects, the success of security administration in your enterprise will depend on how effectively security policy domains are utilized.

There are a number of approaches by which security service implementers can assign objects to domains. We outline some possible approaches to this problem in this section. For the most part, these approaches are taken from our experience in designing a CORBASec product. You first should look for the capability of the CORBASec service of your choice to define a so-called default domain to which all newly created objects are assigned. If this capability is not provided, then the service should supply your security-aware applications with an API to set the object to the domain at creation time. In addition, a security service should provide the capability to move an object to another domain after creation time. Trying to assign all transient objects to specific domains as a system administrative task is not practical because of the scaling problem and because the object references of transient objects are not known at system administration time. On the other hand, assigning important persistent objects to particular domains is both practical and reasonable as these objects are made persistent for a good reason. So, we recommend you use one or more of the following three ways of assigning an object instance to a domain.

- Security-aware servers use a security service API for assigning objects to domains.
- Persistent objects are set using another security service API available to administrative tools.
- All other objects are assigned to a default domain. These may be moved after creation.

The first approach puts the assignment of objects to domains in the hands of the server application developer, which is not necessarily the desired solution. One means of making this approach secure is to have the security service control access to the table of mappings between object references and domains. Thus, a server could be started by an entity that has been authenticated to the security service. The entity, say CustomerAccountFactory, would have rights to set object references for the security aware application to certain limited domains. Needless to say, the domain in which the table with the mappings lives is quite sensitive because it controls what objects can be assigned to what domains.

The granularity of dynamically mapping objects to security domains is application specific. That is, an application may want to associate an object with a domain, or it may decide that all objects created on a particular CORBA server should be associated with a given domain. Therefore, the establishment of the particular dynamic mappings will be left to the application.

Another aspect of dynamic mapping is the removal of records referring to objects already destroyed. Who does garbage collection of objects in domains and when does it occur? How do we know that the object membership in a security domain should be ended? Objects can disappear because of various reasons including a server crash. This is not specified in CORBASec and most probably won't be defined in SDMM either. You will want to know how your CORBASec candidate product addresses this issue because it will affect your administrators and application developers. One possible solution is a Portable Object Adapter, which is a key player in managing the lifecycle of your application objects, and it has a number of policies that can be used by the security service implementation to modify what an application can or can't do. For example, using the LifespanPolicy, the implementation could assure that a mapping is removed from the mapping tables when a process exits in the case of a transient policy.

The process described in the second approach, explicit administration of the domain membership for persistent objects, is controlled by a system administration interface and thus is subject to the same controls as other system administrative interfaces. It is preferable to limit the number of persistent object references for the reasons of scale as well as the practical reasons of maintenance of these object references. Thus, we would expect these objects to be relatively few in number. All remaining objects would be assigned to a default domain.

Again, it is very important that you understand the approach that your security service vendor has chosen to assign objects to policy domains because the OMG has not yet standardized how this is to be done. Once you have assessed the approach, compare and contrast it to the methods described previously and determine if this approach is sufficient for your needs in terms of scalability and security. If it does not meet your criteria, you should seriously consider choosing another vendor or have the vendor modify its approach to meet your needs. This is a critical item and should be high on your checklist of items that are required for a CORBASec service.

As with security attributes and rights, there are always trade-offs between having large and small numbers of security policy domains. Every organization is unique and even for the same organization, security policies can be modeled in different ways using a different number of domains. There is no concrete rule about how many domains you need to have for a given number of objects. Each time you design or redesign your enterprise security infrastructure, consider the following:

- Too many domains make enterprise security configuration difficult to understand and administer.
- Too few domains don't allow implementation of different security policies, especially access control, on the same types of CORBA objects or enterprise beans.
- In domain hierarchies, the extensive use of nonobvious combinators (e.g., intersection or negation) of granted rights can soon get out of hand and make the enforced policies and their behavior impossible for most people to understand.

Delegation

There are situations in which it is necessary for an intermediate object to use the security attributes of the initiating client in a chain of invocations on objects. These situations call for delegation. Delegation allows intermediate objects to act on a principal's behalf.

Strictly speaking, there are two commonly used meanings for "delegation" in the context of distributed applications. One is the delegation of administration (responsibility) from one person to another. The second is the delegation of credentials in a security context that is transmitted from one application to another.

Delegation of credentials in a security context is a well-defined security service that may be used by applications for a number of reasons. Delegation of administration from one person to another is a common security requirement and is a security administrative workflow issue.

To implement delegation of administration from one person to another, you could use delegation of credentials, but this would be an unusual solution. Typically, delegated administration from one person to another is accomplished by granting one person a privilege attribute (i.e., "I grant user Daly the privilege attribute of security officer for the following security domains"). This approach requires that the user's security privilege attributes be updated via a security administration interface. Security policy domains are an effective means to

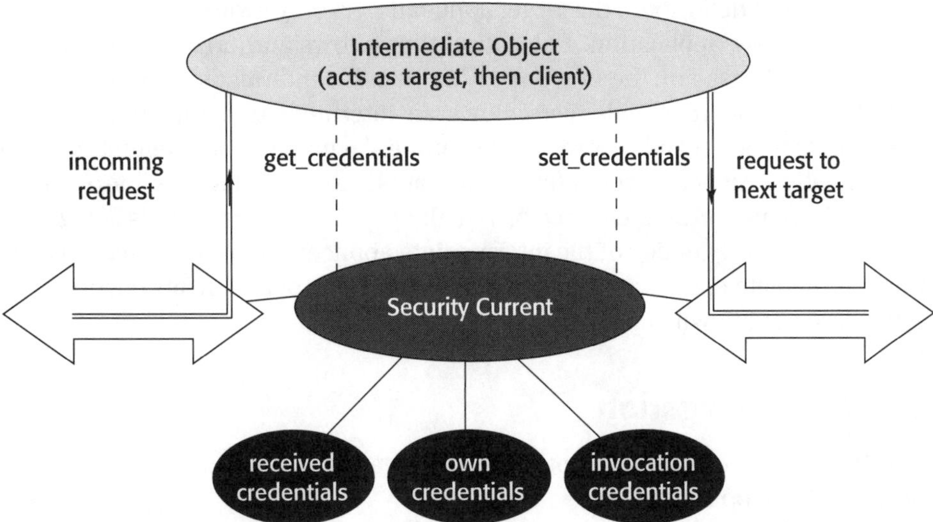

Figure 8.6 Use of credentials by intermediate objects during delegation.

define delegated administration policy because the domain hierarchy naturally matches up with the delegated administration hierarchy. Because delegated administration solutions tend to be product specific, we won't provide additional guidance on this topic.

Delegation of credentials defines how a principal's security attributes are transmitted to other objects to act on the principal's behalf. It is of particular relevance in distributed object systems. Because an object invocation frequently results in a whole chain of calls on other objects, it is common for an intermediate object (or just "intermediate" for short) in the call chain to use a client's privileges, which allows the intermediate to pass the access control checks and perform an operation on behalf of the client.

Figure 8.6 shows that CORBASec provides operations on the security Current interface for intermediate objects to obtain and set credentials. These operations allow manipulations with received, own, and invocation credentials that control the delegation of credentials.

Motivations for Using Delegation

Delegation of credentials can be used to preserve accountability. By permitting the initiator's credentials to propagate through the mid-tier components, the final target (such as a back-end system) can learn the identity of the initiating client. Without delegation, the target application is only aware of the identity of the intermediate application. Delegation thus allows authorization or audit to be performed based on the initiator rather than the intermediate application.

Delegation of credentials also allows an intermediate application object's credentials to be set and controlled at runtime. An initiator's credentials may be dynamically assigned to the intermediate application so that the intermediate application can access a resource on behalf of the client. Credentials delegation allows the security policy of the intermediate application to be flexible because the intermediate application can access resources on behalf of any clients, even if they are not known in advance.

Levels of Delegation

CORBASec supports several options for delegating security attributes to other objects. These options include:

- **No delegation.** The client does not permit its credentials to be delegated to another object.
- **Simple delegation.** The client permits an intermediate object to assume the client's credentials and passes them on or delegates them in subsequent invocations, thus allowing the intermediate application to access objects using the client's credentials. When the client restricts the intermediate object's use of the credentials (i.e., controls which privileges are delegated, or controls which objects may use the credentials), it is known as *restricted* (or constrained) delegation. When the client passes on all privileges to an intermediate object with no restrictions, it is known as *impersonation*.
- **Composite delegation.** The client permits the intermediate object to assume the client's credentials as in simple delegation, but both the client's and the intermediate's credentials are passed in subsequent invocations, thus allowing access checks based on both sets of credentials.
- **Traced Delegation.** The credentials of all the intermediates in the call chain, including the initiator's, are passed.

The initiator can set different credentials when it is accessing a target directly and when its credentials are delegated. Thus, the initiator may limit the credentials when they are delegated, reducing which privileges an intermediate can use when acting on the initiator's behalf.

As one progresses from one delegation mode to another in the order listed previously, the targets may perform more rigorous tests on the origin of the credentials because they have more information available. However, the CORBASec specification does not state the kinds of tests the targets must perform,

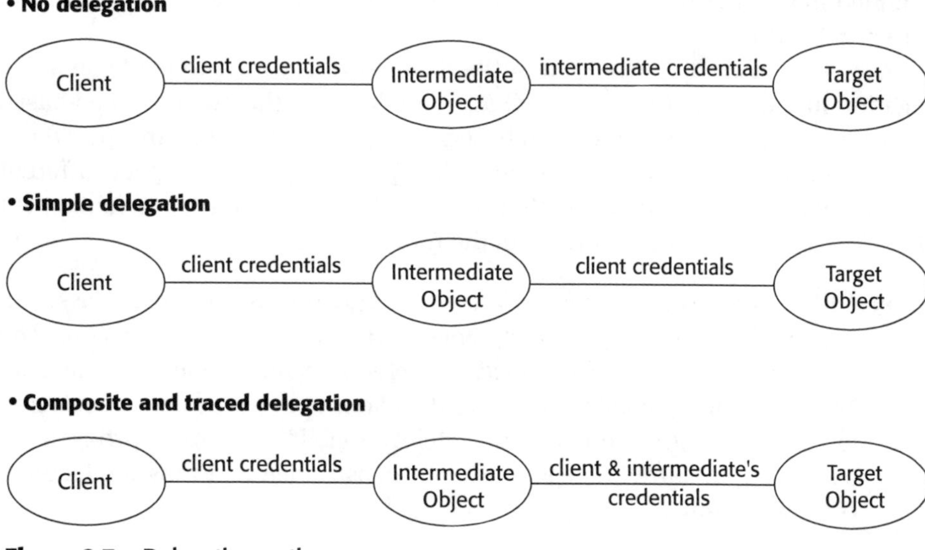

Figure 8.7 Delegation options.

and thus it is up to the security service implementers to determine the tests to be done. For these more rigorous types of delegation, be sure to read the implementers' description of their target tests and follow their instructions closely.

We illustrate the above list of delegation options in Figure 8.7.

Your main concern when using delegation is whether or not the security service implementation provides the checks that are appropriate to the level of security that is needed in your working environment. For example, in a completely closed environment in which all the objects are trusted, impersonation may be adequate. However, in today's large systems, the idea of a completely closed environment is not very likely. Even in a closed environment, the problem of a disgruntled employee cannot be overlooked.

Product Support for Delegation

Not all CORBASec implementations have the same support for delegation. First, different compliance levels of CORBASec require support for different types of delegation, and second, different technologies used to implement CORBASec also have different support for delegation. CORBASec level 1 includes simple delegation, which allows an object to assume the identity of its invoker, whereas CORBASec level 2 requires the ability to constrain simple delegation. (Note the distinction between CORBASec conformance levels 1 and 2, which we defined in Chapter 3, and CSIv2 conformance levels 0, 1, and 2, which we defined in Chapter 6. These are two different sets of conformance levels that are unrelated.)

As you may recall, Chapter 6 described two different ways to implement delegation in the context of the CSIv2 attribute layer: authorization token-based delegation and identity assertion-based delegation. We can now put these pieces together and discuss how the CSIv2 protocol can implement different application level forms of delegation. The CSIv2 forms of delegation implement the CORBASec delegation options in the following way:

- **CSIv2 authorization token-based delegation** uses the PAC passed in the CSIv2 attribute layer to implement *simple restricted delegation.* The PAC allows the client to delegate selected attributes to an intermediate. The PAC's proxy attributes allows the client to delegate only to selected intermediates, thus constraining delegation. If the PAC's proxy attribute is set to "Any," delegation is not constrained and thus implements *impersonation.*

- **CSIv2 identity assertion-based delegation** uses the identity token passed in the CSIv2 attribute layer to implement *impersonation.* The identity token allows the client to delegate its identity (and potentially its attributes) to an intermediate, but the client cannot constrain where its privileges are delegated. A subsequent target may check whether an intermediate that uses an impersonated identity is trustworthy.

Now, let's look at delegation support in the technologies. SPKM, a public key protocol using the RSA cryptosystem based on the Entrust product from Entrust Technologies, does not support delegation at all. Popular Kerberos V5, a secret key (Data Encryption Standard or DES) security technology from Massachusetts Institute of Technology (MIT), supports unrestricted simple delegation. SESAME, a hybrid secret key (Kerberos/DES) and public key (RSA) technology, supports controlled delegation. And, the famous Secure Sockets Layer (SSL) does not support any delegation. You might run into CORBA implementations that only conform to CORBASec Level 1 with the support of simple delegation only, or those that are implemented using one of the security technologies, which play an enabling and at the same time limiting role in supporting delegation. So, when you choose a CORBASec product, be sure to learn exactly what delegation it supports.

In CORBA, delegation decisions are governed by delegation policies that are associated with the domains to which the object belongs. Delegation policy in SDMM is simpler than access policy in that the system walks the tree of policy domains until it finds a delegation policy, and then it stops and uses that delegation policy.

Delegation in EJB

How about delegation in EJB? The EJB security model lacks delegation constraints on credentials and thus only supports impersonation. When a bean's security identity is specified as use-caller-identity, the client's identity is delegated to the bean instance. The bean instance is then permitted to impersonate the client for all invocations. If delegation is inadvertently granted to a bean that is not trustworthy, the bean could potentially reveal the client's confidential information or destroy critical data. As long as beans are all carefully configured, delegation is an acceptable risk. However, in a complex multitier object application, misuse of delegation could compromise security.

Privilege Attribute Certificates (PACs) improve the handling of delegation in credentials beyond what EJB can support. PACs support the notion of constrained delegation, which controls whether intermediates are privileged to use the delegated credentials. By constraining delegation, PACs can reduce the risk of delegation misuse in complex multitier applications. Authorization token-based delegation using PACs is defined at CSI Level 2. This level of conformance is not required for EJB 2.0 compliance, but some vendors may provide this advanced support as a product enhancement.

When and How to Use Delegation

Delegation can be harmful to your system's security. On the other hand, in almost all complex systems, delegation is either needed or it is very difficult to find an alternate solution for. In the rest of this section, we'll give you our recommendations in regard to using delegation at your enterprise, so that you will know what should be taken into consideration when you deploy and configure your distributed security.

Delegation is an important issue to consider when building distributed applications. Although using delegation is tempting to many developers, we recommend avoiding the use of delegation except for auditing or for simple proxies such as Web servers.

General Recommendations

We recommend that each intermediate application should authenticate and have its own credentials statically assigned rather than using delegated credentials. An intermediate will need to have sufficient privileges assigned to access resources on behalf on any of its potential clients. For example, if the intermediate is accessing a database, the intermediate's credentials must be sufficient to access any client's database entry.

ESI SECURITY ASSOCIATION PRINCIPLE: DESIGN FOR FAILURE

As a general rule, delegation is dangerous because it may cause a single point of security failure. If an intermediate server that is permitted to use delegated credentials has been compromised, an attacker could abuse that trust and potentially cause serious system damage. Impersonation is the most dangerous form of delegation, and we recommend avoiding it whenever possible. Constrained delegation is much safer because the number of trusted intermediates is limited. However, even that form of delegation can be abused and should be avoided.

As a result of this approach, the first intermediate component, which is the only one that will have the original client's credentials, will need to enforce the required authorization and audit policies for that client. Without delegation, later components in the call chain will not have access to the client's credentials and so will not be able to make security decisions based on the client's attributes. All components in the call-chain should be properly pair-wise authenticated to preserve end-to-end security along the entire invocation chain.

Avoiding delegation minimizes the number of required back-end user accounts because each intermediate component only uses a single identity for authorization to back-end resources. Thus, a significant additional benefit of avoiding delegation is the reduction of the duplicate back-end user accounts that mirror the perimeter tier user identities.

Delegation can be used with acceptable risk for intermediates that are simple proxies, such as Web servers or load balancers. In these limited cases, the proxy usually needs to be small and highly efficient, so it does not contain the logic needed to enforce authorization and audit policies. The proxy should pass along the unaltered client credentials to a subsequent intermediate for authorization checks.

Risks of Delegation

To enable delegation within EJB and CORBA without compromising the security integrity of the system, the component receiving delegated credentials must be able to trust that the received credentials are authentic—otherwise an attacker could impersonate a trusted principal. To achieve this level of trust, CSIv2 provides mechanisms that protect the security context containing the credentials from tampering by an intermediate application.

Be sure to check whether your security packages used for integrating back-end and mid-tier systems not only support delegation but also provide constraints on transmission of credential tokens to prevent impersonation abuse. If delegation constraints are not in place, all application components must implicitly trust each other to use delegated credentials safely. For small collections of components within corporate network boundaries, this assumption may be reasonable. However, as the number of components grows, particularly as applications are distributed across the multiple enterprises, trusting all applications becomes too risky.

CSIv2 level 2 conformance requires constrained delegation, and vendors are developing solutions based on this standard. If your company adopts this solution, delegation can be used safely. Without support for constrained delegation, we recommend that you avoid using delegation. Furthermore, delegation of security credentials to systems that are outside of your enterprise is particularly dangerous and is never advisable, even if delegation constraints exist.

Summary

Although your organization has complete control over required and granted rights, you should be very careful when defining rights and their semantics. The definitions of required rights must be consistent across the organization, and they must be understood and used by the administrators when they are assigning them to the methods to be controlled.

Security attributes allow you to group principals and apply the same security policies to an entire group. The semantics of each attribute value must be clearly defined between any two disparate entities. Using standard privilege attributes reduces the complexity and makes cross-organization interoperability easier. Strive to find an optimum for your company between too many and too few attributes so as not to lose the required level of granularity and still be able to manage the complexity.

One of the powerful concepts in security today is modeling authorization policies using role-based access control (RBAC), which is a family of reference models in which permissions are associated with roles and users are assigned to appropriate roles. There are four established RBAC reference models: unrelated roles ($RBAC_0$), role-hierarchies ($RBAC_1$), user and role assignment constraints ($RBAC_2$), and both hierarchies and constraints ($RBAC_3$). CORBA and EJB support all of these models. However, additional nonstandardized functionality is required for supporting these models. The main dependence is on the support of roles, their hierarchies, and constraints on them by the authentication environments of both CORBA and EJB.

A distributed computing environment may contain hundreds of thousands of objects to administer, which on an individual basis is impossible. Policy domains, which group objects, is another concept necessary for implementing middleware security in enterprises. CORBASec defines a domain as a set of objects to which a security policy applies for a set of security related activities and is administered by a security authority. Domains may be defined as a proper hierarchy, or they can be federated. Be sure you completely understand which domain compositions are supported by a CORBASec product before you buy it.

As with security attributes and rights, there are always trade-offs between having large and small numbers of security policy domains. Too many domains make enterprise security configuration difficult to understand and administer. Too few domains don't allow implementation of different security policies, especially access control, on the same types of CORBA objects or enterprise beans.

Delegation allows intermediate objects to act on a principal's behalf, which permits authorization or audit to be performed based on the original requester rather than an intermediate application. Not all CORBASec implementations support delegation. First, different compliance levels of CORBASec require support for different types of delegation, and second, different technologies used to implement CORBASec have different support for delegation. The EJB security model lacks delegation constraints on credentials. If delegation is inadvertently granted to a bean that is not trustworthy, the bean could potentially reveal the client's confidential information or destroy critical data.

Using delegation is tempting to many developers, but we recommend avoiding it except for auditing or simple proxies. Although delegation can be harmful to your system's security, for many complex systems it is either needed or it is very difficult to find an alternate solution.

In the remainder of our book we put into practice much of the guidance that we have presented so far. We tie these ideas together by using eBusiness.com as a case study for planning and building an integrated secure component system.

Planning a Secure Component System

This book has taken you through many aspects of building a secure e-business application. In Chapter 1, we first gave you an overview of enterprise security integration and discussed what it means to build an enterprise-class security framework. In Chapters 2 and 3, we explained EJB and CORBA security, which are the two main models for supporting secure application servers, and then followed in Chapter 4 with a description of perimeter, mid-tier, and legacy security technologies that are required to build a complete end-to-end security solution. We covered more advanced topics including investigating approaches for secure interoperability of EJB and CORBA in Chapters 5 and 6, techniques for protecting application-level resources in Chapter 7, and scaleable security policies that deal with attributes, domains, and delegation in Chapter 8.

We've given you a lot of information about many different technologies, and we know that with so many pieces for you to put together, it's not easy to know where to start. Our final two chapters will hopefully make your job easier by looking at the big picture of security integration. We will take a step back from the detailed analysis of technologies needed to create secure applications and look at how to deploy secure applications in the context of planning a secure *system*. This chapter goes through each of the steps that are needed to achieve end-to-end Enterprise Security Integration (ESI). We'll use eBusiness.com as our case study for applying ESI.

Making the Jump from Application to System

You might think that once you've designed and implemented your application, your work is almost done. As far as security goes however, your work has just begun. Security is not a simple add-on to an application. Security cuts across all system layers; not only the application layer, but also the middleware, operating system, hardware, and network layers. Consequently, when you think about making your application part of a systemwide deployment, you'll need to consider how security should be configured in each system layer so that you will achieve the end-to-end security solution that you expect.

Interaction of Applications

In most large systems, it's unlikely that your application will act alone. You will need to consider how your application will interact with other existing applications and what security implications there might be in those interactions. Let's say, for example, that your application does not directly communicate with end users, but instead relies on a separate program that provides Web-based presentation layer functionality. Because the presentation layer communicates with end users, it needs to support authentication of those users, and then pass relevant authenticated data to your application for authorization and audit enforcement.

This simple dependency raises a number of security questions. In what form will the credential information be passed from the presentation layer to your application? How much do you trust this other program to perform authentication for you? Do you have to worry about hostile attackers spoofing the presentation program so they can defeat your authorization checks and penetrate your system? Does the presentation program need to worry about a compromise in *your* application, which mean that users' data may not be properly protected? These are crucial questions when a separate company controls the presentation layer, which is common in Web portals that provide single sign-on to many back-end applications across the network.

What Is Security?

When moving from an application view to a system view, you first need to determine what security problem you are trying to solve. New system level security requirements may surface that are not apparent when looking only at your application. Different systems vary their emphasis on security; some service providers believe that availability is most important for their systems, even if it's at the expense of data confidentiality. Others make data integrity the most critical requirement.

ESI AUTHORIZATION PRINCIPLE: APPLICATION DRIVEN

It's always important to let your business requirements drive the selection of security technologies. We are amazed to see the number companies that start out by first picking a security product, and then struggle to make the product fit their needs. You should avoid the easy mistake of presupposing what technology you should use before you understand the problem you're trying to solve.

Your first course of action in planning an integrated security solution is to decide exactly what security means to you. Examining business level drivers for security is the first step of this process. Once you know what your business needs are, you can then identify the security technologies that best solve your company's needs. We'll talk further about security requirements for eBusiness.com in the "Determining Requirements" section of this chapter.

As mentioned earlier, you may need to take more into account than just your own business needs. E-business applications commonly cut across many different companies or lines of business, forming security policy federations. E-commerce sites depend on outside services to check the validity of credit card purchases. Supply chain management requires sensitive manufacturing data to be shared among many participants. If you are developing e-business applications that are deployed across many different companies, be prepared to work with each of the companies to define cross-company security agreements. Each company will need to maintain its own autonomy to manage and administer its own security, but also work under some constraints to share security data, such as public key certificates. You should also be prepared for lawyers to be involved because serious liabilities accompany federated security agreements across companies.

In addition to identifying your security requirements, you also need to determine the level of *trustworthiness* needed in your system. That is, you need a sufficient level of confidence that your system is as secure as you want it. Checking that the applications in your system function as required is well understood—you perform component and integration testing until you are confident that the system behaves correctly. Security testing, however, is much more subtle.

Security is a negative property—when we say that a system is secure, we mean that the chance of something bad happening (i.e., a security compromise) is very small. It is very difficult to show that nothing bad can happen in a system without performing exhaustive testing, which is impractical for all but the simplest systems. The difficulty of security testing has been demonstrated many times over the years. Programs such as Web browsers and operating systems may be widely used by millions of people without incident. Then one day someone discovers a security flaw that was in the program all along. That program,

ESI AUTHORIZATION PRINCIPLE: PUSH SECURITY DOWN

By relying on security products rather than building your own security in the application, you increase the trustworthiness of your system. You can focus your security efforts on configuring and administering those security products instead of writing security code.

which functioned normally and was previously perfectly acceptable, is now fatally flawed. In this case, functional testing may have been adequate although the program is clearly not trustworthy.

So how do you make sure that your system security is trustworthy? It's not easy to achieve, and perfect trustworthiness is generally impossible. The best approach is to leave security to the experts. Their systems won't be perfectly secure either, but they have one advantage—their code is likely to be exercised by lots of people, so the flaws are more likely to have been detected. Security experts should also be more sensitive to common programming errors (buffer overflow is a classic example) that are the root cause of many flaws, so their systems should be better tested and more robust.

If you can't find a commercial solution to your security needs and you have to roll your own, be prepared to spend a lot of effort to establish the trustworthiness of your code. Define a specialized security test plan and a security specification that is separate from functional testing. Remember that you'll probably never know if an attacker exploits a security vulnerability in your system, so get the most assurance you can. For the best confidence in your security solution, hire an outside group that specializes in security assessments and penetration testing, and let them thoroughly examine what you have built.

Security Evolution—Losing Control

Defining the security technologies needed for a single application can be straightforward because most things are under your control. When moving to a system view, however, you most likely will *not* have control of security technology.

Most large companies today have decentralized control over information technology (IT) in general and over security technology specifically. Although there may be a central IT group, it usually does not mandate what security must be used across the enterprise. Each business application group goes out in search of the best security technologies and deploys them independently to meet their own business needs.

This approach works fine until the various groups want to hook their applications together, which they eventually will want to do to solve an e-business need. When interoperability is attempted, security is invariably one of the major obstacles because of incompatible technologies. The basic solution is simple enough: Some of the applications will have to change security technologies to match up with the others. The cost of this evolution can be expensive and time-consuming and can require major changes to the applications.

Even small companies have problems dealing with evolving security technology. Although a small company may uniformly deploy security products across applications, companies must still cope with changing technology. Over time, all companies need to migrate to new security technologies to protect against new threats and to maintain their competitive advantage. In addition, companies are always pursuing ways to interoperate with their suppliers, customers, and suppliers through business-to-business (B2B) marketplaces that have their own security requirements. Each time you look at a requirement for a new security technology, your simple application may not be so simple anymore.

Public key infrastructure (PKI) is an example of an evolving security technology. Although PKI is not widely used for authenticating clients today, it is just a matter of time before we see its widespread use as the cost of smart cards continues to drop. Can your e-business applications migrate to PKI without major modifications? If they can't, they have not been designed to handle security evolution.

The best way to deal with evolving security technologies is through a security framework. We presented the concept of an ESI framework in Chapter 1, and we'll describe how the framework applies to eBusiness.com later in this chapter.

Dealing with the "ilities"

Getting a single isolated application to function properly is not a big challenge. Getting it to work in the context of a system that needs to behave predictably day in and day out is a major undertaking. It's the nonfunctional system requirements, the "ilities," that make system building so tough. We're talking about issues like manageability, extensibility, reliability, availability, scalability, and of course security. (We know security doesn't end with "ility", but who's perfect?)

Security has a major impact on the other "ilities." Security is a challenge for manageability because security adds complexity to a system. Security policy, in fact, is one of the most difficult aspects of system management. Security affects system extensibility as we just explained in the previous section on security evolution. Security also impacts system reliability; in particular, a security service can be a single point of failure if it is not properly designed. Security and availability go hand in hand because availability is itself an aspect of security in many systems. Denial of service attacks that consume system resources are common, and security mechanisms need to be in place to protect against these kinds of attacks. In addition, proper configuration of a security policy is critical to ensure availability; if the security service denies access when it shouldn't, the entire system will be unavailable. Scalability, like reliability, is also greatly affected by the security solution. All sensitive application data must pass through security enforcement code; if the security architecture is not designed to scale, a bottleneck will result. We'll explore the relationship of security and the other "ilities" later in this chapter.

eBusiness.com's Approach

Consider the following scenario: eBusiness.com realizes that an enterprise security strategy needs to be in place as part of its e-commerce application development effort. It recognizes that its approach to security has been ad hoc and would like a more structured approach in the future. The company has an experienced security IT group that understands perimeter security, such as firewalls, network security, intrusion detection, and operating system hardening. However, this group is not accustomed to application-level security issues, and they do not understand middleware, such as EJB or CORBA. eBusiness.com has a good business application development group that is experienced in building distributed component systems. As this group builds more sophisticated applications, such as this e-commerce application, the development group knows that security is a critical issue. The development group has looked to security IT to supply the infrastructure for securing component-based applications, but security IT doesn't know how to help. In the meantime, management is worried about the business risk of new e-business deployments and is looking for reassurance that the company has the best security practices in place to protect them against fraud, lawsuits, and other business risks.

Fortunately, eBusiness.com management realizes that the way out of its predicament is to encourage its security IT and business application development groups to work together and create an interdisciplinary approach based on ESI. eBusiness.com creates an ESI task force that has members from both groups; the task force creates a security framework that is the basis of its enterprise security strategy. The framework supports the current deployment of the eBusiness.com e-commerce application and will evolve over time to encompass new security technologies as the company builds and integrates new applications.

For eBusiness.com, creating the application code that implements the class model described in Chapter 1 is the easy part. The company then needs to address many of the issues we discussed earlier as it plans the e-commerce application integration and deployment. We'll first address the system level requirements, both security and nonfunctional, that must be considered when integrating the eBusiness.com application with the supporting infrastructure. Based on these requirements, the eBusiness.com technical team defines the security framework in terms of security APIs, protocols, and security policies.

Determining Requirements

Let's first look at the overall requirements for eBusiness.com in terms of functional, security, and nonfunctional requirements. Functional requirements define how the eBusiness.com application should behave in terms of its basic functionality; that is, implementing a system that allows various customers to select and order goods over the Internet. Security requirements define the eBusiness.com system security properties, which by now should be familiar to you. Nonfunctional requirements define the other required system behaviors, the "ilities", beyond functional and security requirements.

Functional Requirements

Because this is a security book, we're going to assume that the eBusiness.com developers know how to build a correctly functioning application. The basic description of the example's functionality was provided in the "Example of a Secure Component Architecture" section in Chapter 1. This should be all you need to know about what the eBusiness.com example does. As a quick recap, a customer first authenticates to the security service, and then gets a list of products and prices using the *ProductFactory* interface. The customer then places orders for products into his or her account using the *CustomerAccount* interface and sometime later settles the order with a credit card number. In addition to the basic ordering interactions, the application interfaces also support administering customer and member accounts, and setting product prices.

Security Requirements

eBusiness.com has many different business level security requirements that need to be enforced by the system. We admittedly contrived our example to combine many security concerns into one simple example, but these security requirements are illustrative of common security issues that we have encountered in real-life businesses.

As a starting point, we should point out that it's frequently very difficult to tell exactly where functional requirements stop and security requirements begin. In many e-business applications, the primary purpose of the application is a financial transaction, which is fundamentally about security. Even so, it's important to try to make the distinction between security and functionality whenever possible. Why bother? As discussed previously in this chapter, one of our basic principles of ESI is to push security down in the architecture. We separate security from application functionality so we can allow the security infrastructure to work for us. It's far better to let a robust security product enforce security for your application than having to reinvent the wheel.

eBusiness.com looks for every opportunity to offload the burden of security functionality from its applications. In this particular application, it has several business driven security requirements that can be enforced by security products, as we'll explore in the following sections.

Limit Visitor Access

First, eBusiness.com would like to permit access for unauthenticated visitors, as long as that access is strictly limited. If casual Web surfers happen to stumble across eBusiness.com, they should be welcomed and should not immediately encounter the "Enter User ID and Password" warning that might scare them off. Of course, if the casual visitor is welcomed, so is the hostile attacker because it will be very difficult to distinguish between someone who is "just browsing" and a hacker looking for a security hole. To address this issue, eBusiness.com defines a very limited authorization policy for unauthenticated users; they may see a list of eBusiness.com's products, but they may not see product prices.

This rather open philosophy could leave the site open to problems, such as denial of service attacks, where a coordinated attack might flood the site with so many requests for product information that it would slow down or stop service to legitimate users. Firewalls and proactive intrusion detection products may be used to detect, filter, and minimize the damage caused by these kinds of attacks.

Eliminate Administration of New Customers

A second business driven security requirement is to minimize the burden on eBusiness.com's security administrators wherever possible. One of the drivers of e-business is to reduce the number of staff required to support customer interactions. This purpose would be defeated if companies had to add administrative security staff to just deal with customers. As a result, a common model used is *self-registration*, in which the user adds himself or herself as a new customer. For the eBusiness.com application, unauthenticated users are allowed to create themselves as new customers, so administrator intervention is not required.

Again, this open approach may be good for business, but it does open up eBusiness.com to possible attacks. The self-registration program, which in this case is *CustomerAccountFactory*, must be carefully written to check the credentials of new users before admitting them as customers. For example, eBusiness.com requires a credit card to be supplied, and the application performs some basic credit checks on the card to reduce the chance that the card has been lost or stolen. CustomerAccountFactory must be a highly trusted security-aware application because it will be interacting with the underlying security service to create new authenticated principals. Consequently, Customer-

AccountFactory must be well tested to ensure that it is trustworthy; if a hacker could exploit an error in this code, he or she could create new users at will, which would not make eBusiness.com very happy.

Grant Members More Access

The next business requirement for eBusiness.com is to give its members access to special product deals that are not available to ordinary customers. The distinction between customers and members could have been made within the eBusiness.com application, but the application developers recognized that the supporting security service was easily capable of making the distinction and had the ability to extend this model to other classes of users in the future.

To address this requirement, we group users and products, as we discussed extensively in Chapter 8. We set up a simple role-based access control (RBAC) policy that grants a basic set of access rights to all users who are customers. We then set up a role hierarchy that grants additional rights to users who are members; they are allowed to see prices for special products. The role hierarchy also simplifies administration for customers and members because it allows eBusiness.com staff to grant these additional privileges to a user simply by switching the user's role. In this case, the supporting security service is a very good match for the business requirement.

Protect the Accounts of Each Individual

eBusiness.com wants to ensure that the data in every customer and member account is protected so that one individual cannot access another individual's account. However, strictly speaking this business requirement is not needed to protect eBusiness.com because if a customer accidentally pays for the wrong account, eBusiness.com still gets paid. The requirement is mainly to ensure the privacy of everyone's account information.

Privacy is a particular kind of security policy that protects user data. Unlike an enterprise security policy, which is controlled by a company to protect its own corporate data, a privacy policy is controlled by an individual to protect his or her own personal data. The view that privacy data should be controlled by an individual might surprise you because today there are few constraints placed on companies to regulate the sharing of their huge stores of consumer data. In most cases, these companies do not have genuine privacy policies in place. The trend we see, as driven by emerging government regulations all over the world, is to give back to consumers the control of their own data. Companies hold data on behalf on individuals, and those individuals will eventually dictate who is allowed to see their data and for what purpose.

Privacy is a rapidly growing topic in its own right and is too big and complex to address in this book. We will summarize by pointing out that the security mechanisms that have been explained in this book are also used to protect the privacy of an individual's data. Cryptography, such as the use of Secure Sockets Layer (SSL), protects the data privacy as it travels over the Internet. Access policies control who in a corporation is permitted to have access to an individual's private data.

To ensure privacy, eBusiness.com wants to enforce fine-grain access control to customer and member accounts. After looking at a variety of products, we have decided that access control at the level of individual accounts will not be enforced by a security product, but will instead be enforced within the *CustomerAccount* and *MemberAccount* application code. The CustomerAccount and MemberAccount application servers will call a RAD server to perform the authorization check. The RAD server ensures that individuals can only get access to their own accounts based on a policy that matches up account numbers and owners, as we described in Chapter 7. Although this solution not may perform as fast as embedding the authorization code in the application, prototyping demonstrates that the RAD server satisfies eBusiness.com's performance requirements and has a much higher degree of security assurance.

Administrator Control of Critical Functions

eBusiness.com also wants to ensure that certain critical application functions are only controlled by its administrative staff. Only eBusiness.com is allowed to set prices and to administer customer and member accounts. (As we will see in a moment, however, even staff members have limits on what they can do.) Product pricing is central to this application and must be highly controlled; if a hacker could break in and set product prices, it would be a disaster.

We enforce this policy by only allowing staff members to access the *setPrice* operation on the *Product* interface. This policy can be enforced by the underlying security service and does not require application level code.

Restrict Administrators Abilities

Finally, eBusiness.com wants to limit the ability of its own administrative staff to commit fraud. In particular, eBusiness.com does not want to allow its staff to settle an order (i.e., pay for an order using a credit card). If a staff member could settle orders, he or she would be able to manipulate a customer account in any fashion. The staff member might be tempted to create a fictitious customer account, and then use a stolen credit card number from another account to order merchandise. The goods could be shipped to a location of the staff member's choice and then be resold, making the fraudulent purchases very difficult to trace.

Preventing eBusiness.com's staff from settling orders is an example of a *separation of duties* policy. Separation of duties policies distribute trust among several people, making it less likely for a compromise to occur. In this case, for example, the staff member could still commit fraud by colluding with a person outside of the company who would pose as the fictitious customer. Although this approach might be possible for one or two people, the number of people required for a large-scale operation makes it likely that the staff member would get caught.

We enforce this policy by only allowing customers and members to access the *settleOrder* operation on the CustomerAccount and MemberAccount interfaces. This policy can be enforced by the underlying security service and does not require application level code.

Nonfunctional Requirements

The nonfunctional requirements that eBusiness.com wants to address are manageability, extensibility, reliability, availability, and scalability. All of these topics have many complex aspects, and because this book is not a complete guide to system architecture, we will not attempt to cover them in depth. However we will address the relationship between each of these topics and security. In particular, we will discuss the nonfunctional requirements that eBusiness.com imposes on its security services.

Manageability

eBusiness.com wants to ensure that security is easy to manage in operational use. The enterprise security architecture should support a management framework for its components, users, resources, and enabling technology. The enterprise security architecture should also support centralized and delegated administration of security components. The framework standardizes the management approach for many security components including:

- Monitoring
- Failure restart
- Installation of software upgrades
- Administration
- Auditing for accountability

Extensibility

eBusiness.com has a variety of requirements for the extensibility of the security architecture and the eBusiness.com application. The security architecture should have the ability to support different security policies and extend those policies over time. The system should have the flexibility to adjust to changed circumstances (such as new business policies and procedures) without requiring changes to the eBusiness.com application code. If the eBusiness.com application does need to change, the security architecture should be able to accommodate application changes without making major changes to the security infrastructure.

In addition, eBusiness.com needs to be able to respond quickly to a rapidly changing business environment. As a result, the security architecture should be able to evolve over time due to:

- Changes in demand for the eBusiness.com application services
- Corporate reorganizations, acquisitions, mergers, or partnerships
- Introduction of new security technologies

Reliability

The eBusiness.com enterprise security architecture must be a highly reliable system due to its critical role in ensuring the security of the e-commerce application. eBusiness.com wants to ensure that the security service is at least as reliable as the application. In this context, reliability means the ability of the system to continue operations without failure. Typically, the reliability of a system is measured in terms of Mean Time to Failure (MTTF) and Mean Time to Repair (MTTR).

In practice, security service reliability is dependent on the reliability of the underlying software and hardware. eBusiness.com ensures security software reliability by purchasing products from reliable security vendors that have good quality control procedures in place and well-demonstrated track records of success. eBusiness.com ensures hardware reliability by using a redundant architecture that avoids a single point of failure. Software and hardware redundancy also supports availability and scalability, so we explore the topic further in the next two sections.

Availability

eBusiness.com wants to ensure that their system is always available. The e-commerce site must be accessible 24 hours per day, 7 days per week. The site must continuously support large numbers of transactions per second and typically subsecond response times.

The eBusiness.com high availability plan considers the entire security architecture to identify and reduce any single points of failure. Included in the availability plan are network components, firewalls, Web servers, security servers, and the eBusiness.com application server components. The availability considerations apply to both software and hardware components in the architecture. To ensure high availability, the enterprise security architecture incorporates the following capabilities:

- Redundancy of software and hardware
- Failover (automated, hot standby, cold standby)
- Disaster recovery
- Replication
- Backups
- Load balancing

Scalability

Scalability requirements for eBusiness.com's enterprise security architecture are driven by its business application requirements. Because eBusiness.com expects to continue to grow, the company wants to be sure that all applications will be able to expand to handle larger volumes of customer orders. Scalability describes the ability of the system to support variations in the size of the workload without design changes.

The multitiered component-based architecture that is the basis of eBusiness.com applications includes two features that directly improve performance and scalability:

- **Load balancing.** Application server middleware hides the server's actual location, facilitating the allocation of processing loads across multiple mid-tier servers. The mid-tier servers can act as concentrators for client connections and thus manage growth in the number of concurrent client data requests.
- **Hardware and software architecture flexibility.** Decoupling the business logic from the presentation, data access, and security logic permits flexibility in allocating the software components to physical computing resources. The components can reside on the same platform or be distributed across several platforms.

Applying the Framework

Once eBusiness.com has defined the functional, security, and nonfunctional requirements for the application, it's time to determine how to apply the ESI framework. The framework helps us structure our strategy for enforcing security and will guide us on the kinds of products we will need. The security services identified in the framework will then be the basis for the deployment of the integrated security system that we discuss in Chapter 10.

As discussed in Chapter 1, the ESI framework specifies the interactions among the security services and application components that use those security services. The framework security APIs are called explicitly by security-aware eBusiness.com components, such as *CustomerAccountFactory* and *CustomerAccount*, and implicitly by most of the other components. A high-level view of the security framework is shown in Figure 9.1.

To implement the security requirements that were described previously, we will build the eBusiness.com framework defined in this figure. The framework consists of application components that implement the three tiers of the eBusiness.com application, security APIs that encapsulate the security services, core security services, and the framework security facilities that support the core security services. In this section, we provide a quick overview of each of these components, which are then explained in considerably more detail in Chapter 10.

Normally, at this stage, eBusiness.com would select a specific set of commercial products to implement all of the required services. Because there is a broad choice of products that implement these services and we intend this book to be relevant for a variety of deployed architectures, we stop short of naming specific selected products. We have provided examples of these products throughout this book; many alternatives are listed in Chapter 4.

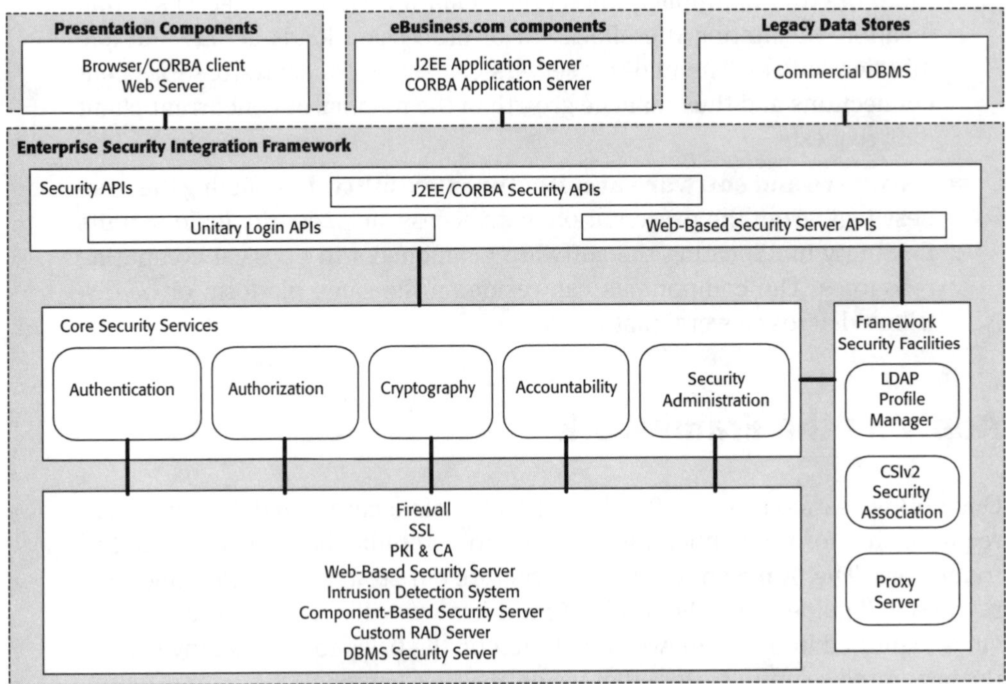

Figure 9.1 ESI framework for eBusiness.com.

Application Components

eBusiness.com has built this application to support Web access to an existing commercial data store, and the application components shown in Figure 9.1 define the functionality necessary to support this goal. eBusiness.com users access the application primarily via a Web browser, although CORBA clients for corporate customers are also supported, as discussed in Chapter 10. The Web server services requests from browsers and forwards them to the J2EE application server. CORBA application servers are also used as support to allow wrapping of non-Java legacy applications. The actual accounting and billing data is stored in a back-end commercial database management system (DBMS).

Security APIs

The security APIs are the interfaces that all eBusiness.com applications, whether security-aware or security-unaware, use for security support. The APIs selected by eBusiness.com are primarily based on the J2EE and CORBA security standards, which are likely to be the most widely adopted standards for component security. Note that because the philosophy of both of these standards is to hide as much security from the application as possible, the APIs that are actually exposed to security-aware applications are very simple. Integration of security services into a J2EE or CORBA environment can be a very complex task. Because this integration has already been taken care of for you by a number of application server vendors, there is little for the application developer to worry about in this area.

eBusiness.com also uses a web-based security server to handle authentication and authorization of HTTP requests to the Web server. As a result, the security framework must also encompass these APIs. Unfortunately, these APIs are currently proprietary and product specific; however, they are designed to integrate easily with Web servers using standard plug-ins, so they do not necessarily need to be exposed to other applications.

eBusiness.com also wants to use a Unitary Login API to securely store password data for access to the DBMS. Because there are no standard APIs in this area, eBusiness.com developers defined their own API, similar to the one described in Chapter 5. This topic is explored further in Chapter 10.

Core Security Services

The core security services provide the wrappers that implement the framework security APIs and encapsulate specific security products. eBusiness.com has selected the products in the following list to implement its system:

- Firewall
- SSL
- PKI & CA
- Web-based Security Server
- Intrusion Detection System
- Component-based Security Server
- Custom RAD Server (eBusiness.com could find no commercial implementation of RAD, so the developers built their own simple implementation that is customized for their application.)
- DBMS Security Server

Uses of these technologies are discussed in Chapter 10.

Framework Security Facilities

The framework security facilities provide support for the core security services. eBusiness.com has selected the products in the following list to implement its system:

- **LDAP directory service.** Supports user and application security profile storage and retrieval
- **CSIv2 security association.** Supports the security protocol for secure interoperability among application server components
- **Proxy server.** Supports CORBA client access to CORBA applications through a firewall

Uses of these technologies are discussed in Chapter 10.

Summary

In this chapter, we took a step back from our detailed analysis to look at how to deploy secure applications in the context of planning a secure system. We first discussed the shift in view when you move from building an application to building a system. We talked about issues such as interacting securely with other systems, trustworthiness, and security evolution. We then went through eBusiness.com's approach to building its e-commerce application as a case study in deploying security. We discussed eBusiness.com's functional, security, and nonfunctional requirements. We finished by describing how we used ESI to define a security framework for eBusiness.com.

The ESI framework helped us structure our strategy for enforcing security and guided us on the kinds of products needed to satisfy eBusiness.com's requirements. Now that the security services have been identified in the framework, they will form the basis for the deployment of the integrated security system. We conclude this book with a discussion of issues related to building an integrated security system.

CHAPTER 10

Building an Integrated Security System

When the Internet first became popular with corporations, they used their Web sites as electronic billboards to advertise their products. People in the perimeter clicked on a company's URL and received a static HTML page with information about the company. A corporation could handle this type of one-way interaction by placing the computer holding the static Web pages outside the company's internal network. The only security required was to limit users to one directory on that one machine, which was not connected to the company's internal network.

As time went on, firms found it desirable to let customers place orders using HTML forms. At that point, the interaction became two-way; that is, information flowed from the customer to the company as well as from the company to the shopper. Security was needed to authenticate a person so that a sale could be recorded. Also, companies found it more efficient to move the computer that customers were accessing into the mid-tier to more easily process the order. Dedicating a server for this purpose and limiting outside access to that server by means of a firewall permitted corporations to handle this somewhat higher level of interaction with their customers.

As companies discovered potential cost savings in e-business, they naturally wanted to use it more in their business practices. E-commerce moved to business-to-business transactions, in which the person on the perimeter needed access to internal information to complete a transaction. For example, a supplier of windshields for an automobile company would need access to engineering drawings for the windshield area of the car models for which they will be supplying windshields. Although the auto company wants the windshield supplier to access the engineering drawings for the windshield area, it would not want the supplier to see the plans for the "Super Gizzmo" engine enhancement that will blow away its competitors when it is released. With these new requirements for interaction, security requirements increased dramatically. Not only did companies need authentication, but they also needed authorization. Additionally, some of these external suppliers would be using a combination of their browsers and a mixture of Java and CORBA programs to get updated price lists, place their sales orders, and get the internal information needed to effectively do their job.

Today, we are in this third stage of e-business requirements in which we want to let customers, suppliers, and partner companies into the mid-tier as well as allow them to access information from the legacy tier. As the host company demands that more functionality be available to the outside company, it is discovering a need for finer-grained authorization. This finer authorization granularity is needed to support the separation of incoming company requests from each other and from the host company's information, which outsiders should not be able to access or manipulate.

Up to this point we have presented you with theory, practical advice, and examples of security in EJB and CORBA. We have also shown you how to make these two models interoperate between themselves and how to make them interoperate with different security models used in the perimeter and with different models used with legacy applications. We now move to a more practical example and talk about using what you have learned to see what is necessary to implement eBusiness.com's security infrastructure. Of course, implementing and deploying a large enterprise's e-commerce security is a major effort with many details to be decided. We will not go into the detailed design decisions for a full deployment; instead, we focus more on helping you understand the requirements of an end-to-end secure deployment. Although the focus of this book is EJB and CORBA, there are other security mechanisms that are necessary to enforce end-to-end security. Therefore, in this final chapter, we present a high-level view touching briefly on a number of different security subjects.

In order to provide end-to-end security and meet eBusiness.com's requirements, the security architecture must encompass perimeter, mid-tier, and legacy security. Security within the enterprise, that is, mid-tier security, addresses security in applications and their underlying infrastructure. Without mid-tier security measures, there is no protection against insider attacks. Insiders include anyone who has access to internal network resources including today's customers and partners. Mid-tier security poses complex and difficult problems in large-scale, distributed systems. One way to gain confidence in planning and deploying a secure distributed system is to use standardized models that have been thought through and designed by security experts.

Many of the world's best security experts have worked for years to produce the comprehensive CORBA and EJB security standards. Commercial software vendors have similarly drawn on years of experience to produce the middleware security products that are coming to market based on these specifications. Consortia such as the Object Management Group (OMG), the Java Community Process (JCP), the Open Group, and the Internet Engineering Task Force (IETF) have invested significant intellectual resources to successfully identify the security issues specific to distributed systems and develop robust security architectures specifically to address these issues. These groups start with security precepts developed in the past (like the C2 criteria in the Orange Book), and interpret and expand them to apply to today's large-scale, distributed, object-based architectures.

This chapter pulls together the principles you learned in the previous chapters and uses them to discuss how an enterprise security system is constructed. We start with the Enterprise Security Integration (ESI) framework that was the result of eBusiness.com's security planning exercise that we described in Chapter 9. We use the security services defined in the eBusiness.com ESI framework to demonstrate how to use what you have learned. We also touch on some of the security aspects that are outside the scope of EJB and CORBA to clarify the all important concept of end-to-end security.

Security Architecture

The security architecture of eBusiness.com implements most of the principles espoused in this book, albeit in a somewhat simple example to enhance clarity. The application security architecture relies on a commercial perimeter security product to authenticate Web users and control access to HTML pages. It relies on SSL/TLS and CSIv2 security to provide secure transfer of user privileges and access control, and it relies on security servers for centralized administration. Additional security functionality, such as auditing, is also a necessary part of the underlying security middleware used by eBusiness.com.

The security services provide the access control checks to support eBusiness.com's security policies. Figure 10.1 shows the security design for eBusiness.com.

The architecture for eBusiness.com uses the security-unaware principle, that is, the security related functionality is transparent to the application developer. For instance, the figure depicts the flow in which an EJB authorizes a call via the security service. This authorization is initiated by the interceptor in the EJB Container and does not require the application developer to call any explicit security related APIs.

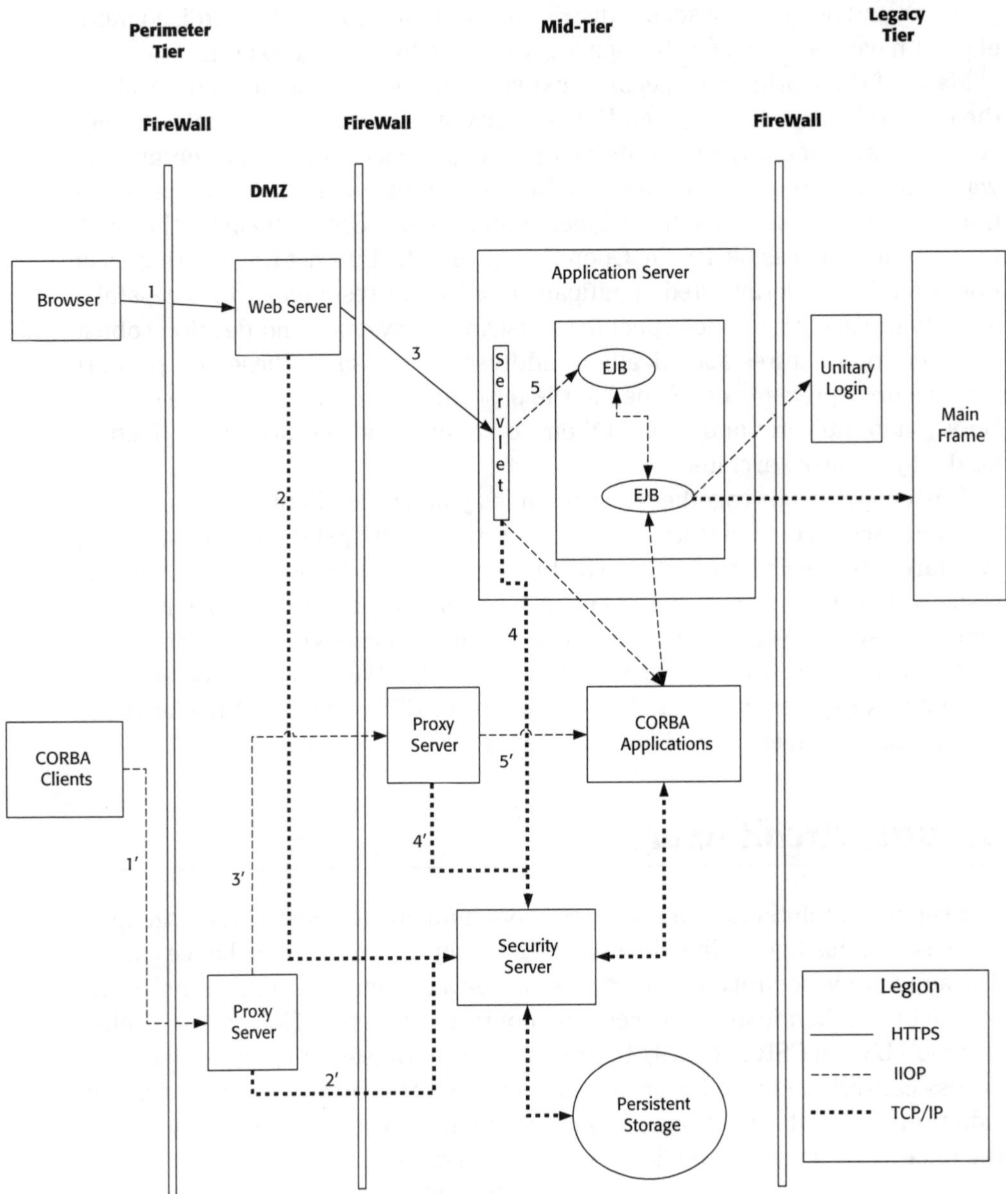

Figure 10.1 End-to-end security model.

There are two places in which the eBusiness.com applications can make explicit calls to the security service. First, eBusiness.com's application servlets can make an explicit call to the secure servlet to set up a secure session. Second, eBusiness.com's EJBs can call the security Unitary Login service to support access to the database servers. If there are a series of servlets that call each other, only the first servlet needs to be trusted and needs to make the security service call. The secure servlet is part of the preprocessing necessary to add the security-based authentication of users. The Unitary Login service provides a secure repository of back-end system authentication data and passwords. It is used to securely retrieve database passwords to allow an application to log in to the database server. Not all EJBs call the Unitary Login service; only those EJBs that require access to the database need to make the explicit security API call.

The following steps, corresponding to the labels in Figure 10.1, outline the activities that take place for a browser to call on an eBusiness.com EJB:

1. The user logs into the Web server. The commercial Web security services, augmented by one of the commercial perimeter security products, are used to authenticate the user and create several cookies.
2. When the user tries to access a Web page, the Web server first checks the page requested by the user. The perimeter security product is used to control access to Web pages based on the user's identity.
3. The userID and cookies are passed from the Web server to the application server as part of the standard HTTP communication.
4. The EJB authentication mechanism works with the security service to determine whether or not the user should be authenticated. The cookies are used to supply authentication evidence to the security service. If the cookie represents a legitimate and current user of the system, the user is authenticated to the EJB environment. No additional user intervention is required beyond the initial user identification and authentication exchange with the perimeter security product registry.
5. The secure servlet invokes on the selected EJB.

In the CORBA scenario, the security server creates and returns the user's credentials, which contain a user ID certificate and a Privilege Attribute Certificate (PAC). The PAC, as you remember, is an X.509 style certificate that contains the user's privileges. The privileges include the user's role, organization, and access ID. The PAC will form one part of the access control decision. Use of a PAC makes possible a "push" model of security, which is generally considered more efficient and scalable than the "pull" model.

The EJB authentication in the container sets the credentials for the thread such that the client's credentials are available for each subsequent invocation. This permits the user's identity to carry through from the servlet to the EJBs.

Figure 10.1 depicts the invocation from the servlet to an EJB. The EJB interceptor intercedes in the invocation and first checks whether access should be allowed. EJB access decision then calls the appropriate APIs to check whether access is permitted. Note that the application developers do not need to include calls to the security APIs within their code. The container invokes the access control checks set by the deployment descriptor.

For each invocation, the security service applies access control security policies as appropriate. Because the security service also provides audit and delegation, these security policies may be applied as well if desired. The security access controls may be applied to other resources as well as EJBs.

The Unitary Login service is used to support access to the database servers. The Unitary Login service provides a secure repository of back-end system authentication data and passwords. It allows different applications to have their own passwords for the various databases. Each EJB that requires database access retrieves its appropriate password from the Unitary Login service. The Unitary Login service eliminates the need for the applications to store unprotected, cleartext passwords in order to log in to existing applications, like any of the numerous commercial DBMSs. It provides a secure means to store and retrieve passwords in a protected manner (e.g., encrypted).

The security Unitary Login service can also be used to support access to mainframe systems. For example, FTP passwords can be securely maintained in the Unitary Login repository.

The administration of the standard security information (e.g., required rights, access policies) is entered via a security administration tool supplied by the security service. The specific steps to administer the system are dependent on the security middleware product chosen and the deployed system.

Deploying the Example

After the planning and preparation described in Chapter 9, we are ready to roll out our e-business implementation. Figure 10.1 showed the complete end-to-end security architecture for eBusiness.com's security installation. The implementation supports both browsers and CORBA clients in the perimeter tier. Customers and members use browsers to access the eBusiness.com site. We also introduce a new class of users, called *corporate customers*, who use a mixture of browsers and custom CORBA applications to access the eBusiness.com site. Corporate customers are companies that have a preferred arrangement with eBusiness.com for high volume orders. As a result of introducing corporate customers, there are two paths initiated in the perimeter, which are shown in Figure 10.1. The first path starts with a customer or member using a browser shown in the upper-left side of the figure. The second path (found in the lower-left part of Figure 10.1) depicts a corporate customer initiating a request using a CORBA application.

The Underlying Protection Layer

Before getting into the discussion of the various paths that a user may take to access eBusiness.com, we will take a look at the underlying protection layer. We use SSL at the transport layer to give us data integrity and confidentiality. (We'll use the more familiar term SSL to mean the standardized TLS variant of SSL in the rest of this chapter.) SSL is used end-to-end, that is, from the perimeter through the mid-tier to eBusiness.com's legacy database on its mainframe

Saying that SSL is used end-to-end does not mean that it is used in every transaction nor that it is used the same way for each type of user. For example, when a user makes a call simply to request information, we do not require them to use SSL. How do we achieve this? If you remember from Chapter 5, in which we described how SSL and HTTP work together, we stated that the server sends an error message back to the browser requesting a username and password. This message also requests that SSL be turned on by the browser. So the simple answer is that the server does not require SSL for requests for simple information data. The server knows that it is a request only for information by the URL that is sent by the browser, that is, the URL points to an information only page. We put this intelligence in a Web server in the demilitarized zone (DMZ) as shown in Figure 10.1.

Chapters 1 and 2 described the existing types of eBusiness.com users: customers, members, and staff. We will treat our new corporate customers differently than our regular customers and members. Although the noncorporate customers and members can employ usernames and passwords, corporate customers are required to use SSL certificates because they usually transact higher dollar orders than our other customers. The use of SSL certificates results in stronger authentication than a username and password, which we feel we need for these high value transactions. We can afford the occasional loss of $10 or $20 dollars, but not a loss of $10,000. The trade-off of a possible small loss is balanced by the reduced hassle to our noncorporate customers when we do not require them to purchase SSL certificates. This is a risk management decision that our design team decided on during the planning stage.

From the customers point of view, our use of SSL gives them the confidence to pass their credit card numbers and other personal data knowing that they are encrypted and thus protected from hackers.

There are a couple of other things that we have to do for our users. We have to keep their credit card numbers and other personal information safe once they reach our system. Consequently, we do not want to keep the numbers on our Web server in the DMZ while we process their orders. This work should be carried out in the mid-tier. In addition, we store the user information that we have collected from them when they registered with eBusiness.com in the legacy tier. In some cases, this may include credit card numbers if users have given us permission to do so. As we all know, privacy is an important topic that is not going to go away, nor should it. Therefore, we will store all user data in a protected database in our legacy tier. Depending on the other type of protection, it would be a good idea to encrypt the privacy data. We'll revisit this issue when we talk about legacy security.

Perimeter Security

Our first step in securing eBusiness.com is to secure the perimeter of our site with regard to our users. These users are not within our secure perimeter boundary. Our customers and members will be using browsers to sign on to our site, look at our merchandise, and make their purchases (we hope). Corporate customers will be using heavy clients, that is, CORBA or EJB applications, as well as browsers to access our site. It should be noted that the trend is moving away from "heavy clients" like CORBA or EJB applications and toward "light clients," such as browsers using HTTP and possibly using Simple Object Access Protocol (SOAP).

In order to serve these users better, our company has moved our digital dealings with them into the mid-tier where they can place orders, have the order filled, be billed, have their credit cards charged, and update their personal information. This means that users will be accessing the machines and programs in our mid-tier. Although these users are our customers and business partners, we do need to be concerned about their ability to access sensitive corporate data in our mid-tier. In addition, there is data about each user, which if one user could access another's personal data, would be a disaster for our business. Therefore, user access to information must be controlled. eBusiness.com will use a layered approach of multiple lines of defense for its security. We will not put all of its security at one location in our system, which could become a single point of failure.

It's not sufficient to enforce access control simply based on the three groups: customers, members, and corporate customers. Customer A must get customer A's bill and only customer A's bill so having just the customer group will not work in this case. If both customer A and customer B were in the customer group and authorization was done solely on a group basis, then A could see the data of B since B is also represented by group customer. Consequently, we have to enforce authorization by user when protecting user data. On the other hand, we can use the role "member" to allow access for all the people in that group to buy special products. Accordingly, we will have to keep track of individual identities that come in from the perimeter as well as roles that are assigned to these individuals.

The first line of defense at the perimeter boundary is the perimeter firewall. The traditional firewall, as we explained in Chapter 4, is no longer adequate on its own. Its protection scheme is too coarse and must be supplemented by finer-grained authorization. However, it still plays a very important part in perimeter defense. The firewall is backed up by a Web server or a proxy server, which can carry out the next line of finer-grained defense that our eBusiness.com needs for its interactions with its users. We discuss the details of the components that play a part in the perimeter defense—the firewall, the Web server, and the proxy server—in the next subsections. But first we will trace different types of users through interactions with eBusiness.com.

Customers and members using browsers in the perimeter communicate with one or more Web servers in the DMZ between the perimeter and the mid-tier as shown in Figure 10.1. This path is labeled as step 1 in the upper-left portion of the figure. The Web server authenticates the incoming client, step 2, using one of a number of third-party commercial, perimeter security products, such as Netegrity Siteminder, Entrust getAccess, IBM/Tivoli PolicyDirector, or Securant's ClearTrust SecureControl. The Web server uses a library supplied by the Web server security provider to parse the HTTP header and extract the security evidence passed from the browser. Be sure to check that your security service vendor supplies this functionality for your Web server.

For corporate clients using a CORBA object, the lower-left portion of the perimeter tier in Figure 10.1, the CORBA object talks with a proxy server over the path labeled 1' in the lower-left part of the figure. (We use the prime notation to distinguish the CORBA path from the browser path.) The IIOP proxy server extracts the authentication evidence in the Generic Inter-ORB Protocol (GIOP) service context from a CORBA client and uses this evidence to authenticate the client using the same perimeter security product that the Web server used (2'). The proxy uses a library supplied by the proxy supplier to extract the authentication evidence and transforms it to the format required by the perimeter authentication service. Once again check to see if this functionality is supplied by your vendor.

Note that the call from the perimeter to the DMZ is protected by the outer firewall. When the call is HTTP, firewalls pass the message to the Web server. For an incoming IIOP call, we open a defined port and configure the firewall to pass all non-HTTP traffic to the IIOP proxy. Of course the firewall will have other rules set by the eBusiness.com administrator, such as deny or redirect all FTP traffic to an FTP server, so some of the non-HTTP traffic will be stopped or redirected by these rules. In the IIOP case, when the call reaches the proxy, it extracts the authentication evidence from the service context and authenticates the client. It is feasible that the Web server and the IIOP proxy are in one server.

There is a remaining problem for the IIOP case and that is the interior firewall. A large company, like eBusiness.com plans to become, normally has a number of internal firewalls, for example, between divisions or for isolating sensitive areas like corporate accounting and personnel. To allow IIOP traffic to pass across internal firewalls, an IIOP proxy needs to be placed behind every firewall. Another solution is to use IIOP firewalls, which are hybrids of traditional firewalls and the IIOP proxy.

Although they have followed different paths, both the browser and the CORBA client have reached the point at which they have been authenticated. In the CORBA case, we have authenticated the client from both IIOP proxies (2', 3', and 4'). Authentication from both proxies may not be necessary if the first and second proxies establish a trust relationship prior to any messages being passed between them. The browser then uses path 3 to call on the servlet in the application server, whereas the interior proxy calls on a CORBA application following path 5'.

So far, we have two lines of defense, the firewall that does course-grained security discrimination and the Web server or CORBA IIOP proxy server that does authentication and acts as the second line of defense.

Before moving on to the mid-tier, we discuss the use of firewalls and Web servers in more detail.

Using Component Security with Firewalls

With the advent of e-commerce and greater use of distributed computing, firewalls are not as effective as when systems in the perimeter were not permitted into a company's mid-tier or were only allowed to access a few computers that were not connected to the corporate network, such as an FTP server or an HTTP server that returned static Web pages. Traditional firewalls, for the most part, are designed to keep people out of your system. E-commerce wants to allow people into your system. That said, firewalls still play an important part in your system's defense.

The main job of perimeter firewalls is to direct traffic to a few systems, which in turn can examine requests and possibly do some authentication and authorization. This firewall may be a router, which directs traffic based on an IP address or specific destinations, such as an FTP server. The perimeter firewall may also be a little more complex and examine the message to determine if it is an HTTP message, and then direct those messages through its HTTP port to the HTTP server.

As we pointed out in Chapter 4, our perimeter firewall also protects us against a number of external attacks, for example, IP address spoofing, TCP SYN flooding, and so on. This is important functionality; however, we will not cover this topic in this book.

We also have an interior firewall to isolate our corporate accounting and billing system. This firewall only permits certain servers from the mid-tier to access the accounting enclave because there is no need for a user to have access to these services.

The IIOP proxy behind the perimeter firewall examines the header information in the incoming message. If it is an IIOP header, it uses CSIv2 security logic to determine what authentication and authorization needs to be done and uses the appropriate security service to carry out these tasks. The proxy server in our eBusiness.com case uses CORBA defined authentication and authorization services to perform these activities.

Using Component Security with Web Servers

We will use a Web server to further refine requests from the perimeter and direct where they will be sent in the mid-tier. The outer firewall shown in Figure 10.1 will direct HTTP messages to our Web server and only to our Web server. As business picks up, we will install additional Web servers to handle the increased load and remove a single point of failure. In either case, the job of the Web server(s) in this design is twofold:

- To authenticate and authorize the incoming request
- To pass the message to the correct server in the mid-tier

To accomplish the first step, the Web server gets the authentication evidence from the client in the HTTP header, and then uses that evidence to carry out the authentication and authorization. As discussed in Chapter 5, security at the perimeter boundary is not standardized. There are a number of ad hoc, proprietary solutions from a number of vendors. We use the solution from Chapter 5 for authenticating and authorizing a user. Specifically, we choose a perimeter security server product, to authenticate a client in the Web server and use the Chapter 5 code to convert the proprietary authentication data to a standardized CSIv2 token.

The Web server then passes the authentication evidence into the mid-tier. The target in this design is a servlet in the application server.

To get a better feel for what's happening so far, let's take a brief look at an example of an ordinary customer accessing eBusiness.com. The customer types http://eBusiness.com into his browser. The message travels through eBusiness.com's perimeter firewall to the Web server. The Web server notices that there is no cookie or username and password in the HTTP header, so it sends an HTTP error message to the browser. In addition, the Web server initiates an SSL session with the browser requesting client authentication. The browser displays a dialog box asking for a username and password from the customer. After the SSL session is set up, the browser sends the username and password to the Web server over the SSL protected connection.

At this point, we could use either the perimeter security products that were discussed in Chapter 4 and 5, or we could use CORBA authentication. In our eBusiness.com design, we will use one of the perimeter security products for authentication.

The Web server uses the authentication evidence sent by the browser to authenticate the user. The authentication is performed by our chosen perimeter security server, which is situated within the mid-tier. Prior to the first attempt at client authentication, a trust relationship is set up between the security server and the Web server. This is accomplished by the security server initiating an SSL session with the Web server using mutual authentication. Mutual SSL authentication using client and server SSL certificates allows the two parties, that is, the security server and the Web server, to obtain their peer's certificate. SSL verifies the peer certificates. Beyond that, the X.500 names in the respective certificates are retrieved and the names are verified against the correct names of the peer, that is, a simple form of authorization. This last step is necessary because SSL, although it verifies the certificates, does not have any knowledge as to what are the acceptable names for each of the trusted servers.

For performance, multiple SSL channels can be set up. As another performance enhancement, we will use the SSL retry mechanism. If an SSL connection is dropped, which means that an SSL session breaks down, using the SSL retry, the two parties can restart the session without the necessity of a full handshake. If a session cannot be restarted, the security server has to start up a new SSL session following the same procedure as when the two processes first started up.

If the user is authenticated, the security server sends back an indication of success to the Web browser along with the user's authentication token. The Web server then passes back to the client the authentication token that will be stored in a cookie on the client, and an initial welcome Web page tailored, in our case, for customers, members, or corporate customers. When the user clicks on a link in this Web page, an HTTP message is constructed containing the cookie and a URL that points from the Web server to a servlet in the application server. In each subsequent HTTP request from the client, the Web server receives the cookie containing the authentication token. The Web server sends the HTTP request and cookie to the security server. If the security server confirms that the client is authorized to make the request on the specified URL, the Web server sends the request on to the application server. We'll discuss what happens in the mid-tier a little later.

Note that there are no standards for the protocol we just went through. In fact, there are very few standards for the perimeter to mid-tier boundary. Make sure that your chosen Web server is able to provide the work needed by your application server. This means the Web server or additional software for the Web server should be supplied or at least coordinated by your security service provider.

A Caution Against Proprietary Solutions

Before going any further, we want to offer a word of caution with respect to using proprietary security solutions. One advantage of standardized solutions is that the algorithms and protocols are written in excruciating detail and published for everyone to see. These solutions can be analyzed by outside security experts to find any potential security holes. This does not mean that a bad implementation of a standard may not introduce a security hole, but it is much more unlikely because the implementers have the blueprints for how to build a standardized product. Also, because the standard is widely available, implementations of it may be examined and tested for conformance to the standard. Consequently, as long as the implementers have followed the standard and the standard is written tightly enough, the security implementation will be secure.

This does not mean that more should not or cannot be done. The next step is for independent bodies to develop security conformance criteria and establish standardized security tests against that criteria. There is some movement in this direction. Government organizations from the United States, Canada, France, Germany, Australia, New Zealand and the United Kingdom have signed the "Arrangement on the Mutual Recognition of Common Criteria Certificates in the Field of IT Security." The Common Criteria (CC) is a security evaluation and testing scheme. Security testing laboratories are being approved with four already approved in the US. Go to http://csrc.nist.gov/cc/ for more information on the Common Criteria.

Mid-Tier Security

The mid-tier is the most complex of the security tiers, as illustrated by Figure 10.2. In the mid-tier, we see a mixture of application servers and CORBA servers as well as servers to handle two types of security administration. In a large deployed system, the mid-tier may contain thousands of applications and multiple application servers with hundreds or thousands of beans. This software is distributed geographically on many different machines. Note that the mid-tier architecture that we describe is only one possible solution among many. Depending on the application server products that you choose, the actual arrangement of servlets, containers, and beans may be different than the architecture defined here.

Not only is the mid-tier complex, but its security is also quite important, as references to studies described in previous chapters have shown that a large number of break-ins are a result of insider attacks on the mid-tier. As e-commerce allows customers, partner companies, and suppliers into the mid-tier, these foreign clients must be allowed access to some methods and denied access to others. Note that we said methods, not just applications. Therefore, in

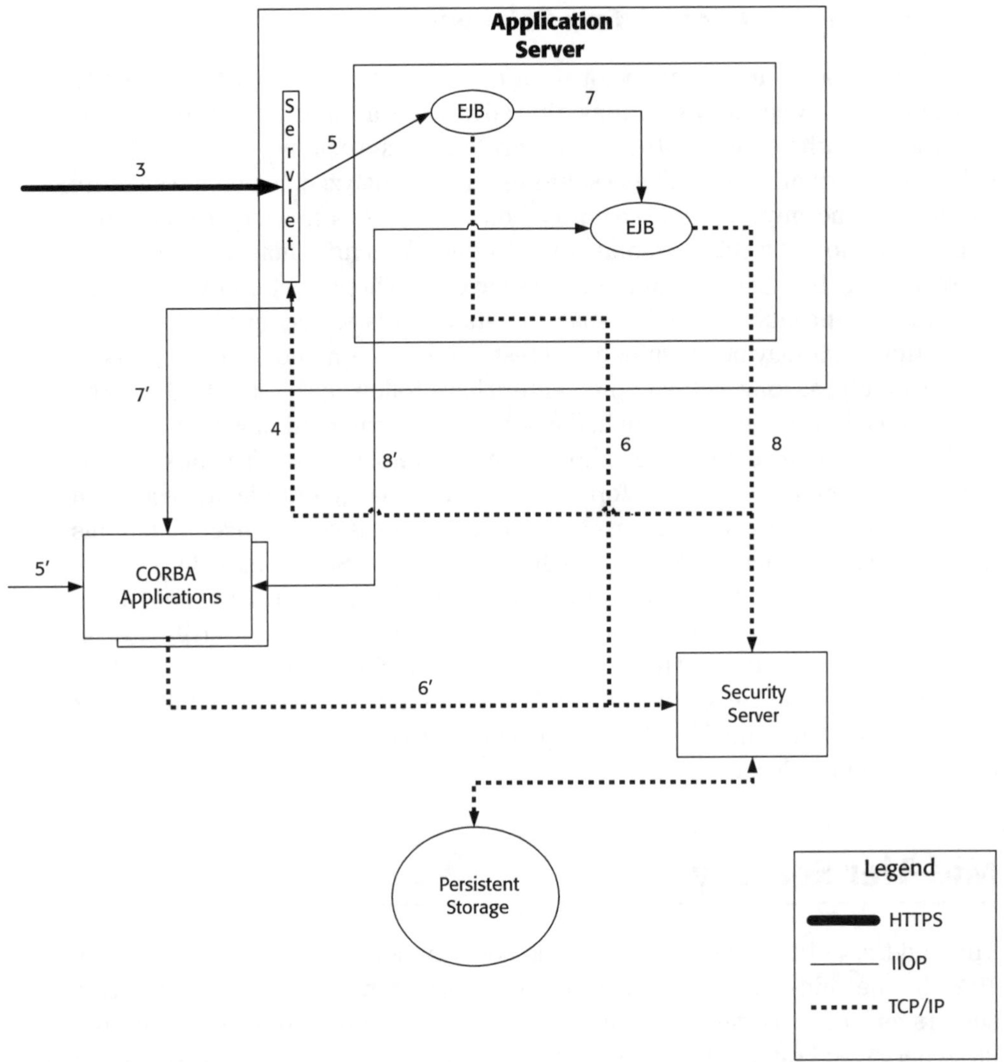

Figure 10.2 Mid-tier security.

addition to a good authentication system, we need a good fine-grained authorization system. Unfortunately, in many corporations, mid-tier security is neglected, and instead these corporations rely only on perimeter security. Let us repeat that this is not adequate with today's trend towards e-commerce.

We will not be so foolish as to ignore mid-tier security with eBusiness.com. Consequently, we continue our story where we left off in our discussion of the perimeter security for eBusiness.com and examine the interactions in the mid-tier. The perimeter calls that come into the mid-tier from the Web server in the DMZ are directed to our application server, which we call the primary application server. Figure 10.2 shows the details of the mid-tier and this application server. In the eBusiness.com situation, there are three servlets in this application server, which receive messages from the Web server. We only show one servlet in Figure 10.2 to keep the diagram simple. In the actual situation, servlet 1 receives calls from customers, servlet 2 receives calls from members, and servlet 3 receives calls from corporate customers. This decision is made by the Web server.

Each of the servlets that receives messages from the Web server establishes a trust relationship with that Web server before any user messages are transmitted from the Web server to the application server. The procedure for setting up this trust relationship is the same as the procedure we used to set up a trust relationship between the security server and the Web server. In our case, this trust relationship is established by first setting up an SSL session between the two with the servlet initiating the connection. All messages between the Web server and the application server flow over these authenticated SSL connections.

After this preliminary discussion, we will follow a message that comes from the browser into the application server. The first thing to notice in Figure 10.2 is the servlet handling the browser's HTTPS messages, path 3. In this example, even though the Web server and the browser have a trust relationship, the servlet could have additional work to do beyond propagating the authenticated user identity. Rather than performing the URL-based authorization check at the Web server as we described, an alternative approach is for the servlet to perform the check. For performance reasons, eBusiness.com could decide to carry out access control by using a number of servlets in the application server rather than at the Web server. Path 4 shows the servlet calling on the security server to carry out authorization of the client using the information extracted from the HTTP header. For better security, we prefer to have the URL-based authorization check enforced by the Web server and a second method-level authorization check in the application server. Having both authorization checks performed by the application server may have better performance, but it would cause a potential system-wide vulnerability if the application server were compromised.

The message from the Web server is directed to the correct servlet in the application server by using the URL extension that the user used in his request. For example, the user clicks on a link in the initial form sent by the Web server. It's this link that contains the complete URL to the application server.

To propagate the authenticated user identity, the servlet needs to extract information out of the HTTP request. To make this easier, the three eBusiness.com servlets are derived from an HTTP superclass furnished by our application container. The container supplies a superclass that takes an HTTP message, parses it, and exposes APIs that our derived class can use to get information such as information stored in cookies constructed by our Web server when it first contacts a user. The format of the security data in the header is not standardized, so there has to be a private protocol between the Web server and the servlet. In our case, eBusiness.com's Web server uses a cookie to store the user's password and the session ID. The session ID is used to keep track of the session set up by this particular user. This is another example of the coordination needed between the Web server and the application server.

The servlet checks the incoming HTTP header data to determine what information the user wants. Note that this information may be in the form of an XML document that is digitally signed. From this request information, the servlet determines what bean is required to satisfy the user's request. For example, if the request is to purchase a particular item, the servlet passes this request to the CustomerAccount bean. This direction information is usually handled by an extension to the URL that the client browser used for the call or by a SOAP-like XML document.

However, before calling on the CustomerAccount bean, the container must determine if this user is permitted to access this particular bean. Because we want to be careful about performance, the container does not reauthenticate the user. If you recall, the container established a trust relationship with the Web server, so the Web server authenticates the user and passes the request to the appropriate servlet. The servlet trusts that the Web server did the proper authentication of the user and passes it to the correct servlet. Nevertheless, the servlet does have some security chores to do. Our container is a version 2.0 EJB specification compliant container, so the token that is passed to the bean must be in the version 2.0 format. This means that the servlet must take the security information it has retrieved from the HTTP header and transform it into a version 2.0 EJB token format. Then, it must insert the token into the service context of the GIOP request header. The IIOP request is then sent to the bean by the container using the normal EJB protocols.

The EJB receives the request, and because we are now in the standardized EJB version 2.0 space, we do not have to do anything special at runtime. Our deployer has set up all the security decisions in the deployment descriptors for the beans in the container. Recalling the discussion in Chapter 2, a version 2.0 EJB container can perform authorization. Therefore, the deployment descriptor requires that the incoming principal, or more accurately, the principal's role is permitted access. If you recall, access is determined by the method-permissions set in the deployment descriptor. The customer, say Mary Smith, is associated with the role customer in a container specific way.

In order to associate Mary Smith with the role customer, we have to go to the documentation of eBusiness.com's application server to determine how the container provider requires us to set the user to role relationships. As described in Chapter 2, this step is container specific as per the 2.0 specification. This task is not a runtime task, but an administrative task that is done before any requests by Mary Smith are made, that is, when Mary Smith registered and set up an account with eBusiness.com. In the eBusiness.com design, we use a different application server for registration requests. Our Web server directs registration requests to the application server using the URL information, which tells it that this is a request for registration. The end-to-end security for registration and acceptance parallels the path that we are describing for a purchase, so we will not go into any details. Of course the logic in the beans vary, but the trust requirements, authentication, and access control concepts are the same.

Note that we have not established any explicit trust relationship between the servlet and the bean. This follows the spirit of the EJB specification, which uses presumed trust between components in a container. We use the term "spirit" because the specification does not explicitly talk about the security of a servlet to bean connection, but it does say that the security between components must use propagation, that is, the components of a single container trust each other. This is not an unreasonable assumption because the container and its components are in a single process.

We are not finished with Mary Smith's purchase. Mary has been approved as a legitimate customer and has placed her order. The next step is to bill her for the purchase. Our billing system is a set of applications that eBusiness.com purchased with its accounting system and is not an EJB application, so we have to bridge over to the billing system. eBusiness.com's billing system is an example of a legacy system discussed in Chapter 5. The next section discusses how eBusiness.com bridges from the EJB application to the billing system.

Before we move on to legacy security, let's look at a corporate customer who is using a CORBA application. We have described the message flow through the perimeter to the proxy server behind the second firewall and then to the CORBA application. Figure 10.2 illustrates the message coming into the CORBA application message path 5' in the lower-left portion of the figure. The message conforms to CSIv2, so all the security is handled by the middleware. The CORBA Security Service validates the authentication evidence and enforces an access control. Path 6' in Figure 10.2 depicts this. The CORBA Security Service was not shown in Figure 10.1 in order to keep that diagram simple.

The work done by the CORBA Security Service is transparent to the application programmer as these applications are security-unaware. Therefore, there is little further to talk about with respect to the runtime. We covered all the steps in discussing CORBA security in the previous chapters. Of course the security administrator will have had to set the policies and attributes for the users. We covered that topic in detail in Chapter 8.

An interesting and an important point in Figure 10.2 is related to paths 7' and 8'. These paths indicate the interoperability between the servlets and the EJB objects with CORBA applications. Because both the application server and the CORBA applications support CSIv2, no additional integration is needed. The servers will interoperate as is. eBusiness.com uses this capability to access Unitary Login to secure the passwords for database access and to access the billing system from the EJBs.

Legacy Security

Now that we have completed Mary's purchase, we want to use the legacy billing system to charge Mary for her purchase and invoice her for the purchase. As we stated in Chapter 5, we could use EJB connectors or the Unitary Login approach for bridging the mid-tier to legacy boundary. We chose to use the Unitary Login approach for eBusiness.com.

If you remember, the first step was to wrap the legacy system with a CORBA application. What this means is that you write a set of CORBA methods that simply forward the calls they receive from the EJB to the legacy function. The CORBA wrapper handles the interoperability and the security. The difficulty is determining which APIs are exposed by the billing system. For example, the billing system might be constructed to interface with other portions of the accounting system and expose all the required interfaces in which case your CORBA system acts as the accounting system and calls the appropriate APIs. On the other hand, the billing system might have a GUI interface in which the user is expected to input the values. In this case, your CORBA application has to emulate external input (i.e., "screen-scraping"). You probably will want to use a professional services (PS) organization from your billing system provider, from an independent firm that specializes in this type of work, or from your CORBA provider to wrap your billing system with CORBA interfaces.

Once we have the CORBA wrapper for the billing system, we need to use the methods described in Chapter 6 to pass the necessary information from the EJB to the CORBA wrapper. Because our container uses IIOP, the job is relatively easy. The bean connects with the CORBA wrapper sending the security information in the service context. The CORBA Security Service verifies the authentication data and performs a normal authentication check by accessing the policy data on a separate security server.

There is one additional complexity, which is transmitting the password needed by the billing system. eBusiness.com applications need to access a DBMS in order to retrieve user data. Most commercial databases require the application to provide a username and password for login. In the past, applications generally stored and transmitted these passwords in the clear because they had no other mechanism to protect and pass this authentication data through the system. Needless to say this was not very secure.

The password that is needed for the database is not the password that Mary Smith used to log in to the browser, but is the password that unlocks Mary Smith's records. In addition, we do not want Mary Smith herself to have access to the database. We only want the application server that is working on Mary's behalf to access the billing information that is stored on eBusiness.com's mainframe. Therefore, Unitary Login authorizes that application server to gain access to the password to unlock Mary Smith's records in the database. The

Unitary Login server uses its internal authorization model to find out whether that application server principal can retrieve the Mary Smith password. In this case, it can, and the accessing bean securely passes the correct password over an SSL connection between the application server and the Unitary Login server.

The passwords stored in Unitary Login are stored in encrypted form and are decrypted by the Unitary Login system, and as we said, passed over an SSL encrypted channel on the network. This improves the security posture of eBusiness.com because sensitive data, that is, the password necessary to gain access to the database, is protected both during storage and when passed over the wire.

In the case of a corporate user's billing, the corporate user's name is not in the portion of the Unitary Login database that is owned by the principal who is doing Mary Smith's billing. This is a more sensitive billing procedure due to the larger dollar amount of corporate bills. Therefore, we have set up access by means of another application server, which is more heavily protected. This application server has a security principal that has extended rights. That is, the application server for corporate users has a higher clearance in eBusiness.com. For example, the application server must be associated with a senior manager in the billing department. In this manner, we can set higher security for corporate accounts than that for customer accounts.

Advantages of Using a Security Server

From an application developer's point of view, security is enabled by linking in a security library and having the middleware take care of security. However, in order for the security service to be able to enforce security, it needs to have access to policies and rules to know what actions to take for a client that wants to access a given resource. The most straightforward way to do this is for the security service to have a separate process to handle administration of the security policy and rules. These policies and rules are used for authentication and authorization as well as other security services, such as delegation, auditing, and nonrepudiation. Any successful attempt to compromise these policies could result in a breakdown of the security of the system, so you can see the necessity of protecting access to setting the policy data. This separate server, usually called a security server (or a policy server), is associated with some persistent store for the data, such as a database or a more popular approach, Lightweight Directory Access Protocol (LDAP).

Setting security policy is a very sensitive process because it is the basis of your security. Having a separate server to handle security removes the procedure from the security runtime and permits independent additions, updates, and modifications to the security data,, making security administration a very secure procedure. The server can be physically protected and all remote access, such as telnet, FTP, and rlogin can be disabled allowing only secure interactions with the security server.

Note that EJB does not use a separate server for the administration of security policy. As we explained in Chapter 2, EJB uses deployment descriptors, which are associated with the .jar files deployed in each container. In this case, you do not have a single point of administration that is afforded by a separate security server. However, as we have also pointed out, the EJB version 2.0 specification does not state how the authorization should be implemented. So, examine your potential application server's implementation of security policy and determine whether it meets your distributed needs now and in the foreseeable future.

Another aspect of security servers is the implementation used for securing the perimeter versus securing the mid-tier. As we stated earlier, perimeter security is not standardized and is proprietary to each vendor. Therefore, the chance of using the same security service for perimeter security and mid-tier is very low, although the two services may be on the same physical server. For example, we might have two security services, a security service used by the perimeter security system and a security service used by the CORBA system in the mid-tier that are both running on the same protected machine. In addition, there may be some areas of overlap in the persistent store used by both services. For example, in eBusiness.com, we use LDAP as the persistent store for both the perimeter and mid-tier policy store. Both security services use the same LDAP structure and data to store persistent information on our users. However, the actual structure and data for policies stored in LDAP are different for each service.

Administration

One of the biggest challenges of security in an e-business environment is the ability to manage the security data for the business. eBusiness.com has thousands of users and hopes to grow to millions of users. It also has a number of applications to handle the buying, selling, billing, and user information for its growing business. Some of this security information can be maintained by human operators, but eBusiness.com will have to automate a vast majority of this data. Because the bulk of the data is related to our customer base, we will automate that data input by having a system that permits a user to register and change his or her personal data online.

The application that registers users must be heavily protected. We do not want one user to modify or even view another user's data. It's not only customers that we have to protect against. We also need to ensure that a random employee cannot access anyone's data. For example, a devious employee may register as a customer, buy a large amount of our products, and then change his access identity to a supervisor in accounting. With this bogus access identity, the employee could then change his charge to a credit. If he could break the administration system, he could assume any identity and do anything he wanted with our system—pretty scary !

So how do we protect ourselves against this kind of an attack? There are a series of steps that you should take:

1. Use a security system that supports a separate administration subsystem.
2. Deploy this system on a separate machine.
3. Shut off remote access by nonsecure or weakly secure means, such as telnet, rlogin, and FTP. Also, do not install any remote access programs, such as PC-Anywhere. You want limited access to this machine.
4. Physically protect the machine and allow only cleared personnel, such as your security administrator, to log in to the machine.
5. Put very tight access controls on the administration programs.

This last point requires a more thorough explanation. Each administration method must be examined. The type of access and who can access that method must be completely thought out. For example, we want a customer to be allowed to modify his or her personal information. The access to the method to change this type of data should be from a separate application. That application should use the full power of the authorization system available to it.

Let's take Mary Smith who wants to change her credit card. She logs into the system and retrieves an HTTP form to change her personal data. She fills in the change request and selects Submit. The response makes its way to the change data application in the system. In this case, the application is a CORBA application supporting CORBA security, or it could just as well be an EJB in an application server. The security system authenticates Mary Smith, and the authorization system allows Mary to access the change_credit_card method. That method uses the Resource Access Decision (RAD) facility, which was described in Chapter 8, to check whether Mary Smith is trying to access her own account. If the RAD system returns true, then the application calls on the administration system.

We don't want to give the customer the rights to change his or her data directly on the security server because that would allow access to the administrative system itself. Although we could protect against inappropriate access at the administrative security server, a more secure way to prevent access is to only permit security administrators access to that server. Therefore, the application that we described in the previous paragraph will be "owned" by the security administrator. This is accomplished by the security administrator logging into the system with authentication evidence known only to the security administrator, and then starting the application. In eBusiness.com, we require a smart card to log in to any application that has access to the administrative system. A smart card is a removable card with a memory chip that contains encrypted authentication evidence. Consequently, not only does the security administrator have to supply a password to decrypt the data, but the authentication evidence is also physically separate from the computer; that is, it's on the smart card.

There are several ways of performing administrative tasks on the security server. A common one is to use a GUI interface that supports graphical capabilities to aid the administrator in carrying out administrative tasks. Another method is to use secure batch tools, which can take information from another source, for example, a mainframe, and perform periodic updates. Finally, if the security product supports an administrative API, it's also possible to write a custom security-aware application that makes calls to the API. In all these cases, only the security administrator should be allowed access using protections similar to those we described for eBusiness.com.

For all but small companies, the amount of security data is usually very large, and maintenance is a major task. When eBusiness.com reaches its million customer milestone, there will be a lot of customer security data. Security administrative tools are supplied by your middleware supplier; so check the administrative capabilities that your middleware provider gives you to be sure that they will support maintenance of your security data as your business grows. As you well know, customers are always changing something whether it is their credit cards, billing addresses, or even their names. So don't underestimate the work entailed in security data maintenance.

Multiple Security Servers

An important requirement of the security administrative service for a large installation is the ability to have multiple security servers. You don't want one point of failure in a critical task like security. This means that the middleware supplier should have solutions for supporting simultaneous changes by different administrators on these various security servers. Support for simultaneous update includes solving all the problems of input timing conflicts, transaction rollback, failover, and replication.

One of the biggest problems that your security service must solve for you is synchronization between multiple security administrators. eBusiness.com expects to have a number of security servers located in different countries, and each of these different locales will have different security administrators. The problem to be solved is what happens when two or more of these administrators attempt to change the same set of security data. Does the system support atomic input of the data? Does it support notification between the administrators of an attempt at simultaneous input and a way for them to choose the correct input? This is a difficult problem, but there has been a lot of work on these types of problems in computer science. The bottom line is to determine what support your potential security provider has supplied, how well have they implemented the solution, and if the solution meets your needs. Neglecting this area can lead to severe problems as your installation grows to enterprise scale.

Authentication

There is another area with respect to a security server that you might overlook, which is the authentication of the security servers themselves. Because the security administration service is critical to the security of your whole enterprise, an attack that substitutes a bogus security server could be crippling to your defense.

The solution is as simple as it is important. Have your administrative service authenticate itself to the processes that use it and have each process that uses the administrative service verify the identity of the authenticated service. This means more than mutual SSL authentication. As we have described, mutual SSL authentication proves that the target is who it says it is, but does not determine if the authenticated identity is an acceptable identity. Consequently, you must do an authorization check on the administrative service. In traditional authorization, the target authorizes the client to perform some activity. However, in this case, we want to guarantee that the target is a legal administration server. This can be accomplished by the client checking against an access control list (ACL) maintained by the client. If you recall, we warned that ACLs could cause scaling problems. This would not be the case in this situation because the number of administration servers would not be large, probably less than half a dozen in a large enterprise.

There is one important caveat that you should be aware of: This important check is not supported by many security service providers. Be sure that your provider supports a way to verify your administrative services.

Securing the Infrastructure

Throughout this book, we have been concentrating on the security service itself with an implicit focus on securing the application. However, this is not the complete story. In any distributed system, not just CORBA or EJB based systems, there is an infrastructure of supporting services that are necessary to make the system work.

One of the most ubiquitous services is the naming service. Your client application has to magically find a server that has implemented the method that you want to call. This magic is supplied by the naming service. The naming service supplies an object reference to the client, which uses the information in the object reference to find the correct server. What if the naming service returns to your client an object reference to a bogus server? How do you know whether you are really talking to a legitimate naming service and not a fraudulent one?

Naming is not the only infrastructure service that you have to worry about. There are other infrastructure services that a distributed system may depend upon. Some of these are dependent on the particular middleware system that you are using, whereas others, like naming, are in all systems in one way or another. We will look at the naming service as a representative of the infrastructure services and show what should be done to secure it. At the outset, we regrettably have to say that many implementations do not secure these services. This can leave a big security hole in your system, which could very well be exploited by malicious attackers. So once again, we advise you to use the information that we provide and find out what infrastructure services are supplied by your middleware vendor or vendors and also find out whether and how they have secured them.

Naming

Naming is an infrastructure service that has to be in every distributed system in one form or another. CORBA has a detailed specification on the CORBA Naming Service, but no specific security specification for the naming service. CORBA security assumes that an ORB vendor will use the security service itself to secure the service. EJB, from version 2.0 of the EJB specification forward, mandates the use of the CORBA Naming Service with the same assumption regarding security. J2EE also supports another naming service, the rmiregistry, for pure RMI calls.

All naming services perform two basic functions:

- Registering an object reference sent to it from some server
- Transmitting this object reference to a client when the client asks for directions to an object on some target

Each of these functions have different security problems.

The naming service has to be assured that the servers that register its object references are not forged servers. If a bogus application that collects credit card numbers is able to register its object reference with the naming service, then when the application sends the client's credit card number to the registered application, for example, the eBusiness.com system, the card number goes to the fraudulent application, which in turn could e-mail the credit card number to a thief. We can stop this attack quite easily by requiring that access to the naming service be security enabled and that the authorization service permit access only to the authenticated security administrator. This means that the owner of the credit card registration program must be a security administrator that has been authenticated to the security service.

In our eBusiness.com case, we are especially sensitive to credit card theft because of the damage it could do to our business. If such a breakdown happened, it would undoubtedly reach the nightly news reports and just as surely kill or severely damage eBusiness.com. Therefore, we have decided to use a smart card front-end to our authentication system for our naming service as well as other sensitive applications, e.g., the administration services mentioned earlier. The second security issue with naming, assuring that the client is accessing a legitimate naming service, is handled by the normal security system, which we made sure was installed in the naming service to solve the first problem. In eBusiness.com, the naming service uses an SSL certificate in conjunction with a smart card for the authentication front-end. The client does authorization as well as SSL authentication as described in the discussion of the security service to be sure that it is talking to a legitimate naming service.

Once we are happy with our authentication and authorization design for naming, there is one more security aspect to check—Has our middleware provider secured the naming service? As it turns out, the provider that eBusiness.com had initially chosen did not. Because this is such a critical operation in our system and we want an out-of-the-box security solution, we will go with another middleware provider that provides a secure infrastructure.

Given a naming service secured as described, let's trace a call from the client browser that contacts our Web server, which is also SSL enabled, to the naming service. The Web server performs an SSL handshake with the client browser. The browser automatically checks that the Web server is an acceptable server unless the client has disabled this check in his browser. (You've probably seen the dialog box that asks if you trust this company.) We have warned our users not to turn this check off. Our Web server in turn performs an SSL handshake with the naming service, and the Web server checks the security name in the naming service's SSL certificate to ensure that the naming service's principal is legitimate. This check is beyond the scope of that carried out by the SSL system and is similar to that carried out in the browser, that is, the Web server compares the security name in the SSL certificate against a list of legitimate security administrators. This latter check required some additional work by our Web server supplier, but because we expect rapid expansion of the eBusiness.com system with multiple name servers for performance, we took the extra precaution now of using an ACL list rather than a single principal name.

Persistence of Security Data

As you might imagine, eBusiness.com will have quite a bit of security data if our plans work out for our company to have millions of customers, thousands of products, and hundreds of suppliers to say nothing of a number of our own employees. Security data has to be kept on all these entities. This naturally leads you to think of some sort of database and of course securing the persistent store.

A popular form of data store that is used by a number of security providers is the LDAP, which we discuss next.

LDAP

More and more companies are releasing LDAP systems, for example, Netscape, Oracle, Microsoft, IBM, and Novell. In addition, a number of the security systems support LDAP as a persistent store for security data. There are a couple of reasons for this. LDAP presents a hierarchical data store, which matches the structure of the data from a security system, and LDAP supports SSL protection and both username and password and certificate authentication, again matching the protocols used in many security systems.

Let's first take a look at user data. In security systems, users are identified by X.500 names, which have a hierarchical data structure. For example, Mary Jones might have an X.500 name of CN=Mary Jones, CITY=Burlington, ST=MA, and C=US. Using this schema for the X.500 customer names allows us to break down our customers by country, state, city, and individual. Figure 10.3 shows the hierarchical nature of eBusiness.com's customer persistent store.

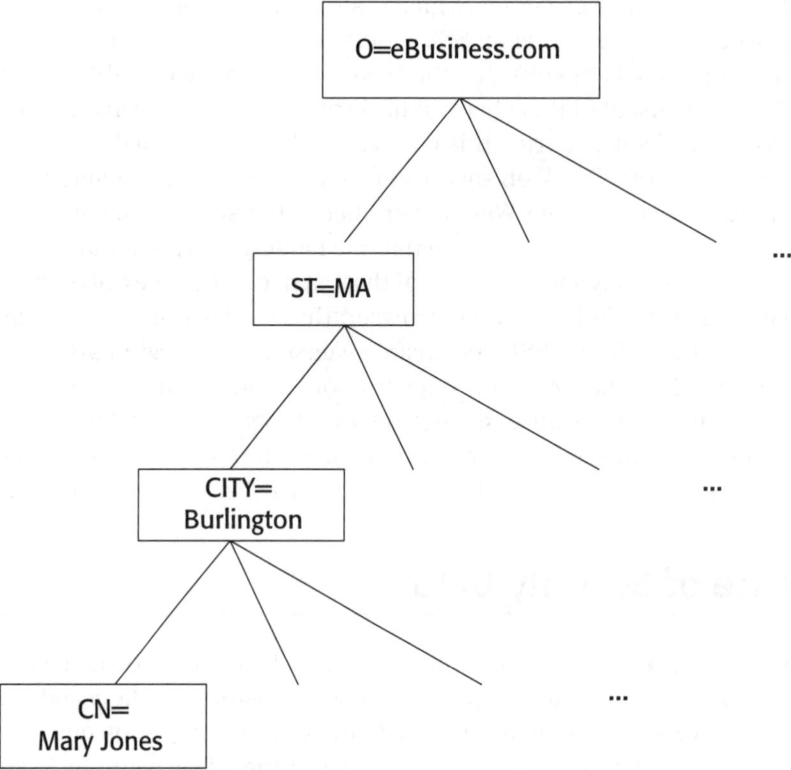

Figure 10.3 eBusiness.com customer LDAP schema.

This hierarchical schema for an LDAP directory tree is supported by the LDAP APIs and is used for more than security purposes. For example, it can be used for employees' telephone numbers, office numbers, and other business related information. At eBusiness.com, we break our customers down by each level in the hierarchy, for example, by country, state, and so on, so that we can use this breakdown to help us in our marketing. Another use is to help our delivery of customer purchases. As we grow, we can automatically keep track of geographic growth and use this information to locate our distribution centers.

On the security side, the type of schema used for our customers matches the format of the customer names in their X.509 SSL certificates, making this a seamless match as we move toward client certificates. In addition to the node names in the LDAP structure, each node can hold a set of attributes, which are key/value pairs. (This is another example of an overloaded name. An LDAP attribute is not a security policy attribute, although a security policy attribute could be placed in an LDAP attribute value field.) LDAP attributes are where the telephone numbers and office numbers are stored.

Your security service could define a password attribute in the Common Name (CN) LDAP node and use that attribute to store the user's password, preferably encrypted. In order to store the password, the LDAP schema has to be expanded. The schema is controlled by an object class, which lists the required and allowed attributes; for example, the schema that we used for our customers is the Person Object Class. This object class requires the CN and the surname (SN). So, in addition to the CN=Mary Smith, the security service has to have SN=Smith. But back to the password. The security provider could define a derived object class from the Person class and define an allowed attribute Password, or it could use a standard derived class that contains the password attribute. The reason that it may define its own object class is so it can define additional attributes, for example, a unique customer ID. In our case we wanted our own schema in order to have the flexibility to add other marketing attributes.

There are a few things that you should look for in your security provider's LDAP implementation if they use LDAP. We have seen some instances in which the provider uses one of the standard fields for its own use—for example, putting the password in an attribute field that it *guessed* its customers would not use. Because you will probably be using the LDAP store for uses other than security, such as the uses in eBusiness.com, be careful, as you might have a need for this same field either now or in the future.

A second thing to look out for is the type of connection between the security server and the LDAP server. LDAP supports SSL and simple password protection. If your security service does not use SSL and the LDAP server is distributed, that is, not on the same physical machine as the security service, then your security data is passed in the clear and is susceptible to snooping. The preferred security approach is to use a system that supports an SSL connection to the LDAP server. As usual, this should be looked at from a risk management point of view. What problems would you face if your security policy data was compromised? Be sure to check the type of connection from the service to the LDAP server that your security provider supports.

Not all your sensitive data will be handled by LDAP, even if that is your persistent store for your security data. In our analysis of our security system, we realize the distinction between policy data and functional data. Specifically, we transmit users' credit card numbers as functional data, whereas our policy data includes information such as user passwords. In the eBusiness.com design, the credit card numbers are stored in the legacy tier in a relational database, and the connection to that database uses the security service protection including SSL protection. User passwords are stored encrypted in LDAP and are passed as security policy data. At eBusiness.com, our risk assessment is such that we cannot afford to have our security policy data, for example, user passwords, compromised. Therefore, we demand a security service that supports an SSL connection when passing policy data. An alternate solution would be to have the LDAP server on the same physical machine as the security server and to isolate that machine. However, this limits the distributed capabilities of LDAP.

Relational or Object Databases

Most LDAP implementations use a database beneath the LDAP APIs to store your security data. Therefore, there is not a big difference in the persistent store for your security data whether your security service provider uses a database directly or through LDAP. The provider's choice is reflected in the system level effects, such as performance and fault tolerance. The provider's choice of persistent store could also show up in other ways, such as additional costs if you have to purchase a third-party persistent store or the replication, distribution, and failover capabilities of the security system as a whole

There is one security aspect of the provider's choice in persistent store that we discussed in the previous section, which is how the transmission of the security policy data is protected. Just as with LDAP, the connection with the database chosen by your security provider must supply a secure channel to that database. This might be harder for the provider using an older database and thus might be skipped. However, it is critical that you find out what protection scheme the provider is using for this connection and make sure that it meets your security requirements.

The provider might be doing its own encryption of the data. If so, find out what encryption algorithms it is using and what type of key exchange it is using. The algorithms may be too weak and easy to break, or they may not be acceptable in the countries in which you are or may be doing business. Another question to ask is—can you change the algorithms and substitute new ones? In general, it is better if the provider uses a standard security connection rather than roll its own, but the provider may have a good reason to use its own system.

File Systems

Another way that the security service provider could store security data is by using the file system. This can be the least secure method depending on what additional protection schemes the system is using. In many cases, the provider's use of the file system only relies on operating system protection—for example, setting the protection on a file to an operating system administrative owner.

There are two problems associated with a security service that relies on the security capabilities of the file system:

- Attackers have studied operating system security in depth and have discovered weaknesses. Although these weaknesses are addressed as they become publicly known, operating systems are very complex beasts, and this complexity works against developing a secure operating system.
- The programs that write to the file system store must have the permissions to access that store and are thus susceptible to compromise themselves.

Our general advice is to shy away from a security service that relies solely on operating system protection for its persistent store, and look to solutions that combine operating system and cryptographic protection.

Security Gotchas at the System Level

In addition to paying attention to the way your security service provider implements and secures the underlying services, you should pay attention to the overall operation of the security service as a whole. The two main system areas that can be severely affected by the addition of security are scaling and performance.

We'll touch on each of these areas in the next two subsections.

Scaling

The security solutions for distributed systems usually employ a security server to handle requests for authentication, authorization, and audit policies. The CORBA specification explicitly talks about security policy, whereas the EJB specification does not dictate the format of the security policy. Nevertheless, in both object models, many implementations employ some sort of security server.

Let's take a look at what a security server is expected to do and why it can be a critical item in affecting the scaling capabilities of your system. There are two competing principles at work. On one hand you want to be able to centrally administer your security data. On the other hand, funneling all the maintenance and requests through one server, especially for a large highly interactive company like eBusiness.com expects to become, can put an extreme load on that one server to say nothing of the single point of failure that a lone security server would impose on the system. Another aspect is the geographic distribution of the system in which you would want security servers geographically distributed. The latter two requirements point to multiple security servers, whereas the first is most easily satisfied by a single security server.

One way for multiple security servers to act as a central point of administration is for them to be stateless or to support very little state, which can be coordinated between the different security servers. A second requirement of multiple security servers is that maintenance be coordinated. For example, when our system administrator in London wants to update the same policy that our system administrator in New York wants to update, the security system should handle the multiple steps of a policy update from the two administrators as a separate, atomic update for each administrator. Because this could wind up in a last update wins situation, there needs to be notification of the updates between the distributed authorities.

The solutions to this class of problems are known, but they are not easy to implement. Therefore, this is another area that you should look at closely; that is, how your security provider has implemented solutions to this scaling problem.

Another potential scaling problem for a heavily distributed system is *key management*, which is how the system stores and retrieves the cryptographic keys needed for encryption and integrity. There are commercial systems that your provider can use such as those from Entrust and Baltimore Technologies. Again, we would prefer that your provider use a firm that specializes in this technology rather than doing this itself as it takes specialized skills that your provider may not have.

Other than in the previously mentioned areas, EJB and CORBA services are specified as distributed systems from the ground up; that is, they are either distributed services like naming, or they are expected to be linked into each application. So, as long as your security provider executes a good implementation of the service and handles the security server and key management as we described, your security system should scale well.

Performance

When discussing performance, the phrase that comes to mind is, "There's no free lunch." In order to have effective security in a distributed system, work has to be done by the system, which means computing time. Once again, risk management comes into the picture. The tighter and more fine-grained you want the security to be, the bigger the performance hit.

For the same level of security, there are a number of factors that can effect the performance of the security system. Some of these include:

- Encryption algorithms
- Underlying transport
- Policy granularity
- Caching

There are two types of encryption: *public key* and *symmetric key*. Symmetric key encryption is much faster than public key encryption, but symmetric keys do not scale as well as public keys. In each of these encryption types, different algorithms have different performance characteristics. When encrypting large amounts of data, implementations usually exchange a symmetric key using a public key to protect the key exchange. The details of encryption are too arcane for most, so our suggestion is to look at the performance numbers for the systems under consideration and compare them with other systems.

The implementation of the underlying middleware transport is another mechanism that can seriously affect performance because the security system itself is distributed and uses the transport to do its work and get the data it needs.

The more fine-grained the policy, the more work the security system must do and thus the slower the performance. This is a trade-off that you can use when designing your overall security system. For example, in some cases performing authorization at the application level is appropriate, whereas in other cases authorization at the interface or even method is required for adequate security.

Caching can boost performance by orders of magnitude if it is well integrated into a security service. For example, an access decision could entail multiple trips to the security server and from there to the persistent store for each piece of data. This offers multiple opportunities for caching the data to improve performance. However, caching can cause a security problem if not done properly. For example, if a break-in is discovered, you will want to flush the cache or that party or parties will continue to have access until the cache times out. If your provider has not implemented an emergency cache flush, you will have to bring your whole system down to remove the cached values. Another problem with a badly designed caching system is the lack of control over the timing of updates to the security data values. Has your provider given you the ability to control the updates to the cache?

In the end, what you, the user of a security service, are concerned with is the overall performance in your environment. It's the job of the security provider to balance the performance of the system against the functionality of the security. It's your job to assess the overall performance of the system. However, the security and system trade-offs in the various parts of the system make the subject of performance highly complex. Therefore, be sure that the performance characteristics that you examine match the type of work that your system will be asked to do. A performance number that measures the performance of calling the same method 100,000 times is not very useful if your system does separate method calls to a large number of methods with very little repetition.

Finally, it is best to get performance numbers from a third party. However, these are hard to get, so you will probably have to do your own comparative performance tests. There is a need for companies that perform independent security performance tests of distributed application server environments, and we expect to see them entering the industry market soon.

Summary

We have reached the end of our long journey to uncover the intricacies of EJB and CORBA security. Our intention was to give you an understanding of basic principles of distributed security as applied to these two popular component models. This field is moving at "Internet speed," so the most valuable and lasting approach is to understand how security is established in a distributed system and to then use this knowledge to choose a current security technology that satisfies your needs. To that end, we concentrated on providing you with the practical theory and understanding of the underlying security functionality of these two component models. However, these two models in isolation will not solve all the security requirements for an enterprise level, distributed system. Therefore, we placed these models in the bigger picture of end-to-end security, which is the real world in which they live. For updates on the latest developments in component security technology, we encourage you to visit our Web site at www.wiley.com/compbooks/hartman.

This chapter looked at some of the security decisions that you might consider when deploying an enterprise level security system. We used our fictional e-commerce company, eBusiness.com, as an example to illustrate some of the issues that you might face in choosing and deploying an enterprise level, distributed security system. We began with an overview of the security architecture eBusiniess.com used. We then described how that architecture could be deployed by looking at the security from the three descriptive regions that we have used throughout our discussion: the perimeter tier, mid-tier, and legacy tier.

In addition to the core technologies of this book, we touched on additional technologies that an end-to-end enterprise security has to encompass. These included firewalls and Web servers as well as the infrastructure services that are necessary to make a distributed system work. We pointed out that some of the middleware security providers neglect the security of these ancillary but necessary services. The naming service was used as a representative of the infrastructure services. We described how this service could be secured by applying the same security principles and functionality as a user of the security system would apply to his or her applications. Unfortunately, middleware vendors do not consider securing the infrastructure their job in many cases. To their credit, we should make it clear that many middleware vendors are making significant progress securing their infrastructure.

Another component of an enterprise security system, the security policy data itself, is often neglected in discussion of enterprise systems. We discussed this unglamorous part of security and pointed out the problems that can arise from the need to maintain large amounts of security policy data. We also discussed methods for isolating and maintaining this data. One component that is used by a number of security service providers is the security server. We looked at some of the problems and solutions associated with security servers.

We ended our discussion with two additional problems that are present in any large distributed system—scaling and performance—and how they are exacerbated by adding security to a system. We alerted you to be on the lookout for these problems and to ensure that the solutions your security system providers use to alleviate them meet your requirements.

Distributed security, as exemplified by EJB and CORBA security, is a difficult topic. Our congratulations on your determination to master its many facets. Now that you have a good grasp of distributed security, we hope that you will use this knowledge when designing and building robust, secure enterprise systems. The principals that you have learned will also serve you well in choosing between secure and not-so-secure products that your company may contemplate purchasing and in making the numerous tradeoffs that you will face when putting together a secure enterprise system. Distributed security is a rapidly changing field, but by learning the fundamental hows and whys of enterprise security using EJB and CORBA, you will be able to understand and critically assess the applicability of new security specifications, ideas, and products.

Glossary

access control Protection of resources against unauthorized access.

Access Control List (ACL) An association with each resource structure that lists subjects that have access rights for a particular resource.

Access matrix A conceptual model, first introduced by Butler Lampson in his milestone work "Protection" (Lampson, 1971), which helps developers to describe access control policies and mechanisms. In the matrix, there is a row for each subject and a column for each object, and each cell specifies access rights granted to the subject for the corresponding object.

accountability mechanisms Security mechanisms that make sure that subjects are held accountable for their actions toward the system resources and services.

ACF2 Access Control Facility 2, an add-on security software package for mainframes from Computer Associates.

ACL *See* Access Control List.

API *See* Application Programming Interface.

application assembler A role in an EJB lifecycle, which is responsible for combining enterprise beans into larger deployable application units by inserting the application assembly instructions into the deployment descriptors of one or more EJB JAR files provided by the bean provider(s).

Application Programming Interface (API) An interface or calling convention by which an application program accesses other programs.

application server Computing environment used for hosting component-based distributed business applications.

assurance A measure of confidence that the security features and architecture of an information system accurately mediate and enforce the security policy.

asymmetric cryptography A modern branch of cryptography (popularly known as "public key cryptography") in which the algorithms employ a pair of keys (a public key and a private key) and use a different component of the pair for different steps of the algorithm (FOLDOC, 2000).

audit *See* Security audit.

authentication The process of establishing authenticity of the claimed subject identity.

authorization The process of access control decisions.

availability A property of an information system to deliver services and data when they are needed.

backward trust evaluation A CSIv2 term that refers to the evaluation of delegation trust based on rules of the target.

bean An abbreviated name for Enterprise JavaBean.

bean deployer A role in an EJB lifecycle that is responsible for taking one or more EJB JAR files produced by a bean provider or application assembler and deploying the enterprise beans contained in these files in a specific enterprise environment.

bean provider A role in an EJB lifecycle that is responsible for producing enterprise beans in the form of EJB JAR files containing one or more enterprise beans. The JAR files include Java classes that implement enterprise bean's business methods, definitions of the bean's remote and home interfaces, and the deployment descriptor.

class A named description of a set of objects that share the same attributes, operations, relationships, and semantics.

client stub Generated by the IDL compiler as part of the client code that acts as a proxy of the object for the client. The client code calls a locally residing stub, which makes calls on the rest of the ORB using interfaces that are private to, and presumably optimized for, the particular ORB core.

component The fundamental building block of distributed software applications. Each component has one or more interfaces that provide the points of entry for calling programs. An interface, which is defined in terms of operations (also called methods), encapsulates a component and ensures that a component is modular.

composite delegation A form of delegation in which both the client privileges and the immediate invoker's privileges are passed to the target, so that both the client privileges and the privileges from the immediate source of the invocation can be individually checked.

confidentiality A security property ensuring that information is disclosed only to the authorized subjects.

constrained delegation Synonymous with controlled delegation.

container A rich runtime environment that provides an array of application services allowing the application developer to concentrate on building the application rather than the supporting infrastructure.

controlled delegation A form of delegation in which a client can impose constraints on what privileges can be delegated to what intermediates. Also known as constrained delegation or restricted delegation.

cookie A small piece of information sent by a Web server to store on a Web browser so it can later be read back from that browser.

CORBA Common Object Request Broker Architecture. CORBA is an open, vendor independent specification for an architecture and infrastructure that computer applications use to work together over networks.

CORBA Security (CORBASec) The CORBA Security service as defined in OMG 2000a.

credentials A container for a subject's security attributes.

CSIv2 Common Secure Interoperability version 2 (CSI, 2000). A recent addition to the CORBA security specification that defines a protocol for transmitting authentication and authorization data over IIOP.

DAC *See* Discretionary Access Control.

Data Encryption Standard (DES) Popular encryption algorithm standardized by US National Bureau of Standards. It is a product cipher that operates on 64-bit blocks of data, using a 56-bit key. It is defined in Federal Information Processing Standards (FIPS) 46-1 (1988), which supersedes FIPS 46 (1977). DES is identical to the ANSI standard Data Encryption Algorithm (DEA) defined in ANSI X3.92-1981 (FOLDOC, 2000).

data tier A tier in the enterprise computing architecture that usually consists of database servers and mainframe-based repositories providing access to data.

DCE *See* Distributed Computing Environment.

delegation A feature of distributed systems that allows intermediate servers to act on behalf of the originating subject.

demilitarized zone (DMZ) A part of the network that is neither part of the internal network nor directly part of the private network. Typically, this is the area between the public network (such as the Internet) access router and the enterprise bastion host, although it can be between any two policy enforcing areas.

denial of service Prevention of authorized access to a system resource or the delaying of system operations and functions (TIS, 2000).

deployer *See* bean deployer.

deployment descriptor A file that provides both the structural and application assembly information about the enterprise beans in the EJB JAR file.

DES *see* Data Encryption Standard.

digital certificate A certificate document in the form of a digital data object (a data object used by a computer) to which is appended a computed digital signature value that depends on the data object (TIS, 2000).

digital signature A value computed with a cryptographic algorithm and appended to a data object in such a way that any recipient of the data can use the signature to verify the data's origin and integrity (TIS, 2000).

Directory service A distributed service that provides the capability to look up objects by their keys or attributes.

Discretionary Access Control (DAC) An access control model based on "restricting access to objects based on the identity of subjects or groups to which they belong. The controls are discretionary in the sense that a subject with a certain access permission is capable of passing that permission (perhaps indirectly) on to any other subject" (DoD, 1985).

Distributed Computing Environment (DCE) A computing environment standardized by the Open Group that provides the following integrated facilities: Remote Procedure Call, Directory Services, Security Service, Threads, Distributed Time Service, and Distributed File Service.

DMZ *See* demilitarized zone.

Document Type Definition (DTD) A description of the markup elements available in any specific type of XML or SGML document.

DTD *See* Document Type Definition.

e-business The use of the Internet technology to help businesses streamline processes, improve productivity, and increase efficiencies. E-business enables companies to easily communicate with partners, vendors, and customers, connect back-end systems, and conduct commerce in a secure manner.

e-commerce Commerce conducted electronically with the use of the Internet technology. It includes an online display of goods and services, ordering, billing, customer service, and handling of payments and transactions.

EJB *See* Enterprise JavaBeans.

encryption Cryptographic transformation of data (called "plaintext") into a form (called "ciphertext") that conceals the data's original meaning to prevent it from being known or used. If the transformation is reversible, the corresponding reversal process is called "decryption," which is a transformation that restores encrypted data to its original state (TIS, 2000).

Enterprise Application Integration (EAI) A methodological approach supported by a set of technologies that allows flexible integration of applications in order to support enterprise business processes.

Enterprise JavaBeans (EJB) Architecture for component-based distributed computing from Sun. Enterprise beans are components of distributed transaction oriented enterprise applications.

Enterprise Security Integration (ESI) A special case of Enterprise Application Integration that enables the use of many different security technologies, and as a result, provides the framework for secure EAI.

Entitlement A business access rule that describes the decision criteria applied when a user attempts to access an application resource.

Entitlement management Administration and maintenance of the various permissions, roles, privileges, and login rights for an organization's information systems users including suppliers, partners, customers, and employees. Resources include client/server applications, legacy applications, and Web pages.

Entitlement server A particular type of authorization server that can provide entitlement-based fine-grained access control for the mid-tier.

Extensible Markup Language (XML) A markup language standardized by the W3C consortium that defines a simple dialect of SGML suitable for use on the Web.

federation A system in which each party retains most of its authority and agrees to afford the other limited rights.

firewall A hardware device or a software program running on a secure host computer that protects networked computers from intentional hostile intrusion, which could result in a security breach.

forward trust evaluation A CSIv2 term that refers to the evaluation of trust based on rules provided by the caller.

framework A set of services, designs, architectures, or systems that embodies an abstract solution to a number of related concrete problems.

hacker A person who enjoys the intellectual challenge of creatively overcoming or circumventing limitations (FOLDOC, 2000). Frequently, malicious intruders are also called hackers.

HTML *See* Hypertext Markup Language.

HTTP *See* Hypertext Transfer Protocol.

HTTPS *See* Hypertext Transfer Protocol, Secure.

Hypertext Markup Language (HTML) Built on top of SGML, a hypertext document format used on the WWW.

Hypertext Transfer Protocol (HTTP) A client/server TCP/IP protocol used on the WWW for the exchange of HTML documents.

Hypertext Transfer Protocol, Secure (HTTPS) A variant of HTTP used for connecting to HTTP servers using SSL.

IDL *See* Interface Definition Language.

IETF *See* Internet Engineering Task Force.

IIOP *See* Internet Inter-ORB Protocol.

impersonation The act whereby one principal assumes the identity and privileges of another principal without restrictions and without any indication visible to recipients of the impersonator's calls that delegation has taken place (OMG, 2000a). There is still debate over this defintion. For consistency we use the CORBASec definition.

initiator A client who originated a chain of client/server calls.

integrity A security property ensuring that information is modified only by the authorized subjects.

interceptor An object that provides one or more specialized services at the ORB invocation boundary based upon the context of the object request (OMG, 2000a).

interface A boundary across which two systems communicate. In software systems, interface is an agreed upon convention used for interprogram communications including function calls.

Interface Definition Language (IDL) A language for defining interfaces to distributed objects accessible via middleware. It's often used to refer specifically to the IDL defined by the OMG as part of CORBA.

intermediate An object in a call chain that is neither the initiator nor the final target.

Internet Engineering Task Force (IETF) A large, open international community of network designers, operators, vendors, and researchers whose purpose is to coordinate the operation, management, and evolution of the Internet and to resolve short- and mid-range protocol and architectural issues (FOLDOC, 2000).

Internet Inter-ORB Protocol (IIOP) A standard protocol used for communications between CORBA-compliant ORBs over TCP/IP networks. IIOP is defined as part of CORBA.

Internet Protocol (IP) Connectionless, best-effort packet switching protocol used at the network layer for the TCP/IP protocol suite. IP provides packet routing, fragmentation, and reassembly.

Interoperable Object Reference (IOR) A CORBA object reference in a format specified by CORBA that enables interoperability of object references.

intrusion detection A process of monitoring and analyzing system events for the purpose of finding and providing real-time or near real-time warning of attempts to access system resources in an unauthorized manner.

IOR *See* Interoperable Object Reference.

IP *See* Internet Protocol.

Kerberos A system developed by project Athena at the Massachusetts Institute of Technology and named for the three-headed dog guarding Hades. It implements ticket-based, peer entity authentication service and access control service distributed in a client/server network environment using passwords and symmetric cryptography.

lattice A partially ordered set in which all finite subsets have a least upper bound and greatest lower bound.

lattice-based MAC An access control model based on comparing security classifications (which indicate how sensitive or critical system resources are) with security clearances (which indicate subjects that are eligible to access certain resources). It's called "mandatory" because a subject that has clearance to access a resource may not, just by its own volition (i.e., discretion), enable another subject to access that resource. Because a system of security labels (a general name for classifications and clearances) constitutes a lattice, the model is called lattice-based.

LDAP *See* Lightweight Directory Access Protocol.

least privilege principle A security principle that requires users to operate with the minimum set of privileges necessary to do their jobs.

legacy security Security infrastructure and technologies developed and deployed on the enterprise to support old enterprise architecture and does not satisfy the requirements of the current enterprise architecture.

Lightweight Directory Access Protocol (LDAP) A protocol for accessing online directory services, which defines a relatively simple protocol for updating and searching directories running over TCP/IP.

Mandatory Access Control (MAC) *See* lattice-based MAC.

method An association between a name and a procedure, routine, or some other action execution, which is encapsulated in an object in an object-oriented programming language (e.g., Java) or other computing environment (e.g., EJB).

method-permission A permission to invoke a specified group of methods of the enterprise beans' home and remote interfaces. Method-permissions are defined in the corresponding sections of an EJB deployment descriptor.

middle tier A tier in the enterprise computing architecture between the perimeter and data tiers. Middle tier consists of business applications that implement business logic.

middle tier (mid-tier) security Security infrastructure that protects mid-tier systems.

middleware Software that mediates between an application program and a network by managing the interactions between disparate applications across the heterogeneous computing platforms.

mid-tier *See* middle tier.

nonrepudiation Provision of evidence that prevents a participant in an action from convincingly denying his responsibility for the action (OMG, 2000a).

object "A unique instance of a data structure defined according to the template provided by its class. Each object has its own values for the variables belonging to its class and can respond to the messages (methods) defined by its class" (FOLDOC, 2000). In the context of security, object is a synonym for resource.

Object Management Group (OMG) A consortium founded in 1989 by 11 companies to create a component-based software marketplace by hastening the introduction of standardized object software. In 2000, it had about 800 members. The organization's charter includes the establishment of industry guidelines and detailed object management specifications to provide a common framework for application development. The major technologies developed by the OMG members are CORBA and UML.

object reference A data structure used as a handle through which a client requests operations on the corresponding object.

Object Request Broker (ORB) The core part of CORBA middleware that facilitates communications among distributed objects. An ORB is responsible for finding remote objects, handling parameter passing, and returning results, among other things.

OMG *See* Object Management Group.

operation A CORBA equivalent to a method in object-oriented programming languages.

ORB *See* Object Request Broker.

owner-based DAC A Discretionary Access Control model in which for each resource there is a subject who is said to be the resource's owner and who manages the resource's access rights.

PAC *See* Privilege Attribute Certificate.

perimeter tier A tier in the enterprise computing architecture that usually consists of Web servers implementing presentation logic.

perimeter tier security Security infrastructure protecting enterprise resource at the perimeter tier.

policy domain *See* security policy domain.

presumed trust Trust based solely on the assumption that the environment and all its entities are trustworthy. In the context of CSIv2, presumed trust is the acceptance of the client identity based solely on the fact of its occurrence and without consideration of the intermediate's authentication identity. The presumption is that communications are constrained such that only trusted entities are capable of asserting an identity to the target security system.

principal A user or programmatic entity with the ability to use the resources of a system. Synonymous with subject.

privilege *See* privilege attribute.

privilege attribute A security attribute that need not have the property of uniqueness, and thus may be shared by many users and other principals. Examples of privilege attributes include groups, roles, and clearances.

Privilege Attribute Certificate (PAC) A digital certificate that contains privilege attributes of a principal with any associated information needed for delegation and other controls.

profile A set of data describing security and other attributes of a user or application.

proxy A hardware device or software program acting on behalf of or representing other hardware devices or software programs in computing interactions.

proxy server A server acting as a *proxy*.

public key cryptography A popular synonym for asymmetric cryptography.

Pull model A way of obtaining a subject's credentials by looking them up in the security environment using some unique information about the subject, such as its identity.

Push model A way of providing a subject's credentials to a target by embedding them into the context of the client's request.

RACF *See* Resource Access Control Facility.

RAD *See* Resource Access Decision.

reference monitor An access control concept that refers to an abstract machine that mediates all accesses to objects by subjects (NCSC, 1988).

Remote Method Invocation (RMI) Part of the Java programming language library, which enables a Java program running on one computer to access the objects and methods of another Java program running on a different computer (FOLDOC, 2000).

repudiation Denial by one of the entities involved in an action of having participated in all or part of the action.

Resource Access Control Facility (RACF) IBM's large system security product available for Multiple Virtual Storage (MVS) and Virtual Machine (VM) operating system environments.

Resource Access Decision (RAD) A specification of application-level authorization service from the OMG. The specification text is available from the OMG as document number dtc/00-06-07.

restricted delegation Synonymous with controlled delegation.

right A named value conferring the ability to perform actions in a system. Access control policies grant rights to principals (on the basis of their security attributes); in order to make an access control decision, access decision functions compare the rights granted to a principal against the rights required to perform an operation (OMG 2000a).

RMI *See* Remote Method Invocation.

RSA A public-key cryptosystem for both encryption and authentication, invented in 1977 by Ron Rivest, Adi Shamir, and Leonard Adleman. Its name comes from their initials (FOLDOC, 2000).

SDMM *See* Security Domain Membership Management.

secret key cryptography Synonymous with symmetric cryptography.

Secure European System for Applications in a Multi-Vendor Environment (SESAME) A European research and development project that was started in late the 1980s. It is also the name of the technology that came out of that project. This technology defines components of a security architecture providing the underlying bedrock upon which full managed security products can be built using the following services defined by the architecture: authentication, authorization, confidentiality, integrity, and audit.

Secure Sockets Layer (SSL) An Internet protocol (originally developed by Netscape Communications, Inc.) layered above TCP that uses connection-oriented end-to-end encryption to provide data confidentiality service and data integrity service for traffic between a client (often a Web browser) and a server. Optionally, it can provide peer entity authentication between the client and the server (TIS, 2000).

security association The shared security state information that permits secure communication between two entities (OMG 2000a).

security attributes Characteristics of a subject (user or principal) that forms the basis of the system's security policies governing that subject.

security audit The independent examination of records and activities to ensure compliance with established security policies.

security authority An entity that establishes security policies.

security-aware application An application that uses security APIs to access and validate the security policies that apply to it. Security-aware applications may directly access security functions that enable the applications to perform additional security checks and fully exploit the capabilities of the security infrastructure.

security context The CORBA security object that encapsulates the shared state information representing a security association (OMG 2000a).

security domain *See* security policy domain.

Security Domain Membership Management (SDMM) An upcoming specification from the OMG that will define the necessary interfaces for managing security domains and object domain membership, as well as their hierarchies and determining security policies governing the objects in those domains.

security enclave A group of machines within an enterprise that is separated from the rest of the enterprise by firewalls.

security policy A set of rules and practices that specify or regulate how a system or organization provides security services to protect sensitive and critical system resources (TIS, 2000).

security policy domain A set of objects to which a security policy applies for a set of security related activities and that is administered by a security authority. The objects are the domain members. The policy represents the rules and criteria that constrain activities of the objects to make the domain secure (OMG, 2000a).

security self-reliant application An application that does not use any of the security services provided by a security framework. A security self-reliant application may not use the security services because it has no security relevant functionality and thus does not need to be secured or because it uses separate independent security functions that are not part of the defined ESI security framework.

security trustworthiness The ability of a system to protect resources from exposure to misuse through malicious or inadvertent means.

security-unaware application An application that does not explicitly call security services, but that is still secured by the supporting environment (e.g., an EJB or CORBA Container).

self-administration An approach in user administration in which users handle many of their own administrative functions rather than relying on an administrator within the enterprise to do it for them. Self-administration provides better service for customers at a lower cost, but comes with significant security risks.

separation of duties principle A security principle requiring that for particular sets of transactions, no single individual be allowed to execute all transactions within the set.

server skeleton Code, usually automatically generated by IDL compilers, which handles parameters and returns results passing to and from a middleware object.

SESAME *See* Secure European System for Applications in a Multi-vendor Environment.

SGML *See* Standard Generalized Markup Language.

simple delegation A type of delegation used in which the client permits the intermediate to assume its privileges using them for access control decisions and delegating them to others. The target object receives only the client's privileges and does not know who the intermediate is (when used without target restrictions, it is known as impersonation).

Simple Public-Key GSS-API Mechanism (SPKM) A GSS-API mechanism defined in IETF RFC 2025 (Adams, 1996), which is based on a public-key, rather than a symmetric-key, infrastructure.

SPKM *See* Simple Public-Key GSS-API Mechanism.

SSL *See* Secure Sockets Layer.

Standard Generalized Markup Language (SGML) An international standard that defines a generic markup language for representing documents.

subject An active entity in the system; either a human user principal or a programmatic principal.

symmetric cryptography A branch of cryptography involving algorithms that use the same key for two different steps of the algorithm (such as encryption and decryption or signature creation and signature verification) (TIS, 2000).

target object (target) The recipient of a CORBA request message. Also, the final recipient in a delegation call chain. The only participant in such a call chain that is not the originator of a call (OMG 2000a).

TCB *See* Trusted Computing Base.

TCP *See* Transmission Control Protocol.

TCP/IP A stack of Transmission Control Protocol over Internet Protocol. It's often used to refer to the entire suite of protocols (such as HTTP, SSL, IIOP) based on this stack.

technology domain A part of an enterprise security infrastructure in which common security mechanisms are used to enforce security policies.

TLS *See* Transport Layer Security.

token An abstract concept used for passing a property or its evidence between cooperating entities.

traced delegation A type of delegation used in which the client permits the intermediate object to use its privileges and delegate them. However, at each intermediate object in the chain, the intermediate's privileges are added to privileges propagated to provide a trace of the delegates in the chain (OMG 2000a).

Transmission Control Protocol (TCP) A transport layer protocol built on top of Internet Protocol. It provides full-duplex, process-to-process connections with reliable communication, flow-control, multiplexing, and connection-oriented communication.

Transport Layer Security (TLS) An Internet protocol that in version 1.0 is effectively SSL version 3.1. TLS, as opposed SSL, is an IETF standard.

trust The extent to which someone who relies on a system can have confidence that the system meets its specifications; that is, that the system does what it claims to do and does not perform unwanted functions (TIS, 2000).

Trusted Computing Base (TCB) The totality of the hardware and software mechanisms that are responsible for enforcing the security policy. The TCB must be tamperproof, always invoked (nonbypassable), and small enough to be thoroughly analyzed. The TCB is usually implemented within an operating system that is under strict configuration control. This architecture permits very tight security because the TCB is the mediator through which all user accesses to resources must pass. Everything within the TCB is trusted to enforce the security policy; everything outside of the TCB is untrusted.

trustworthiness *See* security trustworthiness.

Unified Modeling Language (UML) A third generation modeling language standardized by the OMG and used to specify, visualize, construct, and document the artifacts of an object-oriented software-intensive system under development.

Uniform Resource Locator (URL) A standard way of specifying the location of an entity, typically a Web page, on the Internet.

Unitary Login A security service that provides secure storage and retrieval of sensitive authentication data (e.g., passwords); typically used to access back-end and database systems.

unrestricted delegation Synonymous with impersonation.

URL *See* Uniform Resource Locator.

Virtual Private Network (VPN) A restricted use, logical (i.e., artificial or simulated) computer network that is constructed from the system resources of a relatively public, physical (i.e., real) network (such as the Internet), often by using encryption (located at hosts or gateways) and often by tunneling links of the virtual network across the real network (TIS, 2000).

X.500 An ITU-T recommendation that is one part of a joint ITU-T/ISO multipart standard (X.500-X.525) that defines the X.500 Directory, which is a conceptual collection of systems that provide distributed directory capabilities for OSI entities, processes, applications, and services. (The ISO equivalent is IS 9594-1 and related standards, IS 9594-x.)

XML ***See* Extensible Markup Language.**

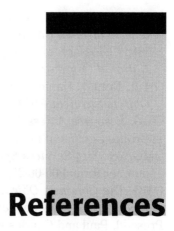

References

Adams, C. *The Simple Public-Key GSS-API Mechanism (SPKM)*. Network Working Group, RFC 2025, IETF, 1996

Bell, D. E. and L. J. LaPadula. "Secure Computer Systems: Unified Exposition and Multics Interpretation." Bedford, MA, *MITRE*, 1975.

Blakley, Bob. *CORBA Security: An Introduction to Safe Computing with Objects*. The Addison-Wesley Object Technology Series. Addison-Wesley, 1999.

CSI. "Common Secure Interoperability, Version 2, Final Submission." Object Management Group. Document number orbos/00-08-04, www.omg.org, 2000.

Coulouris, G., J. Dollimore, and T. Kindberg. *Distributed Systems*. Wokingham: Addison-Wesley, 1995.

U.S. Department of Defense. "Department of Defense Trusted Computer System Evaluation Criteria", DoD 5200.28-STD, 1985.

Emmerich, W. *Engineering Distributed Objects*. John Wiley & Sons, 2000.

Farrell, S. and R. Housley. *An Internet Attribute Certificate Profile for Authorization*. PKIX Working Group, IETF, 2000.

Flangan, David. *Java in a Nutshell: A Desktop Quick Reference (Java Series)* O'Reilly & Associates, 1999.

FOLDOC. *Free Online Dictionary of Computing*. www.foldoc.org, 2000.

Ghosh, Anup K. *E-Commerce Security: Weak Links, Best Defenses*. John Wiley & Sons, 1998.

Lampson, B. W. "Protection." In Proceedings of *5th Princeton Conference on Information Sciences and Systems*, pp. 437, Princeton, 1971.

NCSC. "A Guide to Understanding Discretionary Access Control in Trusted Systems." *National Computer Security Center*, 1987.

NCSC. "Glossary of Computer Security Terms." NCSC-TG-004, Version 1, *National Computer Security Center*, 1988.

Orfali, Robert, Daniel Harkey, and Jeri Edwards. *The Essential Distributed Objects Survival Guide*. John Wiley & Sons, 1995.

OMG. *Resource Access Decision Facility Specification*. Object Management Group. Document number dtc/00-06-07, www.omg.org, 2000.

OMG. *Security Services Specification*. Object Management Group. Document number formal/00-06-25, www.omg.org, 2000a.

OMG. *The Common Object Request Broker: Architecture and Specification*, Revision 2.4, www.omg.org, 2000b.

Prescod, Paul and Charles F. Goldfarb. *The XML Handbook*. 3d ed. Charles F. Goldfarb Series, 2000.

Rauch, W. B. *Distributed Open Systems Engineering: How to Plan and Develop Client/Server Systems*. John Wiley & Sons, 1996.

Roman, Ed. *Mastering Enterprise JavaBeans and the Java 2 Platform, Enterprise Edition*. John Wiley & Sons, 2000.

Ruh, William A., Francis X. Maginnis, and William J. Brown. *Enterprise Application Integration: A Wiley Tech Brief*. John Wiley & Sons, 2000.

Sandhu, R., E. Coyne, H. Feinstein, and C. Youman. "Role-Based Access Control Models." *IEEE Computer* 29(2): 38–47, 1996.

Schneier, Bruce. *Applied Cryptography*. 2d ed. John Wiley & Sons, 1996.

Sun. *Enterprise JavaBeans™ Specification, Version 2.0*. Sun Microsystems, 2000.

Tanenbaum, A. S. *Distributed Operating Systems*. Upper Saddle River, New Jersey: Prentice-Hall. TIS 2000 "Internet Security Glossary" The Internet Society. Request for Comments 2828, 1995.

Index

A

access_allowed(), 218
access control, 18, 29–30, 325. *See also* role-based access control (RBAC) models
  discretionary and mandatory, 248, 249
  middleware, 209–214
  roles for, 32–33
access control lists, 43, 59, 249
access decision models, 142
AccessDecision object, 219, 220–223, 233–234, 238–240
access operation, 220
access rights
  CORBASec, 95–101
  wise use in scalable security policies, 244–246
accountability, 5
  basic principles of, 21
  as core security service, 18
  legacy technologies, 112, 124
  mid-tier technologies, 112, 121
  perimeter technologies, 112, 114, 118
ACF2, 123–124
administration. *See* security administration
administrators, 294–295
admin role, 35–36
all rights, 244
amount attribute, 23
anomaly detection, 118
any rights, 244
APIs. *See* Application Programming Interfaces
application access policies, 88
application assembler, 28. *See also* deployment descriptor
  and EJB lifecycle, 31
  role, 39–47
application audit policies, 88
application components, 299
application-driven authorization principle, 20, 24
  and planning of ESI, 287
  versus push security down principle, 212
Application Programming Interfaces (APIs), 16, 17, 19
  ESI planning for, 299
applications
  in ESI framework, 15–16
  interaction, 286
  making jump to system, 286–290
  writing security into, as bad practice, 34
application servers, 1–3, 14, 27
Applied Cryptography (Schneier), 58
ASN.1 structure, 186

assembler. *See* application assembler
association. *See* security association
association options, 62–64
  CSIv2, 196–197
attributes. *See* security attributes
audit early, not often principle, 21
  CORBASec, 104
AuditEventType, 105
auditing, 18, 54
  and mixed domains, 143–144
audit policies
  CORBASec, 104–105
  and interoperability, 158–159
authentication
  basic principles of, 20
  CORBASec, 84–86
  as core security service, 17–18
  CSIv2 layer, 190–191
  EJB-CORBA differences, 168
  interoperable security layers, 198–201
  legacy tier technologies, 112, 123
  mid-tier technologies, 111, 120, 122
  perimeter technologies, 111, 113, 115–117
  permissions recommended, 58–59
  security servers, 325
authorization
  basic principles of, 20–21
  as core security service, 18
  EJB-CORBA differences, 139–140, 168
  interoperable security layers, 201–206
  legacy tier technologies, 112, 113–114, 117, 124
  mid-tier technologies, 111, 121, 122–123
  perimeter technologies, 111
  permissions recommended, 59
  and roles, 33
  and security identity, 46–47
  and security policy domains, 158
authorization servers, 212–214, 233
authorization token-based delegation, 195, 196
authorization tokens, 185–189
  client, 190
availability, 5
  ESI planning for, 296–297

B
backward trust evaluation, 195, 196
balance cost against threat principle, 20
  and enterprise security technologies, 116
  and interoperability, 145
bandwidth on demand, 6
bean provider, 28
  and EJB lifecycle, 31
  permissions recommended, 57–58
  role, 34–39
beans. *See* Enterprise JavaBeans
biometrics, 117
bridges, 15
  custom, 130
business-to-business (B2B) transactions, 289, 303–304

C
C++, 3
caching, 21
  performance boost, 333
call-backs, 138
callerKey, 38
CancelRequest message, 81
centralized management, distributed enforcement principle, 21
certificate authorities, 115, 147
certificates, 115, 117
Checkpoint Firewall-1, 113
Cisco PIX, 113
ClearTrust SecureControl, 116, 148, 311
client authorization token, 190
client stub, 80–81
client/target interactions, in CORBA, 78–81
CloseConnection message, 81
Coarse-grain entitlement, 122, 123
COBOL programs, 127
code review, 39
collections, 244. *See also* access rights; security attributes; security policy domains
  as mutually suspicious islands, 22
collections for scale principle, 21, 32
  CORBASec, 87, 93
  and scalable security policies, 244
Common Criteria, 315
Common Data Representation (CDR), 178
Common Name (CN) LDAP node, 329
Common Object Request Broker Architecture. *See* CORBA
Common Secure Interoperability (CSI), 182
Common Secure Interoperability v2 (CSIv2), 22, 58, 130, 168
  association options, 196–197
  attribute layer, 185–190
  authentication layer, 190–191

authorization tokens, 185–189
conformance to, 197–198
and CORBASec, 89–91
credentials in, 192–196
and delegation, 280
described, 182–198
ESI planning for, 300
identity tokens, 189–190
overview, 182–185
privilege delegation, 192–196
transport layer, 191–192
component architecture, 2–3
example of secure, 22–25
component authentication/authorization servers, 19
component-based security servers, 119–120
eBusiness.com, 312–315
ESI planning for, 300
component homes (CORBA Component Model), 71
component identity (CORBA Component Model), 70–71
Component Model. *See* CORBA Component Model
components, 2
component technology, 8–9
composite delegation, 278
Concept Five, 26
confidentiality, 4
association option, 62, 197
and authorization, 18
and interoperability, 159
constrained delegation. *See* restricted delegation
construction policies, 88
container provider, 28
and EJB lifecycle, 31
and realms, 49–50
role, 32–33, 51–53
containers, 2. *See also* Enterprise JavaBeans
EJB model, 28–29
container security, 173–174
between containers, 174
container-to-container interoperability, 60–66
content-based filtering, 113
CORBA. *See also* Enterprise JavaBeans
brief review, ix, 76–84
declarative part, 76–78
and enterprise bean objects, 27
in mid-tier, 139–140
object by value capability, 130
object reference, 83–84
$RBAC_0$ using, 252–255
$RBAC_1$ using, 261–263
$RBAC_2$ using, 261–263
run-time part, 78–84
as security technology domain, 134
standard rights, 99
wire protocol, 81–83
CORBA 3, ix–x
CORBA Component Model, ix–x, 2–3, 69
overview, 70–71
CORBA Domain Facilities, x, 72
CORBAfacilities, 72
CORBA IDL interface, 130
CORBA interfaces, 70, 75
CORBA Object Request Brokers (ORBs), ix, 72, 73
responsibilities, 79–80
CORBA security, 71–73. *See also* access rights; security attributes; security policy domains
audit policies, 104–105
benefits, 73–75
declarative, 93–104
delegation support, 279–280
functionality levels, 91–93
identification and authentication, 84–86
libraries, 171–174
programmatic security, 91, 106–108
run-time , 84–93
security policy enforcement, 86–89
security policy types, 88
wire protocol, 88–91
CORBA Security: An Introduction to Safe Computing with Objects (Blakely), 108
CORBAservices, x
core security services, 17–18
ESI planning for, 299–300
corporate customers, 308
credential mapping, 154
credentials, 17–18, 30, 139
in CSIv2, 192–196
credit card authorization services, 5
CrossLogix2, 122
cross-selling, 5
CRYPTOCard, 116
cryptographic products, 19
cryptography. *See also* Privilege Attribute Certificates
authentication permissions, 58–59

cryptography (*cont.*)
as core security service, 18
legacy tier technologies, 112, 124
mid-tier technologies, 111, 121
perimeter technologies, 111, 114–116
CSIv2. *See* Common Secure Interoperability v2 (CSIv2)
Customer, 25
CustomerAccount, 24, 25, 35
interface inheritance, 77
method access, 43–44
runAs-specified-identity, 47
CustomerAccountFactory, 24
customer accounts, 22
CustomerID, 24
customer relationship management, 5
customers, 22, 25
administration of new, 292–293
method access assignment, 42–44
role, 33, 39–40
role definition, 41–42
custom security API, 17

D

data abstraction, 248
database security, 124
data integrity. *See* integrity
decision combinator, 225–227, 234, 240
declarative CORBA, 76–78
declarative CORBASec, 93–104
declarative security, 91
delegation, 18–19, 50. *See also* impersonation; restricted delegation
authorization token-based, 195, 196
CSIv2 layer, 192–196
identity assertion-based, 195, 196
levels of, 278–279
mid-tier technologies, 111, 121
motivations for, 277–278
product support for, 279–280
risks, 282–283
and scalable security policies, 276–277
and security identity, 45–47
using, 281–283
DelegationByClient, 62, 63–64, 197
deleteOrder, 23
demilitarized zone (DMZ), 113, 139, 309
denial of service attacks, 21, 289
deployer, 28, 29
and application assembler, 39–40
and EJB lifecycle, 31
role, 32–33, 47–50
deployment descriptor, 29–30
application assembler, 40–47
bean provider, 35–39
declarative model, 34
and EJB lifecycle, 31–32
using, 54–57
XML-based, 32
deployment tools, 51
deployment wizard, 29
depreciated methods, 36–37
design for failure principle, 22
and delegation, 282
and enterprise security technologies, 110
and interoperability, 137, 189, 191
design principles. *See* application-driven authorization principle; audit early, not often principle; balance cost against threat principle; centralized management, distributed enforcement principle; collections for scale principle; design for failure principle; end-to-end, not point-to-point principle; push security down principle; trust no one principle
DES keys, 114, 280
Diffie-Hellman key exchange, 61
digital signatures, 18, 29, 115
directory services, 19
discretionary access control (DAC), 248, 249
distributed business applications, 1–2. *See also* e-business
distributed component computing, 3
security challenges, 9–11
distributed component security architecture, 10
distributed component technology, 9
Distributed Computing Environment (DCE) cells, 49
Distributed Computing Environment (DCE) security, 120, 121, 124
distributed security, 3, 8–11. *See also* security
distributed trusted computing base, 10–11
document type definition (DTD), 55–57
DomainAuthority interface, 271
DomainAuthorityAdmin interface, 271
Domain Facilities, x
Domain Hierarchies, 271
duty separation, 248, 266
DynamicAttributeService, 215, 230–233

dynamic mapping, 275
dynamic separation of duties (DSD), 267

E
EAI, 13
e-business
  B2B transactions, 303–304
  early forms of, 303
  ESI planning, 287
  new security responsibilities, 5–6
  risks, 4
  security as enabler for, 3–8
eBusiness.com
  access control, 210–212
  application assembler role, 39–47
  bean provider role, 34–39
  declarative CORBA, 76–78
  deployer role, 47–50
  deploying, 308
  granted rights, 100
  infrastructure security, 325–326
  legacy security, 320–321
  mid-tier security, 315–319
  naming, 326–327
  object model, 22–24
  perimeter security, 310–315
  planning for ESI, 290
  $RBAC_0$, 250–259
  $RBAC_1$, 260–266
  $RBAC_2$, 266–267
  $RBAC_3$, 267
  required controls, 99
  Resource Access Decision facility, 214–217
  security architecture, 305–308
  security data persistence, 327–331
  security requirements, 24–25
  security server advantages, 321–325
  underlying protection layer, 309–310
  wise use of domains, 272–274
e-commerce. *See* e-business
E-Commerce Security (Ghosh), 58, 151
EJB. *See* Enterprise JavaBeans
ejbactivate, 53
ejbContext, 52–53
ejbcreate, 53
ejbFind, 53
ejbHome, 53
ejbLoad, 53
ejbpassivate, 53
ejbPostCreate, 53
ejbremove, 53
ejbSelect, 53
ejbStore, 53
Elara, 122
electronic commerce. *See* e-business
Electronic Commerce, OMG Domain Facilities, x
encryption, 18, 29. *See also* cryptography
end-to-end, not point-to-point principle
  CORBASec, 89
  and interoperability, 130
end-to-end security, 12–22. *See also* legacy tier; mid-tier; perimeter tier
  eBusiness.com, 305, 306
enterprise information security. *See* information security
Enterprise JavaBeans, 2. *See also* application assembler; bean provider; container provider; CORBA; deployer; deployment descriptor; security roles
  acceptance of, 27–28
  calling other beans, 28
  container-to-container interoperability, 60–66
  delegation in, 281
  in mid-tier, 139–140
  overview, 28–30
  permissions recommended, 57–60
  players and their duties in lifecycle, 30–54
  portability, 33
  $RBAC_0$ using, 255–259
  $RBAC_1$ using, 263–266
  as security technology domain, 134
Enterprise JavaBeans version 1.0, 28
Enterprise JavaBeans version 1.1, 28, 129
Enterprise JavaBeans version 2.0, 27–28
  container-to-container interoperability, 60–62
Enterprise Security Integration, 3, 303–305. *See also* eBusiness.com
  from application to system, 286–290
  applying, 297–300
  basic principles of, 20–22
  benefits, 19–20
  end-to-end, 12–22
  framework, 15–19
  functional requirements, 291
  nonfunctional requirements, 295–297
  requirements determination, 13–14, 291–297
  security requirements, 291–295
  solutions, 14–15

enterprise security policies, 11
enterprise security technologies, 109–112. *See also* legacy security technologies; mid-tier security technologies; perimeter security technologies
entitlement servers, 122–123
Entrust, 115
environment domain, 133–134
equivalent interface, 70
error checking, 55
ESI. *See* Enterprise Security Integration
EstablishTrustInClient, 62, 63, 197
EstablishTrustInTarget, 62–63, 197
Event Log Monitor, 119
event sinks (CORBA Component Model), 70
event sources (CORBA Component Model), 70
extensibility, 295–296
ExtensibleFamily members, 98
extranets, 4

F

facets (CORBA Component Model), 70
failure, designing for. *See* design for failure principle
federation, 132
file systems, 331
Finance/Insurance, OMG Domain Facilities, x
findByPrimaryKey, 38
fine-grain entitlement, 122, 123
firewalls, 12, 19, 112–114
  component security with, 312–313
  in early e-businesses, 303
  eBusiness.com, 311–312
  ESI planning for, 300
  and interoperability, 136–137
Firewall specification, 138
forward trust evaluation, 196
Fragment message, 82
framework security facilities, 18–19
  ESI planning for, 300
fraud, 4
functional requirements, 291

G

Generic Inter-ORB Protocol (GIOP)
  and CORBA, 81–83
  and CORBASec, 84–91
  eBusiness.com, 311
Generic Security Service (GSS), 190
getAccess, 26, 116, 122, 148, 311
get_attributes(), 106
getCallerPrincipal, 29, 37, 53
getName, 37
getPrice, 23
getProducts, 23
GIOP. *See* Generic Inter-ORB Protocol
granted rights, 96–97, 100, 245
groups. *See* collections

H

hackers, 4
hash, 61, 147
Healthcare, OMG Domain Facilities, x
host monitors, 119
HTML forms, 303
HTTP, 146–147, 170
HTTPS (HTTP running over SSL), 136, 138, 142

I

identification, CORBASec, 84–86
IdentityAssertion, 62, 63, 197
identity assertion-based delegation, 195, 196
identity tokens, 189–190
Identrus, 115
IIOP. *See* Internet Inter-ORB Protocol
impersonation, 45, 46, 278
  CSIv2, 192, 196, 280
  and interoperability, 159
industrial espionage, 4
information security, 7–8
  goals, 4–5
infrastructure security, 325–326
initiating principals, 85–86
insider attacks, 304
integrated security system. *See* Enterprise Security Integration
integrity, 5
  association option, 62, 197
  and authorization, 18
  and interoperability, 159
interceptors, 15, 17
intercompany security, 131–133
interfaces, 2
  RAD, 218–220
Internet, 3. *See also* e-business
  early e-commerce use as electronic billboard, 303
Internet Engineering Task Force (IETF), 305
Internet Inter-ORB Protocol (IIOP), ix, 129. *See also* Remote Method Invocation (RMI) over IIOP

described, 60, 174–175, 178–181
eBusiness.com, 311–312
EJB support for, 3, 27
transport stack, 180
Internet Protocol Security (IPsec), 22
interoperability, 127–128, 167–168. *See also* Remote Method Invocation (RMI) over IIOP; security domains; security technology domains
bridging security tiers, 144–157
combined technology advantages, 170–171
container-to-container, 60–66
of EJB and CORBA, 128–131, 168–174
intracompany/intercompany security, 131–133
mixed security domains, 140–144
modifying architectures for, 161–164
security policy domains, 157–161
security technology domains, 133–140
transport protocols, 174–181
interoperable object references (IORs), 80, 83–84
CSIv2 association options, 196–197
interoperable security layers, 198–206
intracompany security, 131–133
intranets, 4
intrusion detection systems, 118–119
ESI planning for, 300
invocation access policies, 88, 157
invocation audit policies, 88, 157
invocation delegation policies, 88, 157
invocation identity, 38
isCallerInRole, 29, 37, 53

J

.jar file, 29, 39
scoping rules, 49
and security identity, 46
Java Community Process, 305
Java Database Connectivity (JDBC), 164
Java 2 Enterprise Edition (J2EE), 2. *See also* Enterprise JavaBeans
Java in a Nutshell: A Desktop Quick Reference (Flanagan), 129
Java Naming and Directory Interface (JNDI), 38, 172–173
Java 2 Platform Security Policies, 57
Java Remote Method Invocation. *See* Remote Method Invocation
Java Remote Method Protocol (JRMP), 60
Java virtual machine, 176–177
Job Control Language (JCL), 143

K

Kerberos, 58, 120–122, 124
and delegation, 280
Kerberos Key Distribution Center (KDC), 120
key management, 332

L

Lampson's access matrix, 216
lattice-based mandatory access control (MAC), 248, 249
LDAP. *See* Lightweight Directory Access Protocol
least privilege principle, 248, 266
legacy domains, 128
legacy security technologies, 12, 14
described, 111–112, 123–124
eBusiness.com, 320–321
legacy tier, x, 127
integration with e-business applications, 3
interoperability with mid-tier, 152–157
mixed domain, 143
security technology domain, 135–136, 140
libraries, CORBA security, 171–174
Life Science, OMG Domain Facilities, x
Lightweight Directory Access Protocol (LDAP), 116, 124, 321
ESI planning for, 300
and interoperability, 163
relational or object databases, 330
security data persistence, 328–330
listOrders, 23
load balancing, 297
LocateReply message, 81
LocateRequest message, 81
logical roles. *See* security roles
lookup, 23

M

mainframe security, 123–124
manageability, 295
mandatory access control (MAC), 248, 249
Manufacturing, OMG Domain Facilities, x
Mastering Enterprise JavaBeans and the Java 2 Platform, Enterprise Edition (Roman), 32, 129
Master Security Server, 135

Mean Time to Failure (MTTF), 296
Mean Time to Repair (MTTR), 296
MemberAccount, 24, 25
MemberAccountFactory, 24, 95, 101
MemberID, 25
members, 22, 25
  granting more access, 293
  method access assignment, 42–44
  role definition, 41–42
  roles, 33
message confidentiality. *See* confidentiality
MessageError message, 82
message integrity. *See* integrity
Meta-Object Facility (MOF), x
method access, assigning, 42–44
<method-intf> element, 43
method permission, 29–30, 40
  authentication, 58–59
  authorization, 59
  bean provider, 57–58
  transport, 59–60
methods, 2
middleware access control, 209–214
  RAD authorization contrasted, 217
mid-tier, 128
  interoperability with legacy tier, 152–157
  interoperability with perimeter tier, 145–152
  mixed domain, 141–143
  security technology domain, 135, 137, 139–140
mid-tier security technologies, 12, 13, 14
  described, 110, 111, 119–123
  eBusiness.com, 315–319
  in large-scale distributed systems, 304–305
misuse detection, 118
multiple_access_allowed(), 218
mutual authentication, with SSL, 65–66, 314, 325

N

naming, 326–327
  JNDI security, 172–173
  principal mapping, 131–132
  principals, 52
nested elements
  deployment descriptor, 35
  in XML, 32
NetCrusader, 119
network monitors, 118–119
nonfunctional requirements, 295–297
nonrepudiation, 18, 75
nonrepudiation policies, 88, 158, 160

O

object databases, 330
Object Domain Mapping (ODM), 271
object instance assignment, 160
  to policy domains, 274–276
Object Management Group (OMG), 305
  described, ix–x
object reference, CORBA, 83–884
OMG. *See* Object Management Group
OMG Domain Facilities, x
OMG Interface Definition Language (OMG IDL), ix, 76
online services, 3. *See also* e-business
Open Group, 305
operations, 2
Orbix, 26
Order, 23
owner-based discretionary access control (DAC), 248, 249

PQ

packaging security, 171–174
packet-sniffing interception, 11
passwords, 58, 115, 116, 191
  problems with, 61–62
#PCDATA, 56
performance problems, at system level, 332–334
perimeter security technologies, 12, 14
  described, 109–110, 112–119
  eBusiness.com, 310–315
perimeter tier, 128
  interoperability with mid-tier, 145–152
  mixed domains in, 141
  security technology domain, 135, 138
permission. *See* method permission
placeOrder, 23
players, 28, 30
  duties in EJB lifecycle, 30–54
POA object assignment, 160
point-to-point security. *See* end-to-end, not point-to-point principle
PolicyDirector, 26, 119, 148, 311
policy domain. *See* security policy domain
PolicyEvaluatorLocator, 219, 227–230, 234, 236–240

policy evaluators, 215, 224–225, 234, 236–240
Portable Object Adapter (POA), 160
ports (CORBA Component Model), 70
presumed trust, 195
primary keys, 70–71
Principal Authenticator, 162
principal delegation. *See* delegation
principal mapping, 131–132
principals, 28
  CORBASec, 84–85
  naming, 52
  roles, 33–34
privacy, 293–294
Privilege Attribute Certificates (PACs), 132–133, 307
  CSIv2, 183, 185–189
  and delegation, 281
privilege attributes. *See* security attributes
Product, 23
product attribute, 23
ProductFactory, 23, 24
ProductIDs, 23
profile manager, 18
programmatic security, 91, 106–108
protected resource name, 218
protocol vectoring, 113
provider. *See* bean provider
proxy attributes, 193
proxy servers, 300
public key certificates, 28–29
public key encryption, 333
public key infrastructure, 114–115
  ESI planning for, 300
  evolving nature of, 289
  scaling, 58
push security down principle, 20–21, 30
  versus application-driven security, 212
  CORBASec, 74
  and interoperability, 153, 169
  and planning for ESI, 288

R

RAD. *See* Resource Access Decision
Raptor Eagle, 113
$RBAC_0$ (role-based access control) model, 249–259, 268
$RBAC_1$ (role-based access control) model, 249–250, 260–266, 268
$RBAC_2$ (role-based access control) model, 249–250, 266–267, 268
$RBAC_3$ (role-based access control) model, 250, 267, 268
realms, 49–50
receptacles (CORBA Component Model), 70
reference monitor, 212
relational databases, 127, 330
reliability, 296
Remote Method Invocation (RMI), 129–130
  described, 174–178
  transport stack, 177
Remote Method Invocation (RMI) over IIOP, 60, 130
  described, 181
  and interoperability, 168–169, 175
Reply message, 81, 89
Request message, 81, 82–83, 89
required rights, 95–96, 245
requirements determination, 291–297
Resource Access Decision (RAD), 142, 162, 202, 323
  AccessDecision object, 219, 220–223, 233–234, 238–240
  administrative model, 236–240
  advantages and disadvantages, 215–217
  architecture, 220–233
  decision combinator, 225–227, 234, 240
  DynamicAttributeService, 215, 230–233
  eBusiness.com, 214–217
  ESI planning for, 300
  interactions between components, 233–240
  interfaces and data, 218–220
  middleware authorization contrasted, 217
  PolicyEvaluatorLocator, 219, 227–230, 234, 236–240
  policy evaluators, 215, 224–225, 234, 236–240
  runtime model, 236
  specification, 217–233
resource name, 218
resource patterns, 228–229
restricted delegation, 159, 278
  CSIv2, 192, 195, 196, 280
  safety of, 282
reusability, 9
rights. *See* access rights
risk management, 6–7
RMI. *See* Remote Method Invocation
RMI over IIOP. *See* Remote Method Invocation over IIOP
rmiregistry, 178, 326

R,M pair, 42
role-based access control (RBAC) models, 244, 247–250, 268
  $RBAC_0$, 249–259, 268
  $RBAC_1$, 249–250, 260–266, 268
  $RBAC_2$, 249–250, 266–267, 268
  $RBAC_3$, 250, 267, 268
role references. *See* security role references
roles. *See* security roles
root certificate, 189
RSA keys, 114, 280
rules
  and roles, 34
  scoping, 49
runAs method, 38, 64
runAs-specified-identity, 38, 47, 50, 64
  assigning principals to, 48
run-time CORBA, 78–84
run-time CORBASec, 84–93

S

scalability, 297
scalable security policies, 243–244. *See also* role-based access control (RBAC) models
  delegation, 276–283
  and roles, 247
  wise use of attributes, 246–247
  wise use of domains, 268–276
  wise use of rights, 244–246
scaling
  collections for, 21, 32
  ESI planning for, 297
  problems at system level, 331–332
  public key infrastructure, 58
  roles for, 32, 33, 35, 169
screen-scraping, 320
secure attribute service, 183
Secure Inter-ORB Protocol (SECIOP), 183
secure invocation policies, 88, 157
Secure Sockets Layer (SSL), 12, 22, 28–29
  CORBASec contrasted, 74–75
  described, 114–115
  eBusiness.com, 309–310
  EJB 2 support for, 61–62
  mutual authentication, 65–66, 314, 325
  with RMI, 178
SecurID, 116, 122
security. *See also* CORBA; CORBA security; Enterprise JavaBeans; information security
  architecture modification for, 161–164
  and components, 1–3
  between containers, 174
  distributed systems, 3, 8–11
  as enabler for e-business, 3–8
  problems at system level, 331–334
  risk management, 6–7
security administration
  basic principles of, 21
  as core security service, 18
  eBusiness.com, 322–324
  legacy technologies, 112, 124
  mid-tier technologies, 112, 121
  mixed domains, 144
  perimeter technologies, 112, 114, 118
security architectures
  distributed components, 10
  eBusiness.com, 305–308
  modifying for interoperability, 161–164
security associations
  basic principles of, 22
  as framework security facility, 18
  mid-tier technologies, 111
  options, 62–64
security attributes, 70
  CORBASec, 86, 93–95, 102–104
  CSIv2 layer, 185–190
  wise use in scalable security policies, 246–247
security attribute service (SAS), 89
security audit. *See* auditing
security authorities, 134, 135
security-aware applications, 15–16
  APIs, 17
  CORBASec, 75, 91, 92–93
security context, 36
Security Domain Management, 271
Security Domain Membership Management (SDMM) Service, 160, 271
security domains, 49, 51–52, 128, 133–134
  wise use in scalable security policies, 268–276
security enclaves, 113
security environment domain, 133–134
security evolution, 288–289
security identity, 45–47
security integration. *See* Enterprise Security Integration
security layers, 11
security policies, 134, 135. *See also* scalable security policies

CORBASec, 86–89
security policy domains, 49, 133, 134–135
CORBASec, 93–95, 101–102
object instance assignment, 274–276
types of, 157–161
security proxy services, 19
security requirements, 291–295
security-role-ref element, 35–36, 44, 56
security role references, 35–36
assigning roles to, 44–45
security roles, 29–30, 32–34
application assembler, 39–47
assigning method access, 42–44
assigning to role references, 44–45
bean provider, 34–39
container provider, 32–33, 51–53
defining, 41–42
deployer, 32–33, 39, 47–50
separating in sensitive situations, 39
security self-reliant applications, 16
security servers. *See also* component-based security servers; Web-based security servers
advantages of using, 321–325
multiple, 324–325
security service replaceability, 75
security standards, 19
security technology domains, 49
in legacy tier, 140
in mid-tier, 139–140
mixed, 140–144
in perimeter tier, 138
relative security tiers, 133–139
security technology products, 19
security tiers. *See also* legacy tier; mid-tier; perimeter tier
bridging, 144–157
and technology domains, 133–139
security-unaware applications, 15, 16
APIs, 17
CORBASec, 75, 91, 92
Self-administration, 6
Self-registration, 292
separation of duties, 248, 266
SEQUENCE, 186
server skeleton, 81
service context, 60
SESAME, 280
setPrice, 23
settleAccount, 24
settleOrder, 24
ShoppingCart, 23, 24
interface inheritance, 77
simple delegation, 278
Simple Object Access Protocol (SOAP), 141, 310
Simple Password Exponential Key Exchange (SPEKE), 58
simple restricted delegation, 280
single sign-on, 20
SiteMinder, 26, 116, 122, 148, 311
smart cards, 115, 122
SSL. *See* Secure Sockets Layer
staff, 22, 25
method access assignment, 42–44
role, 36
role definition, 41–42
standard security API, 17
stateful connections, 184–185
stateless connections, 184–185
static separation of duties (SSD), 267
Sun Microsystems, 2, 28. *See also* Enterprise JavaBeans
supply chain management, 5–6
symmetric key encryption, 120, 333

T

TAG_CSI_SEC_MECH_LIST, 91
TAG_NULL_TAG, 91
TAG_SECIOP_SEC_TRANS, 91
TAG_SSL_SEC_TRANS, 91
target objects, 78
TCP/IP, 81, 179
technology domains. *See* security technology domains
Telecommunications, OMG Domain Facilities, x
tokens, 113, 116
authorization, 185–189
identity, 189–190
TPBroker, 26
TPBroker Security, 26, 119
traced delegation, 278
transactional entitlement, 122–123
transparency, 9
transport
CSIv2 layer, 191–192
EJB-CORBA differences, 168
permissions recommended, 59–60
Transportation, OMG Domain Facilities, x
Transport Layer Security (TLS), 114
CSIv2, 183, 184

transport protocols, 174–181
transport security mechanisms, 22
TrustBroker, 120
trusted computing base, 9–11
trust evaluation
  backward, 195, 196
  forward, 196
trust no one principle, 20, 46
  CORBASec, 85
  and enterprise security technologies, 111
  and interoperability, 169
trustworthiness, 287

U
unconstrained delegation. *See* impersonation
Unified Modeling Language (UML), x
Uniform Resource Locator (URL), 111
Unitary Login service, 306–308, 320–321
  and interoperability, 154–155, 164
use-caller-identity, 47, 64
user exits, 123
user identification challenges, 132
user IDs, 58, 115, 116
user names, 131–132
user privileges, 15
user propagation, 64
user sponsors, 85
UTF8 strings, 190
Utilities, OMG Domain Facilities, x

V
value type, 130
vendor security API, 17
Verisign, 115
Virtual Private Networks (VPNs), 113
VisiBroker, 26
visitors, 25

W
Web authentication/authorization servers, 12, 19
Web-based security servers, 116–118
  ESI planning for, 300
  using component security with, 313–315
Web browsers, 13–14, 138
  interaction with Web server, 146–147
  passing data from, 148
WebLogic, 26
  security realm, 50
Web servers, 14, 136–137, 138
  critical security position, 151–152
  interaction with Web browsers, 146–147
WebSphere, 26
wire protocol
  CORBA, 81–83
  CORBASec, 88–91
World Wide Web, 12. *See also* e-business
wrappers, 15

XYZ
X.509 certificates, 61, 127, 329
  PACs, 187–188
XML-based deployment descriptors, 32
XML-based Metadata Interchange (XMI), x
XML file tags, 55–57
XML Handbook, The (Goldfarb and Prescod), 32